End

AA
WHERE TO GO IN BRITAIN

WHERE TO GO IN BRITAIN

AA

Produced by the
Publications Division of the Automobile Association
Fanum House,
Basingstoke, Hampshire RG21 2EA

Produced by the Publications Division
of the Automobile Association
Editor **Rebecca King**
Art Editor **Keith Russell**
Assistant Editor **Richard Powell**

Research by the Publications Research Unit
of the Automobile Association

Maps produced by the Cartographic Unit
of the Automobile Association

Based on the Ordnance Survey Maps, with the permission of
the Controller of HM Stationery Office   Crown Copyright Reserved

ISBN 0 86145 028 0 (Hardback) AA ref. 56656
ISBN 0 86145 152 X (Softback) AA ref. 56630

Filmset by Vantage Photosetting Co Ltd, Southampton, Hampshire
Printed and bound by New Interlitho SPA, Milan, Italy

Published by the Automobile Association, Fanum House,
Basingstoke, Hampshire RG21 2EA

Boats have to be pulled high
up the shingle beach at
Hastings because this
seafaring Sussex town has
no harbour

Contents

Introduction 7

How to use this book 8

Alphabetical gazetteer of places to go
in England, Scotland and Wales 10–209

Cities and towns with street plans

Aberdeen 10
Bath 18
Blackpool 23
Bournemouth 27
Brighton 30
Bristol 32
Bury St Edmunds 37
Cambridge 40
Canterbury 42
Cheltenham 49
Chester 50
Chichester 52
Durham 70
Edinburgh 74
Exeter 78
Gloucester 85

Lincoln 114
London 118
Norwich 138
Oxford 140
St Albans 157
Salisbury 158
Shrewsbury 164
Stirling 176
Stratford-upon-Avon 180
Warwick 195
Winchester 202
Windsor 204
Worcester 207
York 208

Area maps
Dartmoor 64
Hadrian's Wall 88
Lake District 108
New Forest 132
Norfolk Broads 134
Pembrokeshire Coast National Park 143
Snowdonia National Park 170

Key Map 210
Road Atlas 211–222

The rolling countryside of
Northamptonshire and
Oxfordshire spreads out below the
ancient hill village of Aynho

Introduction

Britain is packed with exciting places to go and interesting things to discover – magnificent castles where history can be traced as far back as Norman times; ruined forts built by the Romans; elegant stately homes filled with priceless treasures giving a glimpse of a grander past; fascinating cities with ancient houses and churches at every turn; seaside resorts with all the fun of the promenade; sleepy villages to wander around and beautiful countryside to explore.

It would be impossible to include all of Britain's many attractions in one book, so we have picked over 400 of the best from England, Scotland and Wales. The places have been selected because of their accessibility, variety and wide general appeal, catering for as many different tastes as possible. There is something here to suit every occasion – a family day out with the children, a trip whilst on holiday, a weekend away, a school outing, or just a Sunday drive to somewhere new.

With details of opening times accompanying each description where appropriate, street plans of cities and larger towns, twelve pages of road maps clearly locating every place in the gazetteer and hundreds of colour photographs, *Where To Go In Britain* is an invaluable guide to exploring Britain.

How to Use this Book

All the places in the gazetteer are listed in alphabetical order. Each entry has a page number beside it which refers to the road atlas at the back of the book, and a map reference locating the place on the map. For example, Bath *p 212 E4* will be found on page 212 of the atlas in square E4.

When planning a trip to a particular area, use the key map on page 210 to find out which map you need to refer to. All the gazetteer entries are printed in red type on the maps, so it is easy to see exactly where the places of interest are.

With every map there is an alphabetical list of all the places of interest in that area, and beside each name its gazetteer page number and its grid reference. These enable you to turn quickly back to the gazetteer to find out about a place and to pinpoint it easily on the map.

Abbreviations and Ancient Monument Opening Times

NT Indicates properties in England and Wales administered by the National Trust for Places of Historic Interest or Natural Beauty, 42 Queen Anne's Gate, London SW1H 9AS.

NTS National Trust for Scotland, 5 Charlotte Square, Edinburgh EH2 4DU.

AM Ancient Monuments, many of which in England are in the care of the Department of the Environment, 25 Savile Row, London W1X 2BT.

Ancient Monuments in Scotland (with the exception of Holyrood House) are the responsibility of the Scottish Development Department, New St Andrew's House, St James's Centre, Edinburgh 1.

Ancient Monuments in Wales are the responsibility of the Welsh office at Ty-glas, Llanishen, Cardiff CF4 5UP.

Except where otherwise stated, the standard times of opening for all Ancient Monuments, except Scotland, are as follows:

Mar to Apr: weekdays 9.30–5.30   Sunday 2–5.30
May to Sep: weekdays 9.30–7   Sunday 2–7
Oct: weekdays 9.30–5.30   Sunday 2–5.30
Nov to Feb: weekdays 9.30–4   Sunday 2–4

Standard times of opening for all Ancient Monuments in Scotland are as follows:

Apr to Sep: weekdays 9.30–7   Sundays 2–7
Oct to Mar: weekdays 9.30–4   Sundays 2–4

All monuments in England are closed on 1 January, Maunday Thursday, Good Friday, May Day Holiday and 24 to 26 December. Those in Scotland on 25 and 26 December, also 1 and 2 January. Monuments in Wales on 1 January, 4 April, 24 to 26 December and some other Bank Holidays.

Some of the smaller monuments may be closed for one or two days a week.

Churches, cathedrals and abbeys are usually open at all reasonable times.

As far as possible, the opening times given in the book are believed correct at the time of printing. However, as these details may be altered at the discretion of individual establishments, it is advisable to check that they are correct before making a special visit to a place.

Town Plan Key

	London Transport Station
	British Rail Station
	City Walls
	Multi-Storey Car Park
	Parking available on payment *(open air)*
	Official Car Park *(open air)*
	AA Recommended Route *(through route)*
	Restricted Roads
	Traffic roundabout
	One-way street
	Pedestrians only
	Other Roads
	Post Office
	Church
	Cathedral
	Parks and open spaces
	Places of interest described in text
	Tourist Information Centre
	AA Service Centre
	AA road Service Centre
	Convenience
	Convenience with facilities for the disabled

Area Map Key

	Motorway
	A Road
	B Road
	Other Roads
	Boating Centre
	Picnic site
	Nature Trail
	National Park Boundary
	Tourist Information Centre *(summer only)*
	Tourist Information Centre
	Spot Height
	Forest area
	Beach
	Car Park

With its miles of sandy beaches, Weston-super-Mare has grown from a Victorian fishing village to a huge holiday resort with two piers

Abbotsbury

Dorset *p212 E2*

This picturesque yellow-stone and thatch village is located on the western end of the sweep of Chesil Beach.

In the village itself is a huge medieval tithe barn which is all that is left of a Benedictine abbey. Up on the hill just behind the village is St Catherine's Chapel, also built by the monks in the fifteenth century. It is a small, austere building from which there are panoramic views of the surrounding gentle countryside.

It was the monks who established the famous swannery just south of the village. It has existed here for over six centuries and today is the largest in England. The swannery provides a safe breeding ground for hundreds of mute swans and is home for many species of wild fowl.

Another attraction nearby are the sub-tropical gardens about one mile west of Abbotsbury. Sixteen acres of walled grounds enclose numerous unusual trees and an extensive collection of rare shrubs and plants. There are also magnolias and camelias, all of which are proudly surveyed by the resident peacocks, pheasants and turkeys.

Swannery open mid May to mid Sep daily. Also Sun if fine.
Gardens open mid Mar to Oct daily. Sun pm only. Parking available.

Over 500 swans nest and feed on the waters of the Fleet

Aberdeen Grampian *p222 F2*

The Royal Town, or Burgh, of Aberdeen was first patronized by the Crown in the twelfth century when William the Lion granted it two royal charters. Since then it has prospered as a port and become one of Scotland's most important commercial, religious and scholastic centres.

Aberdeen was the main seaport in the north of Scotland as far back as the thirteenth century. Its shipping trade gradually grew and by the mid-nineteenth century the Aberdeen clippers which raced over to China for their cargo of tea had reached their zenith – the *Thermopylae* was reputed to be the fastest clipper in the world and the *Cutty Sark* was built in Clyde to compete with it.

The trawling industry also developed here in the nineteenth century and Aberdeen became an important fishing port. Although vast catches of fish are still handled in the harbour, the oil industry tends to dominate the docks.

Aberdeen is an austere city of grey buildings built from the granite which is quarried locally. However, this severity contrasts with the many parks in the city, all beautifully laid out with flower gardens. Thousands of roses create a blaze of colour every year which have won the city the Britain in Bloom trophy many times.

For ten days during June the Aberdeen Festival transforms the city into a riot of entertainment. Competitions, dancing displays, concerts, vintage car and steam rallies and special markets seem to fill the streets.

Aberdeen Bay

The city stands at the entrance to the valley of the river Dee and the sands here provide wide golden beaches which stretch from the harbour to the Don Estuary. The resort of Aberdeen is located along these two miles of coastline known as Aberdeen Bay. The beaches are backed by Promenades, golf links and extensive recreation and picnic areas. Amusement arcades, a sportsground, an adventure playground and a fairground are all to be found at the end of Beach Boulevard.

King's College
The focal point of Old Aberdeen has always been the complex of university buildings known as King's College which date back to 1494. Its most splendid feature is the dominating tower which supports a huge stone crown built in honour of James IV who aided in the founding of the university. The other gem is the eighteenth-century chapel which is the best preserved example of a medieval college church in the British Isles. Of particular interest here is the wealth of intricate wooden carving inside.

St Machar's Cathedral
The fortification of this fifteenth-century cathedral reflects the political climate of those times. Aberdeen then was a dangerous place to live as it was so open to attack. On the seaward side it was likely to be attacked by the English landing, and on the other side by Celtic Highlanders approaching from the mountains.

The site for Aberdeen's cathedral was allegedly chosen because St Machar, a follower of St Columba from Iona, was guided there in the sixth century after being told to travel until he found a bend in the river resembling a shepherd's crook.

Old Aberdeen Town House
This is the most charming of Aberdeen's Georgian buildings and is situated on an island facing down a street lined with attractively restored houses – the High Street. Displayed above the door are the Lilies of Aulton, the coat of arms depicting heaven, virginity and the Holy Trinity.

Mercat Cross
The oldest part of new Aberdeen is Castlegate, which has been recognised as the city centre for the past 600 years although the castle has long since disappeared.

Situated in Castlegate is the Mercat Cross – undoubtedly the finest burgh cross in Scotland today. It is a circular structure made of red sandstone and has a pillar rising up from the centre of the roof supporting a unicorn made of white marble.

Shiprow
A few steps from Castlegate is Shiprow which may have even

Mercat Cross, built in 1686

earlier origins. Today its main feature of interest is Provost Ross' House which overlooks part of the harbour to which Shiprow descends. Two of the rooms are open and have some interesting old stone carvings in them.

Marischal College
This was founded by the 5th Earl of Marischal as a Protestant rival to King's College, but the two merged in 1860 to become the University of Aberdeen. It is an elaborate building and around the archway through to the quadrangle there is a frieze of shields bearing the coats of arms belonging to past worthies of Aberdeen.

Attached to the college is an anthropological museum with a collection of treasures from all over the world, ranging from whale-tooth necklaces to tom-toms.

Provost Skene's House
About a quarter of a mile away in Flourmill Lane is Provost Skene's House dating from the sixteenth century. The chapel is particularly interesting here as, during restoration work in 1951, a painted ceiling was uncovered illustrating religious scenes thought to be seventeenth century. The top storey of the house has been turned into a folk museum housing exhibits ranging from swords and muskets to domestic items, including a spinning wheel.

St Nicholas' Church
Among the many churches of Aberdeen, St Nicholas' is the main city church and has always functioned as the ecclesiastical centre of the city. It has the distinction of possessing the largest carillon in Britain – a set of forty-eight bells which can either be played mechanically or by hand. They may be visited during the summer after recitals. Other features include the Jameson tapestries and St Mary's Chapel.

Art Gallery
The gallery houses a wide range of visual art spanning painting, sculpture, photography and silverwork. Artists contributing to the collections include Hogarth, Degas, Renoir, Augustus John, and Henry Moore.

James Dun's House
This has been converted into a museum specially for children. It is very much an open exhibition which invites children to take part in the various activities which are organised. Victorian toys, wildlife exhibits and treasures from Scottish history are amongst the contents.

Union Terrace Gardens
There are a number of parks and gardens in and around Aberdeen and this is one of the most central and attractive. Bands play here during summer evenings and there are entertainments for all including four outdoor draughts boards.

Anthropological Museum Marischal College, open Mon to Fri.
Provost Skene's House open all year (except 25, 26 Dec and 1, 2 Jan) Mon to Sat. Refreshments available.
James Dun's House open as above.
Aberdeen Art Gallery open as above, also Sun, pm only. Refreshments available.

The granite clock-towers of Aberdeen rise above the old harbour

Aberystwyth

Dyfed *p216 C1*

Two rivers flow into Cardigan Bay at Aberystwyth – the Ystwyth which gave the town its name, and the Rheidol.

Aberystwyth is a pleasant seaside resort with some attractive nineteenth-century architecture, particularly in South Marine Terrace, Queen's Square and Laura Place.

On the headland between the two beaches are the ruins of its castle. Built in 1277 by Edward I, it soon fell into disrepair and was eventually blown up by the Roundheads in 1649. The headland is attractively laid out with gardens and seats at one or two view-points.

Perched high on a hill overlooking the town is the huge National Library of Wales. It offers unparalleled research facilities on all sorts of Welsh subjects and has over four million books and documents. Here too is the oldest Welsh manuscript in existence – the twelfth-century Black Book of Carmarthen.

Wales is famous for its Great Little Trains and Aberystwyth is the terminus of one of the most popular narrow-gauge steam lines – the Vale of Rheidol Railway, which follows the course of the river Rheidol for twelve miles through some magnificent scenery. It climbs from sea-level up to 680 feet where the line ends at Devil's Bridge. At this famous beauty spot the river Mynach cascades down a 300 foot gorge, spanned by three bridges each at different levels.

Castle open at all times.
National Library of Wales open all year (except Christmas, Easter and Sun). Parking available.
Vale of Rheidol Railway operates Easter to Oct, journey time one hour each way. Parking available.

Abingdon

Oxfordshire *p213 A3*

Abingdon is a pleasant Thamesside town of great historic interest, now relieved from the burden of heavy traffic by a by-pass.

Its origins can be traced back to the seventh century when a Benedictine abbey was founded here. Some of the abbey buildings still remain, notably the long gallery, the thirteenth-century building known as the Checker with its vaulted undercroft, and the adjacent Checker Hall. The Hall has been converted into the delightful little Elizabethan-styled Unicorn Theatre.

Abingdon's County Hall has been described as the 'grandest market house in England', as it is alleged to be the work of a student of Sir Christopher Wren. The first floor of the Hall is now the home of the Town Museum which has collections of local history and archaeological finds.

Other historic buildings in the town include the Guildhall with its fine collection of paintings, the churches of St Helen and St Nicholas' and the sixteenth-century Christ's Hospital almshouses.

Abbey open Mar to Oct daily (except Mon), pm only.
Museum open all year daily (except Bank Holidays), pm only.

Alfriston

Sussex *p214 C2*

This typically picturesque Sussex village has a fourteenth-century church, known as the 'Cathedral of the Downs' because of its unusually large size. Alfriston also has a number of old inns and an enchantingly peaceful village green. Close to the green is the Clergy House. It was first built in 1350 in timber and thatch and used as a residence for priests. Later it became labourers' cottages, but has since been carefully restored retaining many of the original building materials. The large medieval hall is particularly interesting.

One-and-a-half miles north of Alfriston is Drusillas Zoo which specialises in rare breeds of farm and domestic animals. Particularly appealing are the Longhorn cattle. There are collections of small mammals with which children are allowed to play, birds and fish, a playground, a miniature railway and a display of old farm wagons. In a 300-year-old cottage an exhibition traces the history of the zoo. There is also an antique shop here and a shop selling local craftwork, farm produce, honey and jams.

Clergy House open Apr to Oct daily; Nov to 23 Dec. Medieval Hall and shop only Wed, Fri, Sat and Sun. NT.
Drusillas Zoo and Gardens open Apr to Oct daily. Nov to Mar, weekends only. Parking and refreshments available.

Allington Castle

Kent *p213 C3*

This charming thirteenth-century moated castle is set amongst woodlands and green fields beside the river Medway.

Originally built by Stephen of Penchester in 1282, it was intended as a home as well as a military stronghold, and consequently has more the air of a large, well-fortified manor house than a castle. Although it was extensively restored during the early part of this century, structural alterations were kept to a minimum and it still retains its massive gatehouse, inner courtyard, castellated curtain walls and Great Hall.

Today the castle is occupied by the Carmelite Order of Friars who run it as a Christian centre.

Open all year daily (except Christmas Day) pm only. Parking available. Refreshments May to Sep.

Alnwick

Northumberland *p220 F3*

Standing on the banks of the river Aln, this beautiful and ancient market town, provides an excellent base for touring the rugged Northumbrian countryside.

Standing high on a rocky escarpment overlooking the river and dominating the town is the huge castle, an eleventh-century border fortress built for protection from the Scots. This stronghold was the principal seat of the Percy family who virtually ruled the north-east of England for over 600 years.

The interior of the castle differs entirely from the formidable exterior, as it has been redecorated in the Italian Renaissance style. The treasures of the magnificently elaborate staterooms include many objects by renowned

Fine views of Aberystwyth as the cliff railway descends the north cliff

Alton Towers

Staffordshire *p216 F2*

Charles, 15th Earl of Shrewsbury, created Alton in the nineteenth century out of 600 acres of lovely wild woodland in the Churnet Valley. The house which once stood in the grounds was called Alveton Lodge. Charles lived here while his gardens were being landscaped and renamed it Alton Abbey. Later, in 1831, his nephew enlarged the house and called it Alton Towers. Having been used as a training centre during World War II, the Towers then fell into decay and as they were never restored only the shell remains.

However, the gardens which took twelve years to build are magnificent. Lakes, pools, terraces and valleys complement each other perfectly and are covered with thousands of ornamental flowering plants, shrubs and trees.

Various buildings were also installed to enhance the gardens and these include a Chinese pagoda fountain, a Chinese temple and a Swiss cottage. The latter was built for a blind Welsh harpist. From here he played for walkers in the gardens.

More organised entertainments include cable cars, a boating lake, an amusement park, a sea lion pool and a miniature railway.

Open Easter to mid Oct daily. Parking and refreshments available.

The monument in Alton Towers commemorates their creator, Charles Talbot

craftsmen: a pair of cabinets looted from Louis XIV during the French Revolution; and impressive porcelain collection; armoury; and paintings by famous artists including Van Dyck and Titian.

Surrounding the castle are grounds landscaped by Capability Brown which stretch down to the river and the footpath along its banks.

Castle open May to Sep (except Sat) daily, pm only. Parking available.

Alresford

Hampshire *p213 A2*

New Alresford and Old Alresford make up this charming village which stands on either side of the river Alre, a tributary of the river Itchen. New Alresford's aptly named Broad Street, lined with lime trees and Georgian buildings, is one of the finest village streets in Hampshire. North of

The grim walls of Alnwick Castle from the banks of the river Aln

A fully restored N Class 2–6–0 steam loco leaving Ropley Station

the town there is a pleasant walk through watercress beds, and another route follows the south side of the river passing a picturesque fulling mill on the way.

Perhaps the most nostalgic feature of the village is Alresford Station, the starting point of the Mid-Hants 'Watercress' Line, so called because of the large amounts of cress once carried by British Rail from Alresford.

Today a steam railway line runs between Alresford and Ropley along three miles of the old Winchester to Alton line. Both these stations are typical examples of Victorian country-station architecture.

Since the line was re-opened in April 1977, visitors have been able to take a pleasant journey through beautiful Hampshire countryside and to see steam locomotives dating back over the last sixty years, the oldest of which was built in 1920. Most of the coaching stock on the line was built between 1954 and 1956; however, the converted buffet coach was built in 1947.

The oldest coach, built in 1908, is now used as a workshop at Ropley and a variety of steam locomotives are at different stages of restoration.

Open late Mar to Oct weekends only (leaflet available giving details, times of trains etc). Parking and refreshments available.

Arundel's huge castle shows little evidence today of the damage it suffered during the Civil War

Argyll Forest Park

Strathclyde *p219 B4*

This was the first Forestry Commission Forest Park to be created in Britain. It lies on the Cowal Peninsula between Loch Fyne and Loch Long, covering some 66,000 acres of rugged West Highland Countryside, and consists of three forests: Ardgartan, Glenbranter and Benmore.

The scenery here is magnificent, with lofty peaks soaring to heights above 3,000 feet from the shores of sea lochs, their foothills clad in woods of pine and spruce. A network of forest roads covers the park and with their signposted forest walks and numerous picnic sites are ideal for walkers.

Besides the rugged highland scenery the park encompasses the beautiful Younger Botanic Gardens and the nearby Kilmun Arboretum. The Younger Botanic Gardens are situated at Benmore on the southern end of the Park. Their delightful woodlands and fine gardens feature conifers, rhododendrons and azaleas. The Kilmun Arboretum and Forest Plots extend to a hundred acres on a hillside overlooking the Holy Loch.

Younger Botanic Gardens open Apr to Oct daily. Refreshments and parking available.
Kilmun Arboretum and Forest Plots open all year during daylight hours. Entrance and car park at Forestry Commission District Office, Kilmun.

Arley Hall Gardens

Cheshire *p216 E3*

These large gardens cover some eight acres of the Arley Hall Estate. The house is the private home of Viscount and Viscountess Ashbrook. In the walled gardens are yew hedges, azaleas, shrub roses, rhododendrons and herbacious borders. One of the more unusual features here is a long avenue of clipped Ilex trees.

The sixteenth-century barn in the grounds is now a tea room and its roof is supported by seven huge wooden beams.

Open Easter to mid Oct, Tue to Sun and Bank Holidays, pm only. Parking and refreshments available.

Arlington Court

Devon *p212 C3*

Arlington Court was the home of the Chichester family until it was bequeathed to the National Trust in 1949.

It was the last owner, Miss Rosalie Chichester, who left her mark here and gave the house its present character. Her mementoes and trinkets adorn every room. She collected many things, including shells, pewter, porcelain, period costumes and, not least, over a hundred model ships, some of which were made by French prisoners during the Napoleonic wars.

The 3,500-acre park also owes much to Miss Chichester as she established the flock of Jacobs sheep, the Shetland ponies and the heronry which can be seen today from the nature trail. There is also a large collection of horse-drawn vehicles housed in the stable block.

Open Apr to Oct daily (House closed Mon). Park and gardens also open Nov to Mar daily. Refreshments available. NT.

Arundel

Sussex *p213 B2*

Narrow, hilly streets, antique shops and austere Victorian architecture lend Arundel charm and atmosphere.

Overlooking the Arun valley and the town is Arundel's superb castle – home of the dukes of Norfolk for over 500 years. The interior of the eleventh-century castle is packed with interesting treasures including paintings by Reynolds, Van Dyck and Gainsborough. Although it was virtually rebuilt in the nineteenth century, much of the furniture and furnishings are classic period-pieces ranging from William and Mary to Victorian.

Another building of note in the town is the Roman Catholic church of St Philip Neri. It was built to the design of Joseph Hansom, the man who invented the Hansom Cab, in French Gothic style. The church is, in fact, a cathedral since in 1965 Arundel was chosen as the seat of the bishopric of Brighton and Arundel. Light streams through the modern stained glass windows into the spacious interior. The high vaulted ceiling is patterned with alternating stripes of chalk and stone.

Just north of the town lies the Arundel Wildfowl Trust covering some fifty-five acres of wooded land. Many birds not easily visible in the wild can be seen here.

Castle open Apr to Oct Mon to Fri. May to late Aug daily (except Sat), pm only.
Wildfowl Trust open all year daily (except 25 Dec). Parking available.

Audley End

Essex *p213 C4*

Built on the site of a Benedictine abbey, Audley End was at one time the home of the first Earl of Suffolk. The original house, with the two large courtyards, was reputed to be comparable to Hampton Court in its splendour and magnitude. Although much of the building was demolished due to the lack of resources of subsequent earls, it remains one of the most impressive Jacobean mansions in England.

The palatial interiors of the state rooms which remain are particularly magnificent. These include the alcove room, saloon and drawing room, and the exquisite state bed to be found in the Neville Room is still hung with

Capability Brown's lake enhances the distinguished stone façade of 18th-century Audley End

the original embroidered drapes. The house also has a large collection of stuffed birds.

In the rolling parkland grounds are several elegant outbuildings, some of which were designed by Robert Adam. Amongst these are an icehouse, a circular temple and the Springwood Column. A model railway runs in the grounds and over the river Cam.

Open Apr to early Oct daily (except Mon and Bank Holidays). Parking and refreshments available. AM.

Avebury

Wiltshire *p212 F4*

A ring of ancient banks and ditches almost a mile in circumference, and the remains of the largest stone circle in Europe surround the tiny village of Avebury. Many of the stones have now gone, but the line of the outer circle can still be easily followed. Some huge stones, although apparently placed at random, are the remains of two inner circles.

The museum in the village traces the history of the stones and also that of the many prehistoric sites in the area, including the West Kennet Burial Chamber and Silbury Hill one mile south, and Windmill Hill to the north. On the edge of the circle is the Tudor Manor, home of the Marquess and Marchioness of Ailesbury, which contains some fine panelling and plasterwork.

The large garden features a formal Monks' Garden, some interesting topiary work and a magnificent old dovecote.

Museum see AM info. Also open Sun am, Apr to Sep. NT.
Avebury Manor open May and Sep, Sat and Sun. June, July and Aug daily, pm only. Bank Holidays all day.

Aviemore

Highland *p221 D2*

Aviemore, lying between the Monadhliath and Cairngorm mountains, is now the nucleus of Britain's principal winter sports region. The Aviemore Centre, which was developed in 1965, is a huge concrete holiday complex open all the year round.

Within the centre are hotels, restaurants, bars and shops. Recreational facilities include a dry ski-slope, chair lifts, skating and curling rinks, a swimming pool and a go-kart track. The Strathspey Steam Railway can be boarded at Aviemore for the short but very scenic haul to the village of Boat of Garten.

Railway open mid May to Sep, Sat and Sun. July to Aug, Tue, Wed and Thu.

The huge stones at Avebury are thought to have been placed by the nomadic Beaker peoples, as part of a religious circle, in about 1800 BC

Ayr Strathclyde *p220 C3*

Ayr is a busy market town overlooking the Firth of Clyde. Its excellent sandy beaches, attractive fishing harbour and associations with Robert Burns make it one of Scotland's most popular resorts.

Scotland's national poet, Robert Burns, was born south of the town at Alloway and in Ayr his spirit is never far away. The poet was christened at the Auld Kirk and his statue stands near the station, gazing back to Alloway. Relics of his life and work can be seen in the Tam O'Shanter Museum.

The Twa Brigs

These are two bridges close to one another spanning the river Ayr on its path through the town to the Clyde. The oldest of these, the Auld Brig, dates from the thirteenth century and for five hundred years was the only bridge in the town over the river. Burns wrote of it in his poem *The Brigs of Ayr* as 'a poor narrow footpath of a street where two wheel-barrows tremble when they meet'. The Auld Brig was renovated in 1910 and today carries only pedestrians. The second of the Twa Brigs, New Bridge, is a modern replacement of a structure first erected in 1788.

Auld Kirk of Ayr

Now hidden by modern buildings in the High Street, the Auld Kirk dates from 1654 and was built with money given by Oliver Cromwell as compensation for his take-over of the Church of St John. The church was renovated in 1952 and has three galleries

known as the 'Merchants', 'Sailors', and 'Traders' lofts. It still retains its original pulpit, and in the churchyard is a tombstone commemorating the Covenanting Martyrs. In the lych-gate are some heavy iron grave-covers which were commonly used to deter body-snatchers.

St John's Tower

A notable landmark providing panoramic views, St John's Tower is the only substantial remainder of the twelfth-century Church of St John. In 1315 the church played host to Robert Bruce's parliament which was to decide his successor to the Scottish throne. Cromwell incorporated the church into a citadel built in 1652; its remains can be seen nearby.

Tam O'Shanter Inn

An old thatched inn, a brewhouse in Burns' day, stands in the High Street and was bought for the town in 1943. It now houses a Burns museum. This is by tradition the start of Tam's ride as depicted in Burns' famous poem, *Tam O'Shanter*. Every June, the town celebrates the journey with the commemorative Burns Ride. This procession follows Tam's route which ends at the Auld Brig O'Doon, Alloway.

Wallace Tower

This neo-Gothic tower is a conspicuous feature of the High Street. Built in 1832, the 113-foot-high tower incorporates a statue of Sir William Wallace – a fervent champion of Scottish independence.

Burns' Cottage

Burns' Cottage, a two-roomed clay and thatch house, contains many furnishings and domestic implements used in Burns' day. Adjoining the cottage, set in pretty gardens, is the Burns Museum. This has an interesting exhibition of original manuscripts, a copy of the Kilmarnock edition of poems, and other of Burns' possessions, including his family Bible. Nearby stands the Burns' Monument and sculptures of characters from Burns' poems stand in the grounds.

Tam O'Shanter Museum open Apr to Sep Mon to Sat. Oct to Mar pm only. Open on Sun only between June and Aug pm only.
Burns' Cottage & Monument open all year Mon to Sat, Easter to Oct, Sun pm only. Refreshments available.

Balmoral Castle

Grampian *p222 E2*

Balmoral Castle lies in a curve of the river in the beautiful wooded valley of Royal Deeside. It is one of the private residences owned by Her Majesty the Queen and is used by the Royal Family as a summer holiday estate. The estate itself dates back to the late fifteenth century when it was known as 'Bouchmorale', Gaelic for 'majestic dwelling'. It first came into the hands of the Royal Family in 1848 when Sir Robert Gordon, who developed the deer forest and enlarged the original buildings, died suddenly. After leasing the estate for four years it was bought by Prince Albert for the sum of £31,000.

The most striking feature of the house is a square tower rising to eighty feet, which is then surmounted by a turret, extending the total height to 100 feet.

Although the castle is not open to the public the grounds and gardens can be visited when members of the Royal Family are not in residence.

Standing to the east is Crathie Church, the place of worship used by royalty whilst at Balmoral.

Grounds open May to July daily (except Sun). Refreshments available.

Bamburgh

Northumberland *p220 F1*

The small seaside resort of Bamburgh is dominated by its castle standing some 150 feet high on a rocky crag overlooking the North Sea. The town was of considerable importance as a border stronghold against invading Scots, and the castle has suffered much damage throughout its history as a result.

From the 1400s the castle was left to deteriorate and was not restored until the eighteenth century. It has since been completely renovated, and although partly residential, is still open to the public.

The most notable part of the castle is the great square keep

Above: A stained-glass portrait of Burns in his cottage at Alloway
Below: Ayr's harbour forms part of the river which flows into Ayr Bay

The countryside around Balmoral includes Ballochuie Forest, which was added to the estate by Queen Victoria

Bath see page 18

Battle

East Sussex *p213 C2*

Located near the site of the Battle of Hastings is the town of Battle. William the Conqueror built a church here to commemorate his victory in 1066 and the high altar was positioned on the spot where Harold fell. Later, Benedictine monks built St Martin's Abbey close by, although only the gatehouse and the refectory have survived. The abbey house is now a school for girls and the grounds and outer buildings are open to the public. Nothing remains of the Conqueror's church now, but excavations revealed its plan and a monument called Harold's Stone was erected in 1903 on the site of the original high altar.

There are many items connected with the battle, including a half-scale reproduction of the Bayeux tapestry, housed in the Battle Historical Society Museum located in Langton House. The museum also exhibits pieces from the local ironwork industry which prospered in Sussex for over 1,000 years.

Museum open Easter to Oct daily, Sun pm only.

which has a turret at each corner. Within its walls are many treasures including paintings, tapestries, and a cradle which belonged to Queen Anne. Also on view is an impressive weapon collection housed in the armoury. Opposite the church is the Grace Darling Museum. This contains various relics associated with the heroine, including the rowing boat in which she and her father rescued nine survivors from the wrecked SS *Forfarshire* one stormy night in 1838. When Grace Darling died of tuberculosis at twenty-six, she was buried in the churchyard of St Aidan – a thirteenth-century church with a vaulted crypt.

Castle open Apr to Sep daily, pm only. Parking available.
Grace Darling Museum open Apr to Sep daily.

Banham

Norfolk *p213 D5*

Over twenty acres of Norfolk countryside are occupied by Banham Zoo, which specialises in breeding monkeys. Apart from rarer primates, there is a worldwide collection of other animals and birds including otters, llamas, ostriches and seals.

Next to the zoo is a motor museum containing Lord Cranworth's collection of over forty cars, motor cycles and children's pedal cars, all dating from the 1920s to the 1960s. Here can be found Bentleys, famous for their racing success at Le Mans, a rare Gullwing Mercedes and a supercharged Cord.

Zoo open all year. Parking available.
Motor Museum open daily during summer. Parking available.

Bamburgh Castle became a 14th-century stronghold of the Percy family

Barnard Castle

Co Durham *p220 F1*

This historic town on the banks of the Tees is still dominated by the castle from which it takes its name. Originally called Bernard's Castle, it was built by Bernard Baliol around the late eleventh century and quickly gained importance, as did the family when, in 1292, John Baliol was crowned King of Scotland.

In 1569 the castle was besieged during the rising of the Northern Earls and fell into disrepair until 1630 when a large part of the fabric was carried off to build Raby Castle. The ruin that remains covers about six and a half acres on its cliff-top site eighty feet above the river Tees.

The Bowes family were also significant in the history of the town and it was John Bowes and his French wife, Josephine, who built the Bowes Museum in the late nineteenth century. Standing in its own park, the museum looks like an impressive French chateau and contains superb collections of paintings, furniture and porcelain, together with exhibits of local historic interest and a room devoted to dolls and dollshouses.

There are many pleasant walks in the area, one of which follows the river south-east to the lovely ruins of Egglestone Abbey, founded in 1190 for the Premonstratensian Order.

Castle see AM info. Also open Sun am, Apr to Sep.
Bowes Museum open all year daily (except Christmas, Boxing Day and New Year's Day). Sun pm only. Parking and refreshments available.
Abbey see AM info.

The Bowes collected the museum's contents themselves, although they died before its completion in 1892

Bath Avon p212 E4

Secured in the bend of the river Avon between the Cotswold and Mendip Hills, Bath can surely claim to be one of England's most beautiful cities. The Romans built their city around the hot springs and eleven centuries later Georgian architects did the same. Today Bath is a carefully preserved tribute to both those eras.

The origins of Bath are related to the hot springs which probably first reached the earth's surface at this point over one million years ago. However, it took the Romans to discover that the water had some possible therapeutic value and they first utilised it by building the sophisticated baths that, second to Hadrian's Wall, remain Britain's greatest monument to the Roman Empire.

Towards the end of the sixteenth century the hot springs were important to the city because the visitors eventually created more revenue than the established wool industry. Despite this, Bath was not an attractive place to live – the sanitation was appalling and thieving and debauchery were rife.

It was not until the eighteenth century that a gradual change was wrought which transformed Bath to the place we know. The baths became a social centre as well as a source of healing.

When a young dandy named Beau Nash arrived in Bath and became Master of Ceremonies, he impregnated the city with his personality. He was a man of tremendous elegance and style and became the sole arbiter of taste, etiquette and fashion.

Whereas Nash controlled the social structure of Bath, it was one-time postmaster Ralph Allen who instigated the building of the Georgian city. He made his fortune by radically improving the postal system and with the money bought two of the local limestone quarries. With the building material available, Allen, in conjunction with architect John Ward, was thus able to build the city of his dreams.

The Roman Baths

Serious excavations began in the nineteenth century but it was not until 1925 that the full extent of the Roman complex was uncovered. It consisted of the Great Bath, lined with lead, swimming pools, mineral-water baths and a series of rooms heated by hot air under the floors.

Attached to the baths was a temple built as a dedication to the god Sulis Minerva, and fragments have survived to this day. Part of the outside decoration shows, intact, a gorgon's head.

The many treasures which have been retrieved from the ground are housed in the adjoining Roman Baths Museum. Exhibits range from domestic utensils to a bronzed head of Minerva that survived destruction.

The Pump Room

Forming part of the Great Bath complex is the Pump Room. The present building dates from 1796 when the townsfolk decided that a larger room was needed than the one used in Nash's reign. The interior is much the same as it has always been, including the two sedan chairs – one of which was privately owned and the other used as a taxi. The room is filled with tables where either tea or spa water may be drunk to the sound of discreet chamber music.

Pulteney Bridge

This is the only piece of Robert Adam's work in Bath, but it is certainly one of the most beautiful features of the city. The bridge was copied from the Florentine Ponte Vecchio and has the same three arches. It is lined on both sides with shops, and at the back of the arcade is a central window.

Bath Abbey

The abbey is in the centre of the town and it is easy to see why it is called The Lantern of the West. Inside, enormous plain-glass windows above the nave and the choir soar up to the stone fan-vaulted ceiling seventy feet above.

The tower is rectangular rather than square because its foundations were built on the nave pillars of the previous Norman

The Great Bath, below the present street level, still has its original Roman masonry and bases of the huge pillars

Bath's famous bridge spans the Avon

cathedral. The architects of the abbey also designed the chapel at Westminster and the chapel of St George in Windsor Castle

The contents of the abbey include a rare eighteenth-century portable oak font which is still used for abbey baptisms, and more tablets and memorials than any other English church excluding Westminster Abbey; one of these tablets commemorates Beau Nash.

The Assembly Rooms
The upper floors are a fine suite of rooms, which used to be the scene of high society events in the eighteenth century. Eminent figures such as Dickens, Johann Strauss and Liszt were known to grace the rooms. Unfortunately in 1942 the building was gutted by fire and was not reopened until 1963. Since then, however, the Rooms have again provided a sumptuous setting for balls, banquets and conferences.

On reopening, a section was allocated to the Museum of Costume which exhibits the largest collection of costumes in the world. The clothing ranges from the Tudor period to the present day.

Royal Crescent
This magnificent sweep of thirty elegant houses, fronted by a total of 114 Ionic columns, was the first terrace ever to be built as a crescent. It remains one of the finest examples of its kind in Europe.

Number One has been taken over by the Bath Preservation Trust to display Georgian furnishings in an authentic setting.

The Circus
The elegant houses which form the Circus are built in three blocks of eleven, all ornamented by Tuscan, Ionic and Corinthian columns. One complete frieze depicting the arts and sciences stretches across the front of the three arcs.

In the Mews behind the Circus is the Bath Carriage Museum, housed in the original coach houses and stables of the Circus houses. Here thirty-odd carriages are carefully looked after and displayed with all their various accessories such as whips, harness and liveries. Carriage rides are available in the summer.

Burrows Toy Museum
This relatively new museum, opened in 1976, is housed in the Octagon next to the Roman Baths. Curious and amazing toys of all sorts including books and games are on display and provide a fascinating insight into children's lives over the past two centuries.

Victoria Art Gallery and Library
This is housed above the library at the western end of Pulteney Bridge. It is a particularly interesting museum with some unusual collections, including Bohemian glass, mint coins and trade notes of Bath, and the Horstmann collection of antique watches.

Baths and Pump Room open all year (except 25 Dec). Refreshments available Apr to Nov.

The grandeur of Royal Crescent

Abbey open all year (except Christmas)
Assembly Rooms open all year (except 25 Dec), daily. Limited parking available. NT.
Royal Crescent No 1 open Mar to Oct (except Mon) Sun pm only.

Carriage Museum open all year (except Christmas).
Burrows Toy Museum open as above.
Victoria Art Gallery and Library open all year (except Sun and Bank Holidays).

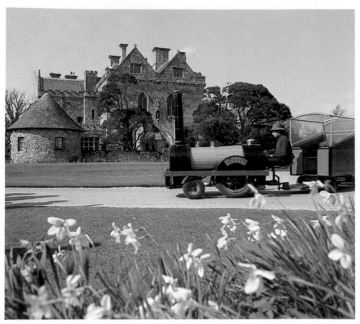

Palace House at Beaulieu with a *Planet* loco replica

Beaulieu

Hampshire *p213 A1*

There are a variety of attractions at Beaulieu comprising the Palace House, the abbey ruins and the National Motor Museum, all set amidst beautiful New Forest scenery. Once through the entrance hall to this complex, the path leads first to the Motor Museum building with its 70,000 square feet of exhibition floor space. Over 300 motor vehicles are displayed here from the magnificent 1909 Silver Ghost to the humble Mini; from the first petrol-driven car of 1895 to one of the most recent Formula 1 racing models. There are comprehensive collections here of motor cycles and commercial vehicles, a few bicycles, prototypes and the huge land-speed record breakers such as Donald Campbell's *Bluebird*. There are also displays of the components and accessories of motor transport and the whole museum is often alive with the sound of engines running and the clatter of spanners from the workshops next door. Work being carried out here may be viewed from a special window in the motorcycle gallery.

Moving on from the world of transport, visitors can either stroll through the pleasant grounds or take a monorail trip to the Palace House. Built in the fourteenth century as the abbey gateway, it was transformed in the nineteenth century and today is a charming blend of historic

building and family home of Lord Montagu.

Behind the house are the ruins of a Cistercian Abbey founded by King John in 1204 and destroyed by Henry VIII. Much of the building is gone now, but the refectory serves as the parish church of Beaulieu village and the Domus building contains an exhibition of Monastic Life at Beaulieu. Other attractions in Beaulieu include veteran bus rides, rallies, steam fairs, a model railway and a monorail.

Open all year except Christmas Day. Parking and refreshments available.

Beaumaris

Gwynedd *p216 C3*

The Norman invaders called this area *Beau Marais*, a Norman-French name meaning fair marsh. Situated on the eastern shore of the Isle of Anglesey was Beaumaris castle, and the town grew up around it. For centuries the town was the administrative capital of the island.

In contrast to many other Welsh castles which are built on limestone rocks or cliffs, Beaumaris castle stands on a vast area of flat ground. This accounts for its grand, spacious layout. The outer walls are surrounded by an octagonal moat which is fed from the sea.

In Steeple Lane, in the town centre, is the county gaol which was built in 1829 by architect and inventor Joseph Hansom. Inside

is a perfect example of a wooden treadmill and this was the last one to be used in Britain. Prisoners serving hard labour in the nineteenth century had to serve between six and eight hours a day on the treadmill, fifteen minutes on the wheel then fifteen minutes rest. Confinement to a sound-proofed cell in total darkness was the harsh punishment prisoners received for offences such as swearing, insolence or refusal to work. High on the outer wall of the prison is the door through which condemned men stepped for execution. The last public execution was in 1862. A documented exhibition of nine-teenth-century prison life gives a complete illustration of the conditions of that time.

The fifteenth-century Tudor Rose in Castle Street is a fine example of Tudor half-timber work. It was bought and restored by artist Hendrik Lek, and today houses an art gallery exhibiting his work and that of his son who is the present owner.

Castle see AM info. Also open Sun am, Apr to Sep. Parking available.
County gaol open mid May to Sep daily.
Tudor Rose open July to mid Sep daily.

Bekonscot Model Village

Buckinghamshire *p213 B3*

This model village, situated within the town of Beaconsfield, has been honoured with several

Royal visits over the years. It contains many working models including an airport, docks, a funfair and a model railway complete with five stations. In a colourful rock-garden setting visitors can walk among miniature houses, shops and churches built to a scale of one inch to one foot. There are also castles, a racecourse and a polo ground – all constructed in minute detail.

Model trains run frequently from Easter to Oct daily (weather permitting). Gardens open all year daily (except Christmas holidays). Parking available.

Belton House Park and Gardens

Lincolnshire *p217 C1*

Belton House has been the home of the Brownlow family since it was built in 1685 to a design by Christopher Wren. The house is decorated with wood carvings by Grinling Gibbons and the furnishings include pieces of porcelain, some Aubusson carpets and many great paintings, including one by Leonardo da Vinci which closely resembles his famous *Mona Lisa*. Of more recent interest is the collection of memorabilia connected with the late King Edward VIII, including, probably, the only portrait painted of him during his brief reign.

The old kitchens stood across the courtyard from the house, and were connected to it by an under-

The windmill and lilyponds in the tiny model village of Bekonscot

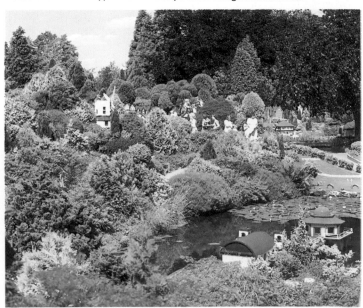

ground railway which still exists.

The grounds vary from formal gardens to deer parkland. They contain a small church housing the tombs of the Brownlows and an orangery. A museum of horse and nature trails, and a children's adventureland are two more recent additions.

Open Apr to Sep daily. Parking and refreshments available.

Belvoir Castle

Leicestershire   *p217 C1*

Home of the Rutland family since Tudor times, the present Belvoir Castle is the third to be built on this superb site above the lovely Vale of Belvoir.

The first castle was Norman, built by Robert de Todeni who

19th-century Belvoir Castle, pronounced 'Beever' Castle

came ashore with William the Conqueror, but this was destroyed during the Wars of the Roses. The second castle met a similar fate during the Civil War and the third, although almost destroyed by fire, was extensively rebuilt and restored during the early nineteenth century.

The exterior of the castle is medieval in appearance with towers, turrets and battlements, but the interior is furnished in a more classical style with painted ceilings, panelling and rich Regency furnishings. Works of art include paintings by Poussin, Reynolds, Gainsborough, Van Dyck, Hogarth and Holbein, and Gobelin tapestries adorn the walls of the Regent's Gallery. There is also a military museum devoted to the 17th/21st Lancers and a Grenadier Guards exhibition.

Between May and September special events take place in the grounds on Sundays such as jousting tournaments, band concerts, falconry displays, folk dancing and steam rallies.

Open end Mar to Sep, Wed, Thu, Sat, Bank Holidays, Sun, pm only. Oct, open Sun pm only. Refreshments available.

Berkeley

Gloucestershire   *p212 E4*

This quiet little Georgian town is dominated by its splendid castle. Built between 1117 and 1153, it remained the ancestral home of the Berkeley family for over 800 years.

The castle has been splendidly preserved and beautifully furnished over the years by the various earls of Berkeley. It was here that the barons of the west gathered in 1215 before setting out for Runnymede to witness the sealing of the Magna Carta by King John, and the deposed King Edward II was gruesomely murdered in 1327 at the behest of his wife and the Earl of Mortimer.

This feudal stronghold is entered by a bridge over a moat and has a solid circular keep. Today visitors can see the dungeon, the fourteenth-century hall, the state apartments with their tapestries and furniture, the medieval kitchens, and the actual cell in which Edward was murdered. There are also Elizabethan terraced gardens, which include a bowling alley, and close by is a large well-stocked deer park.

In the town, the fine early English church, which contains many memorials to the Berkeleys, has a Norman doorway and a detached tower built in 1783. The churchyard contains the grave of Edward Jenner (1749–1823), pioneer of smallpox vaccination, who was born here. A small Jenner museum is housed in a cottage Jenner built for the first boy he vaccinated.

Castle open Apr and Sep daily (except Mon) pm. May to Aug, Tue to Sat daily, Sun pm. Oct Sun only pm. Bank Holiday Mons pm only. Parking and refreshments available.
Jenner Museum open Apr to Sep daily (except Mon, but including Bank Holidays) pm only.

Betws y coed

Gwynedd   *p216 C3*

This oft-painted, much-photographed village has been a busy

15th-century Pont-y-Pair bridge across the Llugwy at Betws y coed

touring centre since Victorian times and shows no sign of losing its popularity. It is set in a fairytale area of wooded slopes and white water where the rivers Conwy and Gwydyr tumble over the rocks and through the valleys.

One of Betws y coed's most famous attractions is the Swallow Falls, an enchanting series of cascades and rapids. Along their course runs a railed footpath.

There are historic bridges here too; the fifteenth-century Pont-y-Pair, Telford's iron Waterloo Bridge, built in the same year as the battle, and the curious Miners' Bridge which climbs from one bank to the other like a ship's gangplank.

In the former goods yard of Betws y coed station is the Conwy Valley Railway Museum exhibiting a number of vehicles which represent each of the pre-nationalisation railway companies. Smaller items on display within the museum building include signalling equipment and models. Among the many walks through the nearby Gwydyr Forest is the Cyffty Lead Mine Trail, taking in the old mine buildings which are currently being restored.

Railway Museum open Easter to Sep daily and Oct weekends. Parking and refreshments available.

The choir of Beverley Minster with its curious illusion of 3-D flooring

A tiered fountain in the formal Italian gardens at Bicton

Beverley

Humberside *p217 C3*

This flourishing market town boasts one of the finest examples of ecclesiastical architecture in Europe, the twin-towered Beverley Minster. The most notable feature of the Minster is the beautifully ornamented Percy tomb, a shrine to the family who once owned much of the land in the area.

The other great church in the town, the church of St Mary, is a worthy tribute to fine English Gothic workmanship. The chancel is particularly impressive with its ceiling of forty panels representing the kings of England up to Henry VI.

Also in Beverley is the museum of the East Yorkshire Regiment, which has many uniforms on display, and a fine art gallery and museum containing local antiquities and interesting Victorian memorabilia.

Another notable feature of the town is Lairgate Hall, famed for its Adam ceiling and delicately hand-painted Chinese wallpaper.

Wednesday Market is a small square surrounded by attractive Georgian houses, whilst Saturday Market contains the Market Cross, bearing four shields: those of Queen Anne; Beverley Borough and the Hotham and Warton families who together contributed to the building costs of the cross.

Museum of the East Yorkshire Regiment open Tue to Fri (except Bank Holidays) pm only.
Art Gallery and Museum open daily all year (except Sun) Thu pm only.
Lairgate Hall open all year, Mon to Fri. Parking available.

Bickleigh

Devon *p212 D2*

The thatched cottages of this charming village lie peacefully on the east bank of the river Exe. It is crossed by an old, picturesque five-arched bridge offering fine views along the river.

Bickleigh Castle, also known as the Court, lies on the opposite side of the river from the village and was built on the site of a Norman castle. All that remains now from that period is the lovely little chapel with its thatched roof. The present building dates mainly from the Tudor period, although it was considerably devastated by Parliamentarians in the Civil War. However, the great hall, armoury and thatched Jacobean wing have survived. For generations it was the home of the Carew family; and Bamfylde Moat Carew, the 'king of the gipsies', was born in the castle and is buried in the village churchyard.

To the north of the village lies Bickleigh Mill Craft Centre and Farm. This picturesque old working watermill is now given over to craft-work including pottery, wood-turning and the making of jewellery and corndollies. It is one of the largest and most comprehensive working craft centres in the west of England. Adjacent to the mill is Heritage Farm, which has working shirehorses, many rare breeds of farm animals and a museum.

Bickleigh Castle open Easter to Sep, Wed, Sun and Bank Holiday Mon. Between July and first week Sep daily (except Sat), pm only.
Bickleigh Mill Craft Centre and Farm open all year daily except Christmas and New Year. Jan to Mar, pm only. Apr to Christmas daily. Parking available.

Bicton Gardens

Devon *p212 D2*

The gardens which form part of Lord Clinton's estate were landscaped in 1735 by Henry Rolle, to the designs of Andre Le Notre, French designer of the gardens at Versailles.

The mile-long narrow-gauge Bicton Woodland Railway provides a good chance to view the lake and one of the finest collections of coniferous trees in Britain, the Pinetum. On the shores of the lake is a nineteenth-century summer house called the Hermitage.

A large countryside museum contains many exhibits of rural life and industry, among them the history of the plough.

Open Apr to Oct daily. Parking and refreshments available.

Bignor Roman Villa

West Sussex *p213 B2*

Evidence was found in 1811 of a Roman Villa at Bignor and the excavations which followed revealed one of the largest villas ever to be discovered in Britain. The buildings, which were inhabited from the second to the fourth century, enclosed a large courtyard and had farm buildings to the rear of them.

There are extensive remains of the Roman mosaic floors and pavements, now protected by wooden buildings. The cold plunge-bath and the floor of its undressing room lie beyond what is now the car park. A museum on the site contains various Roman relics and a plan of the original complex.

Open Mar to Oct daily (closed Mon except Bank Holidays and during Aug). Parking available.

Roman mosaics often depict legends, gods or geometric patterns

Blackpool Lancashire *p216 D4*

Blackpool is England's mecca of entertainment and has attained this position through sheer size, extravagance and wholehearted devotion to the big business of holiday-making. The world famous tower, illuminations and beach are the resort's star attractions, but they merely spearhead the endless amusements Blackpool has to offer.

Over the last two centuries Blackpool has exploded from a small fishing village with a population of less than 1,000, to become one of the largest, most spectacular holiday centres in Europe with well over 150,000 resident inhabitants.

It was the advent of the railway that opened up to Lancastrians and Yorkshiremen the possibility of going away for holidays. With this new-found mobility people flocked to the coast; Blackpool was quick to see the opportunities which existed and the town plunged into the industry of entertainment. Now, during the summer months, approximately eight million people flock to Blackpool and for at least half of them it is their annual holiday resort.

It is difficult to imagine the vastness of a resort which has to cater for such numbers. From the town itself seven miles of sandy beaches stretch southwards, backed by entertainments of every kind. During September and October five miles of the promenade are ablaze at night with dazzling coloured lights. These are Blackpool's famous illuminations.

As well as the promenade display, gigantic animated tableaux are mounted on the cliffs and many of the electric tramcars are transformed into creations such as a Moon Rocket, Mississippi Showboat and the Santa Fe Express. New additions are being made all the time to incorporate current popular fictional characters, such as the Muppets.

Glittering Blackpool Tower

The Tower
Standing 518 feet high is the town's landmark, Blackpool Tower. It is a fairytale showpiece which was built in imitation of the Parisian Eiffel Tower. Weather permitting, a lift takes people up to the top for the tremendous views along the coast.

At the base of the Tower is a huge complex housing the Ballroom; Butterfly Garden; Monkey Jungle; Tropical Garden and the Tower Circus. Amusements for children include Fun Farm and Apollo Playground.

The Space Tower
Another tower has been added to Blackpool's coastline recently, the Space Tower. This construction of tubular steel on the Pleasure Beach has a glass-fronted observation cabin. Which travels up and down the cylindrical tower.

The Promenade
The three piers, each with a sundeck and a theatre, the Winter Gardens and Opera House, the Golden Mile and the only electric trams still operating in Britain, are all characteristic features of Blackpool's seafront.

The piers, trams and Winter Gardens are almost all that is left of the Victorian days that established Blackpool's popularity. The rest of the promenade is crammed with every kind of amusement gimmick and entertainment novelty imaginable. Amongst the latest entertainment complexes are Coral Island, Wonderful World and the Star Entertainment centre. Tram rides can be taken along the length of the promenade.

Stanley Park
Behind the town can be found a more restful aspect to Blackpool's character – Stanley Park. Around the large boating lake gardens are laid out in Italian style and many rose gardens adorn the park.

Next to Stanley Park is Zoo Park, one of Britain's newest zoos. The animals and birds are kept in thirty-eight acres of moated enclosures. The latest addition is a new gorilla house.

Grundy Art Gallery and Central Library
Situated in the town itself, the gallery houses a permanent collection of nineteenth and twentieth-century paintings by British artists.

Tower Buildings open May to Oct daily. Refreshments available.
Pleasure Beach (Space Tower) open Spring Bank Holiday to Oct.
Zoo Park open all year (except 25 Dec). Parking available.
Grundy Art Gallery open all year (except Sun and Bank Holidays). Parking available.

Blair Castle

Tayside *p221 D1*

Beside the highland village of Blair Atholl on the banks of the river Garry, Blair Castle stands amidst its sweeping parkland. It is still the seat of the Duke of Atholl, who is the only British subject permitted to keep a private army, the Atholl Highlanders. The oldest part of the building remaining is the thirteenth-century Cummings Tower which was renovated during the nineteenth century.

Although the present Duke still lives in the castle, thirty-two of the rooms are open to the public. They contain one of the best collections of weaponry in Scotland, many beautiful tapestries, Georgian and Victorian toys, and a marvellous china collection. Several family portraits adorn the walls, and there are many extremely fine examples of period furniture here, including work by Chippendale and Sheraton.

Open Easter weekend, each Sun and Mon in Apr. May to mid Oct daily. Sun pm only. Parking and refreshments available.

Blickling Hall

Norfolk *p218 F1*

This superb example of Jacobean architecture was designed by Robert Lyminge in the early seventeenth century for Sir Henry Hobart.

The splendid interior contains many rooms of the Georgian era. The hall and Jacobean staircase were remodelled by Thomas Ivory and his family who were architects from Norwich, and have life-size carvings of Elizabeth I and Anne Boleyn set into the walls. The long gallery contains a carved Jacobean ceiling. The library is reputed to have one of the finest collections of pre-sixteenth-century books in England.

The exquisite gardens are mainly the work of Humphrey Repton. They contain many formal flower beds and great arcades, an orangery and a temple. Here too is the pyramid-shaped mausoleum designed by the Italian architect, Joseph Bonomi in 1793 for the Earl and Countess of Buckinghamshire.

A crescent-shaped lake in the grounds has been enlarged to stretch almost a mile in length and provides an attractive contrast to the formal gardens.

Open Apr to mid-Oct usually daily, but closed Fri and Mon (except Bank Holiday Mon) during Apr, May and Oct. House closed midday. Gardens only late May to Sep, Mon to Fri. NT.

Bluebell Railway

East Sussex *p213 C2*

The Bluebell steam railway line is operated largely by a volunteer work force of steam enthusiasts and is one of the most successful of its kind in Britain. It runs for five miles through lovely Sussex countryside between Sheffield Park and Horsted Keynes. Sheffield Park Station, built in 1882, is being restored to its original state

The Lily Pool below Bodnant House decorates the third garden terrace

and on Platform 2 is a Museum of Railway Relics. Visitors can also see the signal box and the locomotives which are not in service.

Horsted Keynes station is being restored as well, and it is here that the collection of old carriages and wagons are kept. (See *Sheffield Park.*)

Steam trains run at weekends throughout the year (Sun only in Dec, Jan and Feb), weekends and Wed in May and Oct, daily from June to Sep and daily during Easter week. The museum is open on days when trains are running, and on other days is open for limited viewing. Parking and refreshments available.

Bodiam Castle

East Sussex *p213 C2*

In the fourteenth century when the river Rother was navigable as far as Bodiam and the French were becoming hostile, Richard II granted Sir Edward Dallyngrigge permission to build Bodiam Castle as a military stronghold. From the outside the castle looks very much the same as it did then because its defences were never seriously put to the test. However, since it was besieged in the Civil War the castle has not been inhabited and it is little more than an empty shell. The exterior was restored during the first half of this century by Lord Curzon.

Much of the castle's romantic appearance results from its reflection in the waters of the moat. This is shaped like a lake and is dotted with lovely water lillies. Various objects dicovered during excavations may be viewed in the small museum which is attached to the castle.

Open Apr to Oct daily. Nov to Mar Mon to Sat. Parking available. NT.

Bodnant Gardens

Gwynedd *p216 C3*

These are undeniably the finest gardens in Wales and they occupy a superb position above the Conwy Valley with views across to Snowdon. They were laid out in 1874 and remained in the care of the Aberconway family until donated to the National Trust.

Five large terraces lead down from the house. The canal terrace is perhaps the most beautiful of these, with its open-air theatre at one end and eighteenth-century Pin Mill at the other. The Pin Mill is a small building which was last used as a pin factory in Gloucestershire. It was rescued when practically in ruins and brought to Bodnant. The theatre has a raised grass stage and the

The gables, turrets and open-topped lantern of Blickling Hall

The gaunt shell of Bodiam Castle reflected in the still waters of its wide moat

wings and back-drops are constructed of clipped yew hedges. The gardens are at their best in the spring when the mass of rhododendrons and azaleas are in glorious bloom.

Open mid Mar to Oct daily. Refreshments available Apr to Sep. NT.

Bolsover Castle

Derbyshire *p217 B2*

Bolsover Castle stands some 600 feet above sea level and commands lovely views of the locality. Built on the site of a former Norman keep, the present castle dates back to the seventeenth century when Sir Charles Cavendish had the buildings erected to imitate the earlier romantic medieval style. The battlements, turrets and decorative domes achieved this effect. King Charles I and Queen Henrietta were entertained here after the completion of the lavish staterooms in 1634.

The 170-foot long riding school and gallery, added at a later date by Sir Charles's son, is now used by a Spanish riding school.

See AM info. Also open Sun am, Apr to Sep. Parking available.

Bolton Abbey

North Yorkshire *p217 A3*

The skeleton of this twelfth-century Augustinian priory lies on the banks of the river Wharfe. A foot-bridge spans the river here and there is a way across via stepping stones. After the Dissolution only the nave of the priory was saved which subsequently became the parish church of the village, known as Bolton Abbey. The priory gatehouse was incorporated in the nearby Bolton Hall, home of the Dukes of Devonshire.

So attractive is the spot, that the painter Landseer immortalised it in his poem *Bolton Abbey in Olden Time*.

The abbey may be viewed at any time.

Border Forest Park

Northumberland, Cumbria and Borders *p220 E3*

Only a few main roads give access to these 145,000 acres of forest and fell which extend along the Cheviots and neighbouring hills in Northumberland, Cumbria and the Scottish Borders Region.

The heart of the Border Forest Park is the North Tyne Valley; Kielder North, Mounces, Falstone and Wark make up the four larger forest groups. Peel Fell is the highest peak in the park at 1,975 feet and stands right on the border, affording excellent views over northern England and southern Scotland. Spruce trees account for most of the park's woodlands and provide shelter for the growing wildlife community. Every few years each plantation is harvested and the timber, which visitors can see being felled and trimmed, is transported for use in timber industries.

The area is rich in history, hill circles and hill forts of prehistoric man are scattered over the moors. There are also Roman camps, fortified farmsteads and castles in the park which is crossed by the 250-mile Pennine Way footpath.

Boscastle

Cornwall *p211 B2*

The small fishing village of Boscastle lies in the Valency Valley on the north coast of Cornwall. The main village lies behind the harbour and is surrounded by steep woods. The harbour, built into the cliffs, forms a natural haven for boats. However, its narrow entrance can be difficult to negotiate, especially if the river in spate meets a strong tide which causes a dramatic surge of current.

The Witches Museum close to the harbour exhibits past and present customs of witches and the paraphernalia associated with black magic.

Museum open Easter to Oct daily. Parking available.

Boscobel House

Shropshire *p216 E2*

This modest house in the Brewood Forest was built at the beginning of the seventeenth century by John Giffard of Chillington Hall. It was intended for use both as a hunting lodge and as a refuge against religious persecution (the Giffards were staunch Catholics). Not until some fifty years later was its effectiveness as a place of concealment put to the test. On 3 September, 1651, Charles II's army was soundly beaten at the Battle of Worcester and the Royal escape party reached Brewood Forest. Luckily the owner of Boscobel was with them. Charles spent one tense night in a hiding-hole within the house which can still be seen. The more famous refuge is the Royal Oak in which the King spent his days hiding from the Roundhead search party. A descendant of the original oak in the grounds marks the spot today.

See AM info. Closed lunchtime. Parking available.

Boughton House

Northamptonshire *p213 B5*

Boughton House was erected around a fifteenth-century abbey in a picturesque village built mostly of ironstone and thatch. Sir Edward Montagu was the first to buy the property but there is little left of the original architecture. Four generations later, the house was in the possession of the third Lord Montagu, who was appointed Ambassador to France in 1669, and maintained his fortune by wisely marrying a series of wealthy widows. His love of French architecture inspired him to restore the building in the style of the famous Versailles. The left wing was never completed and was left without floors or ceilings.

Inside the house varying styles of decoration are employed. Mythological scenes cover the ceilings and walls, whilst many of the rooms are oak-panelled in a more sombre manner. Amongst the furnishings are examples of velvet upholstery and marquetry pieces. Italian paintings adorn the walls and there is a splendid collection of luxurious Persian carpets.

The house is surrounded by water gardens and broad avenues of lime and elm trees which include a spacious picnic area, nature trail, and woodland adventure playground.

Open Easter, May Day and Spring Bank Holiday weekends pm only, also Aug to Sep daily (except Fri). Oct, Thu, Sat, Sun pm only.

Originally an abbots' residence, Boughton House was bought in 1683 by Sir Edward Montague (one of Henry VII's executors)

Boscastle was once a busy port with a flourishing seal industry

Bournemouth Dorset *p212 F2*

This distinguished resort was, until the Victorian love-affair with the seaside, a place of wild heathland where the tiny Bourne stream meandered its way to the sea. Today Bournemouth provides all the attractions of a high-class resort with its mild climate, sandy beaches, acres of gardens and fine coastal views.

The sandy shoreline of Bournemouth lies in the shelter of 100-foot cliffs which spread along Poole Bay. These steeply rising cliffs, with their lifts, steps and footpaths leading to the seafront, provide a magnificent background to the town and almost traffic-free promenades. Just to the west of the town these sandstone cliffs are penetrated by a series of deep, wooded valleys called chines that open out to the sea.

The character of this dignified resort is enhanced by the acres of beautiful parks and public gardens which have been landscaped around the natural beauty of the valley and the Bourne stream. Behind the promenades and gardens spreads a modern town of shops, hotels, cinemas and theatres. The two piers, the museums, and the Victorian villas which stand in shaded streets of pine are reminders of Bournemouth's Victorian heyday.

Bournemouth offers the visitor a fine selection of entertainment ranging from variety shows to theatre, cinemas and opera. The renowned Bournemouth Symphony Orchestra has its permanent home at the Winter Gardens, whilst the pier and surrounding areas provide the more traditional seaside amusement arcades, children's pools and playgrounds.

Rothesay Museum

This contains the Lucas collection of early Italian paintings and pottery, English china and furniture. It also has an armoury room, a New Zealand room and a marine room, which includes relics from Sir Cloudesley

One of Bournemouth's gardens

Shovell's flagship HMS *Association*, which sunk in 1707. Here, too, is the British Typewriter Museum, a unique collection of vintage typewriters, which were collected by W. A. Beeching, author of *Century of the Typewriter*.

Russell-Cotes Art Gallery and Museum

East Cliff Hall (housing the museum) is an interesting example of Victorian architecture. It contains period rooms, a section on Oriental art, the Henry Irving theatrical collection and a freshwater aquarium.

Big Four Railway Museum

This museum contains over 1,000 railway items, including one of the largest collections of locomotive nameplates, number plates and work plates in the country. There is also a large working model railway and a shop selling books and models.

The Lower, Central and Upper Gardens

These attractive gardens follow the Bourne stream through the heart of the town. The Lower Gardens form the hub of Bournemouth's seafront. They lie in the valley amongst footpaths and pines and in spring are ablaze with flowering cherry trees. As the gardens follow the Bourne they become the Central Gardens, with their azaleas, rhododendrons and magnolias. The Upper Gardens come next with their pretty willow trees.

Rothesay Museum open all year (except Good Fri, Christmas and Sun).

Some of the fascinating contents of Russell-Cotes Museum

Russell-Cotes Art Gallery and Museum open all year (except Good Fri, Christmas and Sun). Refreshments available.

Big Four Railway Museum open all year June to Sep daily (Oct to May, Wed and Sat only).

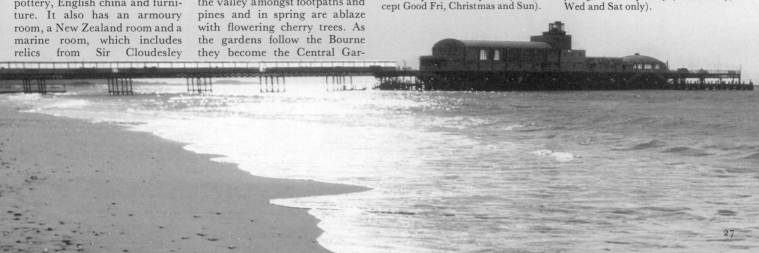

Bourton-on-the-Water

Gloucestershire *p212 F5*

Bourton is a delightful Cotswold-stone village, with the river Windrush flowing through it beside sloping lawns and beneath picturesque low-arched bridges.

Interesting features of this popular spot include the restored parish church which has a fourteenth-century chancel. In the eighteenth-century watermill is a collection of cars and motorcycles ranging from vintage to the 1950s.

In the garden behind the Old New Inn the Model Village portrays Bourton to a scale one-ninth actual size and includes a replica of the river Windrush, working waterwheel, churches, shops and the Inn all in real Cotswold stone.

The nearby Birdland Zoo Gardens covers four acres of ponds, groves and aviaries and is home to some 600 species of foreign and exotic birds.

Motor Museum open all year daily.
Model Village open all year daily. Refreshments available in hotel.
Birdland Zoo Gardens open all year daily (except 25 Dec).

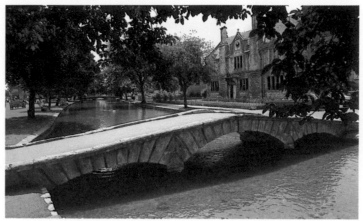

Footbridges over the river Windrush in Bourton-on-the-Water

Bradgate Park

Leicestershire *p213 A5*

This area of woods and heathland was donated to the county of Leicester in 1928 to be used as an open space for public use. There are many pleasant walks through its 850 acres, and the native Fallow and Red deer are protected now where once they were mercilessly hunted.

The area known as Swithland Woods used to contain a prosperous slate-quarrying industry which only declined when cheaper Welsh slate came on to the market in the nineteenth century. The disused quarries are now fenced off for safety.

Standing on the highest point of the park is a tower known as Old John, used by hunting parties and reputedly built to commemorate Old John, a local miller who died in an accident on this hill.

Between the hill and the Cropston Reservoir are the ruins of Bradgate House, built around 1500 by Thomas Grey, 1st Marquess of Dorset. He was the grandfather of Lady Jane Grey, the ill-fated nine-day-Queen who was born and brought up here before the plotting of her family cost her her head. On the edge of the Park at Newtown Linford is Marion's Cottage which serves as the park's information centre and bookshop.

Park open all year, no vehicles allowed except those carrying invalids.
Ruins open Apr to Oct, Wed, Thu and Sat pm only. Sun am only. Parking available.
Marion's Cottage open all year Sat and Sun pm only, also Wed and Thu pm Apr to Oct. Parking available.

Braemar

Grampian *p222 E2*

This summer and winter resort is divided by Clunie Water and surrounded by the heather-clad slopes of the eastern Cairngorms. It is probably most famous for its annual Highland Gathering, an extravaganza of pipe-bands, athletics and, of course, tossing the caber. This event is often attended by members of the Royal Family.

Reminders of Braemar's past exist in the scant remains of Kindrochit Castle near the Cluny Bridge, already a ruin in 1600; in the cottage in Castleton Terrace where Robert Louis Stevenson wrote *Treasure Island*; and in the picturesque Braemar Castle just outside the village.

Built overlooking the Dee in 1628 by the 2nd Earl of Mar, the castle was a gesture of strength against the Farquharsons who later burned it down. Ironically, it was this same family who purchased and rebuilt the castle during the eighteenth century. Still their family home today, the castle has many notable features including the solidly built round tower, star-shaped curtain wall, barrel-vaulted ceiling and the massive iron gateway.

Royal Highland Gathering first Sat in Sep.

Braemar Castle open May to Sep daily. Parking available.

Bramall Hall

Gt Manchester *p216 F3*

One of the finest examples of half-timbered houses in the country, Bramall Hall, is now a museum. Most of the Hall in its present form dates from 1590 and the Davenport family have held the property for 500 years, restoring it in 1819.

The south wing, said to be the oldest, contains the Banqueting Room and Chapel and dates back to approximately 1400. In the master bedroom there is a tapestry worked by Dame Dorothy Davenport which apparently took thirty-six years to complete. She was one of the Hall's owners in the 1590s.

Open all year Tue to Sun and Bank Holidays, pm only. Parking available.

Breamore House

Hampshire *p212 F3*

This red-brick Elizabethan manor was not completed until three years after William Dodington first bought the wooded estate in 1580. In 1856 a fire swept through the interior of the house, and some of the original structure was destroyed.

The Hulses, who owned the property for almost 200 years, collected many treasures which can be seen today. The walls are hung with family portraits dating back as far as the early eighteen

Magnificent views over Braemar, with Clunie Water snaking away into the distance between the Cairngorm Hills

A Victorian cottage kitchen recreated in the Countryside Museum at Breamore House

century. All the furnishings are magnificent, including rare examples of early English mahogany carpentry, unusual Dutch marquetry-work, and an extremely rare feather fan from India.

The grounds contain the Breamore Countryside Museum, which is an interesting exhibition of rural crafts and agricultural machinery, and the Carriage Museum. This has many horse drawn vehicles, and is housed appropriately in the old stables.

Open Apr to Sep, Tue to Thu, Sat, Sun and all Bank Holidays, pm only. Refreshments (teas) and parking available.

Bressingham Gardens and Live Steam Museum

Norfolk *p213 D5*

Bressingham Hall's gardens are said to be the largest of their kind in Europe. Alpine plants and perennials are lavishly displayed in five acres of informal gardens with some 5,000 species of hardy plants. A glittering roundabout accompanied by a brassy steam organ can also be seen in the grounds.

The most comprehensive collection of steam-powered engines in Britain is housed in the Live Steam Museum which exhibits standard-gauge locomotives.

Apart from the locomotives, traction and road engines are on show; in particular a ten-ton machine called *Bertha* which was mainly used in farm work and was the first exhibit to start the steam engine museum.

Another feature of the museum is a separate narrow-gauge railway with miniature trains which give the visitor the chance to take a steam-hauled ride through the Bressingham estate.

Open May to Sep, Sun pm also Thu pm from late May to mid Sep and Wed pm during Aug. Bank Holidays (except winter) pm only. Parking and refreshments available.

Alan Bloom, owner of Bressingham Museum, with the *Oliver Cromwell*

Brighton Sussex *p213 C2*

From a small village called Brighthelmstone tucked away beneath the South Downs, grew the town of Brighton – destined to become one of the most fashionable seaside resorts in the south of England. It reached its heyday in Victorian times but since then its character has shifted away from that of the resort to that of a modern town. Now, rich in cultural and commercial amenities, it remains a popular holiday centre offering a diverse range of entertainment and interests.

The Pavilion – first built in 1787 at a cost of £50,000

Brighton's fame began when a certain Dr Russell published a book in 1750, extolling the curative powers of the sea air, and moved his practice to Brighthelmstone. When the Prince of Wales heard of this and consequently visited the village, it soon became a very fashionable place basking in the glory of royal patronage. A considerable amount of building subsequently took place and the Regency architecture of the eighteenth century gave Brighton the style which distinguishes it from many other resorts. Regency Square, Clifton Terrace and Royal Crescent are particularly fine with their well-proportioned houses, white façades, bow windows and wrought-iron balconies.

Brighton is a curious mixture of styles, however, and offsetting its Regency elegance are the seventeenth-century Lanes, the nineteenth-century pier and the vast ultra-modern marina which is the largest in Europe.

The Royal Pavilion

This curiosity was first built as a classical domed structure to serve as a seaside retreat for the Prince of Wales – such was the fancy he had taken to Brighton. Later, architect John Nash rebuilt the Pavilion after the style of an Indian palace to indulge the exotic taste of the Prince. Inside the flavour becomes oriental and is richly furnished and decorated in the classical Chinese style which was in vogue at the time. The decor is lavish in the extreme; especially splendid is the Banqueting Hall with its forty-five-foot-high domed ceiling, from

Good advertising in the Lanes

Pier, beach and sea – still the great holiday attractions

which hangs a glittering silver dragon dangling from a huge chandelier by its claws. The Great Kitchen is also particularly interesting as it contains hundreds of pieces of cooking equipment for every purpose.

The Lanes

This famous part of the town consists of a maze of narrow streets and alleys lined with bow-fronted one-time fishermen's cottages. Now they sell hundreds of antiques and curios of every description and the browser may stop at any one of the number of attractive pubs and cafés which also abound here.

The Piers and Promenade

The piers and promenade of Brighton are still an integral part of the town's popularity. Although the beach is shingle, it is nearly always crowded with holiday makers in the summer as Brighton is known for its mild sunny climate.

The promenade follows the whole of the front and deck chairs may be hired here in time-honoured tradition. In the 1930s it was extended eastwards from Black Rock as an undercliff path to prevent erosion of the cliffs by the sea. In stormy weather the waves crash over the sea wall in a spectacular fashion.

The pleasures of two piers were once enjoyed in Brighton but now only the newer Palace Pier is open. West Pier was closed when it caught fire and insufficient money was available to repair it. There are still amusement arcades and refreshment stalls on Palace Pier but they are a far cry from the numerous entertainments which flourished in the Victorian era.

Apart from walking along the promenade, the front may be viewed from one of the open-topped double-decker buses that run through the town. As another alternative there is the Volks railway. This was Britain's first public electric railway which opened in 1883. In the summer it provides rides along to Black Rock from the Aquarium. On the route is Peter Pan's Playground where one can stop and enjoy the funfair.

Aquarium and Dolphinarium

There has been an Aquarium in Brighton for over one hundred years and thousands of aquatic wonders can be seen amidst its Victorian subterranean arches. Over 10,000 fish from all over the world can be seen here, as well as penguins, turtles, seals and sealions. As a further attraction there are shows of performing dolphins every day in the Dolphinarium.

Museum and Art Gallery

Next to the Pavilion in Church Street is the Museum and Art Gallery. The buildings were originally stables to the Pavilion – the interior being a far cry from the

one which offsets the treasures housed there now. There are paintings by English and continental masters, as well as a gallery devoted to Fine Art of the twentieth century. Also to be seen here are collections of Sussex archaeology and folk life, natural history, the Willett Collection of English pottery and several wax busts of Georgian personalities.

Booth Museum of Natural History

Stuffed British birds are attractively and realistically displayed here in models of their natural habitat. There are also skeletons here of both rare and extinct animals and over one million pinned butterflies.

Royal Pavilion open all year daily (except Christmas). Refreshments available Easter to Oct.

Aquarium open all year daily. Refreshments available.

Museum and Art Gallery open all year (except Mon, Good Fri, Christmas). Sun pm only.

Booth Museum of Natural History open all year (except Thu and Sat), Sun pm only.

Bristol Avon p212 E4

The Flower of Bristowe, commonly known as non-such, and the phrase 'all ship-shape and Bristol Fashion' give a clue to the city's past. The former was brought here by merchants from the Middle East and the latter reflects the sea-faring history of this bustling centre. Although new shopping centres, car parks and entertainment complexes intermingle with the old buildings, Bristol still has the salty air of a sea-trading port.

Amateur yachtsmen sailing in the shelter of Bristol's harbour

As an Anglo-Saxon settlement, *Brigstoc*, as it was known, grew up around the harbour on the river Avon. Silver coins have been found that were minted in Bristol during the reign of Ethelred the Unready (978–1013) and these indicate the commercial importance of the city even then.

The Normans built a castle on the strip of land separating the rivers Avon and Frome and from the time of the Conquest, Bristowe (the medieval name) grew steadily in importance during the twelfth and thirteenth centuries, doubling in size and increasing its wharfage area to cope with the growth of trade.

Late in the fifteenth century sailors brought from Iceland stories of a distant land to the west. The tales stirred the merchants of Bristol to dispatch their ships in search of these lands, spurred by economic need to find new markets. They were successful and Cabot's Tower, erected in 1897, stands a hundred feet high on Brandon Hill to commemorate the discovery of America by John Cabot in 1497.

Trade grew and flourished but during the seventeenth century Bristol's wealth was bought dearly, for a large part of its income was derived from slave trading. When slavery was abolished in the nineteenth century Bristol suffered a serious setback and found herself in fierce competition with Liverpool.

Bristol is still a busy port and from Prince Street Bridge, Prince's Wharf and Wapping Wharf can be seen where Baltic timber and Dutch merchandise is unloaded. From Hotwells Road a good view may be had of the Albion Dockyards and Cumberland Basin which accommodate ocean-going ships coming in from the Avon.

The Cathedral

The cathedral has stood on College Green since the twelfth century. Originally founded in the 1140s as the church of an Augustinian abbey, Henry VIII granted it the status of cathedral in 1542. The Norman chapter house, the gatehouse, the entrance to the abbot's lodging, the

The cathedral's ornate interior

south-east transept walls and the east walk of the cloister remain from the original building. The superbly carved choir stalls were added in the sixteenth century, and later Grinling Gibbons built the fine organ case.

One particular feature are the bosses in the roof of the north transept and there is also some fine fourteenth-century glass.

In the nineteenth century a nave was built to match the choir. There are fascinating tombs and monuments here and some interesting candlesticks. These were donated in 1712 by the rescuers of Alexander Selkirk, the man on whom Daniel Defoe based his character of Robinson Crusoe.

Museum and Art Gallery

The museum has fine collections of archaeological, natural history, scientific and transport exhibits and the art gallery has displays of ceramics, glass and sculpture. Among the fine art collections are paintings by Sir Thomas Lawrence, a Bristol man. There is also an aquarium in the museum.

Bristol's history, until the Reformation can be found in the St Nicholas Church Museum. There is a special collection of church art and displays of eighteenth and nineteenth-century watercolours of Bristol. A notable attraction is the Hogarth altar piece originally intended for the St Mary Redcliffe church.

Early engraving of the Clifton Suspension Bridge

St Mary Redcliffe

Elizabeth I described this thirteenth-century church as 'the fairest, goodliest, and most famous parish church in the Kingdom'. The nineteenth-century 250-foot spire rests on the thirteenth-century tower and within the church the long nave, open parapets, flying buttresses and huge glass windows resemble the interior of a cathedral. The hexagonal north porch contains carvings of beasts and men which have survived restoration, extension and rebuilding.

The Exchange

Situated in Corn Street this splendid building was designed by John Wood the Elder, famous for his work in Bath. The exchange stands back from the street so its carefully proportioned façade may be more easily viewed.

Outside on the pavement stand four 'nails'. These are bronze pillars on which merchants conducted their business, giving rise to the saying 'to pay on the nail'.

The entrance hall is divided by four Corinthian columns. There are niches along the walls with a frieze of flowers and fruit and a head in the middle of each section. The doorways leading off to the east, west and south have exuberant decorations above them arranged around allegorical heads depicting Asia, Africa and America.

Theatre Royal

Down cobbled King Street, one of the oldest in Bristol, is the longest working theatre in England. Built in 1764–6 the interior is 120 feet by fifty feet and was originally all wood. It has a semi-circular auditorium, which was unusual for that time, and this has been kept.

Also in its original condition is Red Lodge in Park Row. This sixteenth-century house was altered in the eighteenth century

and contains fine oak carvings and furnishings from both periods.

SS *Great Britain*

Prince Albert launched Isambard Kingdom Brunel's *Great Britain* in Bristol in July, 1843. It was the beginning of a new era in ocean travel. The 322-foot-long ship was the largest in the world and also the first one of this size to use an iron hull and be driven by a screw propeller.

Brunel's SS *Great Britain*

Great Britain sailed until 1886 when she was abandoned in the Falkland Islands after being wrecked by a storm. In 1970 she was rescued and brought back to Bristol on a specially constructed raft, and is being restored in the dock in which she was built.

A converted dockside transit shed 400 yards from SS *Great Britain* serves as the Bristol Industrial Museum. Vehicles, both horse-drawn and motorised, aircraft and aero engines and various kinds of manufacturing machinery used locally compete for attention with railway exhibits, which include a full-size locomotive.

Clifton

This elegant, attractive suburb of Bristol is interesting in its own right. Here Brunel's best known work, Clifton Suspension Bridge, hangs like a cobweb between the sides of the Avon Gorge 245 feet above the river. It sways slightly as one walks across it and at night is lit up with fairy lights.

Nearby on the Bristol side of the bridge is the Observatory. Formerly a snuff-mill, it now contains a camera obscura. Beneath is a passage to Giant's Cave which opens out into a ledge high above the river below.

Also in Clifton is Bristol Zoo. This has a good collection of unusual animals incuding the only white tigers in Europe. The grounds are attractively laid out with lawns, lakes and flowers.

Cabot Tower open all year daily.
Museum and Art Gallery open Mon to Sat (except Bank Holiday but open Easter Mon and late Summer Bank Holiday). Parking available.
St Nicholas Church Museum open as above.
The Exchange open Fri for public market.
Red Lodge open as Museum and Art Gallery but pm only.
SS Gt Britain open all year (except Christmas) daily. Parking and refreshments available.
Bristol Industrial Museum open all year (except New Year's Day, Good Fri and Christmas). Sat to Wed.
Bristol Zoo open daily all year (except Christmas). Refreshments available.

Guests, dressed in Dickensian costume, attending a garden party at Bleak House during the Dickens Festival, which takes place in June

Broadstairs

Kent *p214 E3*

During the Regency period Broadstairs was a fashionable 'watering place'; the Victorians continued the fashion by holidaying here and today it is both a popular residential and holiday resort.

The several miles of sand in small bays beneath chalk cliffs make this stretch of coastline particularly attractive.

The town has many links with Charles Dickens. Bleak House, now a Dickens' museum, was his home whilst writing *David Copperfield*. It contains many pieces of Dickens' own furniture, as well as some original editions of his novels, drawings and photographs. Close to Bleak House is the Dickens House Museum immortalised as the home of Betsey Trotwood in *David Copperfield*.

A Dickens Festival is held each year in mid June and the old town with its buildings round the jetty recall Dickensian days as the townsfolk dress up as Dickens' most famous characters and parade through the streets.

Bleak House open Easter weekend then mid May to Sep daily pm only.
Dickens House Museum open Apr to Oct daily, pm only. (Tue, Wed, Thu evenings 7pm – 9pm June to Sep.)

In fine weather several counties can be seen from Broadway Tower

Broadway

Hereford and Worcester *p212 F5*

Broadway, the epitome of a Cotswold village, is built entirely of the honey-coloured local stone. Most of its houses are of Tudor, Jacobean or Georgian origin, and many have been turned into antique shops.

To the east of the village Fish Hill rises to 1,024 feet, surmounted by a fifty-five-foot tower—a folly built in 1800 by the Earl of Coventry. The tower contains an observation room, an exhibition on Broadway and the history of the tower; and the nearby Tower Barn contains a countryside exhibition. This forms the focal point of the Broadway Tower Country Park with its nature trails and picnic areas.

Country Park grounds open all year. Tower and Tower Barn open Apr to Sep daily. Parking and refreshments available.

Brougham Castle

Cumbria *p220 E1*

This imposing building stands on the banks of the river Eamont near its junction with the river Lowther. The oldest surviving part of the castle is the keep. It was built during the latter part of the twelfth century although it was heightened in the following century. The groove for the portcullis can still be seen in the outer gatehouse. On the south wall is an inscription detailing the renovations carried out by the owner, Lady Anne Clifford, and the north wall leads to a guard room. Below the floor is a store chamber which was probably once used as a dungeon.

The Roman fort of *Brocavun*, where two Roman roads crossed, can be seen outside the castle walls. Lady Anne Clifford also rebuilt the nearby church of St Ninian in 1660, as well as St Wilfred's Chapel, the interior of which is decorated with richly carved oak and carved wall scenes.

Castle see AM info. Also open Sun am Apr to Sep. Parking available.

Brownsea Island

Dorset *p212 F2*

This lovely unspoilt island covering 500 acres lies within the sheltered waters of Poole Harbour. It makes a perfect contrast to the bustling seaside resorts just across the water.

About half of the island is a Nature Reserve run by the Dorset Naturalists' Trust and guided tours lasting one-and-a-half

hours are available around it. However, the wealth of wildlife is not just confined to the Reserve. The colony of rare red squirrels may be a little shy, but there are 200 peacocks and large numbers of ducks, geese, waders, heron, gulls and tern to be seen.

It was here that in 1907 General Baden-Powell held a camp for twenty boys which was the small beginning of the Boy Scout Movement.

Open Apr to Sep daily. Reached by boat from Poole Quay or Sandbanks. No dogs. Refreshments available. NT.

Buckfast

Devon *p212 D2*

The village of Buckfast lies within Dartmoor National Park. There is a modern agricultural museum here and an intriguing museum known as the House of Shells. This has exhibits from all over the world which demonstrate the use of shells in arts and crafts.

Perhaps of most interest in the village, however, is the beautiful Buckfast Abbey. It was built between 1908 and 1933 by a succession of small teams of French Benedictine monks. The abbey stands on the site of the original medieval monastery. This was replaced by a Gothic mansion in 1806 which was subsequently incorporated into the present

abbey. Inside there is a particularly fine mosaic pavement.

House of Shells open Easter to late Oct daily.
Buckfast Abbey always accessible.

Buckfastleigh

Devon *p212 D2*

This pleasant little market town lies south of Buckfast in the low-lying Dart Valley.

Buckfastleigh Station is the terminus of the Dart Valley Railway, a steam-operated service which follows the river Dart for seven miles to Totnes. The station at Buckfastleigh is an attraction in itself. It has locomotives undergoing restoration, a large cafeteria, gift and bookshops and an extensive picnic area beside the river. A miniature railway runs for half a mile beside the river and around the picnic area.

The site is still being developed with the construction of new workshops and a museum. During certain Bank Holidays and some other summer weekends Steam Galas are held when the locomotives are joined by traction engines, steam rollers and other vintage forms of transport.

Trains operate during the Easter period, then Sun and Bank Holiday to May; daily from mid May to Aug. Refreshments available.
Miniature Railway operates Easter, then mid May to mid Sep daily (except Sat).

Bucklers Hard

Hampshire *p213 A1*

Walking into Bucklers Hard village is like stepping back in time. Two rows of cottages, unchanged since the eighteenth century, face each other across a wide green which slopes down to the banks of the Beaulieu River. One of the cottages was lived in by Henry Adams – Nelson's shipbuilder. No roads pass through the village and visitors must leave their cars in the nearby car park.

Bucklers Hard was not always so tranquil, however. It was once a busy shipbuilding yard where many of the ships which fought at Trafalgar were built, including Nelson's *Agamemnon*. Remnants of the docks such as slipways and lengths of rusty chain can be seen along the river bank.

The importance of the shipbuilding industry here is illustrated in the Maritime Museum which contains models, drawings, documents and various seafaring relics.

Visitors may also take trips along the river by launch from the village during the summer.

Museum open all year daily (except Christmas Day). Parking and refreshments available.

There are no cars to interrupt the grazing of these New Forest ponies by the roadside in Bucklers Hard

Bungay

Suffolk *p213 D5*

Bungay is a historic market town and a popular yachting centre situated on the river Waveney in the heart of rural Suffolk. Its many interesting buildings include the domed Butter Cross which used to contain a cage where wrongdoers were held.

Saxons once lived within the banks and ditches of the ancient earthworks now known as the Castle Hills, and it was upon this vantage point that Hugh Bigod, Earl of Norfolk, chose to build his castle in 1165. This castle and its successor both fell to ruin and much of the masonry went into road repairs in the eighteenth century. However, visitors today can see the foundations which reach up to the ground floor windows and parts of the curtain wall.

A unique feature of the castle is the unfinished mine gallery. It was begun with the intention of destroying the castle, following Hugh Bigod's rebellion against Henry II. Over the last few decades the castle has been restored and the site excavated.

One mile west of Bungay at Earsham is Philip Wayre's Otter Trust, one of the best collections of otters in the country. The Trust aims to promote the conservation of otters in the wild and to breed them for zoos and wildlife parks.

Castle open all year; guide book and keys available from Sayer's shop or Council Offices, both in Earsham Street.
Otter Trust open Mar to Nov daily. Refreshments and parking available.

Otters are becoming increasingly rare in Britain today

Burford

Oxfordshire *p213 A3*

The wide high street of this picturesque town is lined with old houses and inns of every variety of Cotswold stone. At the bottom of the main street a narrow triple-arched bridge of old Cotswold stone spans the river Windrush.

The Old Tolsey, formerly a toll house, is now an interesting little museum exhibiting local craft work, as well as a dolls house with eighteenth-century décor and furnishings.

South of the town is the Cotswold Wildlife Park where animals and birds live in natural surroundings. Exotic birds and small mammals can be seen in the wal-led garden. and a tropical house contains a variety of colourful birds and many tropical plants. Larger animals including rhinos, zebras and camels can be seen in the African enclosure. An easy and pleasant way of getting around the park is by the narrow-gauge railway.

The park is in the centre of Bradwell Grove Estate and several events take place here during the summer including vehicle rallies and dog shows. Other features here are woodland walks and informal gardens.

Tolsey Museum open Easter to Oct pm only.
Cotswold Wildlife Park open all year daily (except 25 Dec). Parking and refreshments available.

Burton Constable Hall

Humberside *p217 D3*

This fine Elizabethan house, home of the Constable family for hundreds of years, is set amidst two hundred acres of parkland landscaped by Capability Brown.

There are twenty-two acres of lakes, an arched bridge, an island, a bird sanctuary and four acres of lawns and gardens. The grounds incorporate an official country park which has a nature trail and facilities for seasonal fishing, boating and birdwatching. Other attractions include a model railway, a children's playground, a picnic area by the lake, a pets corner and a collection of vintage agricultural machinery, vintage motor-cycles and Lilian Lunn miniature figures.

The great house dates from 1570, although the interior was remodelled in the eighteenth century by craftsmen such as Robert Adam, Wyatt and Lightoler. The superb staterooms, the drawing room with its rare Chippendale furniture and the Chinese room are particularly notable. In the Alice in Wonderland room – once used as a small theatre – is a fascinating collection of dolls.

A cafeteria, gift shop and a caravan site are available in the summer and special events are held in the grounds.

Open Easter Sat to Mon, then Sat and Sun only until Spring Bank Holiday. Thereafter daily (except Mon and Thu), pm only. Parking and refreshments available.

The central block of Burton Constable is built around a courtyard

Bury St Edmunds Suffolk *p213 D4*

Bury, as it is locally known, is a town of colourful history. Here the last King of East Anglia was buried, and King John's Barons swore to force him to accept the Magna Carta. Today it is a pleasantly laid out market and county town with many interesting buildings.

Bury was named after Edmund, the martyred King of East Anglia, whose body was interred in the Saxon monastery thirty-odd years after his death at the hands of the Danes in AD870.

The town has many fine civic and domestic buildings. Angel Hill, for centuries the scene of Bury Fair, is a spacious square which leads into the central complex of the city. On the south side of Angel Hill is the Athenaeum, an eighteenth-century assembly room and formerly the social hub of Regency Bury where Dickens is known to have given two readings. He used the Angel Hotel as a setting in *Pickwick Papers*.

The Abbey
Little remains of this once great and prosperous abbey although there is enough to indicate its former splendour. Behind the abbey gateway and gatehouse, where the portcullis grooves are still visible, lie the abbey gardens flanked by the river Lark which flows under the thirteenth-century Abbot's Bridge. The gardens are filled with flowers, trees, ruins and large areas of grass. Serving now as a bell tower for the cathedral is the solid Norman tower. The ragged remains of the west front of the abbey church have houses built into them.

St Mary's Church
This magnificent fifteenth-century Perpendicular church has a superb hammerbeam angel

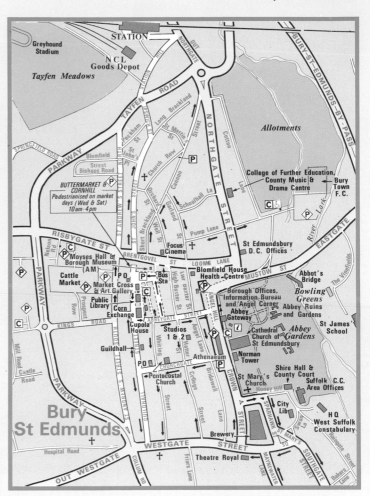

roof in the nave and a wagon roof in the chancel. The chancel contains the grave of Mary Tudor and a fine porch over the north door.

Pentecostal Church
Built in the style of Wren in 1711, and one of the finest nonconformist churches in existence, it retains the original double-decker pulpit and box pews.

Moyses Hall
This twelfth-century flint and stone building is possibly the oldest domestic building in East Anglia. The ground floor is vaulted with stone arches springing

Moyses Hall – the Jew's house in Kipling's *The Law and the Treasure*

from massive pillars. It now houses a museum of local history, archaeology and natural history. Exhibits include Bronze Age weapons.

The Market Cross
The Market Cross, also the Town Hall, dates from 1771 and was constructed to Robert Adam's de-

sign. It was originally built as a theatre but the upper rooms now serve as an art gallery.

The Cathedral
Formerly the parish church, it did not become a cathedral until 1914. Although it has been considerably extended and restored its origins are fifteenth century. It has a fine interior with particularly beautiful stained glass windows.

Angel Corner
This Queen Anne mansion contains the Gershom-Parkington memorial collection of clocks and watches which is one of the largest such collections in Britain.

Moyses Hall open all year daily (except Sun).
Market Cross Art Gallery open all year Tue to Sat.
Angel Corner open all year daily (except Sun, Christmas, New Year and Good Fri).

The 14th-century Great Gate of the abbey in Bury St Edmunds

Caerleon

Gwent *p212 E4*

One of the many places associated with Arthurian legends, City of The Legion and seat of Welsh princes, sits on the banks of the river Usk. Beneath present day roads and houses lies the greater part of the Roman fortress of *Isca*, which was established in AD75 and inhabited until the fourth century. It covered over fifty acres and housed 5,600 men of the 2nd Augustan Legion. The parish church stands on the site of the old Roman basilica which would have been the centre of the fort.

Excavation of part of the north-west corner of the fort has exposed the remains of the legionary barrack block, the only one yet found in Britain, and turrets of the fortress wall. The other area to have been preserved and excavated is the amphitheatre, which actually lay outside the walls of the fort. It was an oval arena hollowed out of the hillside with tiered timber seats, eight entrances and competitors' waiting rooms. Before the amphitheatre was discovered, the site was known locally as King Arthur's Round Table.

A small museum stands next to the church and here all the finds from the site are kept. One of the most interesting exhibits is the remains of a pipe burial – a pipe was left sticking out of the ground to enable relatives to pour wine down it as a religious offering.

Amphitheatre see AM info. Also open Sun am Apr to Sep. Parking available.
Museum open all year daily (except Christmas, New Year's Day and May Day Bank Holiday), Sun pm only.

Caernarfon

Gwynedd *p216 C3*

Caernarfon was an important settlement long before its famous castle was built. The Romans came here in AD78 and built their fort, *Segontium*, on Llanbebig Hill.

Above: Caernarfon Castle, where the first Prince of Wales was born, seen from the banks of the river Seiont

Left: The Roman amphitheatre at Caerleon was able to seat about 6,000 spectators at the gladitorial contests

It was one of the four corner stations of the town which were established to control the Welsh territories. Excavations in the 1920s revealed the foundations which can be seen today, and the Roman museum here contains many of the articles found on the site including many of the personal possessions of the Legionaries.

The castle was part of Edward I's plan to show his supremacy in North Wales. Begun in 1283, it was never completed but is nevertheless one of the most impressive castles in Britain, covering a three-acre site between the Menai Straits and the river Seiont.

Much of the castle's interior was dismantled following the Civil War, but the shell remains intact with its unusual stratified brickwork, battlements and picturesque towers forming an irregular hourglass shape. The walls, up to nine-feet thick in places, were originally extended to encircle the whole of the town, but over the centuries the town has spread far beyond its original limits. Nevertheless the walls are still almost intact, and follow the promenade and quay to the north of the castle

Today the town is a busy market centre with good shopping facilities and the sportsman is well catered for with yacht clubs, golf courses, tennis courts and river and sea fishing.

Castle see AM info. Also open Sun am Apr to Sep. Parking available.
Segontium Roman Fort and Museum open all year daily (except Bank Holidays), Sun pm only. AM.

Caerphilly

Mid Glamorgan *p212 D4*

The industrial market town of Caerphilly is renowned for its cheese and its castle. Although cheese-making has really died out in the town because Devon and Somerset took over as the main producers, the huge castle remains. The first concentric castle to be built in Britain, it is second only to Windsor Castle in size and covers some thirty acres. It was built by Gilbert de Clare, Lord of Glamorgan, in 1266 as protection against invasion from the north. The extensive moats, dams and lakes he created formed a marvellous defence system and now, decorated with swans, provide a beautiful setting for the castle. Parts of the building lie in ruins as a result of repeated attacks and one attempt by Oliver Cromwell in the seventeenth century to blow up the castle caused the slant of one of the huge towers.

Castle see AM info. Also open Sun am Apr to Sep. Parking available.

The double defences of Caerphilly Castle were inspired by experience gained in the Crusades

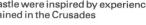

Cambridge Cambridgeshire *p213 C4*

Cambridge revolves around its famous university and there are reminders of this at every turn. The beautiful college buildings and their gardens, students on bicycles, punts on the river Cam and huge bookshops, all blend to create the peaceful scholarly atmosphere of this enchanting Fenland city.

King's College Chapel seen from across the meadows. This masterpiece was begun in 1446 and was not finished until nearly 70 years later.

The scholastic origins of Cambridge date back as far as the thirteenth century. At that time several religious orders had established themselves in and around the town and, as schools were then attached to monasteries and cathedrals, this may have had some influence over the gathering of scholars there, particularly since many had to leave Oxford after disagreements with the inhabitants of the town.

The academic community in Cambridge was quickly established and although it called itself a university, it had not acquired any buildings of its own. The colleges as such began in 1284 with the building of Peterhouse College, which was named after the neighbouring St Peter's church. This was the first of the collection of buildings that give Cambridge its unique beauty. Over the next two centuries eleven more colleges were built, together with hostels to accommodate the students who had hitherto lodged wherever they could find room. As the university became a more powerful and influential factor in the town, disputes arose between the scholars and the townsfolk and as a result the expression 'town and gown' was coined. The situation reached such a pitch that in 1381 several riots occurred.

It is impossible to visit Cambridge and not explore the colleges, and although not all are mentioned here, they are all worthy of exploration and admiration.

King's College

Henry VI was the founder of King's College. He established Eton School at the same time and they share the same coat of arms. In fact, however, the chapel was the only part of his plans that came to fruition and no more was added until the eighteenth century, when the Fellow's Building was built. However, the chapel has remained as the splendid centre-piece to the buildings which have gradually surrounded it. Its ceiling is a superb example of delicate fan vaulting and the Renaissance windows portray the story of the New Testament. Above each one the equivalent story from the Old Testament is depicted. Reuben's magnificent painting, *Adoration of the Magi*, takes pride of place behind the altar.

Queens' College

Both the Queen of Henry VI and of Edward IV founded this college. It is built of red brick, and arching from it over to the opposite bank of the river is the well-known Mathematical Bridge, so named because it was allegedly constructed without using nails – based solely on geometrical principles. However, when a curious Victorian took it apart, he was unable to put it back together again without using iron bolts to secure it.

St John's College

Originally, the site of this college held the Hospital of St John, established in 1135, but after the hospital fell into decay it was converted into a college in 1509. The main gate is decorated with St John, the coat of arms of Lady Margaret Beaufort (Henry VII's mother and foundress of the college), and marguerites to commemorate her name.

Two bridges cross the river from St John's – the Kitchen Bridge and the more famous 'Bridge of Sighs', modelled on the bridge in Venice. The bars in the arched windows were put in to prevent undergraduates getting out at night when codes of conduct were rather more rigid than today.

Trinity College

Two exceptional features of this college are the beautiful ornate fountain of 1602, and the library built by Sir Christopher Wren. Inside the library can be seen examples of Grinling Gibbons' carving and plate dating from the seventeenth century.

St Mary's Church

There are many churches in Cambridge but the official university church is that of St Mary the Great. A climb to the top of the tower affords a good view of the market and most of the main colleges. The clock tower chimes, composed for the Cambridge church in 1793, are the same as the chimes of Big Ben.

The Round Church

One of only four round churches in Britain, it was built to commemorate the Holy Sepulchre and dates from about 1130. Although the conical roof was added in the nineteenth century to replace a crumbling fifteenth-century bell tower, the interior has been carefully preserved and restored.

The Mathematical Bridge crossing the Cam from Queens' College

The Fitzwilliam Museum

This belongs to the university and is the largest museum in Cambridge. Amongst its many collections are those of Roman, Greek and Egyptian antiquities; medieval and Renaissance objects of art; paintings ranging from early Italian to pre-Raphaelite and the French Impressionists; and Meissen china.

Cambridge and County Folk Museum

An extensive and varied selection of items familiar to every family in Cambridge over the past half dozen centuries or so are on exhibition here. The items are di-

The Great Gateway and Nevile Fountain of Trinity College

vided up into groups such as kitchen equipment and children's toys, and a room is devoted to each. In the courtyard is an eighteenth-century shop front which was rescued from the town.

The Scott Polar Research Institute

The Institute was founded to commemorate the great explorer Captain Scott and his comrades. The ground floor of the premises in Lensfield Road have been converted to an interesting display area. Souvenirs, records, photographs and relics of the South Pole Expedition can be seen, as well as the latest findings of Antarctic geographical and geological research.

The River

The river Cam has played an important part in the history and development of Cambridge, and the present charm of the city is intrinsically bound up with it.

The most popular stretch of the river in the city, known as The Backs, passes behind the colleges between well-kept open gardens and lawns. Along here punting, rowing and canoeing may be enjoyed. Further downstream, beyond Jesus Lock, motor boats are permitted.

A familiar sight on the river is that of colleges and schools practising sculling and rowing to the encouraging shouts of their instructors.

For those who prefer to remain on dry land, there are lovely walks and many unspoiled picnic spots along the towpaths, as the river continues on through restful pastoral scenery.

Colleges open to the public on most days, though some restrictions during term times.
Fitzwilliam Museum open all year Tue to Sat, Sun pm only. Closed Good Fri, Christmas, New Year.
Cambridge and County Folk Museum open all year (except Mon and Bank Holidays) Sun pm only.
Scott Polar Research Institute open all year Mon to Sat pm only. Parking available.

Cameron House

Strathclyde *p219 C4*

Cameron House stands on the shore of Loch Lomond, enjoying panoramic views of the large lake. It has been the home of the Smollett family since 1756 and contains many artifacts collected by them over the past 300 years. Special features include a Victorian nursery, oriental curios, fine porcelain and the unique Whisky Galore room which contains bottles of nearly every brand of whisky produced in Scotland. There is also a fascinating collection of books in the Literary Museum named after Tobias Smollett.

Most of the parkland of Cameron House has been set aside as a Wildlife Reserve. Magnificent bears including the Himalayan, Polar, and European brown bears can be seen here in three individual reserves.

A carefully landscaped Waterfowl Sanctuary has a wide variety of colourful waterfowl and there is a pets garden for children.

Open Easter to Sep daily. Refreshments and parking available.

Canterbury Kent *p213 D3*

The birthplace of English Christianity and the seat of the Primate of all England, Canterbury's past reaches back to prehistoric times when Iron Age peoples settled by the banks of the river Stour.

When the Romans invaded Canterbury in AD43, it became a trading centre on the most direct route between London and Europe. The Romans were succeeded by the Anglo-Saxons and in 597 St Augustine arrived to spread the teachings of Christ and build his cathedral. The city, standing on flat land and within reasonable reach of the Channel, was easy prey to invaders and in 851 fell to the Vikings and in 1011 was captured by the Danes. When the Normans arrived they characteristically fortified the city with a wall and castle. A mile or so of the wall remains, but of the castle only the ruined keep has survived.

Although Canterbury was heavily bombed during World War II, it still retains much of its medieval flavour. The massive cathedral bears down on the city from its central position, shadowing narrow streets, old hospitals,

hostelrys and churches, which are scattered amongst the newer buildings.

The Cathedral
Nothing remains of St Augustine's cathedral, nor of the Norman one that replaced it, but the present nave and transepts do stand on the latter's foundations.

It was in this cathedral that Thomas à Becket was murdered and Chaucer's *Canterbury Tales* give a vivid account of pilgrims journeying to his shrine here in late medieval times.

St Michael's Chapel stands off the south-west transept and is now the Memorial Chapel of the Buffs, the Kent Royal East Regiment. Every morning at eleven o'clock a bell is rung by a soldier who turns a page of the Book of Memory which lists the names of men who died in battle. Just short of 250 feet high, the central Bell Harry Tower dates from 1498.

The Old Weaver's House – a picturesque timber-framed building of 1507

The crypt is the oldest part of the cathedral and has a fine vaulted roof which is the largest of its kind in the country.

The cathedral contains many splendid tombs; Henry IV lies beside his queen in Trinity Chapel, and one of the finest tombs is that of the Black Prince, son of Edward III. Above it are replicas of his armour and weaponry. The originals (over 600 years old) are contained in a glass show-case nearby. St Augustine's Purbeck marble chair is also in the chapel and has been used for centuries to enthrone successive archbishops.

Dane John
One of Canterbury's most attractive amenities is centred upon a prehistoric mound which was reshaped in 1790, and turned into a pleasure garden in the nineteenth century. The mound was probably a sister to three further mounds which were once beyond the city wall, and possibly part of

an early defence system.

A column on top of Dane John commemorates the gardens and overlooks a memorial to Christopher Marlow, Elizabethan playwright and contemporary of Shakespeare. Part of the medieval wall skirts the bottom of the mound, and with its round towers, is still an impressive sight.

Westgate

Built between 1375 and 1381 the only surviving city gate now stands across the busy London Road. There was no need for a wall here as the river Stour formed a natural barrier, and the Westgate had its own drawbridge across it.

For many years, the Westgate was used as a prison, but since 1906 has been a museum. The rooms hold a variety of old weapons, handcuffs, manacles, the timbers of old gallows and other reminders of a violent past. Less dour is a penny farthing bicycle and a 1868 'boneshaker'. There is a splendid view across the roof tops of the city to the cathedral from the museum.

Old Weaver's House

Elizabeth I welcomed Flemish refugees of the sixteenth and seventeenth centuries, and gave them permission to ply their trade of weaving in Canterbury. Furthermore they were given a special place of worship in the cathedral, and today, there is still a service held every week in French.

The weavers worked in what is now one of the most attractive

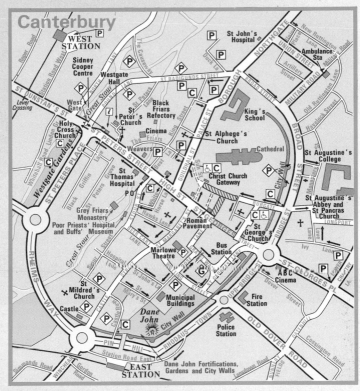

buildings in the city. A white half-timbered building with walls rising up sheer from the river, it has three gables overlooking the road

and five more over the river Stour.

Old bobbins, threads and coins were discovered in the house when it was restored earlier this century, and today a resident weaver using an early Victorian loom carries on the weaving tradition of the past.

Royal Museum, Art Gallery and Buffs Regimental Museum

The museum of the Buffs, tells the story of one of England's oldest regiments. There are collections of medals, uniforms, weapons and trophies pertaining to the Regiment.

The museum also holds a rich store of archaeological finds, including the Roman silver spoon hoard, the Roman coin hoard, Anglo-Saxon glass and jewellery and the silver Canterbury Cross. An art gallery includes work by local artist Sidney Cooper, and collections of engravings and photographs.

Greyfriars

Just off Stour Street are the attractive remains of the oldest Franciscan building in Britain — Greyfriars. It straddles the river banks of this quiet stretch of the river where wild flowers ramble undisturbed.

Westgate Museum open all year Mon to Sat. Oct to Mar pm only.
Old Weaver's House open shop hours.
Royal Museum open all year Mon to Sat.
Greyfriars open summer Mon to Sat pm only.

Canterbury Cathedral dominates its city and rises as a landmark for miles around

Cardiff

Cardiff

South Glamorgan p211 D4

The name of Cardiff conjures up images of docks and industry and rugby football, but it is much more than this. It is an ancient city that was first established by the Romans and parts of their stone walls have been restored.

The Normans chose the same site for their castle which now dominates the modern development of the city centre. It was always an occupied castle, and when military and defensive requirements ceased, it began to be transformed by the addition of new buildings. It is in these newer parts of the castle that the guided tour reveals a wholly nineteenth-century character with its richly ornate décor. One of the most notable features is the banqueting hall fireplace which is surmounted by a medieval castle, complete with a knight on horseback and trumpeters on the battlements.

Within the walls is a vast grassy area where the original Norman keep is perched high on its mound, once surrounded by a moat.

Cardiff is home to one of the largest museums in Britain, the National Museum of Wales, which is primarily concerned with the story of Wales, but also has a fine collection of European art and sculpture, including work by artist Augustus John.

The Welsh Industrial and Maritime Museum in the heart of Cardiff's dockland, houses eight huge engines, including a beam engine and a triple-expansion steam engine.

Outside the museum there are collections of boats, locomotives and cranes.

Castle open for conducted tours all year daily (occasionally closed for special functions).
National Museum open all year daily (except Christmas, New Year, Good Fri, May Day, Bank Holiday), Sun pm only.
Welsh Industrial and Maritime Museum open as above.

Carlisle

Cumbria p220 E2

Situated just to the south of Hadrian's Wall, the city of Carlisle has frequently been the scene of battles between the English and the Scots and in 1092, William Rufus (the Conqueror's son) built the castle here. Although the castle has suffered many conflicts

Colourful Cathays Park, once part of the castle grounds, is now the site of Cardiff's finest public buildings

throughout history, the outer walls, an impressive keep, the main gate and Queen Mary's Tower remain today. The latter houses the Border Regiment and Kings Own Border Regiment Museum, exhibiting trophies, weapons and documents which depict 300 years of the Regiment's history.

Carlisle's red-sandstone cathedral, begun in 1123 as a Norman church, is the second smallest cathedral in England. It boasts one of the finest stained glass windows – the east – in the country, and other notable features include the carved choir stalls, and a painted barrel-vault ceiling. In the cathedral grounds is a thirteenth-century pele tower, called

the Prior's Room. The ceiling is made up of forty-five painted panels bearing coats of arms of well-known Cumbrian families.

Just outside the cathedral stands the fifteenth-century tithe barn built of stone with huge roof beams by Prior Gondibour. It is now the parish hall.

Between the castle and the cathedral stands Tullie House, a Jacobean town house with Victorian extensions which serves as the museum and art gallery. It contains many items relating to Hadrian's Wall, and a collection of Roman and prehistoric relics, together with English porcelain and pre-Raphaelite paintings.

The Carlisle Cross which stands in front of the old Town Hall of

1717 is surmounted by a fearsome lion. Important proclamations are read from its steps, and it was here, in 1745, that Bonnie Prince Charlie declared his father king of Scotland.

The Guildhall in Greenmarket is a splendidly renovated early fifteenth-century timbered building containing displays concerning guild, civic and local history.

Castle see AM info. Also open Sun am Apr to Sep. Parking available. Museums open as castle.
Museum and Art Gallery open Apr to Sep Mon to Sat. Also Sun pm June to Aug.
Prior's Room open all year Mon to Sat (pm only Oct to Apr).
Guildhall open all year Mon to Sat.

Carlton Towers

North Yorkshire p217 C3

The estate here has been owned by the Stapleton's since Norman times, and it is still their family home.

Extensive alterations were made to the exterior of the house during the nineteenth century, and these created a forbidding array of battlements, towers and turrets.

John Francis Bentley, designer of Westminster Cathedral, created the elaborate state rooms. Richly furnished with heraldic detail in their stained glass windows, they are hung with Italian paintings.

In contrast are some delightful smaller rooms with family portraits and photographs, an exhibition of family uniforms and coro-

Tullie House in Carlisle – now used as a museum and art gallery

44

nation robes and an intriguing priests' hiding hole which has recently been opened. The extensive grounds contain several attractive picnic areas.

Open Easter, May Day and Spring Bank Holiday, then June to Sep (closed Tue, Thu and Fri) pm only. Parking and refreshments available.

Carnglaze Slate Caverns

Cornwall *p211 C2*

Near St Neot, the second largest parish in Cornwall, in the beautiful wooded valley of the river Loveny, are the Carnglaze Slate Caverns. Ever since the fourteenth century, the slate from the quarry has been used as a roofing material, but today its uses include building stone, crazy paving and hard core.

The route into the caverns allows the visitor to view the upper chamber, some 300 feet high, which was once used as a rum store. Many drilling holes made by blasting to raise the roof can be seen, as well as the tramway which was built to haul the stone from the depths of the quarry to the surface.

Patches of lichen which collect droplets of water, grow on the roof and reflect the daylight in a most remarkable manner. The underground lake a little further on is a magnificent pool of blue-green water of extraordinary clarity.

Outside the caves stands the proprietor's house, an unusual structure primarily erected to house the machinery once used in the quarry.

Open Easter and Bank Holidays. May to Sep daily, Sun, pm only. Parking available.

Castle Bolton

West Yorkshire *p220 F1*

This romantic-looking castle commands beautiful views of open Wensleydale countryside. It was built in 1379 by Richard Scrope, the Lord Chancellor of England, but not actually completed until nearly eighteen years later.

The gateway and living quarters surround a central courtyard, the entrance being extremely well defended with five doorways and a portcullis at either end. The lord's quarters are spacious and comfortable, and built away from

those of the servants as protection against internal strife. Mary Queen of Scots was held captive here for over five months from 1568–69.

The castle now houses a folk museum in which there is a replica of a Dales kitchen as it would have looked a hundred years ago.

Open all year daily (except Mon). Parking and refreshments available.

Castle Combe

Wiltshire *p212 F4*

Castle Combe, lying deep in a wooded valley, is one of the most

photographed places in the country. The twisting Bye Brook passes under a triple-arched bridge which provides the foreground for the Perpendicular church beyond. Much of the history of the village can be traced in the church, which was built with the help of wealthy clothiers as Castle Combe was an important weaving centre in the fifteenth century.

The church contains a thirteenth-century font, and beautiful fan vaulting. Also inside the church is an effigy to Walter Dunstanville, dated 1270, to commemorate the man who built the original castle from which the vil-

Castle Bolton was dismantled after the Civil War, and one of the four corner towers was lost in a storm

lage subsequently took its name.

The seventeenth-century Dower House, the ancient, roofed market cross, and quaint stone cottages with their uneven mossy roofs, help make this one of England's most beautiful villages.

On the outskirts of the village is a popular circuit for motor racing enthusiasts.

Bye Brook winds through Castle Combe – one of England's prettiest villages

Hawksmoor's magnificent Mausoleum stands in the grounds of Castle Howard

Castle Howard

North Yorkshire *p217 C3*

Castle Howard is one of the largest houses in the country, and everything about it is on the grandest scale. The splendid five-mile-long approach is lined with lime and beech trees, and at a bend a huge obelisk stands to commemorate the rebuilding and replanting of the avenue.

The house was built in 1670 of pale yellow local stone by Sir John Vanbrugh and Nicholas Hawksmoor.

Inside is particularly magnificent although most of the rooms are surprisingly small which give the house a pleasant atmosphere. The marbled entrance hall is lit by a multi-windowed dome – the first to be put on an English house, although the original was gutted by fire in 1940. Near the main staircase hang tapestries by John Vanderbank depicting the four seasons, and paintings by Rubens, Canaletto, Van Dyke and Holbein adorn the walls. The beautiful staterooms are vast and luxurious (only two survived the fire) and are filled with magnificent examples of Sheraton and Chippendale furniture and many fine pieces of porcelain.

In the stables is Britain's largest collection of eighteenth to twentieth-century costume which contains beautiful period-dress lavishly embroidered and trimmed, and costumes belonging to famous artistes.

The grounds surrounding the house extend for some 1,000 acres and sparkle with lakes and fountains, while peacocks strut amongst the parkland. Scattered around the gardens are elegant ornamental structures such as Hawksmoor's circular Mausoleum, and Vanbrugh's charming domed Temple of the Four Winds.

Open Apr to Oct daily. Parking and refreshments available.

Castle Rising

Norfolk *p218 E1*

Situated in this one-time seaport is the castle built by William de Albini, Earl of Sussex, in the twelfth century. The great keep is one of the largest surviving in England, and the exterior walls are decorated with ornate arches. A staircase leads up to the entrance of the castle, which is only two storeys high and once contained a great hall, kitchens, a small, domestic chapel and a gallery.

Also of interest in the village is the Trinity Hospital, now used as alms-houses. The building has a towered gatehouse and chapel and visitors are able to see the rooms furnished with Jacobean furniture and the common-room which has its original fireplace.

Castle See AM info. Also open Sun am Apr to Sep. Parking available.
Trinity Hospital open all year Tue, Thu and Sat.

Castleton

Derbyshire *p217 B2*

This pretty stone village is set in the heart of the magnificent Peak District, amid such famous natural beauty spots as Winnats Pass and Mam Tor.

With its older buildings grouped around the grassy square, the village is overlooked by the ruins of Peveril Castle, now only a shadow of its former strength. It was built in the eleventh century by William Peveril, then later became the property of Henry II, and was featured in Sir Walter Scott's novel *Peveril of the Peak*.

Castleton is most famous for its four caverns which attract countless visitors each year. The Peak Cavern is the largest, extending some 2,000 feet into the mountain, while the Speedwell Cavern is the only one in Britain which has to be toured by boat. The half-mile trip takes visitors to the famous 'bottomless pit'.

The Blue John Cavern is named after the Blue John spar which is found there. It is the rarest rock formation in the country and this area is reputed to be the only source of it in the world. Blue John was mined here as long ago as Roman times and vases made of Blue John were found among the ruins of Pompeii. The Treak Cliff Cavern is also rich in Blue John and includes a solid pillar of it, six feet high.

Castle See AM info. Also open Sun am Apr to Sep. Parking available.
Peak Cavern open Easter to mid Sep daily.
Speedwell Cavern open all year daily (except Christmas). Parking and refreshments available.
Blue John Caverns and Mine open as above. Refreshments available.
Treak Cliff Cavern open as above.

The Blue John Cavern at Castleton. Jewellery is made from the famous spar of blue rock and is on sale in the nearby shop

Cawdor Castle

Highland *p221 D3*

Cawdor Castle is considered to be one of Scotland's finest and most picturesque medieval buildings. It is famous as the scene of Duncan's murder in Shakespeare's play *Macbeth*.

The fourteenth-century tower is the oldest part of the castle, surrounded by sixteenth-century buildings which have been gradually converted, changing what was once a small defensive fort into a large family mansion.

The interior has several attractive rooms giving a good impression of both the family's history and present life at Cawdor. There are tapestries in the family bedroom, specially made in Arras in 1682, depicting biblical scenes; the drawing room has an elegant minstrel gallery and some fine paintings. However, perhaps the most charming room is the blue

Chartwell, home of Sir Winston Churchill from 1922 to 1965

room, a panelled sitting room with a curious ornate fireplace.

The flower and wild gardens are delightful and there is also a pitch and putt course, several nature trails and a picnic area in the grounds.

Open May to Sep daily. Parking and refreshments available.

Charlecote Park

Warwickshire *p216 F1*

An avenue of lime trees leads down from Charlecote village to Charlecote Park, where a large Elizabethan mansion stands. Built in 1558 and the home of the Lucy family since the twelfth century, the house contains many fine furnishings and paintings collected by the family. The great park, set beside the river Avon, was landscaped by Capability Brown, and Spanish sheep and fallow deer peacefully graze here together. It was in this park that a youthful Shakespeare is tradi-

tionally supposed to have poached deer.

Opposite the entrance farm buildings have been converted to house a display of historic carriages, including a carriage once owned by Alphonso XII, the last King of Spain.

Open Apr to Oct, Sat and Sun, May to Sep daily (except Mon but including Bank Holidays). Refreshments available. NT.

Chartwell

Kent *p213 C2*

Sir Winston Churchill bought this unpretentious red-brick Victorian house in 1922 as the home where he could pursue his various interests, and he lived here until his death over forty years later. He extensively altered the house and grounds, building a swimming pool and a wall enclosing some 300 acres of grounds.

The character of the house is that of a real home and still has the air of being occupied. It

was from Chartwell House that Churchill wrote most of his historical works, and the study remains virtually as he left it. On the writing table are photographs of his wife Clemmie, his children and his grandson Winston, and the walls are decorated with a painting of Blenheim Palace, where he was born, and a portrait of his mother and father. An unfinished canvas stands on an easel in the studio, and his paintings that afforded him such pleasure adorn the walls.

At the front of the house a long terraced lawn stretches down to the combe and the lakes that Churchill had built. The flower garden was created by Lady Churchill and is ablaze with fuchsias, lavender and flowering shrubs. White geraniums and tulips give it an informal, pleasant country garden charm.

House open Mar to Nov, Tue, Wed, Thu pm only. Sat, Sun all day.
Garden and Studio Apr to mid Oct, times as above. Refreshments available. NT.

The Emperor Fountain at Chatsworth was built for a visit by Tsar Nicholas I and throws up water 290 feet high

Chatsworth

Derbyshire p216 F3

The ancestral home of the Dukes of Devonshire, Chatsworth House is set in lovely gardens and parkland. It was built in 1687 by the 4th Earl of Devonshire on the site of an earlier house and estate which had been established by the Earl's grandmother, the famous Bess of Hardwick. Coming from a family of modest means, Bess outlived four husbands, becoming progressively richer as she did so. Her fourth husband, the Earl of Shrewsbury, was for some time the keeper of the captive Mary Queen of Scots. Although the house is now a quite different one, some of its rooms are named after the ill-fated Queen.

The house is palatial and the furnishings, décor and state apartments are said to be 'unsurpassed in any house in Europe'. The tour of the house passes through grand rooms with painted ceilings by Verrio and Laguerre (both specialists in that field), exquisite oak panels and carvings and fine sculpture. Both the sculpture gallery and the orangery contain more works of art, and exhibitions of family treasures are held in the theatre gallery.

The gardens were re-landscaped by Capability Brown and subsequent additions and alterations have given them their individual charm. One of the outstanding features is the huge Emperor Fountain which was installed in 1844. An artificial lake had to be created on a hill behind the house in order to supply enough pressure to raise the water to 260 feet. More recent additions include a yew maze which was planted in the early 1960s and a modern greenhouse containing a water-lily pool.

The farmyard at Chatsworth is open during the summer months and the life-cycles of the various breeds of animals are explained.

A woodland walk gives a good insight into the management of forestry on the estate.

House open Apr to Oct daily (except Mon, but open Bank Holiday Mon).
Gardens open daily. House and Gardens also open Sun only early Nov to Dec.
Farmyard open Apr to early Oct daily.

Cheddar

Somerset p212 E3

Famous for its gorge, its caves and its cheese, Cheddar is one of Britain's most popular spots. Gift shops and incongruous modern buildings have sprung up at the foot of the gorge around the entrances to the caves, but no amount of commercialisation can detract from the grandeur of the scenery.

It is best to approach from the north and travel down the gorge where each bend in the winding road takes you deeper into this spectacular ravine, its cliffs rising to some 450 feet on either side. The caves too are a natural phenomenon, a fact which is somewhat disguised by the constructed entrances, the paved floors and the discreet lighting. These man-made additions, however, make it easier to see the magnificent rock formations of stalactites and stalagmites.

Gough's Cave is the most extensive and the most spectacular, stretching into the cliffside for a quarter of a mile. Here evidence was found of inhabitation by prehistoric man over 10,000 years ago. The almost complete skeleton, christened Cheddar Man, which was found here in 1903, now takes pride of place in the museum near the cave entrance.

Further down the road towards the village is Cox's Cave, which also has some beautiful formations, and the man-made Waterfall Grotto with waterfalls and fish tanks set into the rocks. Here too is the entrance to Jacob's Ladder, a steep flight of 322 steps up the face of the gorge. The view from the top is breath-taking.

Cheddar also has a Motor Museum with a large collection of veteran and vintage cars, motorcycles, bicycles and historic motoring accessories.

Gough's Cave open all year daily (except 25 Dec).
Museum open Easter to Oct daily. Refreshments available.
Cox's Cave, **Waterfall Grotto** and **Jacob's Ladder** open Easter to mid Oct daily.
Motor Museum open all year daily (except 25 Dec).

Chedworth Roman Villa

Gloucestershire p212 F4

This is situated in the wooded valley of the river Coln close to the Fosse Way: the Roman road linking Lincoln and Exeter. The villa is the finest and most fully excavated of its kind in Britain, first discovered accidentally in 1864 by a gamekeeper. After excavations in the 1960s, it was apparent that the building ranged from the mid-second century to the early fourth century.

The living rooms and bedrooms, part of which can still be seen, were all served by underfloor hot-air heating. The most remarkable aspect of the house are the baths, which give a clear picture of the elaborate procedures carried out in Roman days. They had steam baths and dry hot baths which worked on the same principles as sauna baths.

Beautiful mosaic floorings have also been unearthed. The dining room pattern consisted of a central octagon with eight main panels surrounding it which were ornately decorated with nymphs and satyrs, and pieces of them remain today. Many other elaborate mosaic pavements have also survived and are on display. The spring which supplied the occupants of the villa with fresh water has a shrine featuring water nymphs built above it.

Open Mar to Oct, Tue to Sun and Bank Holidays (except Good Fri), Feb and Nov to mid Dec, Wed to Sun. NT.

Lime deposits from dripping water cause these formations in Cox's Cave

Cheltenham Gloucestershire *p212 F5*

Cheltenham is a town of spacious elegance. The whole town is a well-proportioned pattern of stately squares, sweeping terraces, broad avenues and well-placed trees and gardens.

Once just a little place on the banks of the river Chelt, its development as a major spa town began with the discovery of a mineral spring in 1715. By 1738 the first pump room was built and fifty years later its future was assured when George III, accompanied by his family, came here to take the waters. The medicinal reputation of the spa grew so rapidly that a select few of the most eminent architects of the day were employed to plan an entirely new town.

On the whole Cheltenham has retained its unique character and the houses and villas still have their splendid Regency ironwork balconies and verandas. Of particular note is Montpellier Walk which is modelled on the Erechtheion Temple in Athens and, lined with female figures, is one of the most unusual shopping precincts in the world. Other fine examples of Regency architecture can be found in Landsdown Place, Suffolk Place, and the Rotunda, which is modelled on the huge Pantheon in Rome. The culmination of this period of planning and design was the Promenade, with its fountain of Neptune, completed in 1825.

Cheltenham is a major centre for music and literary festivals and several of international repute are held here throughout the summer. A contrasting attraction is the race-course at Prestbury Park, home of the Cheltenham Gold Cup, one of the premier National Hunt races which is held in March.

Pittville Pump Room

Built between 1825 and 1830 for Joseph Pitt MP, as a place to entertain his friends, it stands in regal splendour amidst spacious parkland and lakes. The building consists of a great hall surmounted by a gallery and dome, fronted by a colonnade of Ionic columns.

Art Gallery and Museum

The permanent collection here includes Dutch and British paintings, English and Chinese ceramics, pewter, glass, modern art and art and craft exhibitions. In addition there is a large local section which includes regional archaeology, Cotswold crafts, Cheltenham prints, Edward Wilson (companion of Scott to the Antarctic) personalia and general social history items.

Gustav Holst Museum

This modest terraced house was the birthplace of the composer Gustav Holst and he spent the first eight years of his childhood here. The house has been carefully renovated and is now not only a museum portraying the composer's life and music, but also contains fine examples of typical Regency and Victorian rooms.

Cheltenham's Pittville Pump Room dispenses the only drinkable alkaline waters in Britain

St Mary's Parish Church

This, the only medieval building left standing in the town, dates back to the early twelfth century. It is best known for its fourteenth century window tracery and its fine Victorian stained glass.

Pittville Pump Room open May to Sep, Mon to Sat. Sun and Bank Holidays pm only. Parking available.

Art Gallery and Museum open all year (except Sun and Bank Holidays).

Gustav Holst Museum open all year Tue to Sat (except Bank Holidays).

Chepstow Castle on the river Wye

Chepstow

Gwent p212 E4

On the outskirts of old market town of Chepstow, with its steep narrow streets lies an ancient fortress – Chepstow Castle. It stands on limestone cliffs at the Welsh/English border, above the river Wye which forms a natural moat. The castle has spread over the centuries along the natural ridge of land as new defences and buildings were built. Martens Tower was added during the thirteenth century and Henry Marten, a signatory of Charles I's death warrant, was imprisoned in the tower until his death in 1680.

The castle has four courtyards, a forty-foot-high keep and is surrounded by walls which are strengthened by towers. A walk through the dell to its western end reveals a delightful view of the castle and river.

See AM info. Also open Sun am Apr to Sep. Parking available.

Chester *Cheshire p216 E3*

This, the one-time Roman fortress of Deva, is now a dignified mixture of medieval and Victorian architecture. The two-mile circuit of ancient walls, black and white buildings, galleried streets, flights of uneven steps and double-tiered shops, give Chester its unique atmosphere of medieval England.

The Romans chose their site well when they built their stronghold on the river Dee. As it was situated at the head of the tidal estuary on a sandstone plateau, sea-going vessels were able to moor virtually under the walls of the settlement, and the bend of the river protected its southern and western sides. However, when the Romans left Britain, Chester, like so many of their settlements, fell into decay and obscurity and remained so for several centuries.

Under Norman rule Chester was turned into a virtually independent state governed successively by eight earls over a period of 106 years. This ended because the last of these powerful rulers had no male heir and the King, rather than let the city fall into female hands, took over the city and conferred the earldom on his son. Ever since then Chester has been a property of the eldest son of the reigning monarch.

Chester flourished most profitably between the twelfth and fourteenth centuries as a port. Its position on the west coast meant easy trading with Ireland, and a flourishing import and export trade developed. However, this only lasted until the fifteenth century because the estuary began to silt up and was no longer navigable to ships. Trade subsequently declined rapidly and was diverted to the nearby village of Liverpool.

The Walls

These provide a pleasant two-mile walk around the city. The northern and eastern walls are mostly the original Roman structure, but those to the west and south have been replaced over the centuries and their perimeter extends down to the river and the castle.

Towers have been added to the walls at various times; Eastgate is particularly attractive with its ornate clock. Arched over the roads are the four main gates through the walls.

The walls have always been important to the inhabitants of the city and at one time people known as 'murages' were appointed as officials to collect taxes for maintenance.

From the walls are good views both of the city and its environs. To the south-east of the walls is the racecourse known as the Roodee. Originally a harbour in Roman times, the name is derived from two Anglo-Saxon words meaning island of the cross. It has been the scene of horse-racing for 400 years and the Chester Cup is held here annually.

The Rows

These unique shops are probably the most famous features in Chester and have characterised the city since the Middle Ages. Situated in Bridge Street, Watergate and Eastgate Street, they consist of shops on two levels so arranged that the top row is overhung by its upper storeys. The result is an attractive fully-covered shopping precinct which is a delight to explore.

The British Heritage

Part of the Rows, reconstructed exactly as they were in the nineteenth century, can be seen here, as well as an exhibition illustrating 2,000 years of Chester's history.

Roman Amphitheatre

This is the site of the largest amphitheatre excavated in Britain to date. The Roman Garden next to it has re-erected Roman columns, as well as other remains which have been found in the city, including part of an underground heating system.

The Grosvenor Museum

The museum is best known for its galleries of Roman antiquities but it also devotes a considerable amount of space to natural history, local history, costume, furniture and Victoriana.

The Cathedral

Built of sandstone, the cathedral was originally a Norman Benedictine abbey, but when many monasteries were abolished in the Dissolution it was turned into a cathedral. Although it was restored quite considerably in the nineteenth century, architecture spanning eight centuries can be seen in different parts of the cathedral. The stalls which were carved in the 1300s are particularly interesting as they depict in wood a variety of creatures and figures.

The Groves
Alongside the river are the tree-lined Groves providing a pleasant respite from the city centre. In the summer, band concerts are held here and the river is always alive

An engraving of Chester Castle

with pleasure boats.

Behind the Groves are the neat, colourful gardens of Grosvenor Park – donated by the 2nd Marquis of Westminster in 1867 for the enjoyment of Chester's inhabitants.

The British Heritage open all year daily.
Grosvenor Museum open all year daily (except Good Fri and Christmas) Sun, pm only.

Above: The Cross, seen here from Watergate Street Rows
Below: The ironwork clock tower of 1897 on Eastgate

Chichester West Sussex p213 B2

Chichester, standing between the South Downs and the sea, combines the flavour of both. Its busy yachting harbour and weekly cattle market reflect the seafaring and agricultural past of the town.

The Romans called the place *Noviomagus* and in AD200 they built a wall around it of which large stretches remain. Although the remains are mainly medieval, the Roman foundations and core still exist.

Most of the best architecture in the town is Georgian. The area known as The Pallants is particularly elegant and here, and in West Street, are many fine buildings that were once wool merchants' houses. During the fourteenth century wool was Chichester's main source of revenue and a flourishing export trade existed from the town's port. The harbour is now one of the south coast's most popular yachting centres and a path leads down to it from the old canal basin.

The Cathedral

The bishopric, originally at Selsey, moved to Chichester after the Norman Conquest. In 1245 St Richard of Chichester became Bishop and was subsequently adopted as the town's saint.

The graceful 277-foot spire of the cathedral dominates the skyline and is clearly visible from the sea and nearly every point in the city. In 1861 the old spire collapsed in a gale; Sir Gilbert Scott's successful reconstruction preserved the original design however. Some notable features inside the cathedral are the double aisles of the nave with its fine Norman arches and fourteenth-century choir stalls. Two more modern works of art are the vividly-coloured altar tapestry designed by John Piper in 1966 and Graham Sutherland's oil painting, depicting the appearance of Christ to Mary Magdalene on the first Easter morning. The composer Gustav Holst is buried in the north transept.

Roman remains including mosaic pavements have recently been discovered under the foundations of the cathedral and are now kept in the Guildhall Museum. On the south side access can be gained to the formal gardens of Bishop's Palace through a gateway adjoining the cloisters.

District Museum

Exhibits in Chichester museum date from prehistoric to modern times and relate particularly to the town and surrounding area. The Royal Sussex Regiment also have a collection here dating from 1701 – the year it was established. An annexe to the museum is the Guildhall Museum located in Priory Park, which mainly houses Roman relics.

The Market Cross

The city is crossed by four main streets and in the middle stands the fifty-foot high Market Cross, a complex eight-sided arcaded structure crowned with an octagonal stone cupola. It was built in 1500 and provided shelter for countryfolk while they sold their produce. Farmers and growers still gather from a wide area to attend a weekly cattle market here.

Festival Theatre

Just outside the city walls is the distinctive hexagonal-shaped theatre which opened in 1962. It has gained an international reputation for staging the best in classical and contemporary works.

District Museum open all year Tue to Sat.
Guildhall Museum open June to Sep, Tue to Sat pm only.

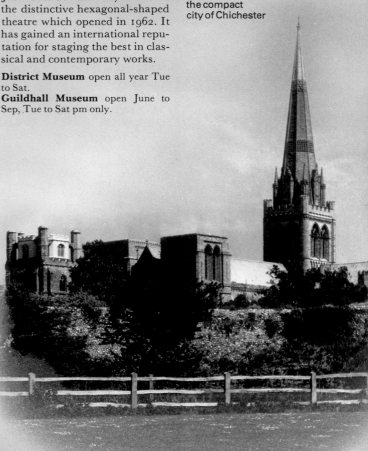

The cathedral spire rises above the compact city of Chichester

Chichester's Festival Theatre

Chilham

Kent *p213 D2*

Chilham's magnificent central square, surrounded by timbered black and white houses, makes it one of the most attractive villages in Kent. Amongst these Tudor buildings is a fifteenth-century flint church which contains several fine monuments, including a group sculpted by Sir Francis Chantrey. He left the large fortune he had accrued to found the art collection now housed in the Tate Gallery (London).

The gates of Chilham Castle stand in the village and through them the hexagonal Jacobean mansion, built in 1616, can be seen. Close to the house is a massive flintstone Norman keep – the only remains of an earlier castle which in turn stood on the site of ancient Saxon fortifications.

The present house is set in a great park overlooking the river Stour, and interesting features and events which take place in the grounds include jousting tournaments, eagle and falconry displays, woodland and lake-side walks and extensive gardens.

Inside the castle is the Kent Battle of Britain Museum which contains a fine collection of memorabilia including propellers, badges, swords and uniforms.

Castle not open to the public.
Grounds and museum open Easter to Oct (except Mon and Fri) pm only. Jousting Suns. Parking and refreshments available.

The gardens of Chilham Castle were landscaped by Capability Brown

Chipping Campden

Gloucestershire *p212 F5*

This ancient town of gabled stone buildings of varying levels has remained unspoilt for centuries. Between the thirteenth and sixteenth centuries Chipping Campden was a major wool centre, and the merchants' prosperity is reflected in the town's beautiful architecture. Perhaps the finest example of this is the Jacobean Market Hall with its pointed gables, open arcade and timber roof.

The impressive 120-foot pinnacled tower on the fifteenth-century church of St James, enhances one of the finest wool churches in the Cotswolds. Inside, kept safely in a glass case, is a rare collection of English embroidery, some dating back to Richard II's reign.

The mid fourteenth-century Woolstaplers Hall in the High Street contains an unusual collection of relics from bygone days, including cine equipment, kitchen utensils, farm tools, coins and exhibits from the wool industry.

Here too is the Campden Car Collection exhibiting over twenty immaculate sports and racing cars built between 1927 and 1963, and a display of photographs of motor sport.
Camden Car Collection open Easter, then May to Sep daily, pm only.
Woolstaplers Hall open Easter, then May to Sep daily.

Chirk Castle

Clwyd *p216 D2*

Chirk Castle stands high on a hilltop on the Welsh border, commanding breath-taking views of the surrounding countryside. It was built as a frontier fortress in a style similar to many other Welsh castles built by Edward I. It is rectangular, with round towers at each of its corners, and surrounds a large quadrangle which is entered through a splendid archway.

Today the castle is an elegant stately home which has been in the possession of the Myddleton family since 1595.

The entrance hall is richly panelled in oak – the work of the English architect Pugin, and is bedecked with weapons and armoury from the Civil War. Beyond is an elegant sweeping staircase after the style of Robert Adam. At the foot of the stairs hangs a portrait of Sir Thomas Myddleton, who bought the castle in 1595. The regal state dining room bears a magnificent brass and crystal chandelier and has been restored to its original eighteenth-century splendour. Rich furnishings abound throughout the chambers, including the Mortlake tapestries, and many interesting paintings adorn the walls, including those of royalty and striking local landscapes.

In the Tudor block are rooms which have been unchanged since Elizabethan days, and the original Tudor room houses a bed where Charles I once slept.

The grounds of the castle are heralded by superb eighteenth-century ornamental gates, wrought with intricate tracery bearing elaborate crests and flower designs, which are the work of the Davies Brothers of Bersham.

Open Easter to Oct, Wed, Thu, Sat and Sun pm only. June to Sep, Wed and Thu all day. Refreshments available. Also open Bank Holiday weekends all day.

Chirk Castle stands in the valley of the river Ceiriog which divides England and Wales

Chysauster

Cornwall *p211 A1*

For nearly 1,600 years the site of this ancient village lay overgrown and neglected. When excavations first began to take place in the 1860s one of the best preserved Iron Age villages in England was discovered. Although only the bottom half of the walls can be seen, it is enough to give a good indication of the layout of the houses. Built with walls fifteen feet thick against the elements they may either have been roofed with thatch or stone. The village was lived in between about 100 BC to the third century AD and the inhabitants probably smelted tin and existed on small-scale mixed farming. A short distance from the houses is an underground chamber, or fogou, which was probably used by the village as a central storage area.

See AM info. Also open Sun am Apr to Sep. Parking available.

Cilgerran Castle

Dyfed *p211 C5*

Romanticism has popularised this striking slate-grey castle. It was from here that the beautiful

Chysauster – where the oval plans of Iron Age houses can be seen

wife of Gerald of Windsor, Nesta, was abducted by an admirer in 1109 and subsequently became something of a legend, often referred to since as the Helen of Wales.

However, the castle has had a turbulent political history; it was fought over and changed hands many times before falling to ruin in 1326. The remaining parts of the curtain walls and the huge twin-towers have been an inspiration to poets and painters such as Turner, and an attraction to countless visitors. Today the ruins dominate the valley of the river Teifi and the quiet old-fashioned village below.

See AM info.

Cirencester

Gloucestershire *p212 F4*

Once one of the chief centres of the wool industry in the Middle Ages, Cirencester became a centre for agriculture when the cloth industry declined during the Industrial Revolution.

Known as *Corinium* by the Romans, the town became the second largest in Britain. The Romans were quick to realise the strategic position of Cirencester, which accounts for the Roman roads radiating from it, including the great Fosse Way and Ermin Street.

In the middle of this mellow Cotswold town is the colourful Market Place where weekly open-air markets are still held. The rest of Cirencester is a maze of fascinating streets lined with quaint old houses including workmen's cottages, almshouses and seventeenth-century bow-fronted shops.

However, the most striking feature of the town is the 120-foot tower of the church of St John the Baptist, built by the prosperous wool merchants, which overlooks Market Place.

A large collection of Roman antiques recovered by archaeologists is kept in the Corinium Museum, and the atmosphere of *Corinium* life is recaptured here for the visitor in a reconstructed dining room, and part of a kitchen in a Roman town house. A cut-away section shows part of an underground Roman central heating system.

The museum entrance looks across to the gateway of Cirencester Park, a 3,000-acre estate belonging to Earl Bathurst. Although the house is not open to the public, the park is available for riding and walking and on most Sundays polo matches take place there.

A Norman arch is all that is left of the abbey, but the grounds make an attractive centrepiece to the town with the river Churn winding through the well kept lawns into a large lake populated by swans and wildfowl.

Corinium Museum open all year daily (except Christmas), Sun pm only. Oct to Apr closed Mon.

Clandon Park

Surrey *p213 B2*

In 1735, the 2nd Lord Onslow commissioned the Venetian architect Leoni to rebuild his Elizabethan family home. The result was a grand, square, red-brick house decorated in a mixture of Baroque and Palladian styles, with Italian, French and English trimmings.

A nineteenth-century porch

In the late 18th century Clandon Park was one of the grandest Palladian houses in England

leads into the beautiful marble hall which is splendidly embellished with Italian plasterwork and fascinating mythological scenes. The staterooms contain plasterwork by Artari and Bagutti and are lavishly decorated; the exact colours and materials of the eighteenth century have been restored where possible. Flock wallpaper from France covers the Palladio room, and the saloon has a

magnificent ceiling in pastel shades. In the hunting room there is a collection of Chinese porcelain birds, and the morning room has satinwood furnishings and pieces of Chelsea porcelain.

Other treasures in the house include a highly ornamented state bed dating from the eighteenth century, with a matching set of chairs, a Chippendale marquetry dressing table, and some early Staffordshire pottery.

Open Apr to late Oct daily (except Mon and Fri) pm only. Also open Bank Holiday Mon but closed following Tue. Refreshments available. NT.

Claydon House

Buckinghamshire *p213 A4*

Claydon House, in the small village of Middle Claydon, has been the home of the Vernay family since 1620. The stone-faced west-wing is the only surviving part of the house, and its sober exterior belies the beautiful rococo state rooms within.

The pink parlour and north hall are particularly fine adjoining rooms. Each is richly embellished with exuberant tracery, magnificent wood carvings depicting fruits and flowers, and birds and beasts on the ceilings and walls. In the fantastic Chinese room is a rare example of eighteenth-century Chinoiserie, decorated with ornate carvings and furniture, and tiny bells hanging from

the walls. The staircase is a masterpiece of wrought ironwork. It winds into garlands and scrolls, and has ears of corn so delicate they faintly rustle as one climbs the stairs.

Florence Nightingale and her sister Frances Parthenope Vernay lived at Claydon for some years, and both have left their impression on the house. Florence's bedroom can be seen in its original Victorian state, and adjoining this is a room containing items from her Crimean mission, and other treasures relating to the military history of the Vernay family.

The eighteenth-century library was created by Frances, although its earlier plasterwork and Ionic doorframes were retained.

Open Apr to Oct daily, pm only (except Mon, Fri and Tue following Bank Holiday). NT.

Cleeve Abbey

Somerset *p212 D3*

The only Cistercian abbey in Somerset, Cleeve Abbey, was founded by the Earl of Lincoln in 1198 and became the most prosperous religious foundation in the county. After its decline, the abbey was sometimes used as a shelter for farm animals and for storage of farm implements but, now in the care of the Department of the Environment, it has been well renovated. The buildings that remain include the refectory, chapter house, common-room and the cloisters, which stand on the banks of the Washford River.

See AM info. Also open Sun am Apr to Sep. Parking available.

Cirencester Park stretches away beyond the house, home of Earl Bathurst, which lies on the western edge of the town

The formal design of the box hedges probably dates from the 1850s, when the present Cliveden House was built

Cliveden

Buckinghamshire *p213 B3*

Cliveden Reach, with its sweeping views, is a beautiful wooded stretch of the river Thames. The grounds of the 327-acre estate of Cliveden contain rambling wooded walks, avenues, terraced gardens and delightful water gardens. Hidden around the grounds are sculptures and statues set in niches and ornamental temples of Italian design.

Cliveden House, former home of the Astor family, has splendid views down to the river and is filled with fine furniture, tapestries and ornaments.

Gardens open all year daily.
House Apr to Oct, Sat and Sun pm only. Refreshments available. NT.

Clovelly

Devon *p212 C3*

The beautiful village of Clovelly is world-famous for its picturesque, unspoilt charm; unspoilt largely because no traffic can enter the village. All vehicles must be left in the large cliff-top car park, and visitors have to make their way on foot down the cobbled streets, so steep that they have been stepped in places.

Pretty, white-painted cottages line the streets, bright with window-boxes and flowering shrubs

56

which somehow defy their north-facing situation, and flower as early and as long as in more southerly resorts.

At the bottom of the cliff-side village is the tiny harbour where fishing boats take shelter, and ancient cannon barrels have been upturned to serve more peacefully now as mooring bollards. Visitors who cannot face the steep climb back to the car park can make use of a Land-Rover service available from the harbour.

All around the village the densely wooded cliffs rise to some 400 feet, providing lovely walks and superb sea views, particularly from Gallantry Bower.

The most attractive way into Clovelly is via Hobby Drive, a three-and-a-half-mile toll road which runs from the main road near Buck's Cross to Clovelly car park, passing through pleasant woodland with panoramic views.

Clumber Park

Nottinghamshire *p217 C2*

This lovely park of nearly 4,000 acres was landscaped by the Dukes of Newcastle. Much of the credit, however, must go to Capability Brown who laid out lawns and shrubberies, planted trees and created the lake all in his own distinctive style.

In the mid nineteenth century

an unusual double avenue of limes was planted, three miles long and containing some 3,000 trees, which remains one of the outstanding features of the park.

The palatial mansion, once the centrepiece of the estate, was demolished in the 1930s, but the lodges and gate-piers remain at the entrances and two garden temples and a fine classical bridge still exist

By far the most impressive remaining structure in the park is the Clumber Chapel, the word 'chapel' doing little justice to the size of the building. Described as 'a cathedral in miniature', it was designed by G F Bodley and is a superb example of Gothic Revival architecture based on the fourteenth-century Decorated style. It is built of contrasting sandstone and white Streetly stone and is surmounted by a graceful

180-foot spire. The interior had the benefit of the finest nineteenth-century craftsmen to create the intricate rood-screen, stone and wood carvings, and stained glass.

Today the whole park is a pleasure ground with shops, cycle hire and fishing available.

Park open all year. Refreshments available weekends and Bank Holidays, also Mon to Thu Apr to Oct. NT.

Cockermouth

Cumbria *p220 D1*

The Cumbrian town of Cockermouth, lying to the west of Bassenthwaite Lake and the distant, lofty height of Skiddaw, is a good starting point for exploring the Lake District. It sprung up around the Norman castle, strategically placed at the junction of the rivers Cocker and Derwent. Much of the castle was destroyed by Parliamentary forces during a Civil War siege, but a surviving older part contains an oubliette, or subterranean dungeon, that was for life prisoners.

The town is particularly famous as the birthplace of the Lakeland poet William Wordsworth. Wordsworth House, the family home, is at the west end of the broad, tree-lined main street where the garden backs on to the river Derwent, which he recalls in *The Prelude*. A simple Georgian house, it contains many of its original features including the staircase and some of the fireplaces and panelling.

All Saints, a nineteenth-century church occupying part of the site of an old grammar school attended by Wordsworth, contains a stained glass window commemorating the poet.

Wordsworth House open Apr to Oct daily (except Thu). Refreshments available. NT.
Castle not open to the public.

Donkeys may be hired to carry luggage up the hill at Clovelly

Colchester Essex p213 D4

The garrison and market town of Colchester stands in the midst of rolling East Anglian countryside, presided over by its lofty Town Hall and an enormous Victorian water tower called Jumbo. The famous Colchester oysters are cultivated on beds in the lower reaches of the river Colne which skirts the northern edge of the town.

The timbers of Old Siege House are riddled with Civil War bullets

Colchester is England's oldest recorded town, and goes back to the seventh century BC when a settlement was first established on the site. Evidence of the huge system of earth works which protected pre-Roman Colchester can be seen to the west and the oldest part of the town is still surrounded by its Roman walls including the Balkerne Gate – the west gate of the Roman town. Later occupations are marked by the Norman Castle, the house of the Flemish weavers in 'The Dutch Quarters' to the west of the castle and the Civil War scars visible on the walls of Siege House in East Street.

Castle and Museum
This Norman castle was built mainly of Roman bricks and constructed on the site of the temple of the Emperor Claudius. The keep, the largest ever built in Europe, is all that remains and now houses the Castle Museum. The museum contains an interesting collection of Roman, Iron Age and medieval relics.

Holly Trees Museum
A fine Georgian house, situated close to the castle, Holly Trees houses a collection of costumes and antiquities. It was purchased for the town by Viscount Cowdray in 1920 and opened as a museum.

Natural History Museum
The museum is situated in the former All Saints church with its fine flint tower, and its existence saved the church from demolition in 1958. Exhibits illustrate the natural history of Essex, with special reference to the Colchester area, and the museum includes a diorama and an aquarium.

Museum of Social History
This interesting museum contains historical displays of rural craft and country life. It is housed in the historic church of Holy Trinity in Trinity Street, and is the only Saxon building left in the town.

The Minories Art Gallery
The Minories is a late Georgian house rebuilt in 1776 from an original Tudor building and is a centre for the visual arts. It has a

The keep of Colchester Castle

continuous programme of concerts, exhibitions and lectures as well as Georgian furnishings and paintings by William Constable.

Bourne Mill
This striking stepped and curved gabled building was constructed in 1591 with stone from St John's Abbey and was originally a fishing lodge. It was converted into a mill in the nineteenth century and can be seen in working order.

St Botolph's Priory
These ruins consist of a great Norman church of which the west front – with a particularly fine doorway – and part of the nave, have survived.

Colchester Zoo
In the forty-acre park of Stanway Hall, with its sixteenth-century mansion and church dating from the fourteenth century, is Colchester Zoo. Founded in 1963, it has a variety of attractions including an aquarium, birdland, all the breeds of large cats, and a model railway.

Castle and Museum open all year Mon to Sat, except Christmas and Good Fri, also Sun pm Apr to Sep.
Holly Trees Museum open all year (except Christmas and Good Fri) Mon to Sat.
Natural History Museum open all year Mon to Sat (except Christmas and Good Fri).
Museum of Social History open as above.
The Minories open all year Tue to Sat; Sun, pm only. Refreshments available.
Bourne Mill open Apr to Sep Wed, Sat, Sun and Bank Holiday Mon pm only. NT.
Colchester Zoo open all year daily. Parking and refreshments available.

Compton Acres Gardens

Dorset *p212 F2*

Thomas William Simpson bought the house at Compton Acres just after World War I and his idea was to surround the house with gardens, designed in such a way that only one of them could be seen at a time. It is not hard to believe that this ambitious plan, begun in 1919, took several years to accomplish.

There are seven gardens in all; English, Heather, Japanese, Italian, Roman, Rock and Water, each with its own individual beauty. Most of them contain a priceless collection of bronze and marble statues which have come from all over the world. There are particularly fine views of Poole Harbour and the Purbeck Hills from the English garden. The careful lay-out of the gardens includes paths and bridges over streams and ponds to avoid steps and stepping stones for the less agile. Many of the plants grown at Compton Acres can be purchased.

Open Apr to Oct daily. Parking and refreshments available.

Compton Castle

Devon *p212 D2*

Battlements and towers lend Compton Castle a charmingly romantic air. Actually a fortified manor house, it belonged to the Gilbert family for six hundred years and the hall, reconstructed in the 1950s, contains an assortment of Gilbert mementoes. Other rooms on view include the old kitchen and the chapel which date from the fifteenth century.

Surrounded by grounds extending to 346 acres, the house is beautifully set in a combe and there is a thatched barn standing next to it.

Open Apr to Oct, Mon to Thur. Parking available. NT.

Compton House

Dorset *p212 E3*

In 1839 an architect from Bath by the name of John Pinch created the present mansion known as Compton House. Although Victorian, the house – featuring gables, tall chimneys, dormer windows and window gables –

Above: The Italian garden at Compton Acres – one of seven designed by owner T W Simpson has a distinctly Tudor appearance.

The Gooden family bought the original house in 1746 and they have owned the estate ever since. During the 1970s one enterprising member of the family, Robert Gooden, transformed the house and grounds into a home for his spectacular collection of butterflies. Locally known as World-wide Butterflies Ltd, the house contains species from all over the world. There is also a natural jungle, where living butterflies fly free, and a tropical palm-house.

Another great attraction of Compton House is the Lullingstone Silk Farm where live silk worms and demonstrations of silk-making can be seen. Silk has been produced by this company for the last two coronations and Queen Elizabeth's wedding dress was made from Lullingstone silk.

Open Apr to Oct daily. Parking and refreshments available.

Compton Castle's magnificent façade was built in about 1500 to protect the earlier house of 1420 from the threat of French invasion

Conwy Gwynedd *p216 C3*

This ancient walled town and its castle stand out against tree-clad hills which rise steeply from the broad estuary of the river Conwy, over which span a trio of very differently styled bridges — a suspension, a tubular railway and a modern road bridge.

The massive town walls, some thirty-five feet high and six feet thick, extend right down to the shoreline and, with their twenty-one crenellated towers, make Conwy one of the most formidable towns in Britain. The Quay is one of the pleasantest parts of the town, now mainly used by pleasure craft and small fishing boats. Fresh fish is sold here and trips to Trefriw, where old wharves remain as reminders of the days when slates were shipped down the river, are available.

The Castle
Edward I drew workmen from all over England in 1283 to build this giant fortress as a means of controlling the newly defeated Welsh armies. It remained as a powerful military stronghold until after the Civil War when, having survived a three-month siege, was surrendered to Parliamentary forces who rendered it useless for military purposes.

Plas Mawr
On the corner of Crown Lane and the High Street stands a perfectly restored Elizabethan house, which is now an art gallery and the headquarters of the Royal Cambrian Academy of Art. Of particular note is the ornate plasterwork which was covered until the nineteenth century and is consequently remarkably well preserved. The banqueting hall is particularly fine.

The smallest house in Britain beside the river-quay in Conwy

Aberconwy
This claims to be the oldest house in Wales, dating mainly from the fifteenth century. Over the years the road level has risen so much that the upper storey has to be approached by outside stairs. Inside an exhibition depicts the life of the borough since Roman times.

St Mary's Parish Church
The church is all that remains of the former abbey which stood here before being moved to Maenan to make way for the castle. It is reached by narrow lanes which lead up to the open grassy churchyard. Inside is a stone figure of the daughter of John Williams, Archbishop of York and a bust of the sculptor John Ginson.

The Smallest House
With its frontage of only six feet and only ten feet in height, its claim to being the smallest house in Britain may well be justified. The only two rooms are linked by an almost vertical staircase and resemble a mid Victorian cottage.

Castle see AM info. Also open Sun am Apr to Sep. Parking available.
Plas Mawr open all year daily (except mid Dec to mid Jan).
Aberconwy open Apr to Sep daily (except Wed in Apr and May). Oct to Mar by appointment only. NT.
Smallest House open Easter to Oct daily.

The ruins of Corfe Castle where Edward the Martyr was murdered in 978

Corfe Castle

Dorset *p212 F2*

Overlooking the village of the same name, are the dramatic ruins of Corfe Castle, a stronghold in the Purbeck Hills which was fortified by Saxon kings. Besieged during the Civil War, the owner's wife, Lady Banks, defended the castle after her husband died, against Parliamentary troops, but it was eventually seized and reduced to its present condition and much of the stone was removed to construct buildings in the village. The ruins cover more than three acres, with the keep at the hill's summit.

The central point of this quaint village is the little square with its church, old inns and houses. In the Middle Ages a marble carving industry existed in the village and the Ancient Order of Marblers still meet in the Council Chamber every Shrove Tuesday. Located in the same tiny buildings as the Chambers is the small museum which shows old village relics and dinosaur footprints one hundred and thirty million years old.

Castle open all year daily, pm only Nov to Feb.
Museum open all year daily.

Cotehele House

Cornwall *p212 C2*

Granite-built Cotehele House, standing in lovely gardens above the river Tamar, is a perfect example of an early Tudor manor house.

Most of the furniture in the house dates from between the six-teenth and seventeenth century and was all collected by the Edg-cumbe family. The hall is decorated with armour, weaponry and hunting trophies, and seven-teenth-century tapestries hang from floor to ceiling in most of the rooms.

The grounds cover over a thousand acres and fall down in terraces of gardens and pools to the valley of the river Tamar where there is a restored water-mill. A mile-long nature trail takes you down these wooded slopes through a mass of shrubs and trees.

Open Apr to Oct, Tue to Sun (House only closed Mon except Bank Holiday Mon); Nov to Mar garden only open. Refreshments available. NT.

Coughton Court

Warwickshire *p216 F1*

This Elizabethan house is situated in pleasantly wooded countryside close to the Forest of Arden. The building, which once had a moat, has a central stone Tudor gatehouse flanked by two half-timbered wings which form an open courtyard to the east.

The house is most famous for its association with the Gunpowder Plot; the wives of the conspirators awaited the result of their husband's conspiracy in the gatehouse dining room. The house is interesting for its Jacobite relics, fine panelling and the early sixteenth-century staircase brought from Harvington Hall in 1910.

Open Apr and Oct Sat and Sun only. May to Sep Wed, Thu, Sat and Sun pm only. No dogs. Refreshments available. NT.

Courage Shire Horse Centre

Berkshire *p213 B3*

Set amidst pleasant Berkshire countryside, the Courage Shire Horse Centre has a fine collection of up to twelve Shire horses. The centre was created to arouse interest in this breed and to help ensure its survival.

The timber-built stables contain a coach house for the show drays and the loose boxes where the horses can be seen. In the display room are many rosettes and shining horse brasses as well as a static exhibition of the ancient craft of barrel-making.

Around the centre is a collection of farm carts and agricultural equipment. Other features of the centre include a farrier's shop, a small animals' enclosure, and a children's playground.

Opposite stands a famous coaching inn, once called The Coach and Horses, but now renamed the Shire Horse Inn, whose deeds go back some 300 years.

Open Mar to Oct daily (except Mon unless Bank Holiday). Parking and refreshments available.

The stone ruins of Criccieth Castle – built in the 13th century

Crathes Castle

Grampian *p222 F2*

Crathes Castle has been the ancestral home of the Burnett family since 1323. Its romantic little turrets and gables were added at the end of the sixteenth century and it was around this time that the magnificent painted ceilings were completed in the Chamber of the Nine Worthies, the Chamber of the Nine Muses and the Green Lady's Room. This is supposed to be haunted, and the ghost is apparently undisturbed by the biblical inscriptions on the beams.

The ghost of the Green Lady is said to walk Crathes Castle

National Heavy Horse Centre and has four shire horses in Victorian stalls, a dray, and showcases displaying harness. A country life museum in the walled area of the park houses farming implements of bygone days.

Other facilities for visitors include a picnic area, a garden shop, a gift shop and a restaurant.

Open all year daily. Parking and refreshments available.

Culloden Battlefield

Highland *p222 D2*

It was here on 16 April, 1746, on the windswept plateau of Culloden Moor that the last battle fought on the soil of the United Kingdom took place. It was between the Jacobites of Prince Charles Edward Stuart and the Hanoverian army, led by the Duke of Cumberland. The defeat of the Prince's men, who were outnumbered by two to one, marked the end of the struggle for supremacy by the Stuarts. The battle is remembered for the particular savagery of the Duke of Cumberland's troops towards the defeated Highlanders, who were slaughtered indiscriminately both in the battle and in the subsequent pursuit. No mercy was shown and over 1,200 men died. This event caused the Duke to become known by Scotsmen as 'Butcher' Cumberland.

A tall cairn erected in 1881 stands at the side of the road, which was constructed across the moor in 1835. On both sides of the road are scattered stones, which mark the graves of the Highlanders and are engraved with the names of the clans that took part. Old Leanach Farmhouse, around which the battle raged, still stands and now houses a museum.

Nearby is the Field of the English where seventy-six of the Hanoverian dead are buried, as well as the inscribed 'Cumberland Stone' which is said to mark the position taken by Cumberland during the battle. The Well of the Dead is reputed to be where wounded Highlanders were butchered when trying to drink.

A National Trust Centre has been erected and houses an audio-visual exhibition, and an information desk.

National Trust Centre open Good Fri to mid Oct, daily, Sun, pm only. Parking available. NTS.

The great hall was restored to its original state during the 1930s and contains a curved granite fireplace dating back to Elizabethan times. Paintings by Jameson adorn the walls of the hall, but by far its proudest possession is the Horn of Leys, a jewelled horn of fluted ivory believed to have been given to the Burnetts by Robert the Bruce. At the very top of the house, stretching across its entire width, is the long gallery with a superbly carved oak ceiling and panelling.

As one of the most visited properties in Scotland, Crathes Castle is equally famous for its gardens, dating from the eighteenth century. A magnificent array of plants glorifies the formal gardens which are separated by dense yew hedges – planted in 1702.Each section has been carefully planned so the colours of the plants complement each other. The rest of the grounds extend almost 600 acres to the north of the river Dee and contain several nature trails.

Castle open May to Sep daily; Sun, pm only.
Gardens and grounds open daily all year. NTS.

A team of four, from the Courage Shire Horse Centre pulling a brewer's dray in the Cart Horse Parade on Whit Monday, in Regent's Park, London

Criccieth Castle

Gwynedd *p216 C2*

Perched high on its headland between two sandy bays, Criccieth Castle looks down over the quiet but popular holiday resort below. Criccieth is the only North Wales resort to face due south and from this unique position the castle enjoys panoramic views across Tremadog Bay to the south and inland to the foothills of Snowdonia in the north.

During the fifteenth century the castle was captured by Owain Glyndwr who then set fire to it; the damage is still evident today from the scorch-marked walls and stones cracked by the heat. Since that time the castle was left to decay, but there are substantial parts of the curtain walls and towers remaining. Particularly notable are the Leyburn Tower and the Engine Tower; the latter is so named because it once con-

tained a stone-throwing machine called an 'engine', to defend its northern face.

See AM info. Also open Sun am Apr to Sep.

Cricket St Thomas Wild Life Park

Somerset *p212 E3*

This beautiful and historic 1,036-acre estate belonged to the famous naval family, the Hoods, between 1757 and 1897. The Park is approached over Windwhistle Ridge and along a tree-lined drive which sweeps down to Cricket House, a fine Ham-stone early nineteenth-century building.

The Wild Life Park is surrounded by the rolling acres of the Cricket St Thomas dairy farms and contains a collection of wild animals and birds. Many of them, which include llamas, wallabies and flamingoes, are allowed to roam free in spacious paddocks. There are sixteen acres of landscaped gardens and a stream was dammed to form the waterfalls and series of lakes.

The park is also the home of the

Culzean Castle and Country Park

Strathclyde *p219 B3*

The powerful Kennedy family's ancestral home has been at Culzean Castle since the sixteenth century, but the present castle was not built until about 1780. It is, in fact, not so much a castle as a palatial mansion, designed by Robert Adam in typical eighteenth-century style with classical lines and an elegant interior.

A collection of Kennedy family portraits hangs on the walls of the castle, which has an unusual circular drawing room and a superb central staircase. The castle tour also includes three rooms set out as a memorial to the late General Eisenhower who was presented with a flat here to use as his official Scottish residence.

The gardens and grounds form the Culzean Country Park, occupying over 500 acres overlooking the Firth of Clyde. It includes a walled garden, an orangery, a camellia house, an aviary and a swan pond. Robert Adam also designed the Home Farm buildings which have now been converted to form a reception and interpretation centre for the Country Park.

Castle open Apr to Oct daily.
Country Park open all year. Centre open Apr to Oct. NTS.

Cwmcarn Scenic Forest Drive

Gwent *p212 D4*

This seven-mile drive through mountain forest, passes through an area which totals 10,000 acres. It includes twenty miles of valleys between the river Ebbw in the north to Newport in the south. Partly a twentieth-century recreation of the thirteenth-century Forest of Machen, the forest is comprised largely of larch, spruce and pine which provide timber for coal mining, local sawmills and the paper and packaging industries.

The drive offers spectacular views of the surrounding countryside as far as the Brecon Beacons and the Bristol Channel. There are forest and mountain paths especially set aside for the walker, along which viewpoints are marked.

Open daily Easter to Oct. Parking available.

Dalemain

Cumbria *p220 E1*

The Hasel family has occupied this historic house, with its distinctive façade of locally quarried dusty-pink sandstone, since 1679. Set in parkland amidst wooded

Left: a monument to local industry along the Cwmcarn Forest Drive vice on 27 September, 1825. This famous locomotive is now preserved in the North Road Station Railway Museum, housed in what is possibly the oldest railway station in the world, certainly the oldest in Britain. The station, built in 1841, has a long plasterwork façade and a cast-iron colonnade and staircase. In the museum are four other nineteenth-century locomotives, a railway coach (c 1845), a chaldron wagon and an extensive model railway layout. There are also paintings, drawings, photographs and railway documents.

Darlington's town museum includes many items of natural and local history, geology and archaeology. One of its more interesting features is an observation beehive exhibited during the summer months. The art gallery contains a permanent collection which includes John Dobbin's painting of the opening of the first public railway.

Among the modern development in Darlington are some interesting historical features, particularly a fine clock tower and the ancient parish church of St Cuthbert. Built by Bishop Pudsey of Durham in about 1180, it contains intricately carved misericords.

Railway Museum open all year daily, Sun pm only. Closed Sun Nov to Easter. Parking and refreshments available.
Town Museum open all year daily (except Good Fri, Christmas Day and New Year's Day, Sun and Thu pm).
Art Gallery open all year daily (except Sun and Bank Holidays).

Left: The grand gardens of Culzean Castle

Locomotion No 1 in the North Road Railway Museum at Darlington

hills, Dalemain lies to the north of Ullswater, on a site which once supported a Saxon settlement. A Norman pele-tower (a tower built to protect crops and livestock) is still the main part of the house, and formed part of the chain of strongholds established along the Scottish marches as a defensive measure against Border raids. Over the centuries the tower has been added to, resulting in the Elizabethan and Georgian mixture seen today.

A museum located in the base of the pele-tower contains military relics of the Westmorland and Cumberland Yeomanry, as well as the militia and volunteer forces which preceded it. In the six-teenth-century cobbled courtyard beside the pele-tower is a countryside museum with many interesting agricultural tools. Other attractions on the estate are the gardens and deer park.

Open Easter to Sep daily (except Fri) pm only. Parking and refreshments available.

Darlington

Co Durham *p217 B4*

The industrial town of Darlington is undoubtedly best known for its railway associations, for it was here that George Stephenson's *Locomotion No. 1* made its first journey as a public passenger ser-

Dartmoor Devon

Dartmoor National Park is one of the few wide open spaces left in the south of England, and its wild beauty is free to all. The moor actually covers some 365 square miles between Okehampton and Ivybridge, Tavistock and Christow, and manages to combine mountains, moors, valleys, woods, market towns and villages.

Many of Dartmoor's ponies are sold each autumn as pets for children

It is the great variety of landscape and colour of Dartmoor which never fails to strike the visitor. Rolling upland, occasionally broken by rugged outcrops of grey granite, rises to summits crowned by massive tors sculptured by centuries of weathering into fantastic shapes, some of which have become strangely recognizable, such as Vixen Tor near Merrivale.

The heather, moss and lichens which predominate in the upland combine to produce soft browns, olives and purples which contrast strongly with the close-cropped green grass along the peat banks of the river valleys, dotted with browsing sheep. Many streams and rivers criss-cross the moor and these rise in the moors to the north and south. The fens and mires provide the headwaters for such rivers as the West Dart and Cowsic in the north and the Avon, Erme and Plym in the south. The going here is too soft for larger animals such as sheep and wild ponies, but, curiously, there are few smaller animals either. It seems an area devoid of inhabitants and even few birds breed here. However, the patient observer can spot the occasional curlew, lapwing or merlin.

The heather and grass moors surround the bogs and it is on these that the wild Dartmoor ponies roam. It is believed these sturdy little animals were first turned out on the moor by our ancestors in the Dark Ages. Although allowed to wander freely over the moor, all the ponies have owners, and are rounded up once a year so the foals can be branded. The open country is ideally suited to riding, and pony trekking is a popular way of seeing the less accessible parts of the moor. Rabbits too, are plentiful here, thanks to the Normans who brought them over from France. The addition of the word warren (as in Trowlesworthy Warren) to many place-names is testimony to the rabbits' long occupation of the

Bowerman's Nose Tor – the name is derived from its curious shape

This noble tower belongs to the parish church of Widecombe-in-the-Moor, scene of the famous Widecombe Fair

moor. The fox is another common inhabitant, and badgers and otters live here undisturbed.

Wistman's Wood, Black Tor Beare and Piles Copse are ancient uplands oak copses, where stunted, gnarled oaks festooned with mosses, lichens and ferns, create a fairyland atmosphere. Other plantations, mostly of conifers, date back to the beginning of this century and the forests at Archerton and Fenworthy and Bellever are even younger. The lower river valleys have their own indigenous oak woods.

Interesting characteristics of this wild tract of land are the relics of prehistoric communities who lived on the moor long before Celtic, Roman and Saxon times.

Spinster's Rock, near Drewsteighton, is a Megalithic tomb which dates from Neolithic times. Remains of villages of the same period are also scattered over the moor and one of these hut circles can be seen at Grimspound on Hameldon. There are also Bronze Age kistvaens (small burial chambers) and standing stones (mysterious monuments where sacred rites were performed). These either take the form of a great monolith such as Beardown Man and Menhir on Petertavy Common, or as long rows of smaller stones – the row which runs between Stall Moor and Green Hill is two and a quarter miles long. On the edges of the moor are Celtic hill-forts of the Iron Age, such as the ones at Cranbrook near Moretonhampstead and at Prestonbury near Drewsteighton.

Medieval legacies to Dartmoor are the wayside crosses marking the old track used by the monks of Buckfast and Buckland Abbeys, and the 'clapper' bridges which were built by the tin miners out of huge granite slabs.

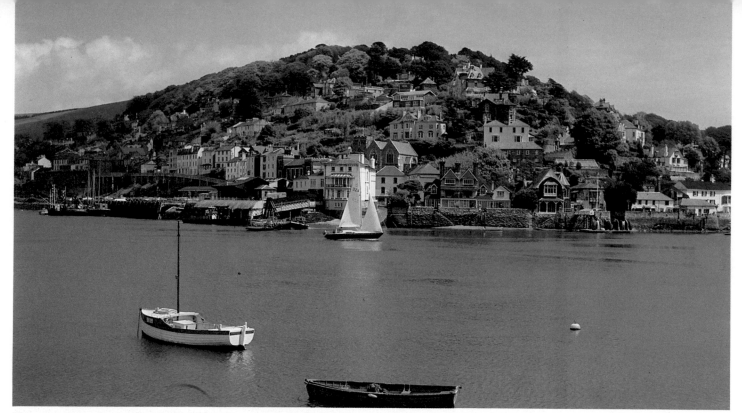

Kingswear, set on the river Dart, is linked by car ferry to Dartmouth on the opposite bank

Dartmouth

Devon *p212 D2*

On the west bank of the beautiful river Dart lies Dartmouth, an interesting ancient town and fishing port with narrow, hilly streets.

The wide tidal river is alive with private, pleasure, and naval craft which must avoid the two car ferries plying back and forth across the Dart at the north and south end of the embankment. A regatta is held here in August and there are regular boat trips to Totnes during the summer. Around the town are a number of fifteenth, seventeenth and eighteenth-century buildings, including those on the waterfront in Bayards Cove with its cobbled quay. On a wooded hill to the north of the town is the magnificent Britannia Royal Naval College (not open to the public). Built in 1905, it replaced HMS *Britannia*, a former training ship for Royal Naval Cadets and here, for the past one hundred years, most of the regular officers of the Royal Navy have started their service careers.

Dartmouth has two castles, one in Bayards Cove, built by Henry VIII as part of his coastal defence system, which has been restored, and Dartmouth Castle opposite, near St Petros Church. The two castles were attached by a chain during times of war to make a barrier across the estuary.

One of the oldest (c 1725) Newcomen Engines (so it is claimed), is housed in a glass-fronted commemorative building in Royal Avenue Gardens. Almost opposite is The Butterwalk, an attractive colonnaded arcade built in the 1630s. On the first floor of number six is a nautical museum which displays over a hundred ship models, as well as other objects of local interest.

Bayards Cove Castle accessible at all reasonable times. Parking available. AM.
Dartmouth Castle See AM info. Also open Sun am Apr to Sep. Parking available.
Newcomen Memorial Engine open Easter to end Oct daily, Sun pm only.
Butterwalk Museum open all year daily (except Sun), pm only Oct to Apr.

Deal

Kent *p214 E2*

This peaceful, old-fashioned seaside resort is tucked beneath the chalk cliffs which border it to the north and south. Here the shingle beach is lined by fleets of fishing boats and its open seascape provides splendid views of shipping passing the notorious Goodwin Sands. These vast, shifting beds lie just five miles offshore and have caused hundreds of wrecks.

Much of the character of old Deal can be found around Middle Street, where narrow lanes run back from the seafront. This eighteenth-century quarter is said to have been the haunt of smugglers.

Deal's first claim to fame is that Julius Caesar made his initial invasion on the beach here between Deal and Walmer in 55 BC. The main historical monument however is Deal Castle, one of a line of defensive forts built by Henry VIII when there was a threat of invasion from France. The castle stands near the foreshore to the south of the town and was built in the symmetrical shape of a six-petalled flower, or clover leaf design, in 1540. Two rings of semi-circular bastions surround the central keep. The castle has been returned to its original architectural form and now houses a small museum exhibiting Iron Age weapons, early pottery and relics of Deal's history. Also of interest here is the Maritime and Local History Museum in St George's Road, which has an interesting collection of items on Deal. Exhibits include local boats, model sailing-ships, maps, photographs and naval relics.

The old Time Ball Tower on the seafront was built in 1854 and indicated Greenwich Mean Time to passing shipping by dropping a large black ball, induced by electric current direct from the Greenwich Observatory itself, down a shaft on the top of the tower at 1.00 pm each day. The time ball ceased to function in 1927 when regular radio broadcasts to shipping became commonplace.

Near the foreshore at Walmer stands Walmer Castle, also built by Henry VIII as part of his coastal defence systems. The castle is now the official residence of the Lord Warden of the Cinque Ports. Over the years many alterations and modifications have changed much of its original at-

The Classical portico of Dodington House seen from the rose garden

mosphere, so that today it is more like a stately home than a fort. It houses a fine collection of items associated with the Duke of Wellington and other Lord Wardens, and is set in magnificent gardens.

Deal Castle See AM info. Also open Sun am Apr to Sep. Parking available.
Maritime and Local History Museum open Spring Bank Holiday to Sep daily, pm only.
Walmer Castle See AM info. Also open Sun am Apr to Sep closed Mon (except Bank Holidays) Gardens closed in winter. Parking available.

Dodington House, Park and Carriage Museum

Avon *p212 E4*

An attractive one-mile drive leads from the entrance gate to Dodington House through gentle Cotswold country which was landscaped by Capability Brown. The estate has been the home of the Codrington family since Elizabethan times, but the original Tudor house was replaced at the end of the eighteenth century. Having made their fortunes in the West Indies, the family commissioned James Wyatt to create a Classical mansion with every facility and convenience available at the time. The exterior is dominated by the huge portico and the curve of the conservatory.

Interesting features inside the house include the grand Imperial staircase, the library, and the lovely little St Mary's Church in the grounds which has direct access from the family's private gallery to the house.

Other attractions within the estate include the stable block housing a carriage museum with a collection of over thirty types of coaches, carriages and harnesses. Carriage rides are available around the estate. There is also a family museum and exhibitions of model aeroplanes and agricultural implements.

The 700-acre park has lovely gardens and a lakeside walk which leads past the enchanting Gothic Cascade House built by Capability Brown. There are also nature trails, a four-acre adventure playground and a narrow gauge railway. A variety of special events take place on certain weekends including steam and vintage fairs, Civil War battles and hot air ballooning.
Open Apr to Sep daily.

Dorchester Dorset *p212 E2*

This pleasant market town, lying in the heart of Thomas Hardy country on the banks of the river Frome, contains many relics of its interesting, and occasionally violent, past. It was here that Judge Jeffreys held his Bloody Assize in 1685, and 1834 saw the trial of the famous Tolpuddle Martyrs.

Despite its ancient origins which stretch back to pre-Roman times, Dorchester has retained very few of its medieval buildings. The exceptions are the Napier Almshouses (founded in 1610 and now converted into shops) and the predominantly sixteenth-century church of St Peter. Most of their contemporaries were destroyed in fires which occurred during the seventeenth and eighteenth centuries, and the greater part of the town has been rebuilt in pleasing grey Portland stone.

However, Dorchester is probably best known for its associations with the author and poet Thomas Hardy who spent most of his life in the area, and immortalised the town as Casterbridge in his novel *The Mayor of Casterbridge*. A life-sized statue of him stands at the top of The Grove.

Dorset County Museum
This contains an interesting collection of archaeological finds and items relating to natural and local history. Exhibits also include the original manuscript of Hardy's novel, *The Mayor of Casterbridge* and a reconstruction of Hardy's study. Relics of Dorchester's other literary figure, William Barnes, noted for his Dorset dialect poetry during the nineteenth century, are also here.

Dorset County Museum

Dorset Military Museum
The museum, housed in the keep which was once the entrance to the Dorset Regiment barracks, covers almost 300 years of local military history. It includes a fascinating collection of uniforms, badges, weapons and souvenirs ranging from a pair of boots and a sword worn during the Charge of the Heavy Brigade at Balaclava, to a desk captured from Hitler's Chancellery in 1945.

Old Crown Court
The six famous Tolpuddle Martyrs stood trial here in 1834. They had formed the Friendly Society of Agriculture Labourers, the forerunner of the Trade Union Movement, and were charged under the Unlawful Oaths Act of 1797. The Martyrs were harshly sentenced to seven years transportation, but were officially pardoned two years later following a public outcry. The Trades Union Congress purchased the Court as a public memorial in 1956.

Judge Jeffreys' Lodging and The Antelope Hotel
When Judge Jeffreys came to Dorchester to preside over the trial of those accused of taking part in Monmouth's unsuccessful rebellion of 1685, he took up lodging in a house in the High Street which has now been converted into a restaurant named after him. His Bloody Assize was probably held in a room at the rear of the Antelope Hotel, which is preserved with its original Tudor panelling. Some 300 men came before Jeffreys and he sentenced seventy-four of them to public hanging and mutilation, and 175 to transportation.

Maumbury Rings
This Roman amphitheatre was built on the site of a prehistoric stone circle. It could accommodate more than 10,000 spectators for the gladiatorial contests and it was the scene of beast-baiting and public executions during the Middle Ages.

Maiden Castle
This huge prehistoric earthwork, consisting of a complicated system of ditches and ramparts, is perhaps, the most famous in the country. Despite its impressive defences, the Romans stormed and seized the castle in AD43.

Dorset County Museum open all year (except Sun, Good Fri and Christmas).
Dorset Military Museum open all year (except Sun, Good Fri, Easter Mon and Christmas), Sat am only from Oct to June. Parking available.
Old Crown Court open all year Mon to Fri (Nov to Apr am only).
Maiden Castle open at any reasonable time. AM.

16th-century St Peter's church in the historic centre of Dorchester

The keep of Doune Castle – the residential apartments were never built

Doune

Central *p220 C4*

The superb fourteenth-century castle of Doune with panoramic views of the surrounding countryside, stands near the confluence of the river Teith and Ardoch Burn on the outskirts of the village. The castle was last used by royalty when Bonnie Prince Charlie housed prisoners here in 1746, but has since been privately owned by the Earls of Moray.

The Doune Park Gardens were laid out in the nineteenth century and the walled garden has the traditional fruit, house, spring and autumn gardens.

Situated about one-and-a-half miles west of the village is Lord Doune's collection of motor vehicles, which includes such cars as Bentleys, MGs and Rolls-Royces. There is also an immaculate 1924 Hispano Suiza, and saloon, sports and racing cars of the 1920s and 1930s. They are all displayed in appropriately converted farm buildings in the grounds of the Doune estate. All of the vehicles are in pristine condition and some compete in the Doune Hill Climb events which take place in April, June and September.

Castle open Apr to Oct daily (except Thu in Apr and Oct). Parking available
Motor Museum open Apr to Oct daily. Parking available.

Dover

Kent *p213 D2*

Dover, looking out over the English Channel, has been the Gateway of England for some 2,000 years. During the second century, it was the headquarters of the Roman fleet in Britain and is now our busiest passenger port. Ships were guided to the harbour by a lighthouse, and the one which still stands on the famous white cliffs as part of the castle is known as the Pharos.

The castle was built during the second half of the twelfth century on the site of an earlier castle and has been remarkably well preserved. Two walls with numerous towers protect a formidable massive keep which stands ninety-five-feet high, forming an almost perfect cube with walls up to twenty-one-feet thick.

Some interesting features within the castle are a 300-foot well with remains of the medieval plumbing, and a collection of weapons and armour. Cut into the chalk cliffs beneath the castle are a series of underground passages, first constructed during the siege of 1216 by Prince Louis of France. They were extended during the early nineteenth century and were put to use as an air-raid shelter during World War II. When Napoleon's army were gathering on the French coast and Dover once more became a garrison town, Crabble Mill was built to provide flour for the troops. The six-storey mill driven by the waters of the river Dour ceased working in 1890, but has now been restored and includes a museum of milling.

Dover has many other historic buildings including tiny St Edmund's Chapel and the Town Hall which incorporates the thirteenth-century Hall of Maison Dieu and a museum. It was not until 1970 that the exciting discovery was made of Roman remains beneath the streets of Dover. A part of the site has since been permanently excavated to show extensive remains of a fine town house, its richly painted walls still standing up to ten feet high in places. Also on show is a section of the hypocaust, or underfloor heating system, displays relating to Roman Dover, and items found during excavation.

Castle and underground passages see AM info. Also Sun am Apr to Sep.
Crabble Watermill open Easter then Spring Bank Holiday to Sep, Wed and Sat pm only; Sun and Bank Holidays all day. Children under 14 admitted Wed and Sat if accompanied but *not* when machinery is working.
Town Hall (including Maison Dieu and museum) open daily (except Wed and Sun).
Roman Painted House open Mar to Nov, daily (except Mon).

Drayton Manor Park and Zoo

Staffordshire *p216 F2*

Drayton was the home of Sir Robert Peel in the nineteenth century, but the manor house has since been demolished. In the extensive grounds are two lakes teeming with small pleasure craft, and a replica of a stern wheel paddle boat. On the lower and smaller lake is a cruise through the Jungle and Lost World, which has life-size model animals and natives. Amongst the magnificent lions, leopards and bears in the zoo are lovable monkeys, exotic birds, paddocks, a farm section and children's corner. There is also an amusement park and a miniature railway along the lakeside, with passenger compartments hauled by a scale model of a nineteenth-century North American locomotive.

A chair lift operates from the main gate across the park and affords an aerial view of the estate and lakes which in all cover over 160 acres.

For the nature lover there is a marked trail and walks through forty acres of woodland.

Open Easter to Oct daily. Parking on parkland and refreshments available.

Dover Castle on the lofty site where an Iron Age fort once stood

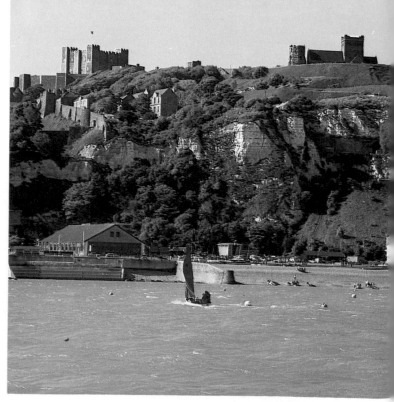

Drumlanrig Castle

Dumfries and Galloway *p220 D3*

The cost of building Drumlanrig Castle in about 1680 was so great that the horrified owner, the 1st Duke of Queensberry, spent only one night there. The castle is now the property of the Dukes of Buccleuch.

It is a superb Renaissance building of pink sandstone with lead cupola turrets and ballustrading overlooking the Nith Valley. Its works of art include Rembrandt's *Old Woman Reading*, and there is also some fine Louis XIV furniture, a silver chandelier which weighs nine stones, and souvenirs of Bonnie Prince Charlie and his highland followers. Lovely walks can be taken through the grounds and there is an exciting adventure playground for children.

Open Easter weekend, then Sat, Sun, Wed and Thu in May and June, also Bank Holidays, pm only. Daily in July and Aug. Parking available.

Dryburgh Abbey

Borders *p220 E3*

Standing on a beautiful wooded horseshoe-bend of the river Tweed is the ruin of Dryburgh Abbey – the site of which was once a holy place for Druids.

It is one of a famous group of

Border monasteries which were attacked by English invaders in 1322, 1385 and 1544. Although there was extensive damage, the west front of the church remains, with its thirteenth-century portal; the transepts, parts of the nave and chapter house have also survived.

The cloister buildings, however, are more complete than those of any other monastery in Scotland, with the exception of Iona and Incholm. Sir Walter Scott, his biographer J. G. Lockhart, and the former Commander-in-Chief of the British Army, Field Marshal Earl Haig, are all buried in the abbey grounds.

See AM info. Parking available.

Dudley Castle and Zoo

West Midlands *p216 F1*

Standing above an escarpment, in the midst of a heavily built-up area, are the impressive ruins of a castle constructed by Roger de Somery in the thirteenth century. This excellent viewpoint is reached by a chairlift which starts from the main entrance 200 feet below the castle.

Housed in the forty-acre wooded castle grounds is Dudley Zoo, famous for the breeding of rare species of animals such as the ring-tailed lemur and the silvery marmoset. The pits which were left after mineral excavations have been cleverly adapted to accommodate some of the larger animals, which include bears, tigers, lions, monkeys and reptiles.

The Land of the Dinosaurs exhibition has lifesize prehistoric monsters, and the children's farm includes a collection of small animals. There is also a fair, and, for the more adventurous, a ski slope.

Open all year daily. Parking and refreshments available.

Dufftown

Grampian *p222 E2*

Dufftown is chiefly famous for its malt whisky distilleries. It was founded by James Duff, the 4th Earl of Fife, and is laid out with two streets running at right angles to a central clock tower, with smaller streets leading off them.

On the northern outskirts of the town stands Balvenie Castle, a

substantial ruin overlooking the river Fiddich. The thirteenth-century castle was originally a stronghold of the Comyns, but was converted to a mansion in the fifteenth century by the 4th Earl. The front entrance still has its original wrought iron gate, known as a yett; and it is the only one of its kind left in Scotland.

A small local history museum in the town contains items of civil regalia and interesting relics from the Mortlach Kirk, which is one of the oldest churches in Scotland.

Perhaps the most famous distillery is the Glenfiddich, situated by the Robbie Dubh – the Black Robert stream. It was founded in 1886 by Major William Grant, and is one of the few distilleries where one can see each stage of the production right through to the bottling process. The visitors reception centre has a bar and Scotch Whisky Museum.

Balvenie Castle See AM info. Parking available.
Dufftown Museum open June to Sep daily. Parking available.
Glenfiddich Distillery open all year (except 2–3 weeks over Christmas and New Year). Parking available. Guided tours Mon to Fri.

Dumfries

Dumfries and Galloway *p220 D2*

Affectionately known as Scotland's Queen of the South, Dumfries is delightfully situated on the broad waters of the river Nith.

In 1791 the poet Robert Burns made his home in Dumfries. He wrote some of his most famous songs here and the house where he died in 1796, now called Burns' House, has been made into a museum in his honour. Many of the poet's personal belongings can be seen here, and the road in which the house stands has been renamed Burns Street.

Not far from the house is St Michael's churchyard, where Burns, his wife Jean Armour and their five sons lie buried in the now famous mausoleum. St Michael's Church itself dates from 1744 and a brass plate in the church marks the pew where Burns sat. A fine statue of him, erected in 1882, stands in front of the present Greyfriars Church.

The central point of the town is an eighteenth-century complex of buildings known as Midsteeple, comprising the old municipal buildings, courthouse and prison. A tablet on the wall inscribed

The six-arched Old Bridge over the river Nith at Dumfries. Down river is the Caul – a weir built to drive grain mills in the 18th century

with distances includes Huntingdon, and this serves as a reminder of the times when Scottish cattle drovers herded their animals south to trade in the lucrative English markets. Another detail on the steeple is a relief map of the town, showing it as it was in Burns' days.

Unusually housed in a restored mid eighteenth-century windmill in Church Street, is the Dumfries Museum with a camera obscura on top of it. The museum itself has a large collection covering local history, archaeology, geology, birds and animals. Close by is yet another museum in the seventeenth-century Old Bridge House, on the end of the medieval bridge. Here period rooms portray the local way of life of the past. The Old Bridge or Devorgilla Bridge itself, now closed to traffic, is a six-arched stone structure and the most famous of five bridges which cross the river Nith on its course through the town. Another attraction here is the Caul, an early eighteenth-century weir, which lies just downstream from the bridge and was built to provide power for riverside grain mills.

Burns' House open all year. Mon to Sat am only, Sun pm only, but closed Sun from Oct to Mar.
Burns' Mausoleum open as Burns' House by arrangement with curator.
Dumfries Museum and Camera Obscura open all year, daily (except Tue) Sun pm Apr to Sep only.
Old Bridge House Museum open Apr to Sep, Mon to Sat (closed Tue), Sun pm only.

Dunrobin Castle

Dunster's yarn-market. The town was a busy trading point in the 17th century

Dunrobin Castle

Highland *p221 D3*

Built in 1275, Dunrobin is the oldest castle in Scotland which is still inhabited and has been the home of the Dukes of Sutherland for 500 years. Most of the existing building was designed in 1856 by Sir Charles Barry, architect of the Houses of Parliament, although much of it was restored after a fire in 1915.

Inside are some fine tapestries, paintings by Reynolds and Canaletto and Louis XV furniture, and various trophies and regimental colours belonging to the 93rd Sutherland Highlanders.

In the grounds a magnificent formal garden borders a hundred-yard terrace.

Open May to Sep, daily, Sun pm only. Parking and refreshments available.

Dunster

Somerset *p212 D3*

The unspoilt village of Dunster lies off the main road, two miles from Minehead. The wide main street is overlooked by the well-preserved castle which stands in a prominent position, surrounded by trees, commanding excellent views of the Bristol Channel, Exmoor and the Quantock Hills.

Originally built by the Earl of Somerset, the castle was the home of the Luttrells for some 600 years. The seventeenth-century plasterwork ceilings and the beautifully carved balustrade of the staircase, depicting a stag hunt, have been well preserved. In the banqueting hall there are some unusual Dutch painted leather panels and portraits.

At the centre of the village is a yarn-market built by George Luttrell when the trade cloth was flourishing. The fifteenth-century church has monuments to the Luttrells and a fine rood screen. A twelfth-century dovecote with a revolving ladder to reach the nesting boxes stands in a walled garden attached to the church.

Castle open Apr to Sep daily (except Fri and Sat); Mar, Oct and Nov, Tue, Wed and Sun pm only. Parking available. NT.
Old Dovecote open Easter to mid Oct daily.

Durham Co Durham *p217 B5*

County town, cathedral city and seat of a university, Durham is one of Britain's most pleasing cities to explore, with the cathedral and castle standing together high on a rocky outcrop surrounded by steep wooded banks leading down to the river Wear.
Gathered about these two Norman giants are old buildings spanning several centuries, pleasant lawns and gardens.

The origins of Durham are related to St Cuthbert who was one of the founders of Christianity in northern England. His shrine was brought to Durham in 995 after being removed from Holy Island in 875 to escape Viking raids, and by 998 a church had been built to house it.

Legend has it that the coffin became immovable on a neighbouring hill until the saint revealed his chosen resting place to his followers in a vision. The spot quickly became a place of pilgrimage, and the pilgrims brought the wealth which enabled the town to grow.

The history of Durham is a peaceful one, although it was a military base from Norman times when the castle was built, until the seventeenth century. The only battle fought in the vicinity was in 1346 when Philip VI of France, having lost a war against Edward III, exhorted his Scottish allies to invade England. Edward III's wife, Philippa, raised an army in her lord's absence and defeated the invaders at Neville's Cross, named after one of her commanders, now a suburb of the city.

The oldest regatta in England is held in Durham, and the renowned miners' gala on every third Saturday of July fills the city with marching feet and music.

The Castle

This was the Bishop's fortress until 1831, when the university was founded, and it now houses University College. The oldest part of the castle is the beautiful little Norman chapel. Original paving, laid in a herringbone pattern, lies under a vaulted roof and the heads of the pillars are carved with geometrical designs, serpents, flowers, human figures and leopards.

The senate room, placed directly above the Norman chapel, is one of the best of the splendid apartments in the castle, and has a sixteenth-century Flemish tapestry depicting the life of Moses.

Monks of Lindisfarne chose the site of the cathedral in Saxon times

In 1840 the battlemented keep was rebuilt to house students and it still serves this function. Opposite is the great hall, a magnificent dining room in which royalty has been entertained since 1322, decorated with carvings and banners.

The Black Staircase, built by Bishop Cosin in 1663, is mainly made of oak with pierced panels of richly carved willow. It rises fifty-seven feet through four storeys. There is much fine carving in St Tunstall's Gallery and Pudsey's Gallery which are connected by the staircase.

The Cathedral

The Cathedral Church of Christ and Blessed Mary the Virgin was built between 1093 and 1133. The vast interior of this, the finest Norman building in Europe, is breathtaking. What first strike the visitor are the great round pillars, seven feet in diameter. They are adorned with bold zigzag carvings which lead the eye up to the earliest rib-vaulted ceiling in the country. A splendidly elaborate stone screen stands behind the high altar and here too is the shrine of St Cuthbert, whose body was laid there in 1104. He is in good company with the Venerable Bede who lies at the opposite end of the cathedral. The fourteenth-century throne of Bishop Hatfield is the tallest known.

Otherwise practically unspoiled Norman architecture, the only two major additions, the Galilee chapel built between 1170 and 1175, and the Chapel of the Nine Altars built between 1242 and 1280, successfully enhance the beauty of the cathedral rather than detract from it.

The Galilee chapel has a roof supported by clusters of Purbeck marble and stone of remarkably light construction, giving the chapel an airiness distinct from the rest of the cathedral. The Chapel of the Nine Altars, built for women worshippers who were denied access to the rest of the cathedral, has pointed arches and richly carved pillar heads.

In the monks dormitory, a timbered hall 194 feet by thirty-nine feet, is a display of the cathedral's prized possessions, including illuminated manuscripts, a collection of crosses and the reconstructed oak coffin of St Cuthbert.

Town Hall

This Victorian hall was built by public subscription and opened in 1851. Relics of Count Boruwalski, a Polish dwarf who died in 1837 at the age of ninety-eight, are kept here, including his violin which he played adeptly. He was buried in the cathedral and an inscribed brass, rejected by the Dean for its wording, states he 'mesured no more than three feet three inches in height, but his form was well proportioned and he possessed a more than common store of understanding and knowledge'.

Durham University

All around the Palace Green the collection of buildings ranging from the fifteenth to the twentieth century, once courts, hospitals, almshouses and residences, now houses the university. It was the third university to be founded in England and has inherited an aura of antiquity and distinction rivalling Oxford and Cambridge.

Durham Castle stands guard high on a wooded terraced hill above the city

Gulbenkian Museum

Housed within the School of Oriental Studies on Elvet Hill, this collection of oriental art and archaeology is the finest in England. The displays in the multi-level hall of Egyptian and Mesopotanian antiquities, Chinese and Japanese pottery and porcelain, exquisite jades, ivories, textiles and paintings are stunning. Particularly interesting are the colourful Tibetan paintings or tankas; a Tibetan magician's apron of human bones, and a fifty-feet-long series of carved teak panels from a Burmese palace.

Durham Light Infantry Museum and Arts Centre

The history of the Light Infantry Regiment is traced back to 1758 in the museum, with exhibits that include uniforms, medals, armoury and Victoria Crosses won by the regiment. The Arts Centre has family exhibitions and films.

Castle open first 3 weeks in Apr, then July to Sep, Mon to Sat. Rest of the year Mon, Wed and Sat pm only. Occasionally closed for University functions.
Town Hall open all year daily (except Sun).
University Grounds open all year daily.
Gulbenkian Museum open all year daily (except Sat and Sun Christmas to Easter). Sun pm only.
Light Infantry Museum and Arts Centre open all year Tue to Sat and Bank Holiday Mon, Sun pm only.

Dyrham Park

Avon *p212 E4*

This long, low, many-windowed mansion overlooks a beautiful 263-acre deer park. The house was built between 1691 and 1702 for William Blathwayt, Secretary at War to William III, and the furnishings have hardly changed since Blathwayt first completed them, according to his house-keeper's inventory of 1710.

During his career, Blathwayt frequently visited Holland. Consequently many of the furnishings are Dutch, and include several pieces of blue and white Delft-ware, beautiful bird paintings by Hondecoeter and leather wall hangings from the Hague. Blath-wayt also had connections with the American colonies which enabled him to obtain some fine cedarwood for one of the stair-cases. There is Virginian walnut panelling in the Diogenes room.

The orangery which is attached to the house resembles the style of Versailles with its massive Tus-can columns. Formal pleasure gardens, laid out by George London, feature terraces with fountains, cascades and a canal. The deer park, as it is now, dates from the late eighteenth century, but Fallow deer have roamed the estate since Saxon times. It is thought that Dyrham comes from the Saxon word 'doer-hamm' meaning deer enclosure.

Open Apr, May and Oct daily (except Thu and Fri) pm only. June to Sep daily (except Fri) pm only. Refreshments available. NT.

East Bergholt

Suffolk *p213 D4*

On 11th June, 1776, John Constable – one of Britain's best-loved landscape artists, was born in East Bergholt. When talking of his home village, Constable once said 'these scenes made me a painter' and some of those scenes have scarcely changed from the day he committed them to canvas. His famous painting *The Hay Wain*, was modelled on Flatford Mill – the family home. Willy Lott's cottage, lived in by a friend

of Constable, stands near the mill.

Flatford Lock resembles the locks in some of Constable's paintings and a restored Stour lighter – a flat bottomed barge – can be seen on request.

In the village itself are many cottages dating back to Elizabethan times, and the church has a number of interesting features, including memorials inside to Constable and his wife, and a bell-house stands in the church yard. This is a timber building dating from the sixteenth century, and the bells are hung upside down and rung by hand.

Flatford Mill and **Willy Lott's Cottage** not open but exteriors viewable at all times. NT.
Flatford Lock open at all times.

Eastbourne

East Sussex *p213 C2*

Eastbourne is a popular south coast resort which has retained much of its nineteenth-century elegance. Rather than bingo halls and amusement arcades, its promenade is backed by splendid hotels and beautiful gardens, notably the Carpet Gardens. Along with all the usual seaside attractions, Eastbourne plays host to international tennis tournaments and, during the summer season, top military bands perform daily on the seafront bandstand encircled by a large covered arena.

There are some pleasant walks from Eastbourne, particularly westwards to Beachy Head which rises to 534 feet and helps to shelter the resort from sea winds.

During the early nineteenth century, when Napoleon was threatening to invade Britain's shores, Eastbourne was in the front line of defence and some of its fortifications can still be seen. The Circular Redoubt was the most extensive, and now contains the Sussex Combined Services Museum which illustrates the military history of Sussex. There is access to the gun platform and the area also includes an aquarium and the popular Treasure Island Play Centre. Tower 73, or The Wish Tower, incorporates a Martello tower and is the home of the Coastal Defence Museum where Napoleonic defence methods and equipment are displayed. Nearby is the Lifeboat

Easton Farm Park

Suffolk *p213 D4*

A working farm is the focal point of this country park near the picturesque village of Easton.

Early farm machinery and country bygones are on show in the Victorian farm buildings, built by the Duke of Hamilton in 1870 as a model dairy farm. The dairy itself is sparkling clean, decorated with floral tiles and a fountain. Visitors may observe the collection of farm livestock, including some rare breeds such as St Kilda sheep and longhorn cattle, and watch demonstrations of steam machines and horse-drawn equipment.

There are nature trails in the park through woodland and riverside meadows, and other features here include an apiary, a children's pets paddock, an adventure play pit and a craft shop. Coarse fishing is also available.

Open Good Fri to early Oct daily. Parking and refreshments available.

Left: Willy Lott's cottage, an enchanting 17th-century house on the banks of the river Stour owned by Constable's father

Below: The many colourful cliff gardens at Eastbourne provide one of the resort's most attractive features

Museum which, when opened in 1937, was the first one in Britain.

Eastbourne is justifiably proud of its parks and gardens and it is within one of these that the Towner Art Gallery is situated. This lovely Georgian manor house contains a fine collection of nineteenth- and twentieth-century British paintings and Georgian caricatures.

Circular Redoubt open May to Sep daily. Oct to Apr Mon to Fri. Parking available.
Coastal Defence Museum open Easter to Sep daily. Parking available.
Royal National Lifeboat Museum open Easter to Sep daily.
Towner Art Gallery open all year daily (except Good Fri, Christmas Day and Boxing Day), Sun pm only. Parking available.

Edinburgh Lothian p220 D4

Watched over by the great castle, the Old Town of pre-eighteenth century Edinburgh huddles about the foot of Castle Rock, while to the north stands the gracious New Town of Georgian buildings, broad streets, squares and circuses.

The Castle

Edinburgh's history centres around its castle and records show that Castle Rock was a tribal stronghold as early as 600 BC. Very little now remains of the original eleventh-century castle, and the present building is a mixture of additions made until the seventeenth century.

On the eastern side of the Palace Yard are the royal apartments, among them the tiny bedroom where Mary Queen of Scots gave birth to a son who became James VI of Scotland and James I of England.

The great hall, built by James IV, now houses a fascinating collection of weapons and armour. In the Crown Room displays of Scottish regalia include the crown, the sceptre and the sword of state.

The famous Military Tattoo takes place under the castle walls and is the highlight of Edinburgh's annual international festival held in late summer. All the arts are included in the official programme which attracts thousands of visitors from all over the world every year.

Holyroodhouse and Abbey

The abbey, now a picturesque ruin, was founded in 1128 by David I and the Palace was built for Charles II in 1671. Mary Queen of Scots spent six years of her reign here during which time her jealous husband murdered her secretary, David Riccio. The place where he fell is marked by a brass tablet.

One hundred and eleven portraits of Scottish kings hang in the picture gallery in the Palace, and the state apartments here are decorated with Flemish tapestries.

Gladstone's Land

This six-storey tenement, completed in 1620, is remarkable for its painted ceilings. The main rooms have been refurbished as a home typical of the period and the ground floor includes a shop front and goods typical of the seventeenth century.

Lady Stair's House

Here important manuscripts and relics of three of Scotland's most famous literary figures – Robert Burns, Sir Walter Scott and Robert Louis Stevenson – are housed. They include Scott's writing desk and printing press and Stevenson's riding accessories.

Museum of Childhood

In this unique museum are historical toys, books, costumes, and dolls' fashions providing a picture of childhood over the past centuries.

National Museum of Antiquities

Extensive collections here include treasures from all over Scotland depicting the Scottish way of life from the Stone Age to modern times. Outside, the building is decorated with statues of eminent Scotsmen.

Royal Scottish Museum

Here collections from all over the world cover archaeology, natural history, geology, technology and science as well as the decorative arts. There are also a large number of fossil fish here.

Canongate Tolbooth

When Canongate was a separate burgh from Edinburgh the Tolbooth, built in 1591, was the municipal building and civic centre. It is an interesting building with outside steps, a turreted tower and a projecting clock. Now it is a museum displaying, amongst other things, the Dunbar collection of Highland dress and tartans.

National Gallery of Scotland

This is one of the most distinguished of the smaller galleries in Europe with its collection of Old Masters, Impressionists and Scottish paintings. Exhibits include work by Constable, Van Gogh and Turner.

John Knox's House

The great Scottish reformer and theologian John Knox is said to have lived here from 1561 to 1572. The house was built in 1490 and may well be the oldest in Edinburgh. His day study and his bedroom can be seen on the second floor.

The Cathedral

A church has stood on this site since the ninth century, but most of the existing building of St Gile's Cathedral is fourteenth or fifteenth century. The most recent addition to this lofty structure is the Thistle chapel, built in 1911, which has a superbly carved interior. John Knox is buried in the churchyard and a statue of him stands here too.

The North-East View of EDINBURGH CASTLE

The unfinished Parthenon on Calton Hill was started as a monument to Scotsmen killed in the Napoleonic Wars

Royal Botanical Gardens

Fascinating landscapes of exotic plants are featured here and amidst the beautiful gardens stands Inverleith House which houses the National Gallery of Modern Art. This has many fine twentieth-century paintings and in the garden are sculptures by Barbara Hepworth and Henry Moore.

Mons Meg cannon stands by the chapel door of the castle

Princes Gardens

The huge Scott Monument in the East Princes Street Gardens is 200-feet-high and has a statue of Sir Walter Scott himself beneath its arches. Placed in niches around the monument are sixty-four statuettes of characters created by him in his novels and poems. The 287 steps up to the top lead to fine views over the city.

The Floral Clock at the east end of West Princes Gardens is the oldest of its kind in the world, and is a famous trysting place. It was built in 1903, and over 27,000 plants cover its huge face.

Castle open all year daily, Sun pm only Nov to Apr. Subject to Tattoo requirements. Parking available. AM.

Holyroodhouse and Abbey open all year daily (except Sun Nov to Apr and when occupied by the Royal Family). Also closed for about a month during late spring. Parking available. AM.

Gladstone's Land open Good Fri to late Oct daily, Sun pm only; Nov to Jan Sat and Sun only, Sun pm only. NTS.

Lady Stair's House open all year Mon to Sat, also Sun pm during Festival.

Museum of Childhood open as above.

National Museum of Antiquities open all year daily, Sun pm only.

Royal Scottish Museum open all year daily, Sun pm only. Refreshments available Mon to Sat.

Canongate Tolbooth open all year daily, Sun pm only during Festival. Parking available.

National Gallery of Scotland open all year daily, Sun pm only.

John Knox's House open all year Mon to Fri.

Royal Botanical Gardens open all year. Refreshments available Apr to Sep.

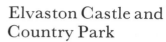

Elan Valley Reservoirs

Powys *p216 D1*

This wild and remote valley, where the river Elan flowed down to the Wye, enchanted the poet Shelley when he occupied a house here with his young wife Harriet, early in the nineteenth century. From the west bank near the mouth of the Nant Gwyllt stream, long stretches of the garden wall can be seen when the water level is low. However, in 1871 the Corporation of Birmingham decided to look to mid-Wales as a suitable source for its water supply and chose the Elan Valley.

Work on forming the great reservoirs began in 1892 by damming the river, and they were completed in 1904. The complex of lakes, which enhanced the beautiful scenery is sometimes referred to as the Welsh Lake District and lies to the west of the little market town of Rhayader. Elan Village in its wooded setting below Caban Coch dam was built by Birmingham Corporation to house the workforce.

Craig Goch, enclosing over 200 acres of the highest part of the Elan Valley, is the topmost reservoir and its stern and rugged shoreline is a popular picnic spot. From Craig Goch the waters cascade over the top dam dropping sheer into the next lake Pen-y-garreg. Its 124 acres are set in wooded surroundings with a fir-covered island in its centre. The long, sinuous shape of Garreg-Ddu follows, with its submerged causeway and woods sweeping across the lake. Caban Coch is the final lake in the complex, which covers some 500 acres and is surrounded by crags and steep, wooded slopes.

Elgin

Grampian *p222 E3*

Elgin is a busy market town and royal burgh lying south of the river Lossie. Well situated for exploring the coast of the Moray Firth to the north, and the hills and Spey Valley to the south, it is also ideal for the trout and salmon angler.

The town has many buildings of architectural interest, the most famous being the beautiful ruins of the thirteenth-century cathedral. Both the town and the cathedral were burnt down in 1390 by Robert II's outlawed son who terrorized the area. However there are well preserved sections of its vaulted roof, and carved stonework can still be seen. Close by is the remaining wing of the fifteenth-century Bishop's Palace and the East Gate of the precincts, which is the only one surviving.

Also of interest in the town are Gray's Hospital, Braco's Banking House and, occupying an island-site in the High Street, St Giles Church with its huge portico supported by six giant columns. The town museum stands at the entrance to Cooper Park and contains a world-wide collection of fossils, as well as a display on the heritage of Elgin and Moray.

Museum open mid Mar to mid Oct Mon to Sat (closed Tue except during July and Aug). Mid Oct to mid Mar Wed and Sat am only.

Elvaston Castle and Country Park

Derbyshire *p217 B1*

When this neo-Gothic mansion was built in 1817, it incorporated an earlier seventeenth-century house to surround a large courtyard. In the middle of this there stands a large water tower.

The entrance hall with its high vaulted ceiling is particularly strikingly decorated in black and gold.

The gardens were landscaped by William Barron, and include a kitchen garden and an old english garden. A remarkable number of trees and bushes, including some rare specimens, were planted in the gardens, and an elaborate topiary garden with yews cut into intricate designs can still be seen today. The church in the castle grounds contains memorials to the Stanhopes who lived here for many years, and an interesting sculpture by Canova, the famous Venetian artist.

The Country Park covers some 200 acres of woodland, gardens and parkland, and is the home of many species of animal and bird life. A marked nature trail and reserve has been developed here, as well as a riding centre, bridle paths and picnic areas around the park.

Castle and **Park** open all year. Parking available. Refreshments available Easter to Oct.

Ely

Cambridgeshire *p213 C5*

Ely is one of Britain's oldest religious foundations, and there has been a cathedral here for some 1,300 years.

Before the Fens were drained for agriculture during the eighteenth and nineteenth centuries, Ely was an island. Today the cathedral rises like a beacon from the flat fenland country, a landmark for miles around. It has always had a measure of good luck, having survived the Dissolution, the Puritans and the Death Watch Beetle. However, the cathedral has had its disasters too. In February, 1322, the Norman tower came crashing down, demolishing part of the choir in the process. Nevertheless, from the rubble

Lovely scenery is very much a feature of the Elan Valley Reservoirs

arose what is now the cathedral's most characteristic feature – the magnificent octagon. The very best medieval craftsmen were employed to create this unique structure which supports an octagonal lantern. The cathedral building is principally Norman, evident in the style of its lofty nave, with some superb intricate stone carving. The most notable example of this is the Bishop Alcock's lovely chantry, built in 1488.

Erddig

Clwyd *p216 E2*

Erddig is set in a magnificent 1,900-acre estate on the south bank of the river Clywedog. This late seventeenth-century red brick mansion has been the home of the Yorke family since 1735. Erddig owes much of its character to John Meller, an uncle of the Yorkes, who acquired the property in 1715. He enlarged the house and furnished it exquisitely with tapestries, oriental porcelain and silver. Its collection of gilt and silver furniture is considered to be one of the finest and best documented in any country house. Especially fine is the state bed, made in London in 1720, and upholstered in beautifully embroidered Chinese silk. The garden has been skilfully remodelled by the National Trust, following the layout of an old engraving of Erddig. It is a fine example of typical eighteenth-century formal design with walks, a canal, a pond and an avenue of lime trees.

Perhaps the most fascinating facet of Erddig is the amount of information about the life of the domestic staff who worked here. The Yorkes were particularly good to their servants and kept their portraits with poetic descriptions of them which are now in the servants' hall. The Trust has also carefully restored the old service equipment and buildings. These include the smithy, sawmill, stable, laundry, kitchens and the bakehouse. There is also an agricultural museum here.

Open Good Fri to Oct (Agricultural Museum July to Oct) daily (except Mon but open Bank Holiday Mon) pm only. Refreshments available. NT.

Evesham

Hereford and Worcester *p212 F5*

Lying at the heart of the market gardening area called the Vale of Evesham, is a small market town nestled in a bend of the river Avon. The river, with its tree-lined walks, lends Evesham much of its peaceful charm.

Two churches have the honour of sharing Evesham's churchyard, entered through an attractive timbered gateway, and between them stands Clement Lichfield's beautiful 110-foot-high bell tower. Abbot Lichfield is buried in All Saints' Church (the oldest of the two) in a marble tomb, although there is no inscription because it was lost during the Puritan régime.

Ely Cathedral's crowning glory – seen from the south side – are the octagon and lantern which were built over 600 years ago

A stroll around the compact town takes in a number of fine old buildings. Probably the best of these is the close-timbered Booth Hall or Round House – now a bank, and Dresden House with its huge iron brackets over the doorway.

The Abbey Almonry in Vine Street is used as a museum of local history which includes many curious old agricultural implements.

Almonry open Good Fri to end Sep daily (except Mon and Wed) pm only.

Exeter Devon *p212 D2*

The charming, historic city of Exeter, capital of rural Devon, has often experienced strife and hardship in the past, but today reigns peacefully as the gateway to the beauty of the West Country.

During the course of its lively history the Danes took the city twice and William the Conqueror laid siege to it for eighteen days in 1068 before capturing it. During the Wars of the Roses, although the citizens were really supporters of Warwick the Kingmaker, they persuaded the victorious Edward IV that they had been loyal to him so successfully that he presented the city with a sword in gratitude. Exeter collected a second sword to hang in the Guildhall from Henry VII for resisting the rebellion in 1497 of Perkin Warbeck, an impostor who claimed succession to the throne.

The town was an important cloth manufacturing and trading centre from Norman times up until the eighteenth century, and Tucker's Hall in Fore Street, which was built for the Guild of Weavers, Fullers and Shearmen in 1471, is evidence of this.

Unfortunately the city was badly damaged by German bombers in May, 1942, and many medieval buildings were lost. In their place new complexes such as the huge Guildhall shopping centre have been built, incorporating much of the Civic Hall of 1838 and the thirteenth-century St Pancras Church.

There are many different aspects to Exeter now, as its huge twice-weekly livestock market, its attractive canal, and its modern university buildings prove.

The Cathedral

Near Southernhay Gardens in the attractive cathedral close, stands the Cathedral of St Peter, notable for the two great Norman towers and fourteenth-century west front which is decorated with a superb array of sculptures. The cathedral was established in 1050, rebuilt by the Normans between 1107 and 1137, and in 1260 demolished except for the two towers, between which the new cathedral was subsequently built. Among the finest features inside the cathedral are the rib-vaulted ceiling, the choir with its finely carved screen, the minstrel's gallery decorated by carvings of a heavenly choir playing musical instruments, the chantry chapels and the fifty-nine-feet-high Bishop's throne, which was carved in Devon oak between 1313 and 1317. A most unusual astrological clock of 1376 adorns the north wall of the transepts.

In the Close, next to the little church of St Martin, stands Mol's Coffee House, where Sir Francis Drake and Sir Walter Raleigh, amongst others, used to meet. The room is now an art shop.

Rougemont and Northernhay Gardens

Running through Northernhay Gardens is a fine piece of the Roman city wall, and the remains of the Norman castle are here too. At the northern most corner of the wall stands Athelstan's Tower, named after a grandson of King Alfred, first King of All England, who had a palace here. An arch in the wall by the tower leads to the Rougemont Gardens. In a corner of these pleasant gardens is

The spire of St Michael and All Angels Church above Exeter

Rougemont House, a fine Georgian town house which has become a museum of prehistoric, Roman and medieval relics.

St Nicholas' Priory

Nearby is the Norman priory of St Nicholas. It has a room with massive Norman pillars and a vaulted roof, a prior's cell, a medieval guest hall with a fine oak ceiling, a Tudor room with an oriel window and a fifteenth-century kitchen. There are also displays of pewter, furniture and wood carving here.

Guildhall

Perhaps the oldest municipal building in the country, the Guildhall, was built in 1330 although the roof dates from 1466 when much rebuilding was carried out. The heavy portico which overhangs the High Street was added in Elizabethan days and the beautiful roof of gilded beams rests on carved figures of bears holding staffs – the badge of Warwick the Kingmaker. Inside is an unusual collection of early civic seals.

Devonshire Regiment Museum

The Devonshire Regiment was gathered in 1685 to help fight an illegitimate son of Charles II when he landed at Lyme Regis to claim his right as heir. Collections of uniforms, medals and weapons reflect its history since that time, until 1958 when it amalgamated with the Dorset Regiment.

Tucker's Hall open all year Tue, Thu, Fri am only (Oct to May, Fri only).
Rougemont House Museum open all year daily (except Sun and Mon).
St Nicholas' Priory open all year daily (except Sun and Mon).
Royal Albert Memorial Museum open as above.
Maritime Museum open all year daily (except Christmas). Parking available. Refreshments Easter and June to Sep only.
Custom House shown by arrangement with HM Customs and Excise – casual visitors usually accepted.
Guildhall open all year, Mon to Sat except when in use for meetings.
Devonshire Regiment Museum open all year (except Sat, Sun and Bank Holidays).

Royal Albert Memorial Museum, Maritime Museum and Custom House

There is a large and fascinating museum dedicated to Prince Albert in Queen Street, which was founded in 1865. Here can be found permanent displays of fine and applied art in the gallery, and exhibits of local industry. Particularly interesting are the collections of Devon paintings and Exeter glass, silver, and local natural history.

The exciting Maritime Museum at Town Quay and Canal Basin has the biggest boat collection in the world. Over a hundred old rowing, sail and steam vessels are on display, some afloat, others under cover. Amongst them is the world's oldest working steamboat and the renowned Ellerman collection of Portuguese craft.

Nearby is the Custom House of 1681, which was the first building in the city to be constructed with bricks. The interior features fine plaster ceilings.

A state barge – just one of the Maritime Museum's fascinating boats

Eye Manor

Hereford and Worcester
p216 E1

This seventeenth-century manor house of brick with distinctive sandstone corners, stands on a hill with a view over meadowland to the hills beyond.

Built by Ferdinando Gorges, a wealthy Barbados slave trader, the house is noted for its nine magnificent plasterwork ceilings which resemble those in Edinburgh's Holyrood House, and beautiful panellings. On display too, are unusual collections of decorative straw-work, period costumes, the Beck collection of costume dolls and many books about the art of the printer.

Open late May to mid Sep, Wed, Thu, Sat and Sun pm, also every afternoon in Aug and Spring Bank Holiday weekend. Parking available.

Farway Countryside Park

Devon *p212 D2*

The park, covering some 130 acres, in unspoilt Devon countryside, opened in 1971. Here visitors can enjoy seeing animals in their natural surroundings, in particular Roe, Red, Fallow and Sika deer. As well as present day farm animals there are some rarer breeds such as St Kilda sheep and red, hairy Tamworth pigs. Other features include a children's pets corner, nature trails and pony and donkey rides.

For the more energetic visitor Ball Hills close to the park is a good place to wander and take in magnificent views of the whole of the Coly valley; a walk along a marked track reveals Bronze Age burial mounds.

Open Good Fri to Sep daily (except Sat). Open Sat of Bank Holiday weekends. Parking available.

Festiniog Railway

Gwynedd *p216 C2*

This narrow-gauge railway was originally built to take slate from the quarries around Blaenau Ffestiniog down to the sea at Porthmadog. At first trucks ran down from the quarries by gravity, but then steam trains eventually came into operation and were used for commercial purposes for over a century.

The line re-opened as a passenger service, with the willing help of railway enthusiasts, in 1955. The trains, hauled by historic little engines, now operate between Porthmadog and intermediate stations to Tanygrisiau. On leaving Porthmadog the trains pass over the Cob, built across the Glaslyn estuary, and wend their way up to a height of approximately 600 feet. The scenery through which they pass is spectacular and includes panoramic views of Snowdonia, Harlech Castle and the sea. They travel up the side of the river Dwyryd valley and the Vale of Ffestiniog, passing through a nature reserve to Dduallt Station. The line continues and goes through a new tunnel prior to running along the side of the Tanygrisiau Reservoir and passing the Hydro-electric power station before reaching Tanygrisiau.

At the Harbour Station at Porthmadog is the railway museum housing ancient rolling stock, maps, and diagrams.

Railway Daily service Mar to Nov, also 26 Dec to 1 Jan and weekends in Feb and Mar.
Festiniog Railway Museum open Feb to Dec all weekends and Mar to Nov when train service is operating. Parking and refreshments available.

Part of the fascinating mosaics at Fishbourne Roman Palace

Fishbourne Roman Palace

West Sussex *p213 B2*

Fishbourne Roman Palace is the largest residence of this period so far discovered in England. It was built in AD70 with many mosaic-floored rooms and is thought to have been constructed round a great central court, half of which is now laid out in its original pattern.

A fire at the end of the third century unfortunately destroyed the whole building and the palace was buried until 1960, when several walls and mosaic floors were accidentally uncovered by workmen laying a water pipe. Finds of the 1960s excavation including the superb mosaic floors, sections of walls and bath and heating systems, are preserved under a modern cover; an adjoining museum explains the history of the palace and surrounding area. Species of herbs and plants grown in Roman times can be purchased from the old palace garden.

Open Mar to Nov daily.

Flamingoland

North Yorkshire *p217 C4*

Over 1,000 birds, animals and reptiles live in the 350 acres of wooded parkland at Kirby Misperton Hall. Probably the most spectacular sight is the flock of pink flamingos standing in a handsome lake edged by willow trees. Many species of animals roam in large paddocks including llama, zebra, wallabies and deer, and some of the tamer animals are housed in the Contact Corner, allowing close inspection.

Linda is one of two engines owned by the Festiniog Railway that were built in 1893 by the Hunslet Engine Co

For model railway enthusiasts, there is a landscaped layout incorporating up to sixteen train sets ranging from vintage steam models to modern diesel electric engines. A replica of the famous *Flying Scotsman* carries passengers through the park.

Other attractions include a fun fair, Gnomeland, an adventure playground and jungle cruise, a raft ride through jungle scenes and Zulu villages. For children there is a real working farm with a milking parlour and a chicken hatchery. Both supply some of the produce made here.

A pottery workshop has recently been established, where each stage of the craft can be watched, and the finished products purchased in the pottery shop.

Open Easter to Sep daily. Parking and refreshments available.

Fleet Air Arm Museum

Somerset *p212 E3*

This interesting museum, situated within the Royal Naval Air Station at Yeovilton, traces the progress of naval aviation since 1903. The collection includes more than forty restored historic aircraft including a Swordfish, a Sea Fury and a Sea Vampire. There are also many engines, ships, aircraft models, armaments, uniforms and photographs. It is interesting to listen to recorded pilot communications on the special telephones provided.

The museum area has recently been extended to include a new exhibition hall which is being developed to cover the progress of passenger supersonic flight. Pride of place has already been given to Concorde 002 which can be inspected inside and out by visitors. On most weekdays flying can be watched from a special viewing area.

Open daily (except 24, 25 Dec) Sun, pm only. Parking and refreshments available.

Folkestone

Kent *p213 D2*

The old and the new mix well in Folkestone; modern development failing to detract from the picturesque charm of the old harbour area. It is both a holiday resort and a busy passenger port with all the facilities and attractions expected of both.

On top of the 200-foot cliffs there is a lovely long stretch of gardens known as The Leas. From here access to the beach is obtained either via pleasant wooded paths or the cliff-lift. Built in 1890, it is one of the few remaining lifts in the country to be operated by water pressure.

More formal gardens have been planted at East Cliff and in complete contrast is a rugged area known as the Warren, where wild flowers abound and many fossils can be found among the cliffs.

Among Folkestone's historic buildings is the interesting parish church of Saints Mary and Eanswythe, founded by the latter in 1138 and still containing her remains. A window commemorates Folkestone-born William Harvey who discovered how the blood circulates round the human body and became physician to James I.

Folkestone's museum and art gallery in Grace Hill specialises in local and Kentish history.

Museum and Art Gallery open all year (except Sun and Bank Holidays).

Forde Abbey

Dorset *p212 E3*

Forde Abbey, home of the Roper family since 1864, lies to the south-east of Chard on the south bank of the river Axe. The magnificent ham-stone structure dating from the twelfth century when it was built by Cistercian monks, embraces a mixture of Tudor and mid-seventeenth-century styles. Much of the earlier medieval stone work is in evidence, in the dormitories for example, and the splendid Tudor entrance tower is particularly picturesque.

Set in beautiful grounds with delightful water and rock gardens, Forde Abbey has a fine south front when viewed from across the lake.

Its most famous contents are the large Mortlake Tapestries, the work of Flemish weavers brought to England by Charles I. They are tapestry copies of Raphael's cartoons, depicting scenes from the Act of the Apostles.

Open May to Sep, Wed, Sun and Bank Holidays, pm only. Parking and refreshments available.

Fort Belan

Gwynedd *p216 C3*

Situated on the northern tip of the small Morfa Dinlle peninsula is the fort built by the first Lord Newborough as defence against Napoleonic invasion. The squat grey walls of the fortress still bristle with ancient cannon, once manned by Newborough's force of 400 Royal Caernarfonshire Grenadiers.

The fort itself has retained much of its original structure, including ramparts, circular sentry posts, gateways, drawbridge, courtyard and battery.

There is a nineteenth-century dockyard belonging to the fort which now houses a small maritime museum, a forge still in working order and a chain-burning stove – still used to burn the rust from ships chains which are then coated with pitch. The chain-burning stove is probably the only one of its kind still in use in the world.

There are also tea rooms, a gift shop, a miniature steam railway, pleasure cruises from the dock and pleasure flights from the fort's airfield.

Open May to Sep daily. Parking and refreshments available.

Fort William

Highland *p221 C1*

Fort William is a popular touring centre lying at the junction of Lochs Linnhe and Eil, at the foot of Ben Nevis, Britain's highest mountain. The town originates from 1655 when General Monk built an earth and wattle fort here as an English military base. This was rebuilt of stone in 1690 by William III, and the town was named after him.

In the High Street is the West Highland Museum, housing many personal belongings of Prince Charles Edward Stuart (Bonnie Prince Charlie), including the famous secret portrait, a picture which only becomes apparent when reflected in a small polished metal cylinder. Also in the museum is a bed in which the Prince once slept, and a sandalwood fan presented to Flora Macdonald on behalf of the Prince, after she had served a brief sentence for helping him to flee to France.

Ben Nevis is probably the most popular mountain in Scotland for both hill walkers and mountaineers. There is a well defined path climbing the Ben, which starts at Achintree Farm about two miles south-east of Fort William. Ben Nevis is not visible from the town itself, but it can be clearly seen from the peak of the 942-foot Cow Hill, which rises behind the town. From here the splendid views incorporate the lower reaches of the spectacular Glen Nevis – a deep and rugged valley on the south face of the mountain, and the beautiful white quarzite peak of Squrr a'Mhaim reaching to some 3,601 feet.

Museum open all year (except Sun).

Ben Nevis provides a magnificent backdrop to Fort William

Cistercian Monks used to teach or study in the cloisters of Fountains Abbey

Fountains Abbey

North Yorkshire *p217 B3*

The largest, possibly the best preserved, and certainly the most famous ruined abbey in Britain is Fountains Abbey, standing majestically beside the river Skell. It was founded in the twelfth century by a handful of monks who had split from their brothers at York. Devoted to a life of poverty, the Cistercians farmed the land and built the large, but austere abbey. Ironically, their farming was so efficient that it eventually became the wealthiest abbey in Britain.

After the Dissolution the abbey and its grounds were sold by Henry VIII to Sir Richard Gresham. It then gradually fell to ruin, some of the stones being used in the building of nearby Fountains Hall. It was saved from total neglect, however, by the new owner's interest in landscaping the area and today its lofty walls share the site with ornamental gardens, ponds, monuments and temples of the hundred-acre deer park. On summer evenings the ruins are spectacularly floodlit.

Open all year (except 25 Dec). Parking and refreshments available.

Framlingham Castle

Suffolk *p213 D4*

The little market town of Framlingham lies in a green valley on the banks of the river Ore. Framlingham Castle stands above the river on the outskirts of the town, for centuries the home of a number of powerful families and successive Dukes of Norfolk.

This site was originally occupied by a fortified house, which was later developed into a castle by members of the Bigod family, the first Earls of Norfolk, at the end of the twelfth century. Its history has been an eventful one, as it was a stronghold of King John in his struggle with the barons, and later the sanctuary of Mary Tudor during the attempt by the Duke of Northumberland to make Lady Jane Grey Queen.

The massive curtain walls incorporate thirteen flanking towers, some of which rise to a height of sixty feet, and are then topped by attractive brick chimneys. The chimneys, added in the sixteenth century by members of the Howard family are all dummies except those on the eighth and ninth towers. In the seventeenth century the castle was given to Pembroke College, Cambridge, by Sir Robert Hitcham. Much of the inside was then demolished and the great hall converted into a poorhouse. Since 1913 it has been open to the public as an Ancient Monument.

See AM info. Also open Sun am Apr to Sep. Parking available.

The high walls of Framlingham Castle rise up above the village

Furness Abbey

Cumbria *p216 D5*

Standing in a deep wooded valley known as the Vale of the Deadly Nightshade is the ruin of the abbey of St Mary of Furness, better known as Furness Abbey.

Founded in 1127 the order was originally Benedictine, then changed to Cistercian in 1147 and became one of the most powerful religious houses in England.

Much of the soft red sandstone ruins which remain are of the twelfth and thirteenth centuries, although the east end transepts and belfry tower were rebuilt in the fifteenth century. Outstanding features are the late Norman arches of the cloisters, three fine transitional arches and the Early English chapter house. In the presbytery the basin used for washing the Communion vessels, and the priests' seats, are among the finest examples to have survived from the twelfth and thirteenth centuries.

See AM info. Parking available.

Furzey Gardens

Hampshire *p213 A2*

In the picturesque village of Minstead are the eight acres of Furzey Gardens with their winter and summer heathers, flowering trees and shrubs. The gardens are of botanical interest throughout the year, but are probably at their best in springtime when they burst into a blaze of colour.

Also of interest here is the 400-year-old thatched cottage with its Will Selwood Art and Craft Gallery displaying work by many local artists and craftsmen.

Open all year daily. Parking available.

Galloway Forest Park

Dumfries and Galloway *p220 C2*

Actually comprised of seven forests, the Galloway Forest Park covers almost 250 square miles of south-west Scotland. It is mountainous country, its highest point being the 2,764 foot Merrick, and hill walkers here are rewarded with some superb views.

The park is well watered with many rivers, streams, tarns and lochs which are particularly popular with anglers for their salmon and trout. These waters also provide much of the beauty of the area, with pretty little streams cascading through wooded glens and glass-like stretches of water surrounded by hills. Large herds of Red and Roe deer live within the forest and birds of prey such as buzzards, kestrels, owls and sparrowhawks can often be seen. Occasionally the native Golden eagle may be seen by the alert observer.

The Galloway area has strong associations with Robert the Bruce who won two battles against the English here in 1307. The Battles of Glen Trool and Rapploch Moss are commemorated with inscribed stones, one by the viewpoint looking down Glen Trool, the other by the Clatteringshaws Reservoir. More modern monuments are the impressive dams and power stations of the Galloway Hydro-Electric scheme. The area is particularly beautiful, taking in mountains, forests and moors. Forest trails and forest walks have been laid out for walkers, and the less energetic can enjoy driving along some lovely quiet roads.

Gawsworth Hall

Cheshire *p216 F3*

This charming black and white Tudor manor with its varying roof levels, is now the home of the Roper-Richards family. The most decorative side of the house with its compass window, faces a courtyard of lawn and flower beds and a lawn beyond. Overlooking the lawns and lake is the north façade, with a sixteenth-century coat of arms of the Fitton family, who were owners of the property for over four centuries.

Of particular interest in the beautiful beamed interior is the bedroom with its fourposter; the carved mantlepieces in the drawing room and library; the tables and seventeenth-century oak coffer in the long hall; the refectory table supported by eight carved bulbous legs in the dining room and above the main staircase the seventeenth-century Waterford crystal chandelier.

The charming little chapel has some beautiful stained glass windows, and over 200 oil paintings and water colours collected over

the centuries are hung throughout the house.

In the grounds is a museum housing a collection of coaches and carriages from the early eighteenth century onwards, and a medieval jousting ground.

Open mid Mar to end Oct daily, pm only. Parking available.

Glamis

Tayside *p222 E1*

Glamis is best known for its romantic-looking castle – associated with Shakespeare's *Macbeth*, the thane of Glamis, who became King of Scotland by killing King Duncan. The lands of Glamis were granted to the Lyon family (Earls of Strathmore) in 1372 and the castle's origins are thought to be fourteenth century. Standing in fine grounds bordered by Dean Water, it was rebuilt in the style of a French chateau during the late seventeenth century by Patrick Lyon, 1st Earl of Strathmore and Kinghorne.

The castle contains fine collections of china, tapestry, furniture, paintings and armour. In the beautiful grounds is a massive sundial with eighty-four dials.

An attractive terrace of restored seventeenth-century cottages in the village houses the Angus Folk Museum. Here a display of local domestic and agricultural life illustrates how people in the area have lived over the past 200 years or so.

Castle open May to Sep Mon to Thu, and Sun, pm only. Also Fri from July. Parking available.
Angus Folk Museum open May to Sep daily pm only and on request. NTS.

Turreted Glamis Castle – once used by kings as a hunting lodge

Glastonbury

Somerset *p212 E3*

This ancient Isle of Avalon, surrounded by mist-covered marshland and colourful legends, has long been associated with Joseph of Aramathea and King Arthur.

It was likely that Glastonbury was founded in Celtic times, but its most popular legend says it was created by Joseph of Aramathea who came from the Holy Land in AD60 to preach the gospel. While leaning on his staff on Wearyall Hill it magically took root and flowered. Joseph took this as a sign that he should settle here, and a wattle and daub church was subsequently built on the site now occupied by the present abbey ruins.

The Arthurian legend has it that both Arthur and Queen Guinevere were buried in the

abbey, and yet another story says that St Patrick was one of the first abbots here.

Without doubt Glastonbury's chief glory is the ruined abbey, and although little of its early history is known, it certainly became one of the richest and most famous in England. The majestic ruins of today consist largely of St Mary's Chapel, the abbey church and various monastic buildings. By far the best of these is the superb Abbot's Kitchen. It was built in the fourteenth century and stands intact with its vaulted domed roof and a fireplace in each corner. The gatehouse now houses a small museum, showing a model of the abbey as it was in 1539.

What was once the principal tithe barn of the abbey is now the Somerset Rural Life Museum. This contains relics of pre-mechanised farming in Somerset and has displays concerning cider making, peat and withy (young willow) cutting.

A walk to the nearby steep, conical hill called Glastonbury Tor, which rises up out of the flat Somerset Plain, provides panoramic views from its top. The tower there is all that remains of the fifteenth-century St Michael's Church. At the foot of the Tor is the Chalice Well beneath which Joseph is supposed to have buried the Holy Grail – the cup used by Christ at the Last Supper.

Abbey (including Abbot's Kitchen and Abbey Gatehouse Museum) open all year.
Somerset Rural Life Museum open all year daily, Sat and Sun pm only.
Chalice Well open Mar to Oct daily (except Thu).

The ruins of Glastonbury Abbey, which was built in the 12th century

Glencoe

Highland *p221 C1*

The fame of the battles at Glencoe has spread far from this remote corner of Scotland, but it is the very remoteness which contributes so much to its rugged beauty. The Glen itself stretches for some seven-and-a-half miles from Rannoch Moor down to Loch Leven through magnificent mountain scenery. Its lofty peaks attract mountaineers, skiers and hill-walkers, but the more leisurely visitor can enjoy the views from special viewpoints, particularly the 1,000-foot summit of the main road at The Study, or Studdie.

Besides being a famous beauty spot, Glencoe is historically important for it was here that on 13th February, 1692 the shameful massacre of the Macdonalds took place. By order of King William III, a party of troops, mostly of the Campbell clan, turned on the families who had been their hosts for twelve days, mercilessly slaughtering men, women and children. Many escaped into the snowy hills of Glen Coe only to perish in the bitter cold. The only crime of the Macdonald clan was that their chief was unavoidably delayed on his journey to swear allegiance to the new King, arriving on the 6th January rather than 1st. A memorial to the Macdonalds stands near the old Invercoe road and another reminder is the Signal Rock near the Clachaig Inn, reputedly the place from which a signal was sent to the Campbells to proceed with the dreadful deed.

Macdonald relics are among the exhibits in the Glencoe and North Lorn Folk Museum, housed in

Mountains tower behind the village of Glencoe as a spectacular backdrop

two heather-thatched cottages. There are also local domestic and agricultural exhibits, Jacobite relics, costumes and embroidery. At the north end of Glencoe is the National Trust's Visitor Centre which provides information and a ranger-naturalist service.

Museum open mid May to Sep daily (except Sun).
Visitor Centre open Good Fri to Oct daily. Parking available. NTS.

Glen More Forest Park

Highland *p221 D2*

The Glen More Forest Park which lies to the north of the Cairngorms National Nature Reserve is sometimes referred to as the Queen's Forest of Glen More. The reserve, one of the largest in Britain, covers nearly sixty-four square miles incorporating Rothiemurchus Forest and the Ben Macdui, Britain's second highest peak. Aviemore, the winter-sports and holiday centre, lies to the west of Glen More.

The forest was originally held by the Grants before passing to the Dukes of Gordon, who used it as a deer preserve. In 1923 it was acquired by the Forestry Commissioners who subsequently established it as a forest park.

The forest of Glen More contains some 9,100 acres of mountainside and 3,400 acres of spruce and pine woods. For centuries it was a completely isolated area and has featured little in history.

When approached from Aviemore via Coylumbridge, the road enters the forest by skirting the shores of Loch Morlich; a central feature of Glen More. Loch Morlich and its surrounding area offers various facilities including bathing, camping and sailing. Beyond the loch to the east lies Glen More Lodge, the National Outdoor Training Centre. Within the park the Forestry Commission has marked a variety of walks and Red deer, Golden eagles, ospreys and reindeer can be seen from them.

Rugged moorland scenery along the Lairig Ghm nature trail in Glen More Forest Park

Gloucester Gloucestershire *p212 F5*

In Roman times Gloucester was a fortified port which guarded the lowest Severn crossing and the legions' route into Wales. Since then the city has had a chequered history as a port, but nevertheless survived to become a thriving export point for local industries.

Since Saxon times the Cross has been the junction of the main thoroughfares of the city which still follow the pattern of the original Roman roads. In the streets leading off from the Cross are a number of interesting buildings including the handsome Guildhall of 1890, the galleried New Inn dating from the fifteenth century and Robert Raike's House, a fine timber-framed house said to have been the home of Raike, the founder of Sunday schools.

The Cathedral

Although mainly Norman in origin, extensive rebuilding has produced an example of architectual development hard to better throughout Europe. The massive Norman pillars dominate the 174-foot long nave with its thirteenth-century vaulting above. The east window is the largest left from medieval England and celebrates the victory at Crécy in 1346 by a glorious profusion of coloured glass saints, popes and kings. The cloisters, with their exquisite fan vaulting, surround a delightful garden which has a well in the middle.

Bishop Hooper's Lodging

This early sixteenth-century timber-framed house is so called because the Protestant martyr sup-

Carved saints adorn the façade of Gloucester's cathedral

posedly stayed here the night before he was burnt at the stake in 1555. It now houses one of the best folk museums in the country and illustrates crafts and industries of the county down to the minutest detail. There is also a section of relics from the Civil War siege of Gloucester in 1643.

City Museum and Art Gallery

Virtually all the finds left from the Roman occupation are kept here, amongst which are fragments of a bronze statue of an emperor on horseback. Many examples of Celtic craftsmanship in bronze are kept here too, including the Birdlip Mirror made in AD25.

Bishop Hooper's Lodging open all year Mon to Sat (except Bank Holidays).
Museum and Art Gallery open as above.

The tomb of the murdered Edward II lies in Gloucester Cathedral

Grasmere

Cumbria *p220 E1*

This unspoilt village sits on the fringe of lake Grasmere, surrounded by high fells, offering protection from cold north and east winds.

Dove Cottage, a simple six-room slated and limewashed stone cottage is delightfully situated on the east side of the lake at Town End. Dating from the early seventeenth century, it was originally a small inn named The Dove and Olive-Bough, serving weary travellers on the old Ambleside to Keswick road. It became the home of William Wordsworth and his family in 1799 and was the scene of some of the poet's most creative years. He wrote most of *The Prelude*, his autobiographical poem, here.

Thomas De Quincy, the essayist, lived in the cottage after Wordsworth left and remained there until about 1830. During this time he wrote *The Confession of an English Opium Eater* and *Recollections of the Lakes and the Lake Poets*.

The cottage is open to the public and has been arranged so the rooms look as they did during Wordsworth's tenancy. Much of the furniture actually belonged to the poet and his family, and the garden, climbing up the hillside at the back of the house, has been carefully kept as it was in Wordsworth's day. Opposite the cottage is the Wordsworth Museum housing a collection of his possessions. An exhibition there displays newly-discovered manuscripts of letters and poems,

Dove Cottage was the unassuming home of the poet William Wordsworth and his family in Grasmere

as well as portraits on loan from the Wordsworth Circle and the National Portrait Gallery. Wordsworth, his wife Mary and sister Dorothy are buried in the churchyard of the thirteenth-century St Oswald church in Grasmere village. The poet is commemorated in the church with a bust by Woolner.

An annual attraction of the village is the Grasmere Sports, held on the Thursday falling closest to 20th August. Wrestling contests, fell-racing and fox-hound training feature among the events.

Dove Cottage and Wordsworth Museum open Mar to Oct daily (except Sun).

Great Dixter

East Sussex *p213 D2*

Great Dixter is a superb example of a late medieval manor house, half-timbered with oak from the Forest of Weald. Built around 1450, it was acquired in 1911 by Nathaniel Lloyd, an architectural historian who employed Sir Edwin Lutyens to restore the building. During this time Lloyd and Lutyens found a decaying sixteenth-century house in Benenden, encased in corrugated iron and in use as a barn. By re-erecting this building at Great Dixter, Lutyens skilfully merged the two to form a sizeable house of great character. Particularly notable is the hall with its timbered roof. The house contains some fine antiques and a late sixteenth-century Flemish tapestry. The delightful gardens complement the house perfectly with yew hedges and a sunken garden.

Open Apr to early Oct. Tue to Sun and Bank Holiday Mon, pm only. Parking available.

Great Yarmouth

Norfolk *p214 E5*

The town lies on a spit of land between the river Yare and the North Sea with five miles of golden sands on its doorstep. All the attractions of a popular holiday resort are in Great Yarmouth, which mingle well with the quaint houses lining the waterfront. To the north-east of the large open

air market place are some interesting almshouses called the Fishermen's Hospital. Nearby is St Nicholas Church, considered to be the largest parish church in England. Originally twelfth-century, the interior was restored after parts of the church were damaged during World War II; the Norman tower and Early English west end have been preserved. Next to the church is Anna Sewell House, a seventeenth-century Tudor fronted building, birthplace of the authoress of *Black Beauty*.

Leading from the town walls (one evening a week during July and August there are conducted tours of these) near the South Quay are The Rows, a number of narrow lanes based on a grid system. Although damaged during World War II air raids, several rows remain, one of which has been renovated, providing a typical example of small town houses in the seventeenth century. Close by is the restored Old Merchant's House, a 300-year-old building exhibiting local building craftsmanship of the seventeenth to nineteenth centuries.

The Tolhouse, which houses the local museum, illustrates the long history of the town. Formerly the civic building and dungeons, the original cells of which can still be seen, the building dates back to the fourteenth century and has been completely restored. Also near here are the fourteenth-century Greyfriar Cloisters and

The waterfront at Great Yarmouth with its old merchants' houses

Elizabethan House, now a museum, which has a late Georgian façade. The interior contains modern furniture, domestic utensils from the nineteenth century, a sixteenth-century panelled room and collections of Victorian toys and Lowestoft porcelain.

There are two piers in the town, each with a theatre, and between the two is the Maritime Museum for East Anglia, showing development of marine equipment past and present. Between the town walls and Britannia Pier is a Victorian house and stables, now called the House of Wax containing a varied exhibition of wax figures. Near Wellington Pier is Merrivale Model Village, set in an acre of landscaped gardens and including a model railway and radio-controlled model boats.

Anna Sewell House open all year Mon to Sat, Thu pm only. Parking available.
Old Merchant's House open Apr to Sep Mon to Fri by guided tour only starting from Row 111 Houses. Ticket includes Row 111 Houses and Greyfriars Cloister. AM.
Tolhouse Museum open all year (except Easter, Christmas, New Year, Sat and Sun Oct to May).
Elizabethan House Museum open as above.
Maritime Museum for East Anglia open as above.
House of Wax open Apr to Sep daily.
Merrivale Model Village open May to Sep daily. Refreshments available.

Greys Court

Oxfordshire *p213 A3*

Three miles west of Henley-on-Thames stands this attractive brick and stone gabled house in some 280 acres of gardens.

In the fourteenth century it belonged to Lord de Grey, who fought at the Battle of Crécy and from whom the house obtained its name. The medieval great tower and the smaller towers still stand, but the present house, with a battlemented bay window on one end, is mainly sixteenth century, although over the years various alterations have been made.

The well-house has a nineteen-foot-wide wooden donkey wheel which was used until 1914 to raise water from the 200-foot-deep well to supply the house with water.

A main attraction of the house is the Carlisle Collection located in the old stables. This consists of miniature rooms filled with dolls house furniture and furnishings.

Open Apr to Sep.
Grounds and Carlisle Collection Mon to Sat, House, Mon Wed and Fri, pm only. Refreshments available. NT.

Grime's Graves

Norfolk *p213 C5*

The 350 or so holes in the ground here are not, in fact, graves but the workings of the largest prehistoric flint mines in Europe. First worked around 4,000 years ago, both Stone Age and Bronze Age man extracted flints from the ground for their own use and for trading throughout southern England. The shafts sink vertically for between twenty to forty feet, and passages lead off following the seams of flint. Some of them link up underground to form a labyrinth of tunnels where primitive man hacked at the rock using antlers as pickaxes. They were excavated for the first time in 1870, and have fascinated modern man for many years and it is now possible to go down a shaft and inspect these ancient workings, although it is wise to take a torch.

See AM info. Parking available.

Guildford

Surrey *p213 B2*

The ancient capital of Surrey, Guildford is a pleasant town and busy shopping centre with an attractive cobbled High Street up the hill. This is lined with historic buildings, including the very decorative seventeenth-century Guildhall with its balcony, bell-tower and ornate gilded clock. Its neighbour, Guildford House,

The clock on Guildford's Guildhall is its most striking feature

built in 1660, is a timber-framed building, with a carved staircase and finely decorated plaster ceilings. It is now an art gallery. Further up the High Street is the Hospital of the Blessed Trinity, better known as the Abbot's Hospital after its founder, George Abbot, who was Archbishop of Canterbury in 1619. A magnificent arched gateway with four turrets leads to an enclosed courtyard in front of this Tudor brick building, which has been in continuous use as an almshouse for old people since it was built.

Guildford's oldest building is the castle, behind Quarry Street, built by Henry II during the twelfth century. Only the square keep remains and it is surrounded by colourful gardens. At the entrance, in Castle Arch, is the town museum containing items of local history and archaeology and needlework. The town's connection with Charles Lutwidge Dodgson – better known as Lewis Carrol, who lived in Quarry Street, is also illustrated here. He died in Guildford in 1898 and is buried in the Mount Cemetary.

One of Guildford's newest buildings is also its most impressive – the Cathedral of the Holy Spirit which looks down over the town from the top of Stag Hill. Completed in 1961, it was built in the shape of a cross with pink bricks made from Stag Hill clay.

The river Wey with its weeping willows provides a lovely setting for the Yvonne Arnaud Theatre, and in summer boats can be hired along the river.

Guildford House Gallery open all year daily (except Sun).
Hospital of the Blessed Trinity (Abbot's Hospital) open May to Oct, Mon, Wed and Sat. Nov to Apr Sat only.
Castle open daily (except Sun). Grounds all year.
Keep open Apr to Sep. Refreshments available.
Museum open all year daily (except Sun, Good Fri and Christmas).

H

Haddon Hall

Derbyshire *p217 B2*

This estate was first owned by William Peveril, illegitimate son of William the Conqueror. The fine stone-built manor situated on the river Wye at the foot of a densely wooded incline was probably originally no more than a modest residence, but through the ages has been developed into a delightful rambling manor house.

Although the Hall was extensively restored in the early part of this century, the same basic materials were used, and it looks much as it did over 300 years ago. Its special features include the long gallery which is beautifully panelled in oak and walnut and has a decorated ceiling. Heraldic panelling and carving decorate the dining room, and the staircase landing is hung with three Mortlake tapestries. Ancient troughs used for water storage are kept in the kitchen, and the butcher's shop contains the original equipment used for salting and chopping.

A small museum has been set up within the Hall which has interesting items found during the restoration. To the south of the house are beautiful stone-walled terraced gardens, a series of lawns, flower beds and yews. Masses of roses adorn the grounds: they can be seen almost everywhere, in formal flower beds and climbing along the stone walls, providing the perfect setting for an English country house.

Open Apr to Sep, Tue to Sat and Bank Holiday Mon, also Sun before Bank Holiday, Sun pm only. Parking and refreshments available.

Hadrian's Wall

Cumbria, Northumberland, Tyne and Wear

The barrier across Britain between Solway and Tyne was built because the Emperor Hadrian wanted to separate the Romans from the barbarians. Roman soldiers, who were also skilled engineers and craftsmen, began work on the wall in AD 122. The wall took just over seven years to complete, and twenty-seven million cubic feet of stone were used in the process.

All that remains of the temple to Mithras at Carrawburgh fort

Huge though the actual wall was, it only formed part of Hadrian's complete defence system. On the north side a steep ditch ran parallel to the wall, whereas south of it ran a flat-bottomed ditch with earth ramparts built up on either side, known as the vallum. The system extended beyond the wall in the form of small forts at one-mile intervals and watchtowers down the Cumbrian coast, outpost forts north of the wall, and a Roman port on the Tyne at South Shields.

On the wall at intervals of 1,620 yards (one Roman mile) there were milecastles, which held between eight and sixty-four men and had gateways opening north and south. Turrets, used as watchtowers, were built between the milecastles every third of a (Roman) mile. In addition to these were seventeen forts, or garrisons, placed strategically on or near the wall which were each manned by troops or cavalry. Altogether the wall garrison consisted of about 15,000 men.

Although the wall has been virtually derelict since the end of the fourth century, the surviving remains are nevertheless quite extensive and very impressive, not least because of their beautiful setting. Working from east to west, the first visible remains are at South Shields which was the port of the Roman wall. In Roman Remains Park, Baring Street, parts of the fort have been preserved, and there is also a museum here of finds from the excavations there.

Just before Heddon-on-the-Wall, about 110 yards of the wall has been preserved, but beyond this point until Shield-on-the-Wall, evidence of the wall has disappeared because the Hanoverians used it in 1781 to construct their military road, and only a few short stretches have survived. However, at Brunton there is a fine piece of wall and a well preserved turret.

The fort at Chesters (*Cilvrnum*), south of the wall on the west bank of the North Tyne, housed a regiment of cavalry. Opposite the north gateway is the headquarters building, with a strong-room beneath the paymaster's office. The Commanding Officer's house, east of the headquarters, had heated rooms and a bath suite. Between the fort and river, set into the riverbank, is a large building which housed the fort baths.

West of Chesters the wall rises

to 1,230 feet, following the geological ridge known as Whin Sill. The central sector of the wall begins here and it runs through magnificent wild countryside. Lonely moors stretch away to the north with the hills of south Scotland and north Northumberland in the distance, while to the south lies the fertile valley of the Tyne.

The next Roman fort to the west is Carrawburgh (*Brocolitia*) where only grass covered ramparts are visible, but to the south a temple of Mithras has been excavated and preserved. He was a God that seemed to appeal to soldiers as a number of temples were dedicated to him.

Beyond Shield-on-the-Wall, where the military road finally leaves the wall, is Housesteads (*Vercovicium*), the best and most exciting of the Roman forts. Its ramparts and gateways have been very well preserved, and the granaries, headquarters, commandant's house, hospital, latrines, some barracks and civilian settlements have been uncovered. The remains of a fourth-century man and woman were found beneath the floor of one of these settlements and their end was

clearly not a happy one as the point of a sword was embedded in the man's ribs. The south gateway tower of Housesteads was a stronghold of the Armstrong's – a notorious gang of cattle raiders and bandits in the sixteenth and seventeenth centuries.

Farther along the wall is the fort at Chesterholm (*Vindolanda*) which was built before the wall in the AD 80s, and subsequently incorporated into the wall system in the AD 160s. There is a military bath-house west of the fort and considerable remains of another civilian settlement. An interest-

An 18th-century engraving of the great Roman wall

ing feature here is a full-scale replica of a section of wall which includes a stone turret. In a valley below the fort is a museum of the site, containing some remarkable finds from the pre-Hadrianic forts, including writing tablets, footwear and leather items.

From the line of the wall at South Shields are magnificent views. The hills of south-west Scotland are visible on a fine day, and to the south Skiddaw, Saddleback and Cross Fell of the Pennines.

Still following the Whin Sill, the wall continues on to Cawfields

where there is a well preserved milecastle, and beyond to the fort at Greatchesters (*Aesica*) with its ramparts, two gateways, barracks and an underground strong-room.

Continuing westwards the wall is rather tumbledown, but at Walltown a lone turret still survives. Beyond the point where the river Irthing intersects it, a fine stretch of wall leads up to Birdoswald fort (*Camboglanna*), where some believe King Arthur fought his last battle. From here to the Solway the land becomes gentler, although no less beautiful, and red sandstone takes over from limestone. Since the wall has provided building materials in the past, few remains of it are visible beyond Walton village, except the ditch and earthworks.

Chesters Roman Fort and Museum see AM info. Also open Sun am Apr to Sep. Parking available.
Carrawburgh Roman Fort open at any reasonable time. Parking available.
Housesteads Roman Fort and Museum see AM info. Also open Sun am Apr to Sep. Parking available.
Chesterholm open all year daily (except 25 Dec). Parking and refreshments available.

Hailes Abbey and Museum

Gloucestershire *p212 F5*

In beautiful countryside, secluded in trees, stand the ruined walls of this Cistercian abbey and its cloisters, founded in 1246 by the Earl of Cornwall. Although relatively little remains above ground, excavations have revealed the massive plan of this once impressive abbey.

The adjoining museum contains roof bosses, armorial tiles and other relics which came to light during the excavations.

See AM info. NT. Parking available.

Hardwick Hall

Derbyshire *p217 B1*

This striking Elizabethan building, surrounded by wooded parkland, was built by Robert Smythson for the famous Dowager Countess of Shrewsbury, best known as Bess of Hardwick.

It is a plain, symmetrical, stone building with four huge towers at each corner, topped with decorative open stonework incorporating the initials of the Countess, ES, and surmounted with a crown. The exterior has such enormous windows that it seems to be more glass than wall. The lavish interior has an abundance

of tapestries and fine needlework, furniture and portraits. It also has magnificent plasterwork and stone and marble fireplaces. Of special interest are the coloured plasterwork frieze and beautiful walls and fireplace in the great high chamber, the fourposter bed in the state bedroom and the seventeenth-century tapestry on the landing of the main staircase.

Open Apr to Oct, Wed, Thu, Sat, Sun and Bank Holiday Mon, pm only. Gardens open during season, daily pm only. Park open all year daily. Parking and refreshments, Apr to Oct, available. NT.

Harewood House and Bird Garden

West Yorkshire *p217 B3*

Harewood House, the West Yorkshire home of the Earl and Countess of Harewood was designed by John Carr of York and decorated by Robert Adam in the eighteenth century.

It is beautifully sited for views over the surrounding countryside and the yellow-stone house itself is set in timbered parkland created by Capability Brown.

The interior is outstanding, offering a glittering display of eighteenth-century craftsmanship, which includes furniture by Thomas Chippendale, said to be

the finest ever made in England. Many of the rooms reflect Robert Adam's passion for designing complete rooms, including the ceilings, mirrors and carpets which complement each other perfectly. A fine collection of Sèvres and Chinese porcelain is also to be seen, as well as many fine paintings including work by Reynolds, Tintoretto, Titian and Turner.

The eighteenth-century stable block has been converted into exhibition rooms showing the history of the house, and next to it children can explore the adventure playground. Between the stables and the lake, covering an area of some four acres, is the Harewood Bird Garden containing over 200 species of exotic birds. In these natural, delightful surroundings many of the birds wander freely on the lawns and amongst the trees. Other attractions within the Bird Garden include a tropical house, a penguin pool and a walk-around aviary.

Open daily Apr to Oct, limited winter opening. Parking and refreshments available.

Harlech Castle

Gwynedd *p216 C2*

Harlech Castle standing, high on a rock, is one of the most imposing fortresses in the country. On one side lies the little holiday town of Harlech, on the other a wide ex-

Harlech is one of the four biggest castles in Wales

panse of sand dunes and the sea.

The castle built by Edward I, was first put to the test just a few years after its completion in 1290 and subsequently suffered repeated attacks. Today it remains as impressive as ever, remarkably well-preserved and still dominating the entire area. From its walls and towers there are panoramic views across Tremadoc Bay, across the Morfa Harlech Nature Reserve to the north and inland towards the mountains of Snowdonia.

Castle see AM info. Also open Sun am Apr to Sep. Parking available.

Harrogate

North Yorkshire *p217 B3*

Harrogate grew up around its eighty-nine mineral springs, and developed to accommodate the fashionable society of the nineteenth century who came to 'take the waters'. Much of its Victorian architecture remains, and the mellow stonework, wide tree-lined streets and colourful gardens lend an air of elegant spaciousness to the busy town centre.

The Royal Pump Room was built in 1842 over a sulphur well which had previously enjoyed the name The Stinking Spaw. This well can still be seen in the basement, and the rest of the building

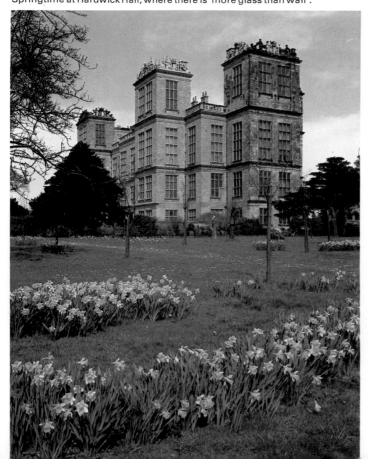

Springtime at Hardwick Hall, where there is 'more glass than wall'.

All Saints Street in Hastings shows some of its Tudor architecture

the town. The extensive grounds, which surround a nineteenth-century country house, include vast areas of parkland and lawns, superb rose gardens and shrubberies of rhododendrons, azaleas and magnolias.

Of industrial and archaeological interest is the half-mile-long Crimple Viaduct one mile south of the town, best viewed from the A61. Built by the York and Midland Railway Company in 1847, it carried the main Leeds to Thirsk line across the Crimple Beck.

Royal Pump Room Museum open all year daily, (except Feb) Sun pm only.
Art Gallery open all year daily, Sun pm only.
Harlow Car Gardens open all year daily. Parking available.
Rudding Park Gardens open Apr to Sep daily. Parking and refreshments available.

Harvington Hall

Hereford and Worcester
p216 F1

This moated, rambling gabled brick house, with stone and mullioned windows masking part of an earlier timber framed building, was one of Worcestershire's great Roman Catholic homes, whose history is linked with the days of Catholic persecution during the seventeenth-century.

In 1630 it was the home of the Catholic Throckmorton family who had been implicated in the Gunpowder Plot. The amazing honeycomb of secret passages, sliding panels, trapdoors, and hidden rooms or attics called priests' holes, where persecuted Catholic priests found refuge or held secret services, can all be seen.

The Hall also contains some re-

markable wall paintings from the Elizabethan or earlier periods, together with fine oak furniture.

John Wall, a Roman Catholic priest and one of the last men in England to be martyred for his faith, frequently used the house as a hiding place. His portrait is in the Roman Catholic church here and a stone lies in the churchyard commemorating him.

Open Feb to Nov, Tue to Sat pm only. Easter to Sep, am only, also open Sun pm. Parking and refreshments available.

Hastings

Sussex *p213 D2*

The old town of Hastings, between Castle Hill and the East Cliff, is an interesting huddle of houses dating from medieval times. Its roots are in the fishing industry which still thrives despite the silting up of the harbour. The motor vessels now used are winched up onto the shingle beach when not at sea, but the tall, narrow, fishermen's huts, are a reminder of past traditions. In these huts the nets are hung to dry and fishing paraphernalia is stored. Nearby is the Fishermen's Museum, built as a chapel in 1854. Now it contains a fascinating collection of photographs, documents and mementos as well as the lugger *Enterprise*, the last vessel to be built in Hastings before the shipyard was closed in 1909. In spite of its change of use, a Harvest Festival service is held annually, and the font is used for christenings.

The two-tier promenade separates a busy road, fronted by shops and hotels, from the beach which is coarse shingle, except at low tide when sand is exposed and rock pools can be explored. Most of the beaches provide safe bathing and are patrolled by lifeguards, and a number of indoor and outdoor swimming pools are provided. Sea trips are available and for those who prefer to row their own boat and there

are vessels for hire both on the beach and at the two boating lakes. Other sports are well catered for, fishing being a favourite pastime, and there is plenty of entertainment, from concert orchestra or brass band to Punch and Judy, with, at Playland, amusements and visual delights to keep the children happy. For those who like to get away from the town, Hastings Country Park provides 520 acres of cliff-top walks with beautiful views of sea and downs.

Hastings is known internationally for its annual chess congress and the Town Criers' Championship, when officials come from all over the country to show off their colourful uniforms and the power of their lungs.

Most people connect the town with the Battle of Hastings where Harold Godwinson got an arrow in his eye and the bastard William became the first Norman King of England. That encounter actually took place six miles inland at the place now called Battle. However, William's arrival is remembered in Hastings itself by the Conqueror's Stone on the seafront near the pier, and is reputed to have been used as a table when he enjoyed his first meal in England, and the ruined Norman castle on the cliff top above the old town, built in 1068 to replace a temporary wooden fort. To commemorate the 900th anniversary of the Norman landing, the Royal School of Needlework designed and made a 243 foot-long tapestry depicting eighty-one major events in British history since 1066; this is now on display in the town hall. Near the castle on West Hill is a series of caves – St Clement's – once used by smugglers, where dances are held on summer evenings.

Fishermen's Museum open Easter to Sep daily (except Fri).
Hastings Castle open Easter to Sep daily.
St Clement's Caves open all year daily.

---

has been turned into a museum of local history. Exhibits include costume, pottery and a lovely antique dolls house containing some 300 household items.

Harrogate's art gallery is in the library and has a permanent collection of oils and water-colours.

On the edge of the town are the outstanding Harlow Car Gardens which contain one of the most comprehensive collections of garden plants in the north of England, all laid out in a pleasant landscape of flower beds, rockeries, woodland and shrubberies.

Another celebrated garden is Rudding Park to the south-east of

The park of Harewood House lost 20,000 trees in the gales of 1962

The rich furnishings in the long gallery are typical of Hatfield House

Hatfield House

Hertfordshire *p213 B3*

Erected early in the seventeenth-century for Robert Cecil, 1st Earl of Salisbury, the house has been occupied by his descendants ever since. Today it is the home of the Marquess of Salisbury.

A brick and stone Jacobean building of mammoth proportions, it has two enormous wings with square turrets at each corner, joined by a colonnaded central section which is crowned by an imposing domed clock tower.

Particularly interesting inside are the elaborately carved screen, the tapestries depicting the four seasons hanging in the marble hall, the decorated plasterwork ceiling, the fine fireplace in the long gallery, and the stained glass of the chapel. Another point of interest is the beautiful carved staircase which has supporting posts adorned with figures, and wooden gates (to prevent children falling down the stairs) on the the first floor landing.

In the gardens is the remaining wing of the original Palace, a royal residence in the early sixteenth century, now used as a tea room.

Open late Mar to mid Oct (except Good Fri and Mon pm but open Bank Holiday Mon) Sun, pm only. Gardens open all year daily. Parking and refreshments available.

Haworth

West Yorkshire *p217 A3*

To the south of the Aire Valley lies an area immortalized in English literature by the novels of the Brontë sisters. At its centre in a valley on the edge of rugged moorland is Haworth, a small, bleak, grey West Yorkshire village. Its narrow streets still contain buildings dating from the sixteenth century, such as the Elizabethan Emmott Hall at the foot of Old Kirkgate. At the top of the steep main street, looking down on the valley below, is a hilltop church and old parsonage.

It was to the bleak Georgian parsonage that the Brontë family came in 1820 and the sisters lived and wrote here until 1849. Now the house is a museum containing the family's belongings including Branwell's portraits of his sisters, Charlotte's sewing box and Mr Brontë's spectacles.

The tower is all that remains of Haworth Old Church, in which the Brontës worshipped, as the rest of the existing church was rebuilt in 1881. A Memorial Chapel was built for them in 1964 and beneath the base of one of the stone entrance pillars is the family vault.

In the village itself at the top of the hill the Black Bull Inn, where Branwell Brontë drank himself to death, may still be seen.

Some two miles west of the churchyard on Haworth Moor, along a favourite footpath of the sisters, lies the Brontë Bridge and waterfall.

Brontë Parsonage open all year daily (except last 3 weeks in Dec) Sun, pm only.

Heaton Hall

Gt Manchester *p216 E3*

This superb country house looks down over the conurbation of Greater Manchester and enjoys a very different view from that in 1772 when it was built. The Earl of Wilton commissioned James Wyatt to design this, the architect's first country house, and the result was one of the finest of its sort in the country. The interior decorations are magnificent and there are eighteenth and nineteenth-century furniture, paintings, ceramics, silver and glass. The music room is particularly notable for its collection of early keyboard instruments, including an organ built by Samuel Green in 1790. The house stands in lovely parkland with lawns, woods, a lake and a playground.

Open all year daily, Sun, pm only. Parking available.

Hereford Hereford and Worcester *p212 E5*

Hereford lies in the rich farmland area of rural England famed for its cider and white-faced red-brown cattle, and the busy market town itself with its famous cathedral, centre around these thriving industries.

Hereford began as a stronghold on the Welsh border around AD 700 and obtained its name from Army Ford. The town's position has caused it to suffer over the centuries from opposing English and Welsh armies, the English finally capturing it in 1645 during the Civil War.

The street plan of Hereford has remained virtually unaltered since its Saxon layout and attractive seventeenth and eighteenth-century buildings now line the streets. One of the pleasantest parts of the town is to the south where it borders the river Wye. Here the cathedral grounds, Castle Green and well-kept Redcliffe Gardens with its bowling green, provide views of the surrounding farmland.

The Cathedral

The pink-stone cathedral church of St Mary the Virgin and St Ethelbert the King dates back to 1080, although the first Bishop was installed in 676. Ethelbert, the Christian King of East Anglia was buried here after being beheaded by Offa, King of Mercia.

The interior is very interesting, boasting one of the finest collections of brasses in any cathedral. It also contains a vast chained library where all the books are chained to the shelves. This dates from the time when books were rare and valuable objects and liable to be stolen. The Mappi Mundi map is kept here too – it is a map of the world as known in 1290, drawn on vellum.

The Old House

Built in 1621, the Old House is a fine restored Jacobean black and white timbered house. It was once part of the picturesque Butchers' Row, which was pulled down in Victorian times by public subscription. Wood carving decorates both the exterior and interior and the outside porch features an amusing butchers' coat

The Old House – once part of
Butchers' Row

Hereford Cathedral's Lady Chapel dates from the 12th century

of arms. The fascinating Jacobean contents include solid oak furniture and paintings of the acting families, the Siddone and Garricks.

Museum and Art Gallery

Although the museum houses mainly modern water colours by local artists, a number of Roman remains are kept here too. Amongst these are sections of tesselated pavements which were excavated from Kenchester, the nearby Roman garrison stronghold called *Magna*.

A natural history and geological section includes domestic items of byegone days and military uniforms and relics.

St John's and Coningsby Museum

Almshouses were added in 1614 to the older dining hall of the Knights of St John (c1170) to form the present museum. Its contents consist of armour and relics belonging to the Knights.

Churchill Gardens Museum and Brian Hatton Art Gallery

The interesting exhibits here include costumes, water colours, glass, porcelain, jewelry and dolls. There is also a Victorian nursery and butler's pantry equipped, as they would have been in those days.

Bulmers Railway Centre

Hereford claims to have the world's biggest cider factory – Bulmers, which was founded in 1887. They now have on the premises of their factory a Railway Centre which is open at weekends during the summer. On Easter Monday and Spring Bank Holiday locomotives can be seen in full steam.

The Old House open all year daily. Sat am only, Sun pm only (closed Sun Oct to Mar).
Museum and Art Gallery open all year daily (except Sun).
St John's and Coningsby Museum open Apr to Oct Tue to Thu, Sat and Sun, pm only.
Churchill Gardens Museum and Brian Hatton Art Gallery open all year daily, pm only.

Herstmonceux

East Sussex *p213 C2*

Although the village of Herstmonceux is noted for its woodcrafts (traditional in this part of Sussex), it is much more famous for its beautiful mellow-brick castle. Formerly a Norman manor house, it was transformed into a castle in 1440 and was one of the first to be designed for residential comfort as well as defensive strength. In 1777 it was largely demolished, but careful restoration in 1913 has recreated its impressive array of battlements and turrets, so that it stands now in perfect condition within its wide moat.

In 1948 the Royal Greenwich Observatory moved here from its outdated premises in Greenwich Park, and it contains one of the largest telescopes in the world.

Grounds and Observatory open Easter to end Sep, Mon to Fri pm, Sat, Sun and Bank Holidays all day. Castle closed.

Heveningham Hall

Suffolk *p214 E5*

One of the finest and loveliest Georgian mansions in the country, Heveningham Hall is set on a hill above its lake and the winding river Blyth. Sir Gerald Vanneck, MP, inherited the estate with its small Queen Anne house from his father in 1777, and had it enlarged by Sir Robert Taylor, court architect to George III. Taylor screened the front with Corinthian columns and added pedimented wings to either side, creating today's imposing building in the Palladian tradition. The Victorian architect James

The beautiful red-brick exterior of Herstmonceux Castle is perfectly mirrored in the still moat which surrounds it

Wyatt designed the Hall's attractive interior, along with some of its furnishings, now considered to be his best surviving work. The magnificent painted decorations are the work of the Italian artist Biagio Rebecca.

Amongst the highlights of the interior are the famous entrance hall, with its semi-circular vaulted ceiling and screens of columns, the dining room, the Etruscan room and the library – all of which contain much of their original furniture and contents.

The grounds including the majestic lake, were laid out by Capability Brown and contain an attractive red-brick crinkle-crackle wall that snakes in and out and so protects delicate plants, and a beautiful orangery by Wyatt.

Open Apr to Oct, pm only Wed, Thu, Sat, Sun and Bank Holiday Mon, also Tue, May to Sep. Parking and refreshments available.

Hever Castle

Kent *p213 C2*

Hever Castle owes much of its present splendour to Lord Astor who spent vast sums of money on restoring it during the early part of this century. The castle dates back to the thirteenth century and in Tudor times was the home of the Boleyn family.

Henry VIII reputedly courted his ill-fated second wife, Anne, here and following her execution he confiscated the castle, later installing the discarded Anne of Cleves.

Lord and Lady Astor modernised the interior of the castle without detracting in any way from its character. The exterior, surrounded by a wide moat, is superbly complemented by the formal gardens which the Astors laid out and filled with Italian sculptures.

There is also an interesting maze using over 1,000 yew trees, and the outstanding topiary work includes a complete set of chessmen.

Castle open Apr to Sep, Tue, Wed, Fri (except Good Fri), Sun and Bank Holidays, pm only. Extra rooms on show on Tue and Fri. Parking available.

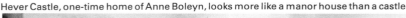

Hever Castle, one-time home of Anne Boleyn, looks more like a manor house than a castle

High Force Waterfall

Co Durham *p217 A4*

The river Tees cascades down over a drop of seventy feet from a cliff of the Great Whin Sill, creating one of the most spectacular waterfalls in England. It plunges into a deep pool enclosed by rocks and shrubs set in a charmingly wooded glen. The best time to see the fall is when the river is in full spate following heavy rain. Access to the falls is by way of a short wooded path which leads down the bank from an entrance opposite the High Force Hotel on the B6277.

A causeway, revealed at low tide, links Holy Island to the mainland

Highland Wildlife Park

Highland *p221 D2*

Amidst mountainous Speyside scenery, the Highland Wildlife Park contains animals that once roamed the Highlands, as well as those species that still do. The drive-through park gives one a close view of free-ranging herds of Red deer, European bison, wild goats, wild horses, Highland cattle and Soay sheep from the isles of St Kilda. Over the hill are enclosures housing bears, wild-cat, eagles, grouse and other mammals and birds. Above the road is the wolf enclosure, where the first cubs to have been raised in the Highlands since 1742 live.

A children's park includes a selection of tame animals, and an Alpine-style chalet incorporates a cafe and souvenir shop overlooking the wildfowl lochan.

Open Mar to Oct daily. Parking and refreshments available.

Hodnet Hall Gardens

Shropshire *p216 E2*

These beautiful landscaped gardens surround the large Elizabethan, red brick house (not open) which stands on the bank of a small valley.

Beginning in 1922, Brigadier Heber-Percy spent over thirty years creating the sixty acres of gardens which are laid out with lakes, pools and sweeping lawns. These provide a perfect setting for the rare shrubs and trees which blend with the blaze of colour roses, rhododendrons and azaleas produce. Primulas, irises and other moisture-loving plants grow beside the water.

Next to the house is a pretty half-timbered seventeenth-century building which is used as a tea-room. The inside is unusually adorned with big game trophies.

Open Good Fri to Sep daily, pm only. Parking available. Refreshments Sun and Bank Holidays and daily May to Aug.

Holker Hall

Cumbria *p216 D5*

This handsome red-sandstone house, ancestral home of the Cavendish family, is a magnificent spectacle. The west wing is particularly fine with its square tower, copper dome and numerous windows of varying sizes and shapes.

The spacious interior has a wealth of carved panelling and woodwork, tapestries and elaborate plasterwork ceilings. Of particular note are the carved twisted columns, made from oakwood taken from the park, of the dining room fireplace. The huge library, an airy room with large windows, houses some 3,500 books. Many are scientific works collected by Henry Cavendish, the eighteenth century scientist who discovered the properties of hydrogen. Several fine paintings hang in the ground floor rooms, including portraits by Richmond and landscapes by Jacob Raysdael. The magnificent staircase has beautiful panelling and elaborately carved balustrades, each one having its own individual design created by local craftsmen. The bedrooms are still furnished in the Victorian style, some with four-poster beds, and toilet sets and wash basins by Copeland and Minton.

The formal and woodland gardens have many different flowering shrubs and trees including a large monkey puzzle tree, said to be the oldest in England. Herds of deer, Shetland ponies, Highland cattle and Jacob sheep roam happily around the parkland. Other attractions here are the Lakeland Motor Museum and an adventure playground.

Open early Apr to Sep, Sun to Fri. Parking and refreshments available.

Holkham Hall

Norfolk *p210 E1*

This vast mansion has remained largely unaltered since its construction in 1734. It was built by William Kent for Thomas Coke, 1st Earl of Leicester, who wanted a fitting home for his remarkable collection of works of art. This he certainly achieved, for the hall and state rooms are truly magnificent with marble columns, a classical frieze and rich furnishings. Old Masters which hang on the walls include works by Poussin, Rubens, Van Dyck and Claude, and the sculpture gallery contains fine marble statues.

The estate was inherited by the Earl's nephew, another Thomas Coke, who was a prominent figure in the Agricultural Revolution. Much of his work concerning soil improvement, crop rotation and sheep breeding was carried out on the Holkham estate. A large monument to Coke of Norfolk, as he was fondly known, stands at the entrance. The gardens include a fine terrace by Nesfield, with a fountain featuring Perseus and Andromeda.

Open Thu June to Sep, also Mon during July and Aug. Open Spring and late Summer Bank Holiday Mon. Parking and refreshments available.

Holy Island

Northumberland *p220 F3–4*

Off the bold, uncluttered Northumberland coastline to the south of Berwick-upon-Tweed, lies Holy Island. This fascinating island, complete with castle and ruined priory, is rich in atmosphere and memory. Often referred to as Lindisfarne, it is commonly regarded as the seventh-century birthplace of English Christianity. For centuries pilgrims crossed the wet sand at low tide to set foot on a place associated with St Aidan and St Cuthbert. Today a three-mile-long causeway enables visitors to drive or walk across at low tide. However, the island is completely cut off from the mainland for some two-and-a-half hours before high tide and remains so for some three hours afterwards. Tide tables are posted at each end of the causeway.

Lindisfarne Castle is a small fifteenth-century Tudor building romantically perched on a pinnacle of high rock, overlooking the tiny harbour. Built as a border fort some of its thick walls were constructed with stones from the ruined abbey nearby. Only ever garrisoned by twenty men, its defences, perhaps fortunately, were never put to the test. The castle fell into ruins in the period after the Civil War, but was acquired by Edward Hudson in 1902 who commissioned Sir Edwin Lutyens to convert it into a comfortable home.

The first Lindisfarne monastery, established by St Aidan in AD 635, was destroyed by raiding Danes in the ninth century. The island then lay deserted until Benedictines from Durham founded the priory two centuries later. All that now remains of the Norman priory are the picturesque red sandstone ruins which look out over the North Sea.

Lindisfarne mead, once the drink of monks, is made on the island and the mead factory close to the priory ruins is open.

Lindisfarne Castle open when tidal conditions permit, Apr to Sep daily (except Fri). Oct, Sat and Sun pm only. NT.
Lindisfarne Priory see AM info. Also open Sun am Apr to Sep. Parking available.

Hopetoun House

Lothian *p220 D4*

As one approaches this Palladian mansion down the long drive, its elegance can be fully appreciated. A wide flight of stone steps lead up to the entrance of the central block, which is flanked by two single-storey wings topped with domed central towers.

Inside is no less elegant with beautiful panelling and plaster ceilings. The two drawing rooms are particularly attractive, one being furnished in yellow and the other in red. Amongst a number of fine paintings here are works by Rubens, Van Dyke, Titian and Canaletto.

The rolling parkland has a specially laid out nature trail, from which Fallow and Red deer and St Kilda sheep can be seen.

Open end April to end Sep daily. Parking and refreshments available.

Hornsea Pottery

Humberside *p217 D3*

This famous pottery attracts many thousands of visitors every year to the guided factory tour, and an inspection of the award-winning designs in their various stages of production. However the factory tour is by no means the only thing to do here. Surrounding the factory are twenty-eight acres of gardens including a landscaped picnic area, a lake, a tea garden and a country craft centre. To keep children amused there is a playground, pony rides, an aviary, a model village and a mini zoo.

The factory shop sells a wide range of Hornsea pottery and bargains can be found on the low priced 'seconds' section.

Open all year daily. Model village open early May to Sep. Parking and refreshments available.

Houghton Hall

Norfolk *p218 E1*

One of the finest examples of Palladian architecture in England is Houghton, built in the eighteenth century for Sir Robert Walpole, first Prime Minister of England and Earl of Orford.

Walpole spent some thirteen years, between 1722 and 1735, rebuilding the original Hall into today's sumptuous masterpiece. His architects were Colin Campbell and Thomas Ripley, and James Gibbs created the striking domes on the four corners of the

Hopetoun House – perhaps the greatest of architect William Adam's houses – was completed in 1748

building. Walpole commissioned William Kent to create the magnificent interior decorations and furniture, including the beautiful painted ceilings. All that Walpole achieved has survived today with the exception of his superb art collection which, unfortunately, was sold to the Empress of Russia after his death.

The present owner of the Hall is the Marquess of Cholmondley whose parents restored the house during this century and also added paintings, French furniture and porcelain.

The exterior of the house is faced in beautiful Yorkshire stone

and its façade has a Classical portico with a richly carved pediment. The Hall is set in a vast park which was laid out by Bridgeman. In the grounds are stables of heavy horses and Shetland ponies, a coach house, pleasure grounds and picnic areas.

Walpole himself is buried in the parish church, a small building of flint and stone which stands in the park. The original village of Houghton also once stood within the park, but was moved by Walpole because it spoilt his view.

Open Easter Sun to Sep on Bank Holidays, Thu and Sun. Sun, pm only.

Mrs Disraeli had Hughenden Manor totally remodelled and faced in brick

House of the Binns

Lothian *p220 D4*

Although this estate is mentioned in documents dating as far back as 1335, the house itself is chiefly seventeenth century. It was then the home of the Dalyell family and in 1681 General Tam Dalyell raised the Royal Scots Greys here. Many of his personal possessions, including his sword and bible, have remained. The magnificently moulded plaster ceilings in four of the main rooms are a particularly attractive feature of the house.

Within the grounds is a beautiful woodland walk which leads to a panoramic viewpoint overlooking the Forth.

Open Easter Sat and Sun, then May to Sep daily (except Fri) pm only. Parkland open all day. NTS.

Hughenden Manor

Buckinghamshire *p213 B3*

This large and dignified house was considerably remodelled in Victorian times by its equally impressive and dignified owner – Benjamin Disraeli, twice Prime Minister and later Earl of Beaconsfield. Disraeli and his wife, Mary Anne, were extremely fond of Hughenden Manor which they bought in 1848, and spent as much time there as possible. Although some alterations have been made to much of the Manor, its furnishings and its contents remain as Disraeli knew them.

His study is quite unchanged and contains many of his personal items, such as letters from Queen Victoria, Mary Anne's diaries, manuscripts of the novels which he wrote here and portraits of his parents. The house is surrounded by lovely parkland with woods, lawns and a stream, and become more formal near the house where a terraced garden was created in the Italian style.

Open Apr to Oct, Wed to Sat, Sun and Bank Holiday Mon, pm only. Mar and Nov, Sat and Sun pm only. NT.

Ickworth House

Suffolk *p213 C4*

Probably one of the most unusual houses in England, is this impressive eighteenth-century mansion lying in the small village of Horringer. Frederick Hervey, 4th Earl of Bristol and Bishop of Derry, conceived the idea from designs by the Italian architect Asprucci. Unfortunately Hervey died in 1803 before the building had been completed, but further work was carried out by his successors.

The centre block of Ickworth is

a 104-foot-high rotunda, decorated with a terracotta frieze. On top is a dome-shaped roof with a balustraded parapet surrounding a central skylight. Semi-circular wings join the rectangular outer pavilions to the rotunda.

The huge rooms are hung with paintings by Reynolds and Gainsborough. A marble statue, *Fury of Athamas*, sculptured by Flaxman, forms the centre piece, and is illuminated naturally from the skylight a hundred-feet above. The house contains many fine pieces of English and French furniture from the eighteenth and nineteenth centuries and pictures by Hogarth hang in the library. Part of the silver collection dates back to the seventeenth century, and includes elaborate designs by French Huguenot craftsmen.

The beautiful park was landscaped by Capability Brown, and magnificent oak and cedar trees provide the house with an effective natural screen.

Open Apr to mid Oct Tue, Wed, Thu, Sat, Sun, Bank Holiday Mon pm. Park open all year daily. Refreshments available. NT.

Ingatestone

Essex *p213 C3*

The Tudor, Georgian and Victorian buildings of the long village of Ingatestone are complemented by the fifteenth-century red brick tower of its parish church. Close to the church is

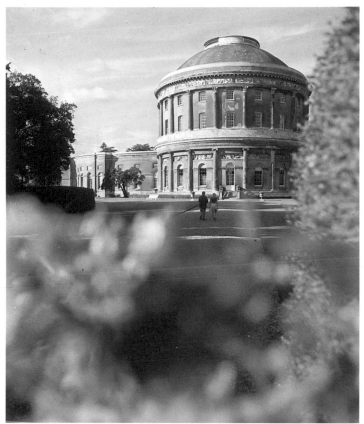

Frederick Hervey built Ickworth to house his great art collection

Ingatestone Hall, an E-shaped Tudor mansion with stepped gables. It was built in about 1540 for Sir William Petre, Tudor Secretary of State, and is now the home of Lord Petre.

Since 1953 the north wing of the hall has been used to display Essex archives and annual exhib-itions based on a theme of Essex history. In the long gallery there is late eighteenth-century and early nineteenth-century furniture, a rare harpsichord and Essex armorial china.

Open Easter to early Oct, Tue to Sat and Bank Holiday Mon. No dogs. Parking available.

Ingatestone Hall was the manor of the Benedictine nuns of Barking Abbey before the Norman conquest

Inveraray Castle

Strathclyde *p219 B5*

Standing in beautiful country on the edge of Loch Fyne, Inveraray Castle looks more like a French château than a Scottish castle, with its light-coloured brick walls, round towers and tall conical turrets. It was built during the eighteenth century on the site of an earlier castle for the Dukes of Argyll, chiefs of the powerful Campbell clan.

Inside there are portraits by Landseer and Gainsborough, Beauvais tapestries and Louis XIV furniture. The armoury hall contains a huge collection of early Scottish weaponry including the dirk handle and sporran which belonged to Rob Roy.

In the grounds is a Spanish cannon salvaged from the sunken Armada vessel, the *Florida*, and pleasant walks may be taken in the well-wooded parkland.

There are excellent views of the whole area from the top of the Inveraray Bell Tower, standing 126 feet high. It contains vestments and campanology (bell ringing) exhibits and the ten bells which hang in the bell chamber are rung daily during Inveraray Week at the end of July.

Castle open Apr to Sep daily, Sun pm only. Closed Fri Apr to June. Parking and refreshments available.
Bell Tower open Spring Bank Holiday to Sep daily, Sun pm only. Parking available.

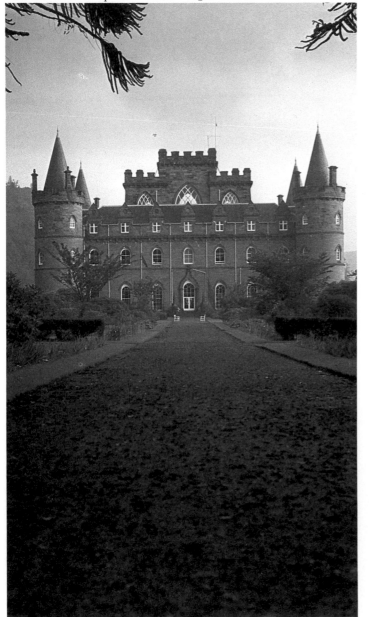

Impressive Inveraray Castle – an early example of neo-Gothic architecture

Inverewe Gardens

Highlands *p221 B3*

The little West Highland village of Poolewe stands where the salmon-filled river Ewe flows into the head of Loch Ewe after its short journey from Loch Maree. One mile north of the village, on a rock promontory jutting out into Loch Ewe, lie the gardens of Inverewe House. Originally barren land supporting no more than a lone dwarf willow, the gardens were founded by Osgood Mackenzie in 1862. In order to establish the right conditions, soil had to be brought to the site and rows of trees were planted to act as wind breaks against the salt-laden Atlantic gales.

The gardens, with their magnificent mountain background, offer something of interest all year round. However, benefiting from the warm, moist climate of the Gulf Stream they are at their best from May to early June. Among the many rare and sub-tropical plants are flowering eucalyptus trees, Australian tree-ferns and Monterey pines. The gardens include a Visitors Centre.

Open all year daily. Visitors Centre open Apr to mid Oct daily, Sun pm only. Parking and refreshments (Apr to Sep) available. NTS.

Inverness

Highland *p221 D2*

Inverness, Capital of the Highlands, lies partly ringed by mountains on either side of the grassy tree-lined banks of the river Ness. The town has long been the historical and administrative centre of the Highland region and its origins can be traced back to the fourth century by the vitrified fort standing on the summit of Craig Phadrig to the west of the town.

One of the oldest buildings in Inverness today is Abbertarff House in Church Street. It dates from 1593 and contains the last remaining example of turnpike stairs, an ancient type of spiral staircase. The house is now the headquarters of The Highland Association, and holds an exhibition illustrating the origins and history of the Gaels, a Highland craft shop and Information Centre.

The present castle (now housing a Sheriff Court House and administrative offices) dates from 1834, although there has been a castle on this site since the twelfth century. A statue of Flora Macdonald stands on the castle esplanade. It was erected in 1899 and shows her looking southwards towards the hiding place of Bonnie Prince Charlie whom she helped escape after his defeat in 1746.

In front of the Town House, a Gothic-style building where Lloyd George and his cabinet met, is the Clach-na-Cudaiann (stone of tubs), where the women of Inverness used to rest on their way back from the well loaded with full tubs of water. Tradition has it that a seer predicted that so long as the stone was preserved Inverness would flourish.

Just off Shore Street is Cromwell's Clock Tower, the only part of the large citadel built by Cromwell's army to escape demolition on the restoration of Charles II. The Tolbooth steeple in Church Street, built in 1791, is the former jail steeple where dangerous prisoners were kept.

St Andrews Cathedral, built in 1866, is richly decorated with illuminated windows and carved pillars. Other religious houses include the High Parish Church which was rebuilt between 1770 and 1772, although the fourteenth-century vaulted tower remains from an earlier building. In the churchyard a bullet-marked stone marks the place where the Duke of Cumberland's victorious army summarily executed prisoners after the Battle of Culloden, fought just six miles away.

Handloom weaving can be seen at a workshop in Tomnahurich Street and at Holm Mills tartan and tweed spinning and weaving can be watched. The Northern Meeting Park is the venue for entertainment during the summer months and among the attractions here are pipe band concerts, Highland and Scottish dancing. The town also boasts a particularly fine theatre in the Eden Court. The Museum and Art Gallery in Castle Wynd depicts the history of the Highlands, and the art collection includes many views of old Inverness.

Abbertarff House open all year Mon to Sat, am only Wed and Sat.
Isle of Skye Handloom open Mon to Fri.
Holm Mills Mill and showroom open Mon to Fri, showroom only Sat am.
Museum and Art Gallery open all year Mon to Sat.

Ironbridge Gorge Museum

Shropshire *p216 E2*

The Ironbridge Gorge Museum represents a unique monument to the Industrial Revolution. It was here, in 1709, at Coalbrookdale, that Abraham Darby first smelted iron using coke as a fuel instead of charcoal, and the Museum illustrates the growth of the iron and allied industries which blossomed in this area, following the experiment.

In the midst of this complex the impressive Ironbridge spans the gorge. Designed in 1779 by Abraham Darby III, this was the first bridge to be constructed entirely of cast-iron and each segment of its 378-ton structure was produced by local workmen.

Blists Hill Open Air Museum occupies a forty-two-acre woodland site with buildings and machines which trace the industrial and social history of the area. Particularly interesting is the 1,000-yard-long tunnel known as the Tar Tunnel under Blists Hill. This gives access to the artificial wells of natural bitumen.

Coalbrookdale Furnace and

The old kilns and buildings of Coalport pottery at Ironbridge

Museum of Iron is a collection of indoor and outdoor exhibitions, including the original furnace used by Abraham Darby. It illustrates the history of the Coalbrookdale Company which progressed from producing iron cooking pots, to the construction of the first iron boiler for a locomotive, the Ironbridge itself, and the iron gates which stand between Hyde Park and Kensington Gardens in London, made for the Great Exhibition of 1851.

Coalport China was manufactured, in what is now the China Works Museum, from the late eighteenth century until 1926 when the company moved to Staffordshire – where they still operate. The works once covered both banks of the Shropshire Canal,

used for the transportation of goods, and many of the original buildings have been restored to form this museum which includes workshops, ovens, kilns and displays of porcelain.

The Severn Warehouse and Visitor Centre – a nineteenth-century building and its adjoining wharf, has been restored and the Warehouse now contains displays and slide shows which introduce the history of the Ironbridge Gorge.

A useful Tourist Information Centre has been installed in the old Ironbridge toll-house.

Open all year daily.

The river Ness flows towards the Moray Firth past Inverness Castle

Isle of Wight *p213 A1*

This compact little island is perfectly suited to the traditional family holiday by the sea with its miles of sandy beaches, rugged cliffs, unspoilt countryside, high chalk downs, little old villages and seaside resorts.

The mainly 14th-century church in the delightful village of Godshill

The island was Queen Victoria's favourite holiday resort and she died at Osborne House, her much loved family home near Cowes. It is now open to the public and among the Victorian opulence and Indian finery can be seen domestic reminders of the Royal Family's daily life.

Cowes itself contains many fine Georgian and Victorian buildings, but is most famous for its yachting tradition. Situated on the mouth of the river Medina, the town is renowned throughout the world for Cowes Week, when the famous yacht races draw competitors from all over the globe.

The Maritime Museum in Beckford Road illustrates the maritime history of the island with models, photographs, paintings and books.

Cowes is the home of the Royal Yacht Club and the club house stands on the site of a castle built originally by Henry VIII. Twenty-two brass cannons stand on the semi-circular platform of Victoria's Parade, and are used to start races and fire royal salutes.

Beyond East Cowes behind Old Castle Point lies turreted Norris Castle, set in attractive grounds. Its rooms, crammed with pictures, furniture and armour are open to the public during the summer months.

Carisbrooke was capital of the island long before Newport (the present capital), because Carisbrooke Castle, built by a kinsman of William the Conqueror shortly after the Conquest, was the home of the 'Governor' of the island. Visitors can walk round the high parapets, see the chapel and museum, or visit the fascinating wheel-house, where a donkey turns a wheel to draw water from a 160-foot-deep well.

Brighstone and Godshill are picture postcard villages complete with thatched cottages, cafés and gift shops. Godshill has a Model Village in the Vicarage gardens, a small but interesting Natural History Museum, and a Birdland with gardens in the shape of the Isle of Wight, aviaries, gnomes and models.

One mile to the south of Godshill are the ruins of Appuldurcombe House, damaged by a German landmine in 1943. This shell of a grand mansion is surrounded by beautiful grounds landscaped by Capability Brown.

Another inland village of the island is the pretty, unspoilt Calbourne. Winkle Row – a group of ancient cottages – is a popular subject for photographers here. The Caul Bourne stream flowing through the village used to power Calbourne Mill, which stopped grinding flour in 1955, and is now a Rural Museum. The quiet well-ordered grounds are paraded by peacocks, and the mill-pond is well stocked with water-fowl.

The chief coastal resorts are on the south coast, except Ryde and Seaview. Ryde, on the north coast and east of Cowes, was turned from a small village into a fashionable holiday resort in the early nineteenth century, and is still as popular today. There is five miles of sandy beach, a pier nearly half a mile long with an electric railway, and an esplanade which leads to pleasant gardens, a boating lake, aviaries, aquariums and parks.

Seaview, farther east, is a quieter resort and more residential. The Flamingo Park bird sanctuary has an attractive collection of native and foreign water-fowl.

On the eastern tip of the island is the quiet village of Bembridge, best known as a yachting centre. Here there is a lifeboat station, a windmill owned by the National Trust, and a small Maritime

Museum – all open to the public.

Inland from Bembridge is Brading, once a seaport on the tidal river Yar in the nineteenth century. The Town Hall has a stone lock-up, a whipping post and stocks, and the sixteenth-century building close-by houses a clever and amusing wax museum, which includes a spine chilling torture-chamber. The Lilliput Dolls Museum here has an interesting collection of dolls and toys displayed in a small, charming cottage.

Sandown is the largest resort on the island, and with its neighbour Shanklin forms a continuous holiday complex three miles long. The old village of Shanklin has been restored although most of it has retained its Victorian atmosphere. Shanklin Chine is a commercially exploited river gorge filled with various amusements.

Ventnor, another major resort, is built on terraces leading down a cliff to a small seafront and pier. Its sheltered position gives it a warm, almost sub-tropical climate and exotic plants flourish in the Botanic Gardens. Close by is the fascinating Museum of Smuggling History, and also Blackgang Chine, a pleasure park set on the cliff complete with a gnomes' garden, giant dinosaurs, a maze and an adventure play ground.

The island countryside affords

The Needles and Needles Lighthouse lie off the western tip of the island

many opportunities for pleasant walks, whether on open high ground with magnificent views as on Brighstone Down, or Tennyson Down where the great chalk stacks of the Needles can be seen standing in the sea, or in the cool, shady woodland of Brighstone Forest or Parkhurst Forest.

Robin Hill Country Park, on Arreton Down, covers eighty acres of grass and woodland where a collection of wild and domestic animals roam free. There is also a selection of caged animals here.

Above: The brass cannons of the Royal Yacht Squadron in Cowes

Osborne House open early Apr to Sep Mon to Sat. Parking available. AM.

Norris Castle open Easter, then mid May to early Sep Sat, Sun and Mon; daily during Cowes week. Parking and refreshments available.

Maritime Museum (Cowes) open all year daily (except Sun).

Carisbrooke Castle see AM info. Museum closed Oct to Easter. Also open Sun am Apr to Sep. Parking and refreshments available.

Godshill Model Village open Apr to Sep daily, Sun pm only.

Natural History Collection open Apr to Sep daily.

Appuldurcombe House see AM info. Also open Sun am Apr to Sep.

Calbourne Watermill and Rural Museum open Apr to Oct daily.

Bembridge Windmill open Apr to Sep daily. NT.

Maritime Museum open Easter to Oct daily, then weekends only until Christmas. Parking available.

Flamingo Park Bird Sanctuary open Easter to Sep daily, pm only Easter to May and all Sun. Parking and refreshments available.

Wax Museum open all year daily. Parking available.

Lilliput Museum open mid Mar to mid Oct daily.

Museum of the History of Smuggling open Easter to Sep daily. Parking and refreshments available.

Blackgang Chine open June to Sep daily. Parking and refreshments available.

Robin Hill Country Park and Zoo open Mar to Nov daily. Parking and refreshments available.

J

Jedburgh

Borders *p220 E3*

One of the four famous border monasteries founded by David I, now a roofless red sandstone ruin, stands by this most attractive lowland town.

The abbey is still impressive, with its eighty-six-foot high Norman tower, richly carved Norman doorway, splendid nave and fine rose window. A small museum houses monuments from the abbey and many carved fragments of medieval work.

The original Jedburgh Castle, built in the twelfth century, was a residence of Scottish kings. However, because of its vulnerable position (to English attack) the Scottish parliament decided to demolish it in 1409. The present Georgian building, erected in 1823 on the site of the old castle, became the county prison and is now a museum of penal methods in the nineteenth century.

Mary Queen of Scots came to Jedburgh in 1566, and almost died of illness here. The house in which she lodged, known as Mary Queen of Scots' House, is a picturesque L-shaped, building, built for defence rather than comfort. It stands in pleasant gardens and today is a museum of relics associated with the ill-fated queen.

Abbey see AM info. Oct to Mar closed 1½ days per week.
Castle Jail open Apr to Sep daily, Sun pm only. Parking available.
Mary Queen of Scots House open Mar to Oct daily. Parking available.

Jervaulx Abbey

North Yorkshire *p217 B4*

The ruins of this eleventh-century Cistercian monastery lie in a magnificent garden setting on the edge of the Yorkshire Dales.

The monastery was founded in 1156 by an order not allowed to eat meat, although many bones were found here. Fifteen masons' marks are discernable on remaining stones and the best feature is the wall of the monks' dormitory with its high lancet windows.

Until it was dissolved by Henry VIII in 1538, the abbey thrived and was particularly noted for its cheese making. Although little remains of its former grandeur, the mellowed remains scattered amidst the trees and shrubs which abound here, are enough to indicate the original plan of the abbey buildings.

Abbey always accessible. Parking available.

Jodrell Bank

Cheshire *p216 E3*

In 1957 the first and largest of the two radio telescopes at Jodrell Bank came into operation to track Russian and American satellites and space probes. Two-hundred-and-fifty-feet in diameter and weighing 850 tons, it is one of the largest fully steerable radio telescopes in the world. In 1964 the 125-feet diameter telescope was completed and both are now engaged in a variety of research programmes.

The Concourse Building houses a fascinating exhibition on space

Above: The house at which Mary Queen of Scots stayed when she visited Jedburgh in the 16th century and astronomy, and working models include a twenty-five-foot radio telescope which visitors can operate to pick up radio emissions from the sun. There is also a Planetarium which presents images and explanations of the night sky.

Open mid Mar to Oct daily pm only, Nov to mid Mar weekends pm only (closed Christmas and New Year). Parking and refreshments available.

K

Kendal – the Auld Grey Town – has many grey limestone buildings

Kelling Park Aviaries

Norfolk *p218 E1*

The Kelling Park Aviaries house a fine collection of European and tropical birds in some fourteen acres of exquisite gardens.

Ornamental pheasants, cockatoos, macaws and flamingos are amongst some of the colourful and exotic inhabitants.

Entertainment within the park includes a children's playground, a clock golf course and a picnic area.

Open all year daily. Parking and refreshments available.

Kendal

Cumbria *p220 E1*

Famous for Kendal Green cloth, mint cake and snuff, Kendal is South Lakeland's largest town and its administrative centre. The river Kent flows through the town and it is surrounded by the gentle countryside of the fells on the edge of the Lake District National Park.

Kendal is very conscious of its past and has a particularly good museum, notable for its huge collection of world-wide animals and birds. There is also an exhibition here of Lake District natural history and items of archaeology and geology.

The Abbot Hall Art Gallery and Culture Centre is housed in the skilfully converted eighteenth-century mansion which stands in the Abbot Hall Park. Paintings by such artists as Turner, Reynolds, Raeburn and Romney are displayed here in carefully restored rooms, with valuable pieces of china, glass and silver. The stable block of the mansion has also been converted to house the fascinating Museum of Lakeland Life and Industry. Here realistic model displays illustrate how a family would have lived and how rural craftsmen carried on their trades.

The Castle Dairy in Wildman Street is a very well preserved Tudor building with oak beams and fine carvings. It is now a licensed restaurant but is open to visitors during the afternoon. Almost opposite is the Kendal Studio Pottery, an historic building housing a permanent exhibition of lakeland-stone pottery and paintings by local artists.

Just to the east of the town is Kendal's most historic feature – the castle. It dates back to the twelfth century and was the birthplace of Catherine Parr, Henry VIII's sixth wife. Although scant remains exist today it is well worth the pleasant walk to its summit.

Museum open all year daily, Sat and Sun pm only. Parking available.
Abbot Hall Art Gallery and Museum open all year daily (except Good Fri and two weeks over Christmas/New Year) Sat and Sun pm only. Parking and refreshments available.

Kenilworth

Warwickshire *p216 F1*

The town of Kenilworth lies between Coventry and Warwick in an area commonly regarded as the heart of England. It is a pleasant residential area with a number of charming half-timbered houses dating from the fifteenth century. The interesting remains of an Augustinian Abbey may be seen in Abbey Fields and, close by, the mainly Perpendicular parish church of St Nicholas with its fine Norman doorway.

The town's chief glory, however, is Kenilworth Castle, immortalised by Sir Walter Scott in *Kenilworth*, his historical novel of Elizabethan England. The novelist once stayed at the Kings Arms and Castle Hotel in the Square and used the castle as the setting for many of the events in the book.

It is situated on the north-west edge of the town and is remarkable for its size, having been referred to as the grandest fortress ruin in England. Built by the Norman de Clinton family in the twelfth century on an original Saxon site, the castle was remodelled by John of Gaunt in the fourteenth century and Robert Dudley, Earl of Leicester, entertained Queen Elizabeth I there in the sixteenth century. From the seventeenth century onwards the castle fell into ruin, but nevertheless conveys an impression of past great strength. The massive keep, its walls over seventeen feet thick in places, still stands although damaged by Parliamentary forces during the Civil War. A sixteenth-century gatehouse, known as Lord Leicester's Buildings, and parts of the banqueting hall, also survive.

See AM info. Parking available.

Below: One of the huge radio telescopes used for research purposes at Jodrell Bank

Keswick

Cumbria *p220 D1*

Keswick stands between Skiddaw and Derwentwater on the river Greta. A market town of intriguing narrow streets and buildings of old grey stone, possibly its finest building, dominating the Market Place, is Moot Hall, built in 1813.

Fitz Park Museum and art gallery in Station Road contains manuscripts and relics of the author Hugh Walpole, and of Robert Southey (a notable poet of the nineteenth century) who both lived in Cumbria. There are two manuscripts by Wordsworth here as well. Apart from its literary collection, the museum also has geological exhibits and a scale-model of the Lake District. The art gallery includes works by Turner and Wilson Steer.

On the west side of the town, there are excellent views of Derwentwater from the churchyard of St John's. The church was built in 1838 and is the burial place of Hugh Walpole. North-west of the town centre is the parish church; memorials here include one to Canon Rawnsley who was vicar at the church for twenty-five years and co-founder of the National Trust, and another to Robert Southey.

To the south-west of the town on the west shore of Derwentwater is Lingholm, with its formal gardens and one-and-a-half-mile woodland walk full of azaleas and rhododendrons.

East of Keswick is a prehistoric circle of thirty-eight stones, ten of which form a rectangle within the ring. It is called the Castlerigg Stone Circle or Druids Circle.

Fitz Park Museum and Art Gallery open Apr to Oct Mon to Sat.
Lingholm open Apr to Oct daily (except Sun). Parking available.
Castlerigg Stone Circle open any reasonable time. AM and NT.

Kidwelly Castle

Dyfed *p212 C4*

Roger, Bishop of Salisbury, built the castle in about 1130, which was subsequently deeply involved in the struggle between the rebellious Welsh and the English Crown. A well known incident here was the battle between the Normans and Welsh in which the Welsh army was led by a woman, Gwenllian. At the time the Normans were in occupation, and during her unsuccessful attack,

A long colourful herbacious border runs along the hillside arboretum in Killerton House Gardens

she and one of her sons died. The battlefield still bears her name, Maes Gwenllian, and Welsh bitterness for her 'murder' remained strong for centuries.

Strategically placed above a steep slope leading down to the river Gwendraeth, the extensive ruins of the castle stand in lovely countryside. The twelfth-century plan consisted of a rectangular inner ward in which there was a great hall and a chapel.

In the fourteenth century a semi-circular outer ward was added including the three-storeyed south gatehouse. Also built between the inner and outer wards at this time was another hall and kitchen, and the great ovens can still be seen here.

See AM info. Also open Sun am Apr to Sep. Parking available.

Killerton House and Gardens

Devon *p212 D2*

Home of the Acland family since the Civil War, the property was given to the National Trust by Sir Richard Acland in 1944. Visitors can see here the Paulise de Bush costume collection, shown in a series of rooms furnished in different periods from the second half

Ashness Bridge, near Keswick, is one of the many marvellous viewpoints found in this area

of the eighteenth century to the present day.

Imaginative use of the natural landscape provides Killerton House with attractive hillside gardens sweeping down to open lawns. Delightful walks can be taken through a fine collection of trees and shrubs. On the east side of the garden is a neo-Norman chapel modelled on the Lady Chapel of Glastonbury.

Open all year daily. Parking and refreshments available. NT.

Kilmarnock

Strathclyde *p220 C3*

The busy industrial centre and market town of Kilmarnock is the home of the Burns' Federation and it was here that Scotland's national poet had his first collection of poems published in 1786 by John Wilson.

The Burns' Museum in Kay Park contains an outstanding collection of original manuscripts and relics, including a copy of the first Kilmarnock edition. The museum is housed in a Victorian tower built of red sandstone, to commemorate the poet. From the top are panoramic views of the town and distant Arran.

Situated in Elmbank Avenue is the Dick Institute, a fascinating museum of rural life including an art gallery and collections of Scottish arms and armour.

About one mile to the north of

the town is Dean Castle, set in some forty-two acres of gardens and parkland which include nature trails. The castle, beautifully restored, contains exhibitions of armour and early musical instruments.

Burns' Museum open May to Sep daily, pm only. Oct to Apr Sat and Sun pm.
Dick Institute open all year daily (except Sun). Parking available.
Dean Castle open mid May to mid Sep daily, pm only on weekdays. Refreshments available.

Kilverstone New World Wildlife Park

Norfolk *p213 D5*

Displayed in the very attractive grounds of seventeenth-century Kilverstone Hall are several birds and mammals from North and South America. The Hall is the home of Lord and Lady Fisher, who, with the curator, have collected all the animals and hope to breed some of the rarer species.

There is also a pleasant riverside walk, a picnic area and a walled garden in which a water tower was built at the beginning of the century. In the park are Chinese water deer as well as Fallow and Sika deer. Of particular interest are the miniature horse stud, pets corner and adventure playground.

Open all year daily. Parking and refreshments available.

King's Lynn

Norfolk *p217 D1*

The low-lying Norfolk coast sweeps in a great arc from Gorleston-on-Sea to The Wash. Some two miles south of the mouth of the Great Ouse, which flows into the Wash, lies the ancient port and market town of King's Lynn, formerly called Bishop's Lynn before it became royal property.

Once a walled city of considerable importance, King's Lynn received its first charter from King John in the twelfth century. Parts of the old city walls remain and the town's medieval streets contain many attractive buildings, such as the timber-framed Hampton Court in Nelson Street. The tall octagonal tower of Greyfriars in St James's Street is all that survives of an original thirteenth-century building. Adjoining the twelfth-century St

Margaret's Church is the Saturday Market Place and to the north-east of the large Tuesday Market Place stands the later Church of St Nicholas. It was around these two markets that the town gradually expanded and, although now car parks, markets are still held here on Saturday and Tuesday.

The elegant Customs House was built by local architect Henry Bell in 1683. The town was a glass making centre between the seventeenth and nineteenth century and visitors may still see glass being manufactured at the Wedgwood Glass Factory in Oldmeadow Road.

Lynn Museum in Market Street contains items of natural history and local archaeology. Temporary exhibitions are held throughout the year and of special interest is the collection of medieval pilgrims' badges.

Located in King Street, the Museum of Social History displays costume, ceramics, glass, toys and domestic items.

Lynn Museum open all year Mon to Sat (except Good Fri, Christmas, New Year's Day and Bank Holidays. **Museum of Social History** open all year, Tue to Sat (except Bank Holidays).

Knebworth House and Country Park

Hertfordshire *p213 B4*

Knebworth house was first built amidst its vast park in 1492, but the present house was largely rebuilt in 1843 by the statesman Lord Lytton, author of *The Last Days of Pompeii*.

The interior is full of treasures, spanning 500 years of English history, such as furniture, family portraits and personal relics of past inhabitants, including some

of Lytton's manuscripts. The great hall is a magnificent room – the plasterwork of the ceiling and the carved screen are both Jacobean, whereas the panelling in the hall is seventeenth century.

The seemingly boundless grounds provide picnic areas, riding facilities, a children's narrow-gauge railway and a skate park. The sixteenth-century tithe barn has been converted into a charming restaurant.

Open Apr to Sep daily (except Mon), also Bank Holidays and Sun in Oct. Parking and refreshments available.

Knole

Kent *p213 C2*

Knole, one of the largest private houses in England, is a great mansion of grey-brown Kentish stone on the outskirts of the ancient town of Sevenoaks. Knole is

Knebworth House was decorated with battlements, gargoyles and heraldic symbols when it was transformed into a Gothic mansion in the 19th century

Now a Tudor house, Lacock Abbey was originally an Augustinian nunnery. It was the last religious foundation to be dissolved at the Reformation

a house of complicated architecture with irregular roof lines, topped by slim brick chimney-stacks, battlemented towers, turrets and gables. The building is spread out over some four acres on the contours of the rounded hill, or knoll, from which it takes its name. The house consists of seven courtyards, corresponding to the days of the week, fifty-two staircases for the weeks in the year, and 365 rooms for the days of the year.

It dates mainly from the fifteenth century and was both an archbishop's and a king's palace before becoming the home of the Sackville family for ten generations. Its magnificent state apartments with their richly plastered ceilings are furnished mainly with original Jacobean and Caroline furniture together with priceless art collections, carpets, tapestries and silver. The mansion's unique interior includes three long galleries – each with their own state bedroom; two state beds; a great hall; the ornamental great staircase; a crimson drawing room; the old billiard room and the ballroom.

The garden plan has changed little since the seventeenth century and covers some twenty-six acres enclosed within its massive Elizabethan wall. The gardens are laid out with formal walks and flower beds, shrubs and trees. Beyond the gardens lies the large park which is open to the public and covers some 1,000 acres. Here, among its hills and valleys, are clumps of broad oaks, tall beeches and herds of Fallow and Japanese deer.

Open Apr to Nov Wed to Sat, Bank Holiday Mon and Sun, pm only. House closed Dec to Mar. Gardens open first Wed in the month, May to Sep. Parking available. NT.

Lacock

Wiltshire *p212 F4*

Lacock is a village of cobbled streets, old mellow houses, many medieval, and none later than eighteenth century. Old inns, weavers' houses, a King John hunting lodge, a pack horse bridge and ford and a fifteenth-century tithe barn, together with a fourteenth-century church, blend together charmingly.

The abbey, founded in 1232 by Ela, Countess of Salisbury, stands on the banks of the river Avon. The cloisters and chapter house survive from the original building, but most is the responsibility of Sir William Sharington, who converted it into a Tudor dwelling house shortly after its suppression in 1539. Notable additions made by him include the octagonal tower, in which there is kept a photostat of the Lacock Magna Carta of 1225, and the stable court, in which the six-teenth-century brew house has been restored.

The house passed to the Talbot family in the seventeenth century, and a century later they added the Gothic-style entrance hallway and great hall.

Near the abbey gates, in the sixteenth-century barn, is the Fox Talbot Museum dedicated to W. H. Fox Talbot whose experiments advanced photography here in 1835.

House and grounds open Apr, May and Oct, Wed to Sun and Bank Holidays Mon pm only. June to Sep daily, pm only. NT.
Museum open Mar to Oct daily.

The east side of Knole. Vita Sackville-West was born here in 1892

Lake District Cumbria

Some of the deepest lakes, the highest mountains, the quietest valleys and the most dramatic panoramas in England are to be found within this diverse landscape covering an area of 900 square miles.

Five hundred million years ago there were no mountains or lakes – but a trough, choked with sediment, lying under a muddy sea. Since then the land has undergone immense changes. Volcanic activity buried it under two miles of ash and lava, earth movements buckled it into a mountain range, which was in turn gradually eroded and drowned in a coral-rich sea. This slowly silted up to create a marshland of pools and mudbanks upon which giant ferns grew. Yet another phase of mountain building followed, and again was the victim of extensive erosion, which this time produced a vast, arid wind-blown desert.

Finally, about twenty-six million years ago movements within the earth's crust raised the land in a great dome, which formed the basis of today's lakeland. The lakes themselves are the most recent addition to the scenery, and will perhaps be the first to change. River sediment is gradually filling the lakes, and in thousands of years time the lakes may have disappeared altogether.

The Lake District has a reputation for being more wet and cold than dry and sunny and it is true that Seathwaite, at the head of Borrowdale, is the wettest place in the country. Yet often the Lake District basks under blue skies while the rest of England shivers beneath rain and fog, and the weather changes quickly – a rainy, overcast morning may be followed by a gloriously sunny afternoon. However beautiful the fells may appear in the sunshine, they take on a wild grandeur in bad weather – the peaks are wrapped in cloud, the rocks running with raindrops.

The great attraction of the lakes, which enthralled the early tourists of the late eighteenth century, is of course the scenery. This is best seen by the walker, but for the less energetic sightseer there is an almost unlimited fund of places to visit which are reasonably accessible to the motorist. There are Wordsworth's homes at Grasmere and Rydal, his birthplace at Cockermouth, Beatrix Potter's home at Hilltop, near Sawrey, there is the tiny Bridge House at Ambleside, the third highest inn in England on top of Kirkstone Pass, the famous Bowder Stone in Borrowdale, the Ruskin Museum at Coniston, numerous old churches and the Roman Fort on Hardknott.

Local customs and events provide plenty of alternative entertainment, such as the rush-bearing ceremonies at Grasmere and Ambleside, or country dancing in the Langdales. There are sports meetings during the summer months where Cumberland and Westmorland wrestling, fell racing and pole leaping can be watched. Hound trailing is a great Lakeland favourite. Specially bred trail hounds are set to follow a course marked by an aniseed-scented trail across the fells. The first dog to return wins, and all are rewarded with a bowl of meat as soon as they finish. There are frequent fox hunts,

Ambleside, Westmorland.

usually followed on foot over such rugged terrain, carrying on the tradition of John Peel, who hunted this region and lived at Caldbeck.

The lakes themselves offer their own variety of pastime. This is water skiing on Lake Windermere and Ullswater – the former also boasts a yacht club and a motor boat racing club, as well as canoeing and other aquatic sports. Skating is often possible on many of the lakes during the winter months, and the sport of curling is still popular.

However the activity most commonly associated with the Lake District is fell walking. Every summit can be reached by walking, although some are more difficult than others, Lord Rake on Scafell perhaps the most difficult. Well trodden paths mark routes on the popular mountains, which are sometimes marked by cairns –

Tarn Hows – a scene typical of Lakeland's tranquil landscape combining water, woods and fells

piles of stones – along the way. However, caution is needed, some clear paths lead straight to the edge of a precipice, worn by those wishing to enjoy the view.

The hard way up the fells provides the rock climber with ample opportunities, and although not on such a grand scale as many other mountainous areas in Europe, the Lake District has several climbs generally respected among the mountaineering community. Skiing is possible on the north-east slopes of Helvellyn during the right conditions, and the Lake District Ski Club have a hut and a ski tow high above Glenridding.

For the naturalist there are Red deer in Gowbarrow Park and Fallow deer in the woods, such as those between Windermere and Coniston Water and in the numerous Forestry Commission plantations. Foxes thrive despite the hunts, and otters and badgers are present although seldom seen. The now rare Red squirrel has one of its few refuges in the Lake District, and can be seen in the Windermere woods and in Borrowdale. Of all the Lakeland birds the Golden eagle must be the most publicised and, in recent years, this magnificent creature has returned to breed after an absence of about 200 years. The

buzzard, often mistaken for the eagle, is common, and the resident falcons are the kestrel and the rarer peregrine. The raven is the most characteristic bird, its sombre plumage and coarse cry typify the brooding wildness of the high fells. Of the smaller birds, the Meadow pipit and

wheatear are the most interesting, although along the stream valleys the delightful dipper may be seen.

Around the lakes the stalking heron is a familiar sight fishing in the shallows, and coots and moorhens are probably the commonest birds on the lakes.

One of the Haverthwaite Railway's two Fairburn 2-6-4 tank engines

Lakeside and Haverthwaite Railway

Cumbria *p216 D5*

This steam operated railway carries passengers through the lovely wooded hills of south lakeland between Haverthwaite and Lake Windermere. Most of the trains connect at Lakeside Station with the popular Lake Windermere steamers. The railway's collection of twelve steam and two diesel locomotives includes two rare 2-6-4 class 4 Fairburn tank engines, together with both passenger and freight rolling stock.

Open Easter then Sun only until end Apr. Daily from May to early Oct, then Sun only until end Oct. Parking and refreshments at Haverthwaite station.

Lambton Pleasure Park

Co Durham *p217 B5*

Lambton was first opened in 1972 as a Lion Park, but has since undergone extensive development as a major tourist attraction.

By driving through the safari park elephants, lions, bears, zebras, White rhinos and other large game can be seen freely wandering in open countryside.

Yet more animals are housed in the new walk-through zoological garden. Within the 'walkabout' areas eland, ostrich and wildebeest are among the creatures to be observed at close quarters.

Children are well catered for here. The large adventure playground includes an Astroglide, Sky Pulley, Domestic Animal Stockade and there are many other amusements such as donkey rides. Also in this part of the park are souvenir shops, an amusement arcade and a licensed Safari Restaurant. Dogs are not allowed in the park, but kennels are provided.

Beside the river Wear, which runs through the 200 acre park, is Lambton Castle. Parts of this nineteenth-century romantic reproduction of a medieval stronghold are open to the public, and the smaller animals and birds of Lambton's collection are kept here.

Open Mar to Oct daily. Parking and refreshments available.

Lancaster

Lancashire *p216 E5*

The old, grey city of Lancaster lies westwards of the lovely moorland scenery of the Trough of Bowland, to the east of Morecambe Bay, with the mountains of the Lake District as an impressive backdrop. Essentially Georgian in appearance, the city nestles at the foot of its Norman castle and ancient priory which look down from the vantage point of Castle Hill. The castle was built in the eleventh century, and, although much altered since medieval days, has been used as a prison for centuries. The great Shire Hall has an impressive display of heraldry and the drop room contains the brutal relics of early prison life.

Standing side by side with the castle is the ancient fourteenth-century parish church of Lancaster, which was founded as part of an eleventh-century Benedictine priory. It is notable for its Saxon doorway and magnificent oak-canopied stalls from Cockersand Abbey.

In the Old Town Hall, an outstanding Georgian building, are the exhibits of the City Museum which include archaeology, maritime history and local paintings. The early uniforms, medals and photographs of the King's Own Royal Lancaster Regiment are on display here as well.

Judges' Lodgings Museum, a seventeenth-century town house, formerly the home of visiting Assize Judges, is now converted into a museum which illustrates the household life of a prosperous eighteenth to nineteenth-century Lancaster family. The Museum of Childhood, incorporating the Barry Elder Doll Collection, is also housed in the building.

To the east of the city in Williamson Park stands the Ashton Memorial, the gift of Lord Ashton in 1909 who also provided the city with its magnificent Town Hall. The green dome of the memorial is a well known landmark and its higher galleries provide panoramic views of the surrounding countryside.

Castle open Easter to Sep daily.
Priory and Parish Church open daily all year.
City Museum open daily (except Sun, Christmas and New Year).
Judges' Lodgings Museum open Easter to Sep pm only Tue to Sun, including Bank Holidays.

Lanhydrock House

Cornwall *p211 B2*

The simple lines and warm brown stone of Lanhydrock House present a pleasing image of a seventeenth-century great house. Yet only the north wing and a part of the west wing are truly seventeenth century, as the rest of the house was rebuilt after a disastrous fire in 1881.

The showpiece of the house is the 116-foot long gallery in the original north wing, with its outstanding plaster ceiling vividly illustrating early scenes from the Old Testament. The ceiling was created by local craftsmen in about 1650.

Inside is delightfully informal, hats and coats hang on hatstands, photographs are proudly displayed on desks – the atmosphere is that of a private home. The kitchen and buttery, full of curios, are particularly fascinating.

Great magnolias grace the outside walls and to the front and one side formal gardens of lawns, rose beds, clipped cypresses and shrubberies are splendidly laid out and immaculately kept. Pleasant walks give access to the parkland which slopes gently away from the gardens, and here stands a half-mile avenue of beeches and sycamores – a landmark among the many other flowering trees and shrubs.

Open Apr to Oct daily. Gardens only Nov to Mar during daylight. Refreshments available (except Christmas to Mar.) NT.

Launceston Castle

Cornwall *p212 C2*

Launceston Castle stands in a dominating position on a hill above the town, surrounded by a public garden. It is a well known local landmark and the topmost wall provides fine views over the wild expanse of Bodmin Moor.

The remains of the circular shell keep and central tower have stood on this spot since the thirteenth century. The original castle here was a primitive motte-and-

Oak timbers with clay and wattle fillings characterise Lavenham

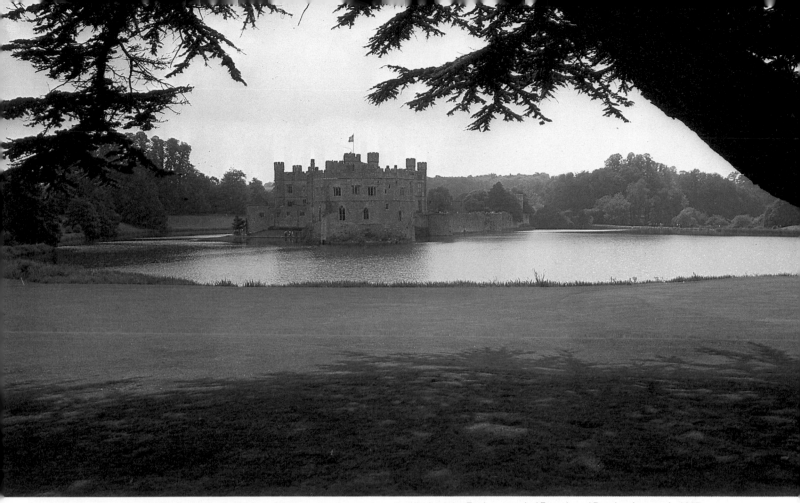

Leeds Castle, where Henry VIII's first wife, Catherine of Aragon, lived, and where the diarist John Evelyn guarded French and Dutch prisoners in 1665

bailey, established by William the Conqueror's half-brother, Robert of Mortain, when he became Earl of Cornwall shortly after 1066. Richard, a subsequent Earl of Cornwall, is thought to have built the present structure between 1227 and 1272.

Although the castle fell into disrepair after the Civil War one tower was kept in use as a prison. It was, it appears, an evil, filthy place and its most famous inmate, George Fox, the Quaker leader, was unfortunate enough to be incarcerated there for eight months during 1656, on a charge of distributing 'subversive' literature. Public executions were carried out below the castle walls until 1821.

See AM info. Also open Sun am Apr to Sep. Parking available.

Lavenham

Suffolk *p213 D4*

The attractive little town of Lavenham is probably one of the most photographed in England. It is noted for its ornate timbered houses, some of which date back to the fifteenth century when the town was an active centre of the Suffolk wool trade. Lavenham blue cloth became famous and a

certain sort of horse blanket is still called a Lavenham rug, but the trade declined during the period when the more notable worsted industry sprang up in neighbouring Norfolk. The Angel Hotel, containing fourteenth-century wall paintings, and the Swan Hotel, which incorporates the old Wool Hall, have survived from this period and a number of ancient weavers' and merchants' houses are to be found near Church Street.

The Church of SS Peter and Paul, with its 141-foot square-buttressed tower, stands at the top of the High Street. It is considered to be one of the finest in the county, with a spacious nave containing some early Flemish carving, notably that adorning the tomb of Thomas Spring who, together with the 14th Earl of Oxford, contributed to the building costs of the church. The church bells are another well-known feature, and the tenor bell, made in 1625 by Miles Graye of Colchester, is famous for its almost perfect tone.

The half-timbered Guildhall, built in 1529, was originally the headquarters of the Guild of Corpus Christi which was responsible for the local cloth trade, and a full length figure of the 15th

Lord de Vere, founder of the Guild, is set into one of its corner posts. The Guildhall has since, in turn, been used as an almshouse, a workhouse and a prison and Dr Rowland Taylor, Archbishop Cranmer's chaplain, was held captive there in 1555 before he died at the stake. Inside are exhibits relating to the history of Lavenham and the local wool trade.

Little Hall (fifteenth century) is the only furnished house open to the public in Lavenham and contains the Gayer-Anderson collection of antique furniture, pictures and books.

Guildhall open Mar to Nov daily (closed Fri in Mar and Nov). NT.
Little Hall open Easter to mid Oct Sat, Sun and Bank Holidays, pm only.

Leeds Castle

Kent *p213 D2*

Two islands in a lake formed by the river Len provide a picturesque setting for Leeds Castle. It was named after Led, the chief minister of Ethelbert IV, King of Kent, who inhabited the area during the ninth century, given to the Crèvecoeur family by William the Conqueror, and rebuilt by them in stone in 1119 to form an

unassailable fortress. The castle reverted to the Crown in the late thirteenth century and earned the name Lady's Castle, following its occupation by a number of Queens of England. Eleanor of Castille and Margaret, the first and second wives of Edward I, Philippa of Hainault, queen of Edward III and Catherine of Valois, wife of Henry V, were some of its well-known occupants. In 1926 Leeds Castle was acquired by the Hon. Olive, Lady Baillie, who, until her death in 1974, was responsible for a great deal of renovation. She finally bequeathed the castle to the Leeds Castle Foundation, a charitable trust concerned with the furtherance of medical research.

Features within the castle of particular interest include the twelfth-century Norman cellar, Impressionist paintings and house-keeping records for the year 1422 – kept by Joan of Navarre (second wife of Henry IV), the King's private chapel and Henry VIII's banqueting hall. The surrounding parkland contains rare swans, geese and ducks, aviaries and a golf course.

Open Apr to Oct Tue, Wed, Thu, Sun and Bank Holidays (daily throughout Aug), pm only. Parking and refreshments available.

Leicester

Leicestershire *p213 A5*

The railway of 1832 linked Leicester to the coalfields, thus transforming an ancient, compact, county town into a sprawling industrial city.

Early remains include an impressive memorial to Roman times – Jewry Wall, believed to date from AD 130. It once formed part of a complex which included a public bath and shops. The Jewry Wall Museum contains finds from the excavation carried out here as well as other items ranging from the prehistoric period to 1500.

Little remains of the Norman castle with the exception of the motte and great hall; the latter is preserved behind a façade built in 1695 and is now used as a law court.

There are many fascinating museums in Leicester. Near the old castle is Newarke Houses Museum, which contains a social history of the county from 1500 to the present day. The fifteenth century Magazine gateway close by houses the Museum of the Royal Leicestershire Regiment and displayed here is a collection of mementoes, battle trophies and other relics.

Three other museums in the town are of special interest. In the museum of Technology in Corporation Road giant beam engines can be seen, whereas in contrast, the Wygston's House Museum offers English costume ranging from 1769 to 1924 shown in a late medieval building with some later additions. The Leicestershire Museum and Art Gallery in New Walk, with its display of eighteenth to twentieth-century English paintings and drawings, also houses a unique collection of German Expressionist paintings and exhibitions of ceramics, natural history and Egyptology.

Ecclesiastical buildings of special interest include the beautiful church of St Mary de Castro, which is of Norman origin but was enlarged in the thirteenth century. Of particular note here are the five sedilia, or priests' seats. St Martin's Cathedral, a thirteenth to fifteenth-century church became a cathedral in 1926. The splendid bishop's throne reaches almost to the roof in diminishing tiers adorned with tracery.

On the south-eastern outskirts of the city are the University Botanic Gardens, which include amidst their sixteen acres rock gardens, rose beds and a herb garden.

Jewry Wall Museum and Site open all year (except Good Fri and Christmas) daily, Sun pm only.
Newarke Houses Museum open as above.
Museum of the Royal Leicestershire Regiment open as above.

Leighton Hall

Lancashire *p216 E5*

In 1822 Leighton Hall was acquired by Richard Gillow of the famous furniture-making family, whose descendants still own it today. It is a fine example of a neo-Gothic mansion with an elegant staircase, a series of family portraits and wood panelling. However, the feature which distinguishes Leighton Hall from many other houses is the superb collection of Gillow furniture. Unusual pieces include the altar in the private chapel, a games table and a unique cabinet decorated with religious panels and Italian ivory statuettes.

Many birds of prey are kept and flown in the grounds when the weather is suitable.

Open May to Sep Tue to Fri and Sun pm. Grounds and bird displays only Tue and Fri pm. Parking and refreshments available.

Lelant Model Village

Cornwall *p211 A1*

South of the charming village of Lelant, situated on the estuary of the river Hayle, is this interesting model village. Standing in landscaped grounds are scale models of historic Cornish buildings and a museum displaying various crafts from the county's colourful history; special attention is given here to smuggling, shipwrecks and tin-mining. Other features within the grounds include water gardens and a junior assault course. An art gallery exhibits paintings by local artists, which are for sale.

Open Easter to Oct daily. Parking available.

Levens Hall

Cumbria *p216 E5*

This fine Elizabethan mansion was developed from a thirteenth-century pele tower – a border defence tower. Much of its character today can be attributed to James Bellingham who bought the Hall in 1580 and had it decorated with richly carved panels and superb moulded plaster ceilings. A substantial part of the furniture also dates from this time and there are some interesting family relics including a pair of the earliest English-made pistols in existence.

Levens Hall Gardens are famous in their own right for their wealth of topiary work and they remain very much as they were laid out in 1692. The former brewhouse now houses a unique steam collection and on certain days traction engines can be seen working. There is also a plant centre and a gift shop here.

Open Apr to Sep Tue to Thu, Sun and Bank Holiday Mon, pm only. Garden and plant centre open daily. Parking and refreshments available.

stands in the market square. Here, too, is a statue of Johnson's friend and biographer, James Boswell. Dr Johnson is buried in Westminster Abbey but there is a bust of him in the south transept of Lichfield Cathedral.

Johnson Birthplace Museum open all year (except Public and Bank Holidays, other than Late Summer Holiday) Mon to Sat, also Sun pm May to Sep.

Lilford Park

Northamptonshire *p213 B5*

Deer herds roam freely over the 220 acres of parkland which surrounds a magnificent Jacobean Hall. Although the Hall is not open to the public, the grounds are and hold many attractions for the visitor.

At the end of the last century the Hall was the home of the 4th Baron Lilford, who created the great aviaries and gardens out of his love for birds. Now the aviaries have been rebuilt and stocked with hundreds of birds, including the Lilford crane and the Little owl – a native of Europe

A magnificent display of daffodils offsets the grandeur of Lilford Park

which was first established in Britain through birds released from here.

The park also contains a flamingo pool, a children's farm, an adventure playground, ponies for riding and pleasant riverside walks with picnic spots along the banks of the Nene.

In the stable block and old coaching house is a museum, crafts and antiques centre, and other facilities include a gift shop and log cabin cafeteria.

Open Easter to Oct daily. Refreshments available.

The yew topiary at Levens Hall is a survivor of the formal gardens so popular before the 18th century

Lichfield

Staffordshire *p216 F2*

The city's beautiful red sandstone cathedral dates from about 1200 to 1340 and is dedicated to St Mary and St Chad. It has the distinction of being the only English cathedral with three tall spires, and, known as the Ladies of the Vale, they are a beloved local landmark. One hundred and thirteen statues grace the grand west front, although only five of them are the originals.

Inside, just before the Lady Chapel, is a sculpture by Chantrey known as the *Sleeping Children*, a memorial to children of the cathedral cleric who perished in a fire in 1812. The Lady Chapel itself contains a lovely sixteenth-century stained glass window. The St Chad Gospels (seventh-century manuscripts) are the cathedral's most treasured possessions.

An old house in the cobbled market square of Lichfield is the birthplace of one of the town's most notable characters, Dr Samuel Johnson, man of wisdom and wit, and compiler of the first Dictionary of the English Language in 1755. The house is now a museum dedicated to Johnson's life and works, and a statue of him

The three spires of Lichfield Cathedral, the tallest almost 260-feet-high, can be seen from every approach

Lincoln Lincolnshire *p217 C2*

The three majestic towers of Lincoln's cathedral dominate the sky line of this ancient city and rise as a spectacular landmark above the Lincolnshire plain. Narrow cobbled streets wind down through quaint old buildings and antique shops, to the banks of the Witham.

The Romans called the town *Lindum Colonia*, used it as the centre of their control over east England, and turned it into one of the finest towns in Britain. They built colonnaded streets and a stone built sewerage system unique in Britain. They encouraged agriculture by draining fenland and boosted trading opportunities by digging the Fossdyke canal, which links the rivers Witham and Trent.

During the Middle Ages Lincoln prospered on the wool trade, as the city had a right to tax the wool merchants. However, after the fourteenth century when the wool trade began to decline, the city's fortunes fell with it and it was not until the mid nineteenth century with the advent of the Industrial Revolution, that Lincoln's second boom period began.

Lincoln has many ancient buildings of interest. On Steep Hill stands the oldest domestic building still in use in Britain, the twelfth-century house known as Aaron the Jew's House, named after a well-known money lender of that period. Close by is the Jew's House, built about 1170; it is a fine Norman house notable for its superb decorated doorway and chimney.

Leading off The Strait is an attractive timbered black and white building called The Cardinal's Hat, probably named in honour of Cardinal Wolsey, who was Bishop of Lincoln in 1514.

Newport Arch spans the ancient Roman road – Ermine Way, and is unique in being the only Roman gateway still used by traffic. The remains of another Roman gate, the east gate, are visible in the forecourt of the Eastgate Hotel. Here is the massive north tower, once part of a double carriageway gate, built in the third century AD. Further relics of a Roman past are indicated

A survivor of the Roman wall, Newport Arch, is still used by traffic

by inscriptions in the roadway at Bailgate, which mark the positions of the columns of a façade 275 feet long. This was cut by the road linking the east and west Roman gates.

The Cathedral

Completed in 1092 by the Normans, a fire destroyed the roof in 1141, and in 1185 an earth tremor brought down the main structure.

Bishop Hugh began the rebuilding in 1192, building five chapels behind the high altar and worked his way towards the west front which had survived. When the nave was completed and joined to the Norman front, the alignment of the vault wasn't accurate, and the irregularity can be seen to this day. The five chapels were later demolished to make way for the beautiful Angel Choir and to create a setting for the shrine of St Hugh.

The present cathedral tower was completed in 1310. It was originally crowned with a wooden spire which reached 540 feet above ground level, but this fell during a storm in 1547.

Notable are the two Eyes (windows) of the cathedral. Dean's Eye at the north end of the transepts dates from 1225, and contains vividly coloured glass. Bishop's Eye at the south end is fourteenth century and is filled with a mosaic of eighteenth-century glass fragments.

The arcading was designed by Christopher Wren, and above it is Wren's library, containing first editions of *Paradise Lost* and *Don Quixote*.

The Castle

This castle featured in the struggle between King John and his barons, and the cathedral holds one of the four original copies of the Magna Carta. It was stormed for the last of many times in 1644 during the Civil War, when the Royalists surrendered to the Roundheads.

The building encloses about six acres of lawn and trees with a wall up to ten feet thick and double that in height. There are two artificial mounds within the grounds, on top of one is the Observatory Tower, on the other Lucy Tower, which formed the main stronghold of the castle. At the northeast corner is Cobb Hall, added in the fourteenth century as a prison cell. Its roof remained a place of public execution until 1868.

Greyfriars and City Museum

Originally a two-storey church of the thirteenth century, and made a free school in 1574, this oldest surviving church of the Franciscan order is now a fascinating museum of local antiquities and natural history. Special exhibits include a prehistoric boat found buried near the Witham, and a huge punt gun used by wild fowlers on the fens.

The Museum of Lincolnshire Life

Here the visitor obtains an insight into the county's social and industrial history from Elizabethan times to the present day. The exhibits also include the traditional devices of poachers.

The Usher Gallery

The gallery contains a remarkable collection of antique watches, glass, ceramics, exquisite miniatures and over fifty paintings by Peter de Wint, the artist who was born in Staffordshire and worked in Lincoln.

Stonebow and Guildhall

The Stonebow is a 500-year-old Tudor Gothic gateway, above which stands St Marys Guildhall, popularly known as John of Gaunt's Stables. Built about 1180, it was the meeting place of medieval social and religious guilds.

In one of the rooms some of the city's treasures are kept, including a sword probably presented by Richard III, and another given by Henry VII. Also here are the Mayor's Mace and other trappings of state. The City Council still meets in the hall and are summoned as they have been for centuries by the Mote Bell, cast in 1371.

Castle open all year (except Christmas) daily, Sun pm only. Closed Sun Nov to Mar. Parking available.

Greyfriars City and County Museum open all year (except Good Fri and Christmas) daily, Sun pm only.

Museum of Lincolnshire Life open Feb to Nov daily. Sun pm only. Parking available.

Usher Gallery open all year (except Good Fri and Christmas) daily, Sun pm only. Parking available.

Stonebow and Guildhall open all year, first Sat in each month, other times by arrangement with the Publicity Officer of Lincoln.

Right: a view of Lincoln Cathedral. The building before the west front is the ancient Exchequer Gate

Below: One of the many cobbled streets which are fascinating to explore in this ancient city

Little Moreton Hall, 400 years old, retains its original furnishings

Littlecote House

Wiltshire *p213 A3*

Flowing through the lovely gardens and parkland of Littlecote House is the river Kennet, and in the spring and summer the rich water meadows are alive with the blooms of wild flowers and the voices of birds.

Henry VIII is thought to have courted Jane Seymour at Littlecote, a legend substantiated by their initials entwined in a stained glass window of the Tudor great hall. Another legend concerns the ghost of a lady-in-waiting. She bore a child of the master of the house, Wild Darrell, who promptly threw it on the fire. Her spirit is said to walk still, looking for her child.

The house is a building of enormous size, and it was Wild Darrell who built the magnificent long gallery, 110 feet long, hung with buff coats, arms and armour which belonged to a garrison of soldiers who stayed here during the Civil War.

The chapel is distinctly Puritan, reflecting the beliefs of the Pophams, who succeeded Darrell, and is the only one of its kind to survive intact.

The house of mellow stone and flint lies in woodland, and in the grounds excavations have uncovered the remains of a Roman villa and a large mosaic which was lifted in 1978 and is now a permanent display.

Part of the grounds are incongruously given over to a simulation of America's wild west. It is easy to forget surrounding Wiltshire here with the live shows, replica buildings and western museum.

Open Apr to Sep, Sat, Sun and Bank Holidays pm only. Refreshments available.

Little Moreton Hall

Cheshire *p216 E3*

This black and white timbered building is probably one of the best known of its kind. Little Moreton Hall, or Moreton Old Hall as it is sometimes known, rises majestically above the surrounding countryside, its slightly leaning gabled walls casting a picturesque reflection in the waters of the moat which surrounds it. The house is reached by an arched stone bridge and a timbered gatehouse guards the entrance to a cobbled courtyard. From the quadrangle there are lovely views down to the immaculately kept gardens and a small grassy hill upon which a watch tower once stood.

The Hall was originally built by William Morton the elder in the early fifteenth century, roughly in the shape of a capital H with the great hall as its central feature. His son added the gatehouse a few years later and in turn his son John was responsible for the magnificent Elizabethan long gallery, which is probably the most impressive part of the building. The gallery measures sixty-eight feet by twelve feet, and particularly fine are its huge fireplaces, oak beamed roof and leaded windows. Another special feature of the interior is the enormous kitchen with its open range and collection of pewter utensils.

Open Mar to Oct. Mar, Sat, Sun pm only, Apr to Oct daily, (except Tue) pm only. NT.

Llanberis

Gwynedd *p216 C3*

Llanberis, a little grey town in the shadow of Snowdon, attracts thousands of visitors each year who come to explore this popular mountain area. Just outside the town stand the ruins of Dolbadarn Castle which once commanded the valley. It is thought to have been built by Llewelyn the Great, but fell into disrepair after Edward I established his supremacy in Wales.

More recent history has left a greater mark on Llanberis, for this was one of the major slate-producing areas in North Wales. The Vivian Quarry Trail follows the footsteps of the quarrymen, including the splitting and dressing sheds and blast shelters. The North Wales Quarrying Museum goes one step further and here, in the former central workshops, much of the original machinery is preserved. There is also the fifty-four-foot diameter waterwheel which at one time supplied most of the power needed for the workshops. The cinema/gallery provides a film and photographic illustration of the quarrying industry and many aspects of the social history of the nineteenth-century workers.

Llanberis is also the terminus for two of the famous railways of North Wales. Undoubtedly the best known is the Snowdon Mountain Railway, established in 1896 specifically for the purpose of carrying tourists to the top of Snowdon. It is the only rack and pinion steam railway in Britain and Swiss locomotives provide the power for the easiest, if not the cheapest, way to the summit. In contrast the Llanberis Lake Railway follows the valley along the north bank of Llyn Padarn, using the old Dinorwic Quarries to Port Dinorwic line.

Dolbadarn Castle See AM info. Also open Sun from mid morning July to Sep. Parking available.
North Wales Quarrying Museum open daily Easter to Sep (except May Day). AM.
Snowdon Mountain Railway operates from early Apr to early Oct daily. Parking and refreshments available.
Lake Railway operates from Easter to Sep, trains run frequently. Parking and refreshments available.

Llandaff Cathedral

South Glamorgan *p212 D4*

During the latter half of the eighteenth century Cardiff began expanding, gradually incorporating a whole series of communities within its boundaries. One such community was the tiny cathedral city of Llandaff which became a part of Cardiff in 1922.

Tightly grouped around its ancient cathedral and lying some two-and-a-half miles from the city centre, Llandaff has nevertheless retained the air of a separate community. Bounded by the river Taff and busy main roads, the cathedral occupies the site of an earlier sixth-century church founded by St Teilo. The present cathedral was began in the twelfth century on the instructions of Urban, the first Norman Bishop of Llandaff, and continued down the centuries. At various times over the years the cathedral has suffered from periods of abuse and neglect, from storm damage and from devastation by a German landmine in 1941. Its history has been chequered with misfortune to such an extent that its survival is surprising. An impressive feature of Llandaff Cathedral is the sculpture by Sir Jacob Epstein, *Christ in Majesty*, which dominates the interior. Cast in aluminium, the inspiring figure soars above the nave. Outside the cathedral, to the south-west of the presbytery aisle, stands a tenth-century Celtic cross discovered in 1870. Also to be seen in the cathedral grounds are the remains of a thirteenth-century bell-tower and the ruins of the former bishop's palace. Sacked by Owain Glyndwr in 1402, the ground within the palace ruin has been developed into a public garden.

Llandudno

Gwynedd *p216 C3*

In the mid-nineteenth century Llandudno developed from a cluster of mining and fishermen's cottages to a Victorian seaside resort. The town was the brainchild of Liverpool surveyor Owen Williams, who planned the great sweep of its promenade and its majestically wide streets.

This classic little resort lies on a curving bay, flanked to the west by the massive limestone headland of the Great Orme and on the other side by the smaller headland of Little Orme. The Great Orme towers some 679 feet above sea level, dominating the town and separating its two superb beaches. The summit of this massive headland offers panoramic views and can be reached in a variety of ways; either by Edwardian tramway; a funicular or cable railway almost a mile in length; by modern cabin lift; by foot or by road. A toll road called Marine Drive encircles the Great Orme.

Set on the Orme's northern slopes overlooking the sea is the ancient church of St Tudno, from which the town derives its name. The church dates back to the twelfth century, but it is thought that St Tudno began a Christian Mission here back in the sixth century. Features of interest in the church are the stigmata in the roof above the altar representing the five wounds of Christ, together with the font dating from the Middle Ages.

Just above the town on the lower slopes of the Orme are the Happy Valley Rock Gardens containing rare plants, shrubs and trees interlaced with footpaths overlooking the sea. Nearby Haufe Gardens also overlook the town from the Orme's lower slopes and provide sweeping views over Conwy Bay and Estuary from its terraced gardens.

Tucked away in the town is the Dolls Museum and Model Railway which exhibits a delightful collection of over 1,000 dolls, depicting the different eras and fashions of yesteryear. There is also a collection of prams, cradles and toys together with intriguing lace, chain items and bead purses. Contained in the same building is a large model railway and displays of old tin plate. Also of interest is the town's other museum, the Rapallo House Museum and Art Gallery, which is situated at Craig-y-Don. Standing among ornamental gardens, the museum contains a traditional Welsh kitchen, Roman relics, armour and weapons, porcelain, together with its art collection and sculpture.

There is a memorial stone of the white rabbit from *Alice in Wonderland* consulting his watch on the west promenade, because Lewis Carroll decided to write his famous story whilst holidaying in Llandudno.

Cabin Lift operates from Happy Valley to Great Orme summit.
Great Orme Tramway operates from Victoria Station, Church Walks in the town to Great Orme summit. Continuous daily service throughout summer season.
Dolls Museum and Model Railway open Easter to Sep daily, Sun pm only.
Rapallo House Museum and Art Gallery open May to Aug Mon to Fri.

Llywernog Silver-Lead Mine

Dyfed *p216 C1*

It is about 200 years since the first prospectors began to dig in these Welsh hills for ore, but the real boom occurred during the 1870s and that era that is now being re-created at Llywernog. A Miners' Trail has been laid out around the seven-acre site with information plaques near the main features. Although most of the tunnels are still flooded or clogged with rubbish, one underground section, Balcombes Level, can be visited as part of the trail. However the roof is very low, the floor uneven and the tunnel narrow, so only the sure-footed should attempt this section. The rest of the trail is above ground and includes several waterwheels, winding gear, the main engine shaft and head-frame and gunpowder magazine. The Crusher House contains the last of the Cornish roll-crushers in Wales and in the Jigger Shed is a triple-compartment jig, powered by a fourteen-foot diameter water wheel.

The main building on the site is the nineteenth-century Count House which contained the office, workshops for carpenters and blacksmiths, stores and secondary power supplies. The building has been restored as a museum and includes reconstructions of underground scenes, a working smithy and, upstairs, the California of Wales Exhibition which illustrates all types of metal mining in Wales.

Open Easter to Sep daily. Parking and refreshments available.

Loch Lomond

Strathclyde *p220 C4*

This Queen of Scottish Lakes is in fact the largest lake in Great Britain. It stretches for twenty-four miles, its width varying between three-quarters of a mile and five miles. Of its thirty islands, the most significant are Inchmurrin with its ruins of Lennox Castle and Inchcaillach where a former nunnery stands in ruins near the burial place of the MacGregor clan.

Gentle slopes in the south give way to more dramatic mountain scenery further north. Amongst this is Ben Lomond, which can be climbed from Rowardennan, a long rather than a difficult climb, but well rewarded by the superb views from its summit. A pleasant way to view the loch is by taking one of the popular steamer trips from Balloch. Places of interest around the shores include Cameron House.

On the west side of the loch, just south of the picturesque village of Luss, is Rossdhu House, occupying a promontory jutting out into the loch. The Colquhouns' family seat has been here for many centuries but the present mansion dates from the eighteenth century. An unusual feature here is the boxing room, which contains a collection of china figures and prints relating to famous boxers. Around the house are attractive lakeside walks, a picnic area and a bathing beach.

Rossdhu House open Easter, then May to mid Oct daily. Parking and refreshments available.

Tarset Pier on Loch Lomond. The loch is one of three famous for the rare powan, or freshwater herring

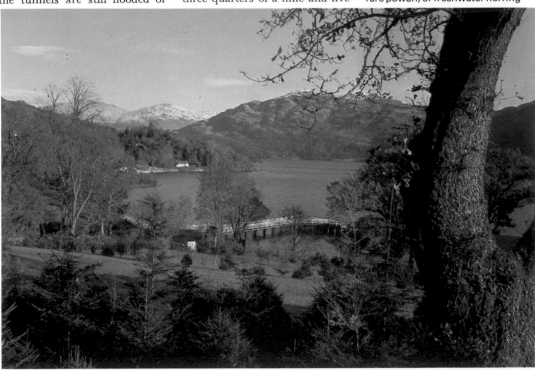

London

No other area of Britain is as rich in history, traditions, and cultural associations as London. Throughout the capital there are great mansions, venerable old buildings, quaint houses, unrivalled collections of art treasures, tremendous sweeps of glorious parkland, and colourful ceremonies to suit every possible taste and mood.

The palace of Hampton Court stands majestically on the river Thames

British Museum

The collection which began one of the world's largest and most varied treasure house was founded in 1753 and, since then, has grown to include every conceivable kind of artefact from all over the world.

Exhibits not to be missed include the superb Elgin Marbles from Athens, the mummies and sculpture in the Egyptian Galleries, two of the four existing original copies of the Magna Carta, and the beautiful seventh-century Sutton Hoo Treasure from a ship burial discovered in Suffolk.

Open all year daily (except Christmas, New Year's Day, Good Fri and May Day Holiday), Sun pm only. Refreshments available.

Buckingham Palace

Originally built in 1703 for the Duke of Buckingham, this most famous of royal homes was purchased by George III in 1762. On her accession to the throne in 1837, Queen Victoria moved the Court here from the Palace of St James, and it has been the London home of the reigning monarch ever since.

The imposing east wing of the building, which faces down The Mall, was added in 1847, and the façade was redesigned in 1913. The Royal Standard flies above the building when the sovereign is in residence. At 11.30 am every day the ceremony of the Changing of the Guard takes place in the palace forecourt.

Although the palace is not open to the public, many of the art treasures belonging to the royal family can be seen in the Queen's Gallery, whose entrance is in Buckingham Gate. The Royal Mews, in Buckingham Palace Road, is also open to the public. It houses the state coaches and the beautiful horses which draw them.

Queen's Gallery open all year daily (except Mon) Sun pm only.
Royal Mews open Wed and Thu pm (except at certain times) and at other times as published.

Courtauld Institute Galleries

Most famous for its magnificent Impressionist and Post Impressionist paintings, this gallery also contains an excellent collection of Old Master drawings and Italian primitive paintings.

Open all year daily (except Christmas and most Bank Holidays), Sun pm only.

Greenwich

It is from the Thames that the splendid buildings of Greenwich are best appreciated. Nearest to the river, on the site of a palace that was used by successive

monarchs from the fifteenth to the seventeenth centuries, are the buildings of the Royal Naval College, which were mainly the work of Sir Christopher Wren. Beyond this complex is the National Maritime Museum, housed in the Queen's House and its wings. The Queen's House was begun by the architect Inigo Jones in 1618, and is the oldest example of an Italianate house in England. Exhibits in the museum include some of the best seascapes ever painted and many reminders of the great days of British seafaring. On the hill in the centre of Greenwich Park is the old Royal Observatory, now a museum. The park is a royal one and owes much of its elegant charm to the seventeenth-century landscape artist Le Notre. It has areas of wild as well as formal gardens, a great many mature trees, and excellent sporting facilities. Near the Thames are two further reminders of Britain's seafaring tradition – the lovely clipper ship *Cutty Sark*, and *Gypsy Moth IV*, in which Sir Francis Chichester sailed round the world.

Cutty Sark open daily (except Christmas and New Year's Day), Sun pm only.
Gipsy Moth IV open as above.
National Maritime Museum open as above.
Old Royal Observatory open all year daily (except Christmas, New Year's Day, Good Fri and May Day Holiday), Sun pm only.
Royal Naval College open all year daily (except Thu) pm only.

Hampton Court

The extensive grounds of Hampton Court Palace comprise one of London's royal parks. There are wide areas of grass crossed by avenues of stately trees and beautiful, varied formal gardens. In springtime the wilderness garden is a carpet of daffodils, and at all times of the year the herb garden, in the shadow of the tremendous palace buildings, exudes marvellous scents. Near to the famous maze is the rose garden, growing in what was once Henry VIII's tiltyard.

The palace itself is breathtaking both in its size and its beauty. It was built for Cardinal Wolsey during the early part of the sixteenth century, but he did not have long to enjoy it, for in 1529 he felt impelled to give it to Henry VIII for political reasons, and less than a year later was imprisoned for high treason.

Henry considerably enlarged the palace, and it became his favourite residence. No further extensive changes were made until the reign of William and Mary, who commissioned Sir Christopher Wren to rebuild it. In fact, he only rebuilt the eastern and southern parts of the palace, and the rest was left virtually untouched. Today the palace is a vast storehouse of treasures that range from domestic utensils to great works of art.

Open all year daily (Sun pm only Oct to Mar). Parking available. AM.

Hampstead

Hampstead owes much of its character to the Heath. An area of open grassland dotted with trees and interspersed with formal gardens, it covers nearly 800 acres. From Parliament Hill there are extensive views over the whole of the London basin. On the northern edge of the Heath is Ken Wood – the grounds of seventeenth-century Kenwood House. It was enlarged during the eighteenth century by Robert Adam and makes a magnificent setting for the Iveagh collection of Dutch and English paintings.

Hampstead, with its elegant old houses, historic inns, and literary associations, retains a village-like atmosphere that has been lost in

much of the rest of London. One of England's greatest poets, John Keats, lived at Wentworth Place, Keats Grove, for nearly two years, and it was here that he wrote his best poems. The house,

and the one next door – lived in by Keat's lover Fanny Brawne – are open to the public.

Kenwood House open all year daily (except Christmas and Good Fri). Parking and refreshments available.
Keats House open all year daily (except Christmas, New Year's Day, Easter and May Day Holiday) Sun pm only.

HMS *Belfast*

Moored just above Tower Bridge, this 11,000-ton cruiser was the largest ever built for the Royal Navy. She was built in 1939 and has functioned as a floating museum since 1971.

Open all year daily (except Christmas, New Year's Day. Good Fri and May Day Holiday). Refreshments available in summer.

Elegant 18th-century Kenwood House stands in its own grounds on the edge of Hampstead Heath

Houses of Parliament

Officially known as the New Palace of Westminster, this forest of towers, turrets and spires rising from a vast honeycomb of courts, corridors and chambers, stands on the site of a palace which was a royal residence from the time of Edward the Confessor until the reign of Henry VIII.

In 1834 the whole rambling complex was destroyed by fire. A competition was held at once for the design of a new Parliament building. It was won by Sir Charles Barry, whose designs, in an imposing Gothic style, were immeasurably improved by Augustus Pugin – an architectural genius then only twenty-three years old.

During World War II the House of Commons and adjacent chambers were destroyed by bombs, and were rebuilt in 1950 in an uninspired Gothic style.

Westminster Hall, incorporated in the western part of the complex, somehow escaped the fire of 1834, and has what is said to be the finest and earliest hammerbeam roof in Europe. The Hall was originally built by William Rufus, but was virtually rebuilt at the end of the fourteenth century by Richard II, from which time the roof dates. It has been the scene of many great moments in British history, including the forced abdication of Edward II in 1327, the deposition of Richard II himself in 1399, and the trial of Guy Fawkes in 1606.

At the northern end of the Houses of Parliament is the magnificent gilded Clock Tower universally known as Big Ben. In fact, the name Big Ben only belongs to the thirteen-and-a-half ton bell which strikes the hours.

The most important parts of the Houses of Parliament, including the Queen's Robing Room, House of Lords, Central Hall, and House of Commons, may be seen by the public on conducted tours. The public may also, on application, watch the proceedings in both Houses.

Palace of Westminster open Sat and Bank Holidays (except Christmas and New Year), also Mon, Tue and Thu in Aug and Thu in Sep (providing neither house is sitting).
Westminster Hall open Mon to Thu am only (providing neither House is sitting) Sat all day. Open Mon to Sat all day during Recess.

Imperial War Museum

This museum illustrates and records all aspects of the two world wars and other military operations involving Britain and the Commonwealth since 1914. Exhibits include tanks, aeroplanes, models of ships, and reconstructions of famous battles. The collection of paintings and drawings by official and unofficial war artists is unsurpassed in Europe.

Open all year daily (except Christmas, New Year's Day, Good Fri and May Day Holiday), Sun pm only. Refreshments available.

The Palm House in Kew contains a tropical world of exotic flora

Kew Gardens

The superb Royal Botanical Gardens at Kew were begun more than 200 years ago by Princess Augusta, George III's mother. From the small nine-acre garden she planted, the gardens have grown to be one of the largest and most extensive of their kind in the world. Every kind of plant, from tiny alpine flowers to huge trees and delicate exotics that will only thrive in the magnificent Palm House, is to be found here.

Kew even has a royal palace. It is a relatively modest seventeenth-century town house, but for George III it meant escape from the Court life which he so heartily detested. It is now open to the public and houses mementoes of the King and an excellent collection of furniture.

Kew Gardens open all year daily (except Christmas, New Year's Day and May Day Holiday).
Kew Palace open Apr to mid Oct daily. Parking available (AM)

Big Ben dominates the complex of buildings known as the Houses of Parliament

London Zoo

Opened to the public in 1847, London Zoo has established a reputation as one of the world's leading collections of animals. Over 6,000 species, ranging from tiny sea creatures to the largest land mammals, are kept in environments as natural to them as possible, yet giving the public the best possible chance of seeing them. Of special merit are the lion terraces, the elephant and rhino pavilion, the night-time world of the Charles Clore pavilion for small mammals, and the Snowdon aviary, where birds nest, feed and fly as they would in the wild.

Open all year daily (except Christmas Day). Parking and refreshments available.

Madame Tussaud's

One of London's most famous and lasting institutions, this collection of waxworks was opened in 1835. Exhibits include historical figures, politicians, entertainers, and in the Chamber of Horrors reconstructions of hideous crimes.

Open all year daily (except Christmas Day). Refreshments available.

Maritime Trusts Museum, Historic Ship Collection

Set in the elegant surroundings of the restored nineteenth-century St Katharine's Docks, this floating collection comprises a number of British sailing and steam-powered vessels.

Open all year daily. Parking available

The Museum of London

This museum, opened in 1976 in the ultra-modern Barbican complex, illustrates, by means of brilliantly-displayed exhibits, models, and audio-visual effects, London's continually evolving and fascinating story. The museum is arranged chronologically, and the exhibits include a relief model

Polar bears breed happily at London Zoo and the cubs are particularly popular

showing the archaeological levels of the Thames Valley, a reconstruction of the Great Fire – complete with realistically-crackling flames, and the lavishly decorated Lord Mayor's State Coach, which was made in 1757.

Open all year (except Mon and Christmas), Sun pm only. Refreshments available.

National Gallery

Housed in this handsome Classical-style building is one of the finest collections of paintings in the world. The works include examples from all the great European schools of art, including a choice selection of British masterpieces.

Open all year daily (except Christmas, New Year's Day, Good Fri and May Day Holiday), Sun pm only. Refreshments available.

National Portrait Gallery

The aim of this gallery is to illustrate British history by means of portraits, sculpture, engravings and photographs. It is almost incidental to the gallery's function that many of its works are masterpieces.

Open all year daily (except Christmas, New Year's Day, Good Fri and May Day Holiday), Sun pm only.

Natural History Museum

Dinosaurs, whales, fossils, insects, butterflies, mammals, and birds are all to be found in this museum. The creatures are so well displayed that they could well be alive. The Botanical Gallery on the second floor has beautifully-made dioramas illustrating many different types of habitat and landscape.

Open all year daily (except Christmas, New Year's Day, Good Fri and May Day Holiday), Sun pm only. Refreshments available.

The Planetarium

Spectacular representations of the heavens are projected on to the inside of the Planetarium's great copper dome and are accompanied by a commentary.

Open all year daily (except Christmas Day).

Richmond Park

This vast royal park, over 2,000 acres in extent, was enclosed by Charles I as part of a hunting estate and still has large herds of Red and Fallow deer. It has kept its feeling of wild countryside, but several gardens – notably the Isabella Plantation Woodlands and the grounds of Pembroke Lodge – have been laid out. Pen Ponds are popular with skaters in the winter and fishermen during the season.

Stretching across the bottom of the London pages is J C Visscher's *Long View of London*. This engraving, depicting London along the Thames from St Katharine's Docks to Westminster, dates from 1616

Wren's greatest achievement – St Paul's – took 35 years to complete

Royal Parks

Five of London's nine spectacular and unique royal parks are in the very heart of the capital and each has a special character of its own.

St James's is, in some respects, the most attractive of the parks; perhaps because so much is crammed into so comparatively small a space. It has a lake enlivened by water birds of all sorts, flower beds, many kinds of trees, and affords beautiful views of the towers and pinnacles of West-minster through the foliage.

Green Park is principally a place of stately avenues of trees among grass that is bestrewn with crocuses and daffodils in spring. Beyond Hyde Park Corner is Hyde Park itself. Its most outstanding feature is undoubtedly the Serpentine, but it is the feeling of great space and freedom which characterises it. Kensington Gardens are separated from Hyde Park only by a road, but the difference in character is marked. It is a more formal, more enclosed and gentle area than Hyde Park. It shares the Serpentine with Hyde Park, but here it is called the Long Water.

Regent's Park is set apart from the other four royal parks in central London. If Primrose Hill is included in its area, it is, at 670 acres, the largest of the central parks. It was originally a hunting ground (like the others) and was given its present appearance in the early nineteenth century by the great architect John Nash. At the heart of the park is Queen Mary's Garden, a lovely place of water, rock gardens, beautiful roses and overhanging trees. To the north is London Zoo, bounded on its far edge by the Regent's Canal.

St Paul's Cathedral

Sir Christopher Wren drew up plans for a new cathedral on this site almost before the ashes of the old cathedral (razed to the ground during the Great Fire of London in 1666) had grown cold. The building that rose from those ashes is Wren's masterpiece and has a dignity which the surrounding tower blocks cannot diminish.

It is crowned by a beautiful central dome, 365 feet above ground level at its highest point and 112 feet in diameter, which contains the famous Whispering Gallery. There are several hundred monuments in the cathedral, as well as the imposing tombs of such notables as the Duke of Wellington and Lord Nelson.

Science Museum

Of all London museums this is the one most loved by children and their fathers. There are knobs to press, handles to turn, and all kinds of functioning exhibits. The museum has a serious aspect in that it traces the application of science to technology and the development of engineering and industry from their beginnings to the present day.

Open all year daily (except Christmas, New Year's Day, Good Fri and May Day Holiday), Sun pm only. Refreshments available.

Tate Gallery

The Tate Gallery houses the national collection of British works from the sixteenth to the twentieth century, and also traces the development of British and foreign art from the mid 1800s to the present day. British artists represented include Hogarth, Blake, Turner, Constable, and the Pre-Raphaelites. All modern schools of painting and sculpture are superbly represented; and because the Tate buys works almost before they are finished it is often many years ahead of generally accepted tastes in art.

Open all year daily (except Christmas, New Year's Day, Good Fri and May Day Holiday), Sun pm only. Refreshments available.

Tower of London

William the Conqueror built the Tower of London as a reminder to the citizens of the City of his unassailable power. At the heart of the complex is the White Tower, or keep, looking much as it has done for the last 900 odd years. It is one of the earliest and largest buildings of its kind in Western Europe and contains the Chapel of St John, which displays Norman architecture at its simplest and most dramatic.

Over the centuries a powerful and complicated series of walls and towers were built up round the White Tower, gradually transforming the original Norman motte-and-bailey castle into the most important medieval fortification in Britain.

The Tower has been used as palace, treasure house, menagerie and – most famously – prison. Many of the prisoners entered the Tower through the infamous Traitors' Gate and eventually went to their deaths at the block on Tower Green.

The Crown Jewels – most of which were melted down during the Commonwealth and had to be remade for the coronation of Charles II – are displayed in vaults beneath the Waterloo Barracks and a wealth of armour and other military equipment in the White Tower, Waterloo Barracks, and the Tower's Museum.

The Tower is also famous for its Beefeaters, splendidly attired officers; and for its ravens, sinister black birds that strut over Tower Green – scene of many executions.

Open all year daily (except Christmas, New Year's Day and Good Fri) Sun pm only from Mar to Oct, closed Sun from Nov to Feb. Refreshments available.

Victoria and Albert Museum
Exhibits ranging from great works of art to items whose function is simply to entertain and amuse are displayed in this vast box of delights. Among the items on display in the museum's seven miles of galleries are paintings, sculpture, furniture, costumes, armour, locks, ceramics, and, of all things, a large wooden model of a tiger eating a British officer. It was made in the eighteenth century and emits sounds intended to imitate the soldier's groans of agony.

Open all year daily (except Fri, Christmas, New Year's Day, Good Fri and May Day Holiday) Sun pm only. Refreshments available.

Wallace Collection
Perhaps the most famous work of art contained in this elegant eighteenth-century town house is *The Laughing Cavalier* by Frans Hals, but it is also packed with a huge variety of other treasures. These include French paintings and furniture of the eighteenth century, works by Titian and Rubens, and objects ranging from the finest and most delicate porcelain to assorted bric-a-brac.

Open all year daily (except Christmas, New Year's Day, Good Fri and May Day Holiday) Sun pm only.

Westminster Abbey
Henry III began this magnificent abbey church in 1245 to replace a church which had been built during the reign of Edward the Confessor. After Edward's death in 1065, his successor, Harold, was crowned here, and every English sovereign since that time has been crowned in the abbey (with the exception of Edward V and Edward VIII, who were never crowned).

Henry III's church was completed in 1269, and from then until the reign of George III it was the burial place of all English kings and queens. During the late fourteenth and early fifteenth century the nave was rebuilt, but without altering Henry III's overall conception. Between 1503 and 1509 the Lady Chapel was replaced by the majestic Henry VII Chapel – perhaps the supreme example of Perpendicular architecture. The 225-foot-high towers at the abbey's west end were added in the mid eighteenth century by the architect Nicholas Hawksmoor.

The interior of the abbey is one of the finest achievements of English architecture, and over a thousand monuments

The shrine of St Edward the Confessor lies within Westminster Abbey

are crowded into the building; they not only commemorate prominent men and women from every walk of life, but also give a breathtaking view of English monumental sculpture. However, it is perhaps the simple grave of the Unknown Warrior near the west entrance which is the most poignant. His Tomb symbolizes the sacrifice of more than a million British who lost their lives in World War I.

Beneath the cloisters of the abbey there is an undercroft originally used by the monks of the abbey as a resting room, but now housing a museum. Among the many fascinating exhibits here are several wax funeral effigies which figured in the elaborate funerals of famous people buried in the abbey. The oldest is believed to be an actual death mask belonging to Edward II.

Longleat

Wiltshire *p212 F3*

The Marquess of Bath claims there is something for everyone at Longleat and there is certainly enough entertainment to choose from on his country estate.

Longleat House, still the family home, and one of the most famous stately homes in England, is a magnificent Elizabethan building set in sweeping parkland landscaped by Capability Brown. The interior is filled with treasures including tapestries, Spanish leather, Genoese velvet and paintings by famous artists including Titian, Reynolds and Lawrence. The magnificent Venetian ceilings and ornate Italian décor are the results of alterations carried out by Sir Jeffrey Wyatville during the last century. The state bedroom suite, last used by the Duke of Windsor, and the Victorian bathroom, are amongst smaller rooms on view. Many possessions of the household can be seen, including the family's state and garter robes, state coach, and a waistcoat worn by Charles I at his execution.

The fully equipped Victorian kitchens give a glimpse of what life was like 'below stairs'. The scullery is now a kitchen shop selling culinary goods and gifts.

Perhaps the most famous of the attractions at Longleat now is the extensive Safari Park, home of the Lions of Longleat. However, these are by no means the only exotic animals here, and visitors can observe at close range from the safety of their car Siberian tigers, elephants, rhinos, zebra, buffaloes and antelopes.

During the summer months, the Safari boat weighs anchor regularly, and one can cruise amongst wallowing hippos and frolicking sealions, and sail past the Ape Islands.

For the non-seafaring visitor there is a fifteen-inch gauge railway running alongside the lake.

Amusements for children include camel and donkey rides, nineteenth-century dolls houses, a pets' corner with a chimps' tea party, and Leisureland – an exciting adventure playground. The Garden Centre sells many plants actually grown at Longleat.

Open all year daily (except Christmas Day). Parking and refreshments available.

A view of 16th-century Longleat House through some of the more informal parkland on the estate

Melford Hall was sacked by Parliamentary forces during the Civil War

Long Melford

Suffolk *p213 D4*

One of the most outstanding small towns in Suffolk, Long Melford has a delightful main street, lined with fine old shops and houses. Dominating the street is the magnificent church of the Holy Trinity, a huge fifteenth-century building occupying the site of a Roman temple. Many windows illuminate the church, and beautifully worked pillars, columns and stained glass make the interior particularly striking.

At the upper end of the triangular Melford Green is Melford Hall. Completed in 1578, this turreted Tudor manor house was built in brick with attractive contrasting stone decorations. The rooms date from varying periods, and contain collections of fine furniture, porcelain and paintings.

To the north of the village is Kentwell Hall, a mellow Elizabethan manor surrounded by a moat and beautiful grounds. A 300-year-old avenue of lime trees forms a picturesque approach to the tranquil setting of the Hall. Restoration work is presently being carried out, and it is interesting to be able to watch work in progress.

Melford Hall open Apr to Sep Wed, Thu, Sun and Bank Holiday Mon pm. NT.
Kentwell Hall open Mar to Oct Sun, May to Sep also Wed and Thu mid July to late Sep also Fri and Sat. Also Easter week and Bank Holidays Sat to Mon pm. Parking and refreshments available.

Loseley House

Surrey *p213 B2*

An elegant Elizabethan mansion of Bargate stone, tall white windows and decorative chalk corner stones beneath right-angled gables, Loseley is the home of the descendants of Elizabethan statesman, Sir William More.

Elizabeth I and James I stayed here on more than one occasion, and further royal connections are suggested by the painted panels in the great hall, one of them bearing the initials of Henry VIII and Catherine Parr. The hall has a lofty, flat-beamed ceiling and the gallery is made up with various carvings and panelling said to have come from Henry VIII's Nonsuch Palace. Here also is a notable portrait of Edward VI.

The drawing room has a handsome plaster ceiling and an extraordinary chimneypiece, made from a single piece of chalk, and excellent Elizabethan carving is to be found in the library.

The beautiful parkland which surrounds the house can be viewed from the garden terrace and the moat walk. Delicious products of the dairy farm are on sale in the house shop.

Open June to Sep, Wed to Sat. Also Spring and late Summer Bank Holidays.

Lotherton Hall

North Yorkshire *p217 B3*

This early eighteenth-century house was the home of Sir Alvary and Lady Gascoigne. It now houses the admirable Gascoigne collection and English and oriental objets d'art. Of particular interest are the exquisitely decorated gold and silver pieces and the excellent costumes of the fashion display.

Among the collection of eighteenth and nineteenth-century furniture is an octagonal table beautifully inlaid with ivory, mother-of-pearl, various woods, copper and brass. A grand piano and dressing table housed here are also fine examples of the cabinet makers' skill.

Nearby is a small chapel notable for its beamed roof and richly carved pulpit.

Open all year (except Christmas and Mon). Parking and refreshments available.

Ludlow

Shropshire *p216 E1*

Ludlow, former capital of the Welsh Marches, stands on high ground overlooking the river Teme at its junction with the river Corve. Above the town rises the impressive red-stone ruin of Ludlow Castle and the 135-foot-high tower of the parish church of St Laurence.

Famous for its black and white buildings, Ludlow has a regular pattern of intersecting streets. Parts of the old town walls are still visible and Broad Gate, complete with its portcullis slits, is the only original town gate still surviving. Broad Street, considered one of the finest streets in England, has a mixture of Georgian houses and timber-framed buildings including the Angel Hotel, a splendid coaching inn. Other buildings of note include the sixteenth-century Feathers Hotel in the Bull Ring, the fine thirteenth-century Reader's House and the Hosyers Almshouses dating from the fifteenth century but rebuilt in 1758. The church of St Laurence has some very fine carving, including a famous series of misericords, and a fine fifteenth-century window. The ashes of A. E. Houseman, author of *A Shropshire Lad*, are buried in the churchyard.

The eighteenth-century Butter Cross houses the town museum in a room once used as a school. Displaying a fascinating collection of Ludlow's past, the exhibits include examples of arms and armour, geology and Georgian and Victorian domestic items.

Dating from the twelfth-century, Ludlow Castle was built by Roger de Lacey and formed part of a chain of castles erected along the border between England and Wales. During its troubled history it was a royal palace and residence of the President of the Council of the Marches. Although the castle is now in ruins, an unusual circular Norman chapel has survived.

Museum open Easter to Sep. Mon to Sat. Sun, June to Aug only.
Castle open all year daily.

Lullingstone Castle

Kent *p213 C3*

The large sixteenth-century gatehouse with its crenelated towers and parapet could aptly be described as a miniature

Ludlow stands in the boundary area of England and Wales known as the Marches

castle, whilst the castle itself is a large eighteenth-century mansion. The most decorative feature of the exterior is the entrance with its false pillars and open stonework parapet.

Worth noting inside is the panelling and carved balustrade of the staircase incorporating crests of the Hart family. Also of interest is the state drawing room with its plasterwork, barrel vaulted ceiling and portrait of Queen Anne who was a regular visitor here. The extensive grounds have sweeping lawns, shrubs, trees and a lake. About half-a-mile to the north are the remains of a Roman villa with a particularly fine tessellated pavement.

Castle open Apr to Sep Wed, Sat, Sun and Bank Holidays pm only. Parking available.
Villa see AM info. Also open Sun am Apr to Sep. Parking available.

Luton Hoo

Bedfordshire *p213 B4*

This palatial mansion on the southern outskirts of Luton was built in 1767 by Robert Adam, but has been considerably altered over the years. The most significant changes were made at the beginning of the twentieth century, when it was completely remodelled in the French style for Sir Julius Wernher, a South African diamond magnate. His architect, C. F. Mewes, created a perfect setting for Wernher's re-

markable collection of works of art and although a part of the house is now a private residence, the major part is laid out as a museum for the collection. Paintings include works by Rembrandt and Titian and the splendid *St Michael* by Bartolomé Bermejo (c 1480). There are also fine collections of English porcelain and china – with a few pieces from Dresden and China; ivories, metal-work and enamels and superb Fabergé jewels. In the Russian room are the Court Robes and personal mementoes of the Russian Imperial Family and in the dining room Beauvais tapestries are hung in specially designed marble wall insets. The house stands in the 1,500 acre park which was skilfully landscaped by Capability Brown.

Open Easter to Sep Mon, Wed, Thu and Sat, Sun pm only. Parking and refreshments available.

Lydford

Devon *p212 C2*

Lydford, a secluded moorland village, lies on the edge of Dartmoor, where the river Lyd has cut a deep wooded gorge into its valley. It was once an important town and the headquarters of the tin-miners who virtually ruled Dartmoor until the decline of the industry in the seventeenth century.

The village is dominated by the remains of its Norman castle,

which was built by the omnipotent tin-miners in 1195 as a prison to house offenders against its mining laws. The castle's lower floor was once the prison, whilst its upper floor was the Stannary Court. Lydford's role as a prison lasted for many centuries and was notorious for its rough and ready justice, where it is said men were tried after being hanged.

Lydford Gorge is one of Devon's outstanding beauty spots. This deep wooded ravine, about a mile in length, offers a dramatic and unforgettable walk beside the seething waters of the Lyd, with its boulders, dark pools, cascades and long rapids. On either side huge oaks almost roof the gorge and wild garlic, lichens, moss and ferns carpet its sides, flourishing in the humid atmosphere. At its southerly end the Lyd is joined by a tributary at the spectacular ninety-foot-high White Lady Waterfall. In the seventeenth century the gorge was inhabited reputedly by the fearsome family of highway robbers called the Gubbins. The gorge is best approached from the car park beside the bridge at the southern end of the village.

The village church is worth visiting too, just see its fine screen and carved bench-ends. In the churchyard is an epitaph to George Routleigh, the watchmaker.

Castle open at all reasonable times. Parking available. AM.
Gorge open Apr to Oct daily. NT.

Lyme Park

Cheshire *p216 F3*

Lyme Park was the home of the Legh family for 600 years until Richard Legh, 3rd Lord Newton, gave the estate to the National Trust. The house is a splendid example of Palladian architecture built around a central courtyard, and from the outside there is little evidence of the Elizabethan building upon which it was based. The notable exception is the huge Tudor gateway on the entrance front.

Contained within Leoni's enlargement of 1726 is the Tudor drawing room and the long gallery, stretching 120 feet, which has remained unchanged since 1541. The house contains a fine collection of pictures and furnishings and the state rooms are richly panelled with some superb wood carving and tapestries. In the parlour there are four interesting chairs made by Thomas Chippendale and upholstered with the cloth from the cloak worn by Charles I at his execution in 1649. The exterior of the house is imposing, particularly the south front with its huge Ionic portico which looks out across the lake. Surrounding the building is a 1,300-acre park, nine miles in circumference, which is home to a herd of Red deer.

House open Mar to Oct daily pm (except Mon but including Bank Holidays). Park and gardens open all year daily. Parking available. NT.

Lympne

Kent *p213 D2*

The Romans built a fort at Lympne as part of their coastline defence. At that time it was a coastal village, but the sea has since receded.

Built 300 yards from the ruins of the fort, known as Studfall Castle, is Lympne Castle, a fourteenth-century fortified manor house. Although greatly restored in 1905, it retains its Norman appearance. Romney Marsh, the Channel and the Military Canal – dug in fear of invasion from Napoleon – are overlooked by the castle.

Just west of the village is Port Lympne Wildlife Sanctuary and Gardens covering some 270 acres – several of the more exotic animals kept here include wolves, rhinos, African leopards, Siberian and Indian tigers, monkeys and bison.

Within the grounds is a Dutch-colonial-style mansion which is the work of the architect Sir Herbert Baker. Many of the original features still survive, including an hexagonal library where the Treaty of Paris was signed after World War I. The house is set in fifteen acres of elaborate terraced gardens, from where on clear days the French coast is visible.

Castle open Easter to Oct, Sun pm only. July to Sep daily. Parking available. Refreshments Bank Holidays only.
Port Lympne Wildlife Sanctuary and Gardens open all year daily (except Christmas Day). Parking and refreshments available.

Mapledurham

Oxfordshire *p213 A3*

This peaceful, unspoilt village beside the river Thames, backed by wooded hills, is noted for its old cottages and contains a particularly attractive row of early seventeenth-century alms-houses.

Mapledurham House stands majestically beside the river, and is probably the best known feature of the village. Built in pink brick by Sir Michael Blount during the sixteenth century, it is a fine example of Tudor architecture and is said to be the model for the home of Soames Forsyte, in John Galsworthy's novel *The Forsyte Saga*. An interesting feature of the house is the small chapel which, when built in 1789 during a period of strong anti-Catholic feeling, was required by law to have an exterior which could not be easily recognised as an ecclesiastical building.

Mapledurham's other main historic building, also dating from the Tudor period, stands on the river near the weir. The watermill is the last working corn and grist mill on the Thames. One of its two great waterwheels was replaced by a water-driven turbine in 1926 but the other is still in operation and has been restored and still grinds wholemeal flour which may be purchased.

The village church, dating from

the late fourteenth century, has a fine oak-timbered arcaded ceiling and contains memorials to local families, including the Blounts, and the south aisle is still walled off as a Roman Catholic chapel where many of the Blounts are buried.

Mapledurham House open Apr to Sep Sat, Sun and Bank Holidays, pm only.
Mapledurham Watermill open Apr to Sep (except Mon and Fri, but open Bank Holidays) pm only.

Margam Country Park

West Glamorgan *p212 D4*

Margam Park is a delightful place in which to wander – whether over open parkland, through woods, beside quiet lakes or around the orangery, abbey, castle and gardens.

The ruins of the chapter house and abbey church are all that are left of what was once the largest Cistercian abbey in Wales. Close-by is the orangery, reputed to be the largest in Britain. It was built of local stone to house orange and other citrus trees (highly prized in the eighteenth century) with tall, elegant windows and a parapet adorned with numerous stone urns, paralleled by a balustrade of open stonework. In the surrounding gardens many rare and

unusual trees and shrubs flourish.

Margam Castle, now an empty shell, was built in the nineteenth-century, and is a fanciful compilation of turrets, mock battlements, Gothic doorways and windows. In complete contrast, overlooking the castle, is a hill-fort called Mynydd-y-Castell, built by Iron Age people over 2,000 years ago.

The castle park is a haven for wildlife. Wild flowers flourish, and the woods and water attract all manner of birds and beasts, from buzzards to dragonflies. One of the greatest attractions is the herd of Fallow deer, established since the fifteenth century and a delight to watch grazing among the trees.

There are facilities for boating and putting, children's donkey and pony rides, an adventure playground and marked walks. Gymkhanas, horse trials, pony and carriage events, band concerts and archery competitions take place throughout the year.

Open Apr to Oct Tue to Sun, Nov to Mar Wed to Sun. Parking and refreshments available.

Marwell Zoo

Hampshire *p213 A2*

Opened in 1972, Marwell quickly became established as one of Britain's major wild animal collec-

The Living of Mapledurham Church was much sought after, and is now in the possession of Eton College

The splendid library of Mellerstain House – little altered in 200 years

tions and now specialises in conservation and breeding. Over 1,000 animals of a hundred or so species are kept in spacious enclosures which once formed part of the park surrounding Marwell Hall (not open). The many varieties of big cats here include Asian lions, and a magnificent pair of Siberian tigers. There are also camels, giraffes, monkeys, cattle, Przewalski wild horses and several species of deer.

For younger visitors, there is a delightful children's zoo and a playground. The gently sloping site of the park has good walking surfaces, for those who do not wish to drive, and there are pleasant picnic areas around the perimeter.

Open all year daily. Parking and refreshments available.

Melbourne

Derbyshire *p217 B1*

This pretty village gave its name to Lord Melbourne – nineteenth-century statesman and first prime minister to Queen Victoria – and through him to Australia's city.

Lord Melbourne's home was Melbourne Hall, a charming stone mansion, now owned by the

Marquess of Lothian and filled with superb family portraits.

The formal gardens are probably more famous than the house itself. Landscaped by Henry Wise, they form a delightful mosaic of well-cut lawns, terraces and tree-lined avenues scattered with elegant fountains and statues of lead cupids and embracing cherubs. One of the most attractive features of the gardens

is the delicate wrought iron 'birdcage' summer-house by Robert Bakewell, the great Derby ironsmith. Another feature to look out for is the hundred-yard tunnel of yew.

Hall open Apr to Sep Wed, Thu and Sun pm only. July and Aug open daily except Mon and Fri. Parking and refreshments available.

Mellerstain House

Borders *p220 E3*

Robert Adam designed this great Georgian house of honey-coloured stone. When he began his work in 1770 there were already two lower wings built by his father, but the mansion which was to join them was never begun. The result is rather forbidding and rigid, very square and built in an E-shape with a castellated roof line.

However, it is interior decoration for which Adam is most famous, and here he excelled himself. Little has been altered, and the

ceilings, friezes and fireplaces are just as Adam designed them. A particularly fine room is the library. It has a fireplace of green and white marble, white carved wood bookcases, and the white plaster relief of the ceiling stands out against pale green and pink, with medallions in slate grey.

Among the treasures within the house are a Van Dyck portrait, an early painting by Gainsborough, and other paintings by Ramsay, Van Goyen and Constable. They are all hung in Adam's immaculate rooms which are furnished with fine eighteenth-century pieces, and separated by beautifully finished mahogany doors.

The garden terraces were created in 1909 by Blomfield, and look out across the sweeping lawn which slopes to a distant lake fed by Eden Water, with the distant Cheviot Hills as an attractive backdrop.

Open Easter then May to Sep daily (except Sat), pm only. Parking and refreshments available.

Melbourne Hall was rebuilt from ruins of Melbourne Church in the 17th century

Melrose

Borders *p220 E3*

This small, quiet town is best known for what must be the most famous abbey ruins in Scotland, Melrose Abbey – owing much of its fame to the glamour given it by the romantic writings of Sir Walter Scott. Its position on one of the main routes into Scotland meant that during the Wars of Scottish Independence, both the abbey and town suffered repeated plunder and burning by the English armies. Nevertheless, the well-preserved stone ruins, mainly of fifteenth-century origin, give an indication of just how grand and beautiful the abbey was in its prime. The elaborate stonework, flying buttresses, pinnacles and the rich tracery of the windows are among its finest features. The abbey contains the remains of King Alexander II, and the heart of Robert the Bruce is buried near the High Altar. The fifteenth to sixteenth-century Commendators House has been adapted as a museum to display many items excavated in and around the abbey.

Close to the abbey ruins are the unusual Priorwood Gardens, which grow flowers suitable for drying. The National Trust for Scotland run the gardens and have set up a regional visitors centre, shop and picnic area here.

Abbey see AM info. Parking available.
Priorwood Gardens open Easter to mid Oct daily, pm only on Sun. Mid Oct to 24 Dec daily except Sun, pm only on Mon. NTS.

Mevagissey

Cornwall *p211 B1*

Sprawling up the cliff in typical Cornish style, Mevagissey maintains a sense of timelessness that eludes many of the neighbouring fishing villages. Its real charm has to be discovered by walking through the narrow streets between the wooden slatted houses and along the quay, rather than viewing it from a distance. The traditional trade of Mevagissey has always been pilchard fishing and this reached its height in the nineteenth century when the town became very prosperous. Smuggling would have undoubtedly contributed to this wealth too. Now Mevagissey relies mainly on tourism, although after Looe it is still the main centre for shark fishing in Cornwall. In a small folk museum on the north

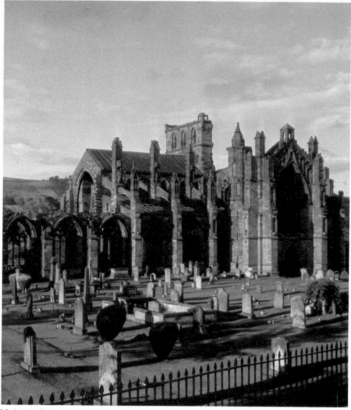

Melrose Abbey was saved by the Duke of Buccleuch in 1822

quay can be seen local handicrafts, fishing tackle, a cider press and agricultural implements. There is also an indoor model railway in the village, laid out through realistic terrain, running British, Continental and American models.

Folk museum open Easter to Sep.
Model railway open June to Sep daily. Oct to May, Sun pm only.

Milton Abbas

Dorset *p212 F2*

In this picture-postcard village, identical pairs of picturesque, square, thatched and whitewash cottages are set behind immaculate wide mown verges and rowan trees, strung out along the curving village street. The Brewery Farm Museum is housed in the old brewery here and contains a marvellous collection of local relics, including agricultural implements, bygones and a collection of old photographs.

A short distance from the village is Milton Abbey, its mansion and abbey church standing side by side in Gothic splendour, in a delightful bowl of farmland and woods. The beautiful Benedictine abbey church dates from the fourteenth and fifteenth centuries, but only part of it remains today – the choir, crossing and transepts, and fifteenth-century tower. The church was sensitively restored by Sir Giles Gilbert Scott and contains good vaulting under the tower and a carved altar screen, together with the white marble monument to Lady Milton (1775) which Robert Adam designed; Lord Milton lies beside his wife.

The fifteenth-century Abbot's Hall of the former abbey was incorporated into today's eighteenth-century mansion by architects Sir William Chambers and James Wyatt, for the owner, Lord Milton. The mansion is now a school and the abbey church its chapel. There is a rewarding walk from the abbey up a hundred or more grassy steps to the Norman St Catherine's Chapel which stands surmounting the hill above the abbey. Lord Milton completely cleared the original village as it spoilt his view although he did subsequently build the present village, which has all the balance and symmetry of an integrally planned village.

Brewery Farm Museum open all year daily. Parking available.
House and Gardens open daily during school summer holidays.

All the atmosphere and excitement of a working fishing port can be found in the harbour of Mevagissey

Monmouth Gwent *p212 E4*

Monmouth, lying at the centre of the Lower Wye Valley, has many interesting buildings and retains much charm from the Georgian era, while maintaining the hectic life of a market town.

Monmouth was probably the site of the Roman fort of *Blestium*, on the route from Gloucester to Caerleon, and Roman pottery and coins have been found at Overmonnow and near the river crossing. The town's recorded history, however, begins with the Normans who established a castle and a priory here within a few years of the 1066 conquest. Eventually the Lordship passed into the Duchy of Lancaster, and so it was as a Lancastrian that Henry V was born in Monmouth Castle in 1387. The walled town which grew up has lasted almost unchanged to this day, although the castle was practically destroyed by Parliamentary forces during the Civil War.

The town became prosperous during the eighteenth and nineteenth centuries, when it benefitted from the vast trade up and down the Wye. Coaching inns were turned into hotels to cater for travellers from England to Wales, or for followers of the fashionable Wye Tour, and the many attractive domestic and religious buildings in the town date from this period. Markets in both agricultural produce and livestock developed, and each year Monmouth holds an agricultural show which is one of the best in the country.

Local History Centre and Nelson Collection

The centre provides information on all aspects of the history of the town and the surrounding neighbourhood, including such articles as the Monmouth Cap and the Borough Weights, Measures and Seals. There is also a good deal of information about C. S. Rolls, co-founder of Rolls-Royce, together with a model of the plane in which he was killed in 1910. He was born at the nearby village of Rockfield and his statue stands in Agincourt Square outside Monmouth's Shire Hall.

Left: The statue of pioneer aviator Charles Rolls of Rolls Royce, and on Shire Hall, one of Henry V, who was born in Monmouth

Monmouth was renowned in medieval times for the Monmouth Cap and was prominent in the art of knitting which originated on the Continent

The Nelson Collection was the gift of Lady Llangattock to the Borough of Monmouth. It contains a very fine and varied collection of Nelson relics, and his fighting sword is the most prized exhibit. There are also several letters, log books, naval documents, prints, engravings and paintings here.

Great Castle House

This was built by the first Duke of Beaufort in 1673, and in about 1875 it became the HQ of the Royal Monmouthshire Royal Engineers, the senior non-regimental unit of the Army. The speciality of the house is the plasterwork in the ceilings.

Monmow Gateway

Guarding the bridge over the river Monmow, the gateway is probably the most famous building in the town. It was constructed at the end of the thirteenth century for use as a toll house, watchtower and prison.

St Mary's Church

Except for the tower and spire, the church was rebuilt in 1736 on the site of the Church of the Benedictine Priory, founded here in 1075. Medieval tiles, a cresset stone, and fragments of a piscina are the only remains of the former priory church.

In the wall of the nearby old priory is a fifteenth-century oriel window, named Geoffrey's Window, after the celebrated Geoffrey of Monmouth who, in about the year 1135, wrote *History of the Kings of Britain*, the origin of much of the Arthurian legend.

Dixton Church

At the entrance to the chancel of this church, small brass tablets show the height to which Wye floods have reached in the past. It was consecrated between 1066 and 1070, and still bears traces of Saxon work.

Castle and Great Castle House exterior freely accessible at any reasonable time. AM. Parking available.
Museum (Nelson Collection and Local History Centre) open all year daily, Sun pm only.

The Elizabethan stone balustrade and Lodge of Montacute House

Montacute House

Somerset *p212 E3*

This must be one of England's loveliest Elizabethan houses, built of locally-quarried golden Ham stone at the edge of a medieval village. It is adorned with carved statues, open-stone parapets, fluted columns, twisted pinnacles, oriel windows and a decorated entrance porch. The gallery, reputed to be the largest of its kind in England, houses a collection of Tudor and Jacobean portraits on permanent loan from the National Portrait Gallery. Of particular note is the stained glass and stone screen in the great hall.

The formal garden with its pavilions is walled with a stone balustrade which looks beyond to open parkland.

Open Apr to Oct daily (except Tue) pm only. Parking and refreshments (Apr to Sep) available. NT.

Morecambe

Lancashire *p216 E5*

The shoreline known as Morecambe Bay is one of the most spectacular stretches of coastal scenery in Britain. The bay stretches for some four-and-a-half miles, and when the tide goes out several miles of sand are revealed. These have been crossed on foot at low tide since Roman times, when the route provided a short cut to the Furness Peninsula – twenty-seven odd miles round the coast. Later the Cartmel monks guided travellers along this 'roadway'. Much later it was traversed by stage coaches and during that time 140 people died. This gives some indication of the dangerous nature of the journey, due mainly to the three tidal rivers and treacherous quicksands which have to be negotiated.

Today the sands can be crossed for fun as an adventure trek between Hest Bank and Grange-over-Sands, under the guidance of the official Sand Pilot appointed by the Chancellor of the Duchy of Lancaster.

Situated on the southern shores of the bay is the huge holiday resort of Morecambe – sometimes called the Naples of the North. It has grown from two villages, Poulton-le-Sands and Heysham. The former was an ancient fishing village until just over fifty years ago, when it began life as a holiday resort. Now there are all the usual seaside attractions, including the huge Marineland Oceanarium and Aquarium. As well as daily dolphin and sea lion shows, there are collections of turtles, penguins and alligators – quite apart from hundreds of kinds of local fresh and salt water fish.

The major attraction at Heysham is the Heysham Head Entertainments Centre – a vast new holiday park, which is a Disneyworld of entertainment featuring a Tropical Bird Collection where exotic tropical birds housed in an area of some 10,000 square feet fly freely all the year round; a Zoo and Animal Walk which contains many of the smaller animals not usually seen in larger zoos. All the animals are in pens or enclosures designed so even very young children can see in without difficulty. Animal Walk is an area of open woodland through which one can walk and observe birds and animals in their natural surroundings; and there is also a go-kart race track here.

Marineland Oceanarium and Aquarium open daily during summer; aquarium only in winter, Sat and Sun only.
Heysham Head Entertainments Centre open late May to Sep daily.

Morwellham

Devon *p212 C2*

This small village on the river Tamar has served as a port to Tavistock since the twelfth century. Morwellham reached its peak of activity in the first half of the nineteenth century as a mining centre and an underground canal was built between town and village as a valuable link from Tavistock to the Tamar.

Now some hundred years later Morwellham Quay has been set up as an outdoor museum and recreation centre. Old workings of the port can be seen, including lime kilns and copper chutes. In the original wheel pit stands a thirty-two-foot water-wheel

The pier and attractions of this major seaside resort are enhanced on summer evenings by the spectacular sunsets over Morecambe Bay which was brought from Dart-moor. There is also an indoor museum depicting the life and industry of the nineteenth century. Other features here include a riverside tramway, slide shows, adventure playground and a craft shop.

Open-air Museum open all year daily. Parking available.

Muncaster Castle and Bird Garden

Cumbria *p220 D1*

The Pennington family have owned the land here since the thirteenth century, but the present castle is mainly a nineteenth century structure which incorporates an ancient tower.

Some Tudor fireplaces were installed and the castle has a fine collection of sixteenth and seventeenth-century furniture, pictures and embroidery. The most interesting piece in the castle is the Luck of Muncaster – a gold and white enamelled glass bowl given by Henry VI to bring luck to the

family, after he was given refuge here following his defeat at the Battle of Hexham in 1464.

From the castle terrace there are magnificent views down the lovely Esk Valley and the gardens are superb. Rhododendrons and azaleas create a riot of colour in the spring, which is rivalled by a collection of startling ornamental and tropical birds. There is also a bear garden with Himalayan bears and a flamingo pool.

One mile from the castle is the interesting Muncaster Mill, where water from the river Mite is carried three-quarters of a mile to turn a thirteen-foot water wheel. This provides the power for the three pairs of millstones, two elevators, flour separators and a sackhoist. Flour milled here can be bought, and a new feature is a fish farm selling trout.

Castle open from Easter to early Oct, Tue, Wed, Thu and Sun, pm. Grounds daily, (except Fri) pm only. Parking and refreshments available.
Muncaster Mill open Easter to Sep daily (except Sat).

Newby Hall

North Yorkshire *p217 B3*

Newby Hall, a Queen Anne house built for wealthy mine owner Sir Edward Blackett at the end of the seventeenth century, lies on the north-east bank of the river Ure.

One of Yorkshire's smaller country houses, and now the home of Major R. E. J. Compton, Newby Hall is set in extensive grounds of parkland and beautifully planned gardens with their flower beds, shrubberies and rare ornaments sloping gently down to the river's edge. The house is famous for its magnificent Roman sculpture galleries, with pride of

William Weddell, owner of Newby Hall in the mid 18th century, filled the house with sculpture collected during his Grand Tour

place going to the beautiful Venus from the Barberini Palace in Rome. No less renowned is the sumptuous tapestry room, as planned by Robert Adam and hung with a complete set of Gobelin tapestries.

Other features of the house include the fine entrance hall and the furniture, much of it made by Adam and Thomas Chippendale.

Situated within the grounds of Newby Hall is the nineteenth-century village church of Christ the Consoler, noted for its Victorian stained glass windows. A miniature steam passenger-carrying railway runs through orchards and alongside the river, from which a small steam launch operates in suitable weather.

Open Good Fri to Sep.
House Apr, May, Sep, Wed, Thu, Sat and Sun pm only. June, July, Aug daily (except Mon).
Gardens open daily.

131

New Forest Hampshire

For many centuries a royal game preserve, the area is no more a natural forest than the regimented plantations of the Forestry Commission, but was planted by order of William the Conqueror in AD 1078 for his favourite sport of deer hunting.

William I's successor, William Rufus, was also addicted to hunting, and the Rufus Stone at Stoney Cross marks the place where legend has it the arrow of one Sir Walter Tyrell, loosed at a fleeing deer, glanced off the trunk of an oak tree to mortally wound the king.

Seven hundred years ago the forest stretched from the Avon on the west to Southampton Water on the east, and from the borders of Wiltshire to the English Channel. That area is now considerably reduced, but the forest still covers 144 square miles and measures twenty miles across at its widest point. The term 'forest' is misleading, as about half of the total area termed forest is open heath, and the area is a delightful mixture of streams, green lawns shorn by ponies, rivers, ponds, cottages, leafy villages and ancient churches.

The forest divides naturally into three areas, each with a different character. The northern area is mostly open moorland covered in heather, furze and bracken – split into five parallel ridges by streams bound for the river Avon.

Here and there thickets, pine woods, old woods and Forestry Commission plantations replace the heather and gorse.

The middle region is truer to what is commonly understood by forest. It is an area of woodlands interspersed with glades – old woods in every state of maturity and decay. Complementing these old woods are thickets and plantations, or enclosures, of young trees. The exceptions are the cultivated lands around Lyndhurst, Minstead and Burley, and a heathland that stretches from Brockenhurst to Thorny Hill to Burley, and then on to Bratley Plain. The woods provide many pleasant walks, and it is only on foot or horseback that the forest can be truly appreciated. The woods are splendid in any season. In the winter they are carpeted with fallen leaves, the branches hang with grey lichen and gnarled roots are covered with vivid green moss hiding fungi and ferns. Spring revitalises the forest with young green and in summer the woods produce flowering honeysuckle foxgloves and banks of tall, cool bracken. New Forest ponies and deer wander freely about the woods.

Bounded on the southern side by a low-lying stretch of cultivated land beside the Solent, the southern part of the Forest lies inland from Sway Common to Butts Ash. It consists of bare heathland, overgrown in places by Scots Pine, cut by well-wooded valleys of numerous streams. Farther inland the land dips down above sea level, and bogs stretch from Hinchesley, Brockenhurst and Beaulieu Road to Ashurst. From here the ground gradually rises northwards to Ramnor Park Hill woods and on to Lyndhurst. Birch and holly are found in the lowlands, the holly once cropped for its berries at Christmas and sent by rail to London.

The Rufus Stone records the death of William II on August 2, 1100

The forest is unique in retaining the ancient Court of Verderers, which administers the laws of the forest. The ten members directly protect the well-being of the commoners and animals – their laws, for example, give wildlife priority on the roads, and there are strict rules against the public feeding the animals.

The forest officers, called Agisters, patrol the forest on horseback dressed in traditional green, watching over the land and enforcing the laws. One of their duties is to cut the tails of the New Forest ponies, to show that the owners have paid their dues – any

found unmarked are impounded and the owner fined. By careful selection of those stallions allowed into the forest, the Verderers have greatly improved the New Forest breed, established since Norman times. All the ponies are annually rounded up in the spring for the marking of any foals and selling at auction.

Right: Market day in Ringwood – a pretty town on the edge of the forest and an ideal touring centre

The variety of wildlife in the forest can rarely be matched in Britain. Matley Bog is an example of an area which is still a sanctuary for rare plants and insects. Red deer, Fallow deer, Roe and Japanese Sika deer live in the forest, and are kept in check by the Forestry Commission and the New Forest Buckhounds which

hunt them during the winter.

Otters inhabit the river Avon and several of the smaller streams, while the solitary badger lives under the big oak and beech woods. The Grey squirrel has here, as in many places, replaced the native Red squirrel, but all the British species of bats, save one, live within the New Forest.

It is a paradise for the birdwatcher, and houses species scarce elsewhere in Britain. The common buzzard, the legendary Dartford warbler, occasionally Montagu's harrier, siskin and pied flycatcher number among the many unusual nesting birds. Green woodpeckers can be heard in the woods, and the jaunty jay and magpie are forever present. Woodlarks, nightjars and nightingales, gold crests, redstarts and marsh tits are a few of the numerous species breeding within the boundaries of the forest in a variety of habitats. Winter visitors include siskins and bramblings, and the coastal haunts of the forest play host to waders and occasionally to rarely seen birds such as osprey, avocet and spoonbills.

The area is also renowned for its butterflies, and species include the Queen of Spain fritillary, Camberwell Beauty, Brown Argus and Silver-Studded Blue.

Newquay

Cornwall *p211 B2*

The town first became prosperous during the sixteenth century as a centre for pilchard fishing. Huer's Hut, on the western headland, dates from this period when the 'Huer' kept watch for pilchard shoals and alerted the fishermen when one was sighted. It was not until the late nineteenth century that Newquay realised its potential as a holiday centre and exploited its 650 acres of beautiful white sands. In spite of a certain lack of character in its buildings, it is now established as Cornwall's largest resort, and as probably the best place for surfing in Britain, attracts international surfing champions.

The main part of the town overlooks Towan Beach which is somewhat sheltered from the Atlantic breakers, and therefore especially suitable for children. It is illegal on any beach to swim when red danger flags are flying. There is a paddling pool at the foot of 'the Island' – a rocky outcrop connected to the mainland by a suspension bridge – and rock pools and caves here fascinate both children and adults. High cliffs make most of the beaches accessible only to the young and fit.

Periodically throughout the summer, several thirty-foot boats race each other round a six-mile course in the bay. These were once Newquay pilot gigs that competed for the lucrative job of landing a pilot on an incoming ship. Deep-sea fishing boats may be chartered at the harbour, which is enclosed by cliffs and two granite piers.

The main amusement area is around Trenance Park, where a boating lake, miniature railway, outdoor swimming pool, trampolines and a zoo are to be found.

Towan Beach and the Island
at Newquay

Other attractions include a golf driving range, a toboggan run, and facilities for bowls, pitch-and-putt and tennis and a golf course on the cliffs above Fistral Bay. There are opportunities for pleasant coastal walks, especially around East Pentire which has lovely views; and the rocky headlands such as Porth, with its island which was a prehistoric camp, are interesting to explore.

Zoo open all year. Parking and refreshments available.

Newstead Abbey

Nottinghamshire *p217 B1*

Founded as an Augustine Priory around 1170 by Henry II, possibly as part of his atonement for the murder of Becket, Newstead Abbey now stands resplendent as a stately home.

After the Reformation, the abbey was sold by Henry VIII to Sir John Byron for the sum of £810. Documentation of this sale has been preserved, along with other deeds relating to the abbey's history. Successive generations of Byrons adapted the monastic buildings into a comfortable dwelling, incorporating much of the medieval architecture into their designs. The west façade of the thirteenth-century priory church, the fifteenth-century cloister and the old chapter house, now converted into a chapel, have survived virtually in their original form.

By far the most famous occupant of the house was the 6th Lord, the poet, who owned the abbey from 1798 until 1817. Many relics of Lord Byron have been retained, including his bedroom containing the gilt four-poster bed which he had at Trinity College, Cambridge, and his writing table. The Byron Gallery houses many of the poet's treasures, such as the helmet he designed for the Greek campaign of liberty against the Turks, in which Byron fought and died.

Newstead Abbey is justly famous for its fine gardens with lakes, waterfalls, rock gardens and a Japanese garden representing the design on a willow-patterned plate. A monument to Boatswain, Lord Byron's beloved Newfoundland dog, stands near the Eagle Pond, with lines composed by the poet engraved on its pedestal.

Open Easter to Sep daily, pm only. Garden open all year daily (except 25 Dec). Parking and refreshments (summer only) available.

Norfolk Broads Norfolk

The Norfolk Broads have become one of the most popular holiday haunts in England – not too far from London and the hinterland of Great Yarmouth. They have become a haven for amateur sailors and all those who enjoy 'messing about in boats'.

The 200 miles of waterways, part lakes and part rivers, weave their way through a quiet and charming countryside in an area bounded by Norwich, Beccles, Lowestoft, Great Yarmouth and North Walsham. In general, the waterways lie away from the roads and often private land separates the motorist from the water's edge. Indeed, between Acle and Yarmouth, where the country is flat, the only evidence of the Broad's existence is the appearance of sails apparently gliding over the flat fields.

However, the land is not in fact entirely flat. In many places steep banks rise from the rivers, and below Norwich, hills rise to the south of the river Yare, and a ridge of high ground to the north separates it from the river Bure where many of the Broads are grouped. Higher ground to the south-east of Norwich causes the river Waveney to make a wide sweep before it joins the Yare at Breydon Water. It is the area west of Great Yarmouth, as far inland as Acle on the river Bure, which is virtually uninhabited, flat marshland, broken only by the sails of boats and the stark silhouettes of windmills – at Horsey, Reedham and Herringfleet there are particularly fine windmills.

Surprisingly, the Broads are man-made. It was not until the post-war years that it was realised that these natural-looking lakes were the result of extensive peat digging by the Anglo-Saxons, who used the peat as a source of fuel. A change in the land and sea levels caused the pits to flood, so creating the shallow lakes known as the Broads. The process of peat formation has resumed, and since the nineteenth century it has been noticed that the 'meres' are shrinking by silting up with dead vegetation. The exception is Breydon Water, the largest of the Broads, which is a tidal landlocked estuary of the rivers Yare and Waveney, separated from the sea by a sandbar upon which stands Great Yarmouth.

The Broads vary considerably in character. Wroxham and Salhouse are surrounded by woodlands and gently sloping grassland leading down to the water's edge, while the northern Broads and Rockland Broad, connected with the river Yare, are fringed by reedbeds. The upper reaches generally are wooded and unspoilt.

In the past, the villagers utilised the Broads for trade, and built trading wherries – broad shallow draught boats with a single tall mast which sailed under the power of one huge brown or black sail. The word wherry comes from the Scandinavian, and betrays the past presence of the Danes, who colonised East Anglia. One of the cargoes these craft carried was possibly the harvested reeds which grow in abundance around the shores of the northern Broads. Many people associate the Broads with the famous local thatching and although not as finely worked and decorative as straw thatch, it lasts a good deal longer. With the mini-revival of thatch as a roofing material, the small band of remaining craftsmen in Norfolk are in great demand, so the craft may well be saved from dying out.

Many of the villages in the area stand back a mile or two from the water and are easily missed, which is a pity as several of them are extremely attractive and nearly all have ancient churches of interest.

Those villages near to the water

have developed thriving boat building and hiring industries, and cater to the amateur yachts'-man's every need. A place of particular interest is the site of the ruins of St Benet's Abbey, which is only accessible by water. Founded in AD 955 on the banks of the river Bure, the Bishop of Norwich still travels there by boat every August Bank Holiday to hold an open-air mass.

The wildlife of the Broads is plentiful, and a number of unusual creatures inhabit the reedbeds, woods and marshland. On the open water the great crested grebe, mallard and teal are a common sight, and semi-tame Greylag and Canada geese are present all the year round. The reedbeds conceal some unusual birds. The rare bittern is not often seen, but its strange booming call heard at night time has sent shivers down many a spine. The charming bearded-tit, or reed pheasant, also makes its home amongst the reeds and lapwing and snipe live on the marshland. In the woods the Green woodpecker can often be heard hammering at bark in search of small insects and grubs, and the noise echoes about the tree-tops. An unusual animal, and something of a pest, is the coypu. Originally from South America this largest of rodents (the size of a small dog) is a strong swimmer, and does

much damage to crops. Due to its semi-aquatic life, a curious adaption is the row of teats along the female's back, allowing the young to cling there and feed while the mother is in the water. For the fisherman, roach, perch, pike, rudd, bream, tench, eels and the occasional trout can be taken.

A bonus for the holiday-maker is the climate. The area boasts the least rainfall in England, although the evening breezes can

be chilly. Because of the mildness of the weather, the Broads are one of the few habitats where the exotic swallowtail butterfly breeds.

Boats are easily hired, and the tourist afloat is well catered for, whether for the day or a fortnight. Few waterways are restricted, and as long as channels are followed and safety rules obeyed, there is no better way to explore this charming corner of East Anglia.

Hickling water nature trail in Norfolk Wildlife Park

Norfolk Wildlife Park

Norfolk *p218 E1*

Founded in 1962 by the famous naturalist Philip Wayre, the Norfolk Wildlife Park is now regarded as the largest collection of European animals and birds in the world. The park tends to specialise in breeding and it can boast a number of firsts in this field – for example, it produced the first European otters bred in captivity in Britain since the nineteenth century, and the first lynx for over thirty years. Rare Eagle owls have also been bred here for a number of years. Animals include beavers, bison, bears, ibex, seals, wolves, Barbary apes, badgers and a large number of European birds, which are displayed in specially constructed aviaries.

The park is also the home of the Pheasant Trust which safeguards rare and endangered species. Swinhoe's pheasant, from the island of Taiwan, and the Mikado pheasant are two whose continued existence has been ensured.

Open all year daily. Parking and refreshments available.

Norham Castle

Northumberland *p220 F4*

The river Tweed, winding its way past the ruins of Norham Castle, marks the boundary here between England and Scotland. A stone fortress called Norham Castle was built during the twelfth century. It replaced a wooden one, and continued to defend this strategic position by a ford in the river. However, border skirmishes over the centuries took their toll, and today the castle stands in ruins with only parts of the lofty keep, gates and inner and outer baileys remaining. Enough remains though to indicate the former strength of the castle with the keep walls rising up to some ninety feet. Towers and turrets are still in evidence around the outer walls.

See AM info.

North Norfolk Railway

Norfolk *p218 E1*

From its headquarters at Sheringham Station, the North Norfolk Railway operates over three miles of track to Weybourne, once part of the Midland and Great Northern Joint Railway, and it is hoped to extend the line as far as Holt. Sheringham station has a collection of steam locomotives and rolling stock, some undergoing and some awaiting restoration. There are several industrial tank engines and two examples of ex-Great Eastern Railway main line engines. Rolling stock includes many suburban coaches, the Brighton Belle, Pullman cars and directors' private saloons, and there is a railway museum – including a model railway.

Sheringham Station open Easter to mid Oct daily. Steam-hauled trains operate Easter and Spring Bank Holiday weekends, then Sun and certain weekdays throughout the summer, until Oct. Refreshment available.

Right: A replica of *Locomotion* in steam at the Beamish Open Air Museum – the original ran in 1825

Below: The evocative ruin of Norham Castle is set high up on rocks above the winding river Tweed

North of England Open Air Museum

Co Durham *p217 B5*

Covering some 200 acres of park and woodland, this fascinating open-air museum at Beamish was the first of its kind in England. It consists of a large collection of buildings imaginatively reconstructed to illustrate the past way of life in north-east England.

Rowley Station, first built in 1867, has been rebuilt on the museum site and includes the station office, furnished as it would have been during the latter days of the North Eastern Railway Company. An N.E.R. Class C locomotive is regularly kept in steam during the summer months. The station is complete with weighbridge, signals, ticket office, waiting room and footbridge.

A Victorian colliery has been recreated here, and features a typical north-east steam-winding engine of 1855. Boilers, originally from Shotton colliery, provide the steam for all the colliery engines. A full-scale working model of *Locomotion No. 1*, a replica of the original built by Stephenson in 1825, can also be seen in the colliery.

The Home Farm, established

for some 250 years, houses a collection of agricultural machinery and tools, including a horse engine, barn thresher and granary. A cart collection is housed in the rebuilt cartshed to the rear of the farm.

Amongst other exhibits are the Foulbridge Cottages, some fully furnished, and nearby is a garage, housing an Armstrong Siddeley car, and a 1938 Morris 8.

Beamish Hall contains an exhibition of articles in store awaiting further development of the museum, including a chemist's shop containing many bottles with their original contents, together with a collection of Victorian toys and games. A classroom set up within the Hall shows the typical desks and writing slates used at the turn of the century. Traditional crafts are demonstrated including Durham quilting and local slipware pottery.

Open all year daily. Closed Mon from Sep to Mar.

Norton Priory

Cheshire *p216 E3*

Norton Priory, the most fully excavated monastic site in Britain, is situated close to Astmoor on the

eastern outskirts of Runcorn. Founded by Augstinian monks in the twelfth century, it flourished until the Dissolution of the monasteries brought about its closure in 1536. Some years later it was acquired by the Brooke family who made it their home, building a Tudor mansion in the outer courtyard. This was replaced in the eighteenth century by a Georgian house which remained until 1928, when it fell into decay. The remains include a medieval vaulted room in which exhibitions are held and a very large model of the priory church may be seen in the cloister.

Now essentially an open-air museum, Norton Priory is surrounded by some seven acres of woodland and set within these is a restored summer house containing a wildlife display. This is made up of such things as animal bones, floor tiles and carved woodwork which have all been found on the site. Excavation work, which began in 1970, still continues at certain times of the year and future developments include the building of a permanent museum adjoining the priory.

Open Apr to Sep Mon to Wed, Sat, Sun and Bank Holidays pm only (also Thu and Fri in Aug, pm only), Oct to Mar, Sun pm only.

Norwich Norfolk p213 D5

Over 1,000 years old, Norwich is a truly English city with an individuality and independence born of isolation. It is still a pleasure to wander among the medieval streets – particularly Elm Hill, the evocative cobbled thoroughfare which is now the centre of the city's flourishing antique trade.

Market day in Norwich, with the castle beyond rising above the town

A large and important city since the Norman conquest, Norwich prospered as a textile centre in the fourteenth century and this industry was revived some 200 years later when settlers came over from the Netherlands and introduced their crafts and skills.

Prosperity and forward-looking attitudes have always characterized Norwich, and the vast modern shopping centre of Anglia Square, and the unusual new buildings of the University of East Anglia, testify to this. However, the preservation of old Norwich is a prime concern of the city, and its different architectural styles complement, rather than detract from, each other. A link between the two is the colourful open-air market that has taken place every weekday since Norman times, and is still very much part of the city's life.

Norwich's Norman Cathedral

The Cathedral

Rising in Norman splendour from the spacious surrounds of the Cathedral Close, the Church of Holy and Undivided Trinity is as magnificent and awe-inspiring as it must have appeared to those who saw it consecrated in 1278.

Apart from the stone vaulting and clerestory windows, the architecture is purely Norman. The survival of the semi-circular east end is unique in northern Europe and houses a stone bishop's throne, possibly 1,000 years old. Beautiful gilded and painted bosses decorate the vaulting and those in the cloisters are particularly outstanding examples of medieval craftsmanship.

Within the Close, which leads down to the river, are many medieval buildings. Some now house a school established in 1553 as the Edward VI Grammar School. Perhaps the most famous scholar here was Horatio Nelson, whose statue stands in the close.

Pull's Ferry, a great beauty spot on the river, is a fifteenth-century watergate which once marked the entrance to a small canal which was built especially to transport building materials to the cathedral.

Strangers' Hall

This ancient merchant's house, the earliest parts dating from about 1320, is now a fascinating museum depicting English domestic life. Built around three courtyards, the house was constantly enlarged and rebuilt by successive wealthy owners, resulting in a delightfully rambling place of many different periods. Twenty-three of its rooms are open to the public, furnished in periods ranging from early Tudor to late Victorian.

Two of the finest rooms have special attractions. The great hall

Norwich

– the most impressive – has a crown-post roof, a minstrel's gallery, an early Tudor bay window, a staircase of 1627 and on its walls hang superb Flemish tapestries, woven about 1485. Adjoining the great hall is the Georgian Room, the dining room of the Assize Judge, who had his official lodgings here. The room is notable for the fine furniture it contains, and the magnificent chandelier made of Irish glass.

Stranger's Hall derives its name from the building's association with Flemish weavers, who were encouraged to settle in Norwich at the end of the sixteenth century to revitalise the textile industry.

St Andrew's Hall

This was the home of the Dominican Friars up until the Reformation, when the Norwich Corporation bought the Hall for use as a public building. The Blackfriars Hall at the east end was originally the chancel of the Friar's church. Events which have occurred here since the sixteenth century include Charles II's knighting of Sir Thomas Browne; the celebration of the opening of the city's railway; and the entertainment of King Edward VII, George V and George VI. The Triennial Music Festival began here in 1824, and has played host to many notable names in the world of music.

Bridewell Museum

The Bridewell Museum is housed in part of a fourteenth-century merchant's house – used as a prison for tramps and beggars in 1583. In the courtyard can be seen various dates and initials scratched by prisoners. Now a museum of local industries, there is a room devoted to agriculture, a room displaying cloths and looms of the old textile industry, and another room of exhibits relating

The water gate at Pull's Ferry

to the boot and shoe industry, including footwear from Tudor times to the present day. Other industries recalled here are metalwork – partly represented by a smithy; the building industry, demonstrating traditional techniques; and clockmaking.

The Castle

Norwich's castle, built in the twelfth century, has one of the finest Norman keeps in England. It consists of a great stone tower seventy feet high decorated by tiers of blank arcading which were carefully restored in 1834.

The castle was adapted as a splendid museum, after being a county jail from 1220 to 1887. In the art galleries of the museum is an unrivalled collection of paintings by John Sell Cotman, and works by other artists of the Norwich School, such as John Crome.

Other exhibits reflect the history and culture of the Norwich region over the centuries. In the Geology Gallery can be seen the fossilised foot of a plesiosaur. The Archaeological Gallery contains beautiful Iron Age gold necklaces, and a wonderfully decorated Roman parade cavalry helmet and visor of gilding metal.

In the keep is a case of bones from local sites – one skull shows the effects of a battle axe. On a more festive note are two large brightly painted snapdragons, built of wickerwork and canvas, once used for state processions.

Weapons, coins, stamps, domestic trivia, glass and many other collections, cater for every interest.

St Peter Hungate

Early this century, the medieval church of St Peter Hungate was threatened with demolition, but fortunately was saved to be used as a Museum of Church Art and Craftsmanship. It now provides an apt setting for the exhibits which include illuminated manuscript service-books, Russian icons, musical instruments (once played in church) and, most unusual, a fourteenth-century coffin complete with a skeleton.

Strangers' Hall open all year (except Christmas, New Year, Good Fri and Sun).
Bridewell open as above.
Castle open all year (except Christmas New Year and Good Fri) daily, Sun, pm only. Refreshments available.
St Peter Hungate Church Museum Open all year daily (except Christmas, New Year, Good Fri and Sun).

Oakhill Manor

Somerset *p212 E3*

The little village of Oakhill lies high in the Mendip Hills. Close by is Oakhill Manor, incorporating The World of Models at Oakhill Manor – a display of models paying tribute to great British engineers of the past, and the British craftsmen who brought their dreams to fruition. A small, private country estate of some forty-five acres, the manor is a fine example of one of England's smaller country houses. Attractively furnished, all the principal rooms and many of the lesser ones have been used to display the magnificently comprehensive collection of models and pictures embracing land, sea and air transport.

The house itself is set in eight acres of wooded and formal gardens, and a miniature railway, complete with stations in Mendip stone, transports visitors from the car park to the manor. The three-quarter-mile scenic route incorporates cuttings, embankments, bridges and even its own miniature Cheddar Gorge.

Open mid Apr to Oct pm only. Parking and refreshments available.

Oban

Strathclyde *p219 B5*

Oban was no more than a small fishing village with a single inn when Dr Johnson and Boswell stayed there in 1773 on their famous tour of the Highlands, but it

has since grown considerably in size and importance. It is now both the Gateway to the Western Isles, with regular ferry services, and a centre for those attracted by the grandeur of the western Highlands. The town has much to offer those who enjoy natural beauty and traditional entertainment, and its magnificent setting combines the delights of a busy harbour with views across the Sound of Mull to a backdrop of blue mountains.

The town stretches along a flat seafront, backed by a wooded escarpment with more buildings on a higher level. Behind these terraces stands Oban Hill with the skeleton of an abandoned Victorian hydro, and Battery Hill with its strange semi-completed edifice resembling Rome's Colosseum. This was built in the 1890s by a Mr MacCaig to provide work for the town's unemployed, but his worthwhile, though eccentric, project was abandoned when he died.

The bay is a popular yachting and boating centre, and is home port to a fishing fleet. Fish auctions are held on Railway Pier, and motor boats take sightseers out to a seal island, and short cruises are available to such places of interest as Iona.

Oban is also the centre of an agricultural area, with a thriving livestock market. Local industry includes MacDonalds Mill, a tweed mill with a historical display and showroom open to the public, a glass factory, and a whisky distillery. At the end of August the Argyllshire Highland Gathering draws the crowds, and other events with a Scottish flavour are the game of shinty, a game similar to hockey, in Mossfield Park, and performances by the Oban Pipe Band.

MacDonalds Mill open Mar to Oct Mon to Sat. Demonstrations Mon to Fri only. Parking available.

Car ferries sail for the Hebrides from the harbour at Oban

Moated Oxburgh Hall was fortified against possible civil unrest

Oxburgh Hall

Norfolk *p213 C5*

Surrounded by a formal moat, this building resembling a fortress was built in the late fifteenth century by Sir Edmund Bedingfeld, whose descendants still live here. The outstanding feature of Oxburgh Hall is the magnificent eighty-foot-high gatehouse which, unlike the rest of the house, was spared from Victorian restoration. Two wings, built around a central courtyard, are decorated with battlements, decorated chimneys, oriels and elaborate windows. The interior is mainly Victorian except for the rooms in the gatehouse which have retained their original form; the King's Room where Henry VII was lodged in 1487 is furnished with a bed dated 1687, and wall hangings with panels worked by Mary Queen of Scots and by Elizabeth, Countess of Shrewsbury. The Queen's Room is hung with an elaborate tapestry of Oxfordshire and Buckinghamshire. A spiral staircase links the chambers and the roof, from which there are fine views over the surrounding countryside. The contrasting Victorian rooms, dark and richly patterned, are filled with memorabilia of the Bedingfelds.

In the grounds outside the moat is an interesting parterre garden of French design, laid out to the designs of Alexandre le Blond.

Open Apr to mid Oct, Tue, Wed, Thu, Sat, Sun and Bank Holidays, pm only. NT.

Oxford Oxfordshire *p213 A3*

Bounded by the Isis and willow-lined Cherwell, this city of ancient spires scattered with high walls, medieval gateways and enchanting college precincts, glories as the oldest and most respected academic seat in Britain.

The history of Oxford's university is almost as old as the origins of the city itself. Although a Saxon settlement (called Oxenford) developed around the place where ox-drovers crossed the river Thames, it was not until the twelfth century that the town really began to grow. This came about when Henry II ordered all English students studying abroad to return to England immediately. For various reasons, many of them converged at Oxford and so the scholarly character of the town was established.

Today there are twenty-eight colleges in Oxford and most of them are within walking distance of the High Street. Student life is always apparent in the city, the streets teeming with students on bicycles, and during summer, the rivers are alive with boats. These are either punts, or rowing boats practising hard for the numerous summer river events.

Ashmolean Museum

The Ashmolean Museum of Art and Archaeology first opened its doors in 1683 and the collection expanded to such an extent that in 1845 the stately New Ashmolean was built to house it.

This, the oldest museum in the country, is famed throughout Europe. The main exhibits are archaeological, of British, European, Mediterranean, Egyptian and near-Eastern origins. Coin collections and medals from all countries and periods are kept in the Heberden Coin Room, and other rooms hold examples of European ceramics, English silver, Chinese and Japanese porcelain, painting and lacquer, Tibetan art, Indian sculpture and paintings, Islamic pottery and metalwork, and Chinese bronzes.

The galleries are hung with Italian, Dutch, Flemish, French and English oil paintings; Old Masters and modern drawings; watercolours; prints; miniatures; and the Hope collection of engraved portraits.

St Edmund's Hall

This delightful small college is everyone's idea of an Oxford College. Once through the little archway this, the last of the medieval Halls, appears as a world in miniature. It is a gentle and scholarly

place, giving the impression of having been rather haphazardly planned, the buildings surrounding a green square overlooked by mullioned windows and golden stone. The little Classical chapel has above it the original college library, which still continues the medieval tradition of chaining up its books.

Magdalen College

Beneath Magdalen Bridge runs the river Cherwell, and beside it stands the college, founded in 1458. From the top of the striking bell-tower, choristers sing at sunrise on Mayday to tired but happy crowds below, in celebration of the beginning of summer. The peaceful haven of the quadrangle is surrounded by cloisters, and above the west walk, venerable manuscripts lie in the library.

The New Buildings of 1773 merge exceptionally well with the old and overlook the Grove – the deer park within the grounds where open-air plays are performed every summer.

Museum of the History of Science

This first home of Elias Ashmole's collection, in which the Ashmolean Museum has its origins, is among the foremost Classical buildings of the city, and has been used since 1939 as the Museum of the History of Sci-

Magdalen Tower and Bridge – the scene of Oxford's May Day celebrations

Radcliffe Camera of 1737, beneath which great subterranean bookstacks store 600,000 books.

Merton College

Merton is one of the three oldest colleges in Oxford, founded in 1264. The old city wall encloses part of the college, and, like many of the colleges, has beautiful gardens. The original Hall, though much altered, still stands but the outstanding buildings are the library and chapel. In the library is the helmet of Sir Thomas Bordley, founder of the Bodleian library, and the chapel is renowned for its thirteenth and fourteenth-century glass, and its choir.

Christ Church College

Cardinal Wolsey founded the college in 1525, on one of the loveliest sites in Oxford, overlooking lush water meadows which sweep down to the rivers Thames and Cherwell. From Christopher Wren's Tom Tower, high above the gateway, rings Great Tom, an ancient bell taken from Osney Abbey. The college

has amongst its buildings the smallest cathedral in England, which contains architectural features from the twelfth to fifteenth centuries.

Trinity College

Trinity is the traditional academic rival of Balliol College. The mainly nineteenth-century building stands at the end of Broad Street, a pleasant, wide road where Oxford's leading booksellers are found.

One of the most notable features of the college is its chapel, which holds an alabaster tomb of Sir Thomas Pope (the founder), and has a screen and altarpiece carved by Grinling Gibbons.

Ashmolean Museum open all year (except Christmas New Year, Easter and during St Giles Fair in early Sep) daily, Sun pm only. Parking available.

Colleges open to the public most afternoons though some restrictions during term times.

Museum of the History of Science open all year Mon to Fri (except Christmas week and week after Easter.

ence. Here is the finest collection of early astronomical, mathematical and optical instruments in the world. Many of the exhibits are artistic as well as scientific, such as the sun-dials and the orreries – mechanisms which represent the motions of planets.

The Sheldonian Theatre

This was designed by Sir Christopher Wren in likeness to a Roman theatre in 1669. From the cupola, practically all the important buildings in Oxford can be seen. The interior of the theatre, with its tiered seats, gallery and Vice-chancellor's chair, is elegantly decorated beneath a beautifully painted ceiling. The university awards its degrees here.

the Apostles, used by the Venerable Bede. Founded by Humphrey, the Duke of Gloucester, in 1480, and reformed by Sir Thomas Bodley in 1598, the library consists of 'Duke Humphrey', the oldest part on the upper storey of the glorious Tudor Divinity School, the huge New Bodleian building, and the

The Radcliffe Camera

The Bodleian Library

The Bodleian Library, second only in size to the Vatican's library, holds in excess of three million volumes and possesses many of the oldest manuscripts in existence. These include a seventh-century manuscript of the Acts of

Oxford

Packwood House

Warwickshire *p216 F1*

Originally a sixteenth-century farmhouse of modest proportions, Packwood House was extended during the seventeenth century and a large range of outbuildings was added to it. The result is a pleasing blend of two styles, carefully restored by the National Trust.

Interior furnishings, both interesting and valuable, include Jacobean panelling, seventeenth-century furniture, Italian needlework and French and Flemish tapestries. The gardens are particularly famous for the layout of clipped yew trees of various sizes, which represent the Sermon on the Mount. Another interesting feature of the gardens is a wall with a series of niches designed to hold beehives.

Open Apr to Sep Wed to Sun and Bank Holiday Mon pm only, Oct to Mar (except 25 Dec) Wed, Sat, Sun and Bank Holiday Mon pm only. NT.

Paignton

Devon *p212 D2*

Paignton has a mild climate, gently-sloping reddish sands, and plenty to offer by way of entertainment. Lawns, play areas and beach huts line the front, with hotels and guesthouses galore on the other side of the esplanade.

The town has developed very swiftly over the last century, effectively obliterating the original village. The Church of St John, on the site of a Bronze Age settlement, was established in Saxon times, and has a Norman font and west door, although the present structure dates mainly from the fifteenth century. Next to it is all that remains of the erstwhile palace of the Bishops of Exeter, known as Coverdale Tower after the sixteenth-century Bishop who translated the Bible into English. Fifteenth-century Kirkham House, which is open to the public, was the home of the family responsible for building the chantry of St John's Church. Oldway

The pretty walled flower gardens of Packwood House

Mansion, built by Isaac Singer and his son with some of the millions derived from their sewing machine company, has a hundred rooms and was modelled on Versailles and the Paris Opera House.

Floats and diving rafts, as well as deck chairs, can be hired from the beaches, and pleasure trips run from the small harbour. South of the pleasure pier is the Festival Hall, surrounded by gardens with a mini-golf course, and beyond the harbour and Roundham Head are the well-kept gardens of Goodrington Cliff, with its zig-zag path leading to a holiday centre and amusement area.

Other delights include the Torbay and Dartmouth Railway with steam trains running between Paignton and Kingswear; open-topped double-decker buses along the front; the Torbay Aircraft Museum just inland at Higher Blagdon, which contains eighteen aircraft dating from 1924 to 1954, an indoor aeronautic exhibition, and a section devoted to World War I aces. Paignton Zoo, set amidst a hundred acres of grounds full of exotic plants, contains a world-wide collection of birds and animals.

Kirkham House open Apr to Sep daily, pm only on Sun. AM.
Oldway open May to Sep daily, Sun pm only, Oct to Apr Mon to Fri only. Closed occasionally for Council purposes. Parking and refreshments (in summer) available.
Torbay Aircraft Museum open all year (except 25 and 26 Dec). Parking available.
Torbay and Dartmouth Railway open Easter, then mid May to Sep daily.
Zoological and Botanical Gardens open all year (except 25 Dec) daily. Parking and refreshments available.

Pembroke Castle

Dyfed *p211 B4*

The castle stands on a rocky promontory lapped by the tidal waters of Milford Haven on three sides. Its towers and circular defensive walls encompass a seventy-five foot high, round keep, unique in its design, with walls some nineteen feet thick at the base. Another unusual feature is the Wogan cavern, a high natural cave in the limestone rock below the Northern Hill, probably used as a store room and boat house.

The wood and turf forerunner of this massive fortress was established by Arnulf of Montgomery towards the end of the eleventh century, as a base from which to subdue the turbulent Welsh. Arnulf retained it until 1102 when his part in the unsuccessful rebellion launched by his brother, Robert of Bellême, against Henry I, led to his possessions being confiscated by the Crown. Pembroke passed into the hands of the Clare family, who were the first Earls of Pembroke. They enlarged and strengthened the castle and a subsequent Earl, William Marshall, Marshal of England, was probably responsible for the construction of the fortress in its present form, building the keep and the Norman hall between 1189 and 1245.

Perhaps the most famous occupants of the castle were the Tudors. Jasper, half-brother of Henry VI, was created Earl of Pembroke in 1453 and his nephew, Henry Richmond, was born there in 1456, probably in a room on the first storey of what is now known as the Henry VII Tower near the gatehouse. Although the young Henry and his uncle were forced to flee the country during the Wars of the Roses, they returned in 1485, gathered their forces and seized the crown of England on Bosworth Field.

After the Civil War the castle fell into disrepair until 1880 when Mr J. R. Cobb spent three years carrying out restoration to the original design.

Open daily all year (except Sun, Oct to Easter and 25 Dec).

The impressive fortifications of Pembroke Castle

Pembrokeshire Coast National Park Dyfed

The most westerly peninsula in Wales is scattered with relics of past peoples, and around every little village or chapel are woven curious legends and often stranger facts. Along the coasts grey seals gambol in grey-blue waters, and fulmars battle with the heady winds. Inland walls, built at the dawn of the Christian era, divide the rich, fertile countryside.

Whitesand Bay near St David's is typical of Pembrokeshire's coast

Over one third of Pembrokeshire is designated a National Park. The area includes the coastal belt, outlying islands and the Preseli Hills. It is a wonderfully varied countryside of imposing cliffs, secret coves and sandy beaches, hills and moorland, wooded valleys and fast flowing streams.

The coast is easily and enjoyably accessible by way of the coastal path which stretches 167 miles from the old fishing village of St Dogmaels on the estuary of the Teifi to Amroth.

Working from north to south, the path first climbs to Cemaes Head and follows high cliffs to Newport, passing by an Iron Age hill-fort at Pen-Castell and fulmar breeding grounds, with fine views over the Newport Sands and the Nyfe estuary. At Newport the town clusters beneath a Norman Castle and the Iron Age hill-fort which crowns the summit of Carn Ingli, where St Brynach is said to have communed with angels.

Heading towards Fishguard the path takes the line of rugged cliffs, and once past the sheltered harbour, near the place where the last invasion of Britain took place in 1797), it continues along the indented coastline of Strumble Head, weaving its way towards St David's Head, a bare, windswept plateau whose coast is the breeding ground for seals, and where peregrine falcons and choughs may be sighted.

The path sweeps round Whitesand Bay with its sixth-century sailor's chapel – one of several from which St Patrick is supposed to have set out from on his last journey to Ireland. Just beyond Porth Clais is the chapel of St Non, mother of St David, where the patron saint is said to have been born during a great gale. Past the tiny inlet and village of Solva, a gay assembly of colour-washed cottages typical of

many along this stretch, the path arrives at Newgale, which has the largest beach in Pembrokeshire, some two miles of golden sands, and at low tide the fossilised remains of the forest which once covered the area can be seen. Beyond, the path turns south along St Bride's Bay to the popular little resorts of Broad Haven and Little Haven.

To the south-west the path rounds the Marloes-Dale Peninsula and takes in Martin's Haven and Marloes Sands on its way to St Anne's Head. Then the path turns northward for Dale, the sunniest place in Wales and a busy yachting centre, and across the estuary to St Ishmael's. There is a second crossing at Sandy Haven, both of which can only be crossed at low tide. The path follows the shores of the vast natural harbour of Milford Haven. Once past the town, the path continues on to the Cleddau Bridge and the southern shore of the estuary, via Pembroke Dock and Pembroke. The path returns to the shore at Pwllcrochan. It continues on round Angle Bay, and the Angle Peninsula to turn eastwards for the home straight.

Before St Govan's Head, a little inland, is Bosherston, famous for its water-lily ponds and its mere, out of which it was believed came Arthur's sword, Excalibur. Deep in a cleft in the cliffs is St Govan's Chapel, probably St Gawaine's cell. A rock by the chapel is said to hold a silver bell, which rings out when the rock is struck.

Past St Govan's Head the path continues along the towering cliffs, until it arrives at Tenby, the only sizeable resort along the coast. Beyond, the path follows the shores of Carmarthen Bay through Saundersfoot to the path's end at Amroth, where ebonised stumps revealed at very low tides are all that are left of a great forest in which some of the earliest men to reach these shores hunted.

A completely different aspect of the park is found on the Preseli Hills. This ridge of rounded hills made up of moorland, heath and bog is a landscape of gorse, heather and bilberry in which the curlew and skylark make their home, noted for its many prehistoric remains. A prehistoric track, known as the Flemings Way, was probably the route along which the 'bluestones' of Stonehenge were transported from the outcrops of igneous rock found in this region. Near Mynachlog-ddu is Garn Fawr, a stone circle of sixteen stones and Moel Drygarn, near Crymmych, is the site of a huge Iron Age hill-fort, within which are three Bronze Age cairns.

An area of outstanding beauty is the Gwaun Valley, which runs from Newport to Fishguard. Along its length are the churches of Cilgwyn, Portfaen, Llanychllwydog, Llanawer, and Llanychaer. Near Llanawer is Parc y Meirw (Field of the Dead) which contains the largest Megalithic alignment in Wales, over 140 feet in length with four of eight pillars standing. The ghost of a lady in white is said to walk among them at night.

Pendennis Castle

Cornwall *p211 B1*

Falmouth, with its important harbour, grew up under the protection of Pendennis Castle, which has seen the town evolve from a tiny hamlet into Cornwall's largest port.

The castle was built in about 1540 by Henry VIII, as part of his coastal fortification against the Continent. It stands on a promontory 200 feet above sea-level – an ideal position from which to defend Carrick Roads. The original castle consists of a circular tower or keep, surrounded by a curtain wall. A large outer enclosure was added by Elizabeth I in 1598, when the Spanish were rumoured to be preparing to launch another armada against England. The castle was in use by the military as late as World War II when it became a coastal defence post. The well-preserved keep is now open to the public, and is entered through an impressive gateway over which the Royal Arms are carved into the stone. Above the entrance is the room from where the drawbridge and portcullis were operated, and the two slots through which the chains passed can still be seen.

Penshurst Place has not had any major alterations since the long gallery was completed in 1607

The two main floors of the round tower housed guns which fired through ports provided with smoke vents. Heavy guns were also mounted on the roof and from the battlements the view of the estuary is dramatic.

A museum of arms and armour is housed in a separate building within the complex.

See AM info. Also open Sun am Apr to Sep. Parking and refreshments available.

These sturdy walls of Pendennis Castle withstood a Civil War siege

Penrhyn Castle

Gwynedd *p216 C3*

Overlooking the Menai Strait, Penrhyn Castle commands splendid views of Beaumaris Bay, Great Ormes Head and Anglesey. G. H. Dawkins Pennant, the wealthy owner of the Penrhyn slate quarries, commissioned Thomas Hopper to build this massive neo-Norman castle, which was completed in 1840. The result is a dramatic and remarkable structure, built of local materials wherever possible: slate from the nearby quarries; oak from the estates' forest; and Mona marble from Anglesey.

The vast and extravagant interior reflects the lavish, opulent hand of the architect, who completely decorated and furnished the castle, mostly in Norman style. The great hall, modelled on Durham Cathedral, is floored with polished slate; the splendid library has deeply recessed windows, and a marvellous ribbed and bossed ceiling. A large collection of nineteenth-century paintings can be seen in the house, together with an industrial railway museum, an exhibition of dolls, and a natural history museum. The castle is set amidst beautiful grounds, and a walled garden contains a variety of rare trees and shrubs.

Open Apr to late Oct daily. Apr, May and Oct pm only. NT.

Penshurst Place

Kent *p213 C2*

Penshurst Place stands unobtrusively in the corner of a wooded park, amid gardens laid out in authentic Tudor style. It is the seat of the Viscount De L'Isle, whose ancestors, the Sidneys, gradually converted Penshurst from a medieval manor house into a sumptuous estate, while still managing to retain most of its original character. Sir Philip Sidney, the well-known soldier and writer, was born at Penshurst in 1554 and writers such as his sister, Lady Pembroke, and Ben Johnson, were associated with the estate during the early seventeenth century.

The oldest feature is probably the great hall, with a sixty-foot-high timbered roof and an octagonal central hearth which can still provide an adequate form of heat. It was built by John de Pulteney, a wealthy wool merchant who was Mayor of London no less than four times.

Next to the great hall is the state dining room where a table is permanently laid with a Rockingham dinner service, made for William IV. A complete tour of Penshurst includes a number of other rooms and galleries containing some fine examples of Elizabethan architecture and furniture, and a collection of historic family documents is on display in the Nether Gallery. An unusual museum of nineteenth-century toys and games is to be found in the stable wing.

A public restaurant overlooks the Italian garden, and the home park, which adjoins the north front of the house, contains varied rare breeds of sheep and a venture park and nature trail, recently commissioned by Lord De L'Isle.

Open Apr to Oct (except Mons) pm only. Parking and refreshments available.

Perth Tayside *p220 D5*

The aptly named Fair City of Perth straddles the banks of the river Tay on the very edge of the Highlands. In ancient times it played an important role in Scotland's affairs, and was the country's capital for a century.

Few of the ancient buildings remain intact, but the city nevertheless retains a unique character with Georgian terraces overlooking the river and parkland. Today, it is the commercial and cultural centre for a wide surrounding area and has a major livestock market famous for its Aberdeen Angus bull sales, whilst its repertory theatre, which is housed in the Victorian Perth Theatre, is reputed to be the oldest in Scotland.

Branklyn Garden

Described as the finest garden of its size in Britain, it covers little more than two acres and contains a unique collection of rare plants from all parts of the world.

Black Watch Regimental Museum

The museum is housed in Balhousie Castle, a restored tower house reputed to be older than the Burgh of Perth itself. It contains treasures of the 42nd/73rd Highland Regiment from 1725 and includes paintings, silver, colours and uniforms.

The Fair Maid's House

This restored house was the former home of Catherine Glover, as described in Sir Walter Scott's famous novel, *The Fair Maid of Perth*. It was a guildhall for over 150 years and a recently uncovered wall here is said to be the oldest visible wall in Perth. The house is now an antique and craft centre.

Museum and Art Gallery

The Classical portico of this purpose-built museum and art gallery houses a varied and interesting collection of items, including natural history, social and local history and a collection of fine and applied art.

St John's Kirk

This imposing kirk is one of the noblest of the grand Scottish burghal churches, and is one of the few buildings to survive from Perth's medieval past. Consecrated in 1243, the choir dates from 1450, the central tower has a fifteenth-century steeple and the nave is c1490. It was here in 1559 that the fiery preaching of John Knox kindled the Reformation in Scotland. In the 1920s the church was restored as a memorial to those who fell in World War I.

The church boasts a set of thirty-five bells, together with fine examples of stained glass. Also on view is a priceless collection of old pewter and silver sacramental dishes.

Kinnoull Hill

The 739-feet summit of this hill commands a fine view of the city and the Tay estuary towards the Ochil and Lomond Hills. A nature trail and numerous wooded paths make this a popular spot for walking.

Branklyn Garden open Mar to Oct daily. NTS.
Black Watch Regimental Museum open all year, Mon to Fri.
Fair Maid's House open all year Mon to Sat.
Museum and Art Gallery open all year daily, Sun pm only.

Perth from the bridge over the Tay. The tower belongs to St John's Kirk

Peterborough

Cambridgeshire *p213 B5*

The geographic position of Peterborough, its fertile surroundings and handy raw materials, have made it a place of importance since Neolithic man first settled here.

The focal point of the old city is the magnificent cathedral, founded as a monastic abbey in 655, although the present fabric dates back to 1118. It is a massive Norman structure with a remarkable early Gothic west front. Its height, the light colour of the local Barnack stone and the double arches which admit daylight to the nave, prevent it from being gloomy. It retains its ancient wooden roof with an odd variety of figures in its painted decoration. Catherine of Aragon was buried here, as was Mary Queen of Scots until her son, James I of England, had her body moved to Westminster. On the west wall of the nave is a memorial to Old Scarlet who dug the Queens' graves. Behind the altar is a carved stone, known as the Hedda Stone because it was thought to commemorate Abbot Hedda who, with his monks, was murdered by Norsemen in 870, though it is now believed to be of an earlier date.

Other old buildings of note are Longthorpe Tower – a fortified medieval house with rare wall paintings, and Thorpe Hall, built during the Commonwealth period. The City Museum and Art Gallery in Priestgate covers local history, and includes articles made by prisoners during the Napoleonic wars.

Multi-purpose leisure centres, swimming pools, a theatre, stadium, and a complex of facilities for outdoor recreation at Orton Mere, are some of the developments connected with the city's expansion. For railway lovers, the Nene Valley Railway operates on a five-mile track between Wansford and Orton Mere, using a variety of steam and diesel locomotives, some of them from the Continent.

Longthorpe Tower see AM imfo.
Museum and Art Gallery open all year (except Good Fri and 25 and 26 Dec) Tue to Sat. Sep to May pm only.
Nene Valley Railway open Apr to Sep Sat and Sun, also midweek June to Aug. Christmas specials every Sat and Sun in Dec. Parking and refreshments available.

The triple-arched west front of Peterborough Cathedral

Petworth

West Sussex *p213 B2*

Petworth is a charming small country town dominated by Petworth Park, its walls some thirteen miles long. Within these walls is a beautiful deer park and the impressive mansion of Petworth House.

Re-built from the former Percy mansion by the sixth Duke of Somerset between 1688 and 1696, only the thirteenth-century chapel remains of the former building. The magnificent 320-foot west front faces a lake and the great park; the south front was reconstructed between 1869 and 1872 to the designs of Anthony Salvin. One of the finest art collections in England can be seen in its state rooms and galleries including works by Gainsborough, Rembrandt and Van Dyck. Perhaps the most notable collection is that of the artist Turner who was a frequent visitor to Petworth House. The most impressive room in the house is probably the carved room with its lovely decoration by Grinling Gibbons.

Open Apr to Oct, Tue, Wed, Thu, Sat, Sun and Bank Holiday Mon, pm. Deer park open all year. NT.

Pickering

North Yorkshire *p217 C4*

Lying on the edge of the North York Moors National Park, Pickering is an ancient market town with some interesting old buildings and historic coaching inns. The parish church is particularly notable, with its huge entrance porch and some of the best preserved fifteenth-century wall paintings in the country.

Agriculture has always been, and still is, important to the area and one of the great pioneers of farming development, William Marshall, lived in Pickering. He converted his home into one of the first agricultural colleges; today the Georgian building houses the Beck Isle Museum of Rural Life. The rooms illustrate, with bygones and folk exhibits, the history of Pickering and the surrounding area.

On the northern edge of the town the castle stands high on its mound. In the twelfth century it was a hunting lodge for medieval kings and a centre for all administration of their forests. Only fragments remain today, but there is still a good deal to see.

A stretch of the Tay, the longest river in Scotland, near Pitlochry

Sections of the wall with towers enclose a now grassy area, and upon the forty-three-foot high motte there are remains of the keep. The chapel is the only structure that has been restored.

One of Pickering's most popular attractions is the North York Moors Railway, which operates out of Pickering Station to Grosmont, some eighteen miles away. Diesel and steam-hauled trains carry passengers northwards, following Pickering Beck through the beautiful forest and moorland countryside of the National Park, including the outstanding Newton Dale. At the station in Pickering visitors can see the loco sheds and viewing gallery.

Museum open Easter to mid Oct daily.
Castle see AM info. Also open Sun am Apr to Sep. Parking available.
North Yorkshire Moors Railway open week before Easter to early Nov. Parking and refreshments available.

Pilkington Glass Museum

Merseyside *p216 E3*

With the natural resources of coal and fine sand available in the area, St Helens became an important glass-producing centre in the eighteenth century and has continued to be so. Attached to the headquarters of the Pilkington Company in Prescot Road is an interesting museum of the history of glassmaking. The displays on two floors include some which show how glass was made, as well as the development of glassmaking techniques, decorating glass, clear and coloured glass, plate glass, mirrors, optical glass and uses of glass in science, technology, transport and building.

Open all year (except Christmas and New Year) daily, pm only Sat, Sun and Bank Holidays. Refreshments available.

Pitlochry

Tayside *p221 D1*

Pitlochry, lying almost exactly in the centre of Scotland, is a popular base for touring. The origins of Pitlochry go back to prehistoric times and evidence of this may be seen on the present golf course where the remains of a 2,000-year-old Pictish fort are to be found.

The town of today is a well-known holiday resort with notable manufacturing interests, namely tweed and whisky. Its Festival Theatre, Scotland's Theatre in the Hills, is internationally famous for its summer presentations of drama, music and art.

To the north of the town lies the Pass of Killiecrankie, notorious site of a seventeenth-century battle. Also to the north lies the picturesque village of Moulin with its ruined fourteenth-century Black Castle. Some one-and-a-half miles south of the town, at the entrance to the Dunfallandy House mausoleum, is the Dunfallandy Stone, a Pictish sculptured slab from the eighth century.

Pitlochry dam, situated some ten minutes walk from the town centre, has a public walkway along the crest which links up with Forestry Commission footpaths. The power station is not open, but there is public access to an exhibition area which contains a viewing gallery and an illustrated history of the development of hydro-electricity in the Highlands. Observation chambers in the 900-foot long fish ladder provide close-up views of salmon returning upstream to their spawning grounds.

About two miles to the north-west of Pitlochry lies the Faskally Wayside Centre, on the shores of the idyllic man-made Loch Faskally. The centre incorporates woodland, picnic facilities, a children's play area and a nature trail.

Power Station Dam and Fish Ladder Exhibition area open Easter to Oct daily. Fish Ladder observation chambers open during daylight hours.
Faskally Wayside Centre open May to Sep daily.

The west front of Petworth House looks out onto a 2,000-acre estate

Plymouth Devon *p212 C2*

An historic seaport with a great maritime tradition – it was from here that Captain Cook sailed round the world; so, many years later, did Sir Francis Chichester, and the Pilgrim Fathers put into Plymouth for repairs before finally departing for the New World.

Sutton Pool beside the Barbican – the old town of Plymouth Drake knew

By far the most famous of all the seafarers connected with Plymouth is Sir Francis Drake, the local boy who became a national hero and of whom the city has been justifiably proud for 400 years. From the Hoe, which he made famous with his legendary game of bowls, his statue looks out across the sea he loved. The Hoe is still a pleasant open space of lawns and flower beds, backed by a row of cannons.

However, Plymouth's maritime heritage is not confined to the history books, for it is still a major base for the Royal Navy at their Devonport dockyard. While the presence of the Navy ensured Plymouth's prosperity over the years, it also brought about the devastation of the 1941 Plymouth Blitz. Nevertheless, from the rubble of bomb damage has risen a new city centre with good shops and civic offices. Fortunately not all of the historic buildings were destroyed, and the area known as the Barbican is an attractive Old Quarter with narrow streets, old houses and a busy harbour.

City Museum and Art Gallery
This interesting museum covers local history, archaeology and natural history. The art gallery has a collection of West Country scenes by local artists, including Sir Joshua Reynolds, together with portraits and collections of porcelain and silver.

Drake's statue, Plymouth

Royal Citadel
Charles II built this impressive fortress and its remaining buildings include the Guard House, the Governor's House and the Chapel. The entrance gateway is still magnificent, and from its ramparts there are superb views across the city and along the coast.

Elizabethan House
An attractive sixteenth-century house in the heart of the old Barbican area has retained most of its original features and contains period furniture.

The Merchant's House
The largest of Plymouth's old buildings to have survived, the Merchant's House now contains a museum which illustrates the development of Plymouth in the Middle Ages.

Prysten House
This was the Priest's House of the nearby St Andrews Church and was built in 1490. One room is dedicated to the Mayflower story, and there is also a model of Plymouth as it was in 1620, and a herb display.

Drake's Island
A prominent feature in Plymouth Sound, this was a fortress and a prison before becoming an Adventure Training Centre. The guided tour includes underground caverns and a museum.

Mount Edgcumbe House and Country Park
Across the Sound from Plymouth is a Tudor-style mansion, extensively restored following bomb damage during World War II and now the home of the seventh Earl of Mount Edgcumbe. Unfortunately the contents and many works of art were also destroyed

and only a few examples remain of a once-large collection of Reynolds portraits. The grounds include formal gardens, over 800 acres of woodland and lovely scenic walks along some ten miles of coastline.

Museum and Art Gallery open all year (except Good Fri and Christmas) daily, pm only on Sun.
Royal Citadel open at any reasonable time at the discretion of the military. AM.
Elizabethan House open all year Mon to Sat, also Sun pm from Apr to Sep.
Merchant's House open all year daily, (except Good Fri and Christmas) Sun, pm only.
Prysten House open all year daily, (except Sun, Good Fri, Christmas and New Year's Day.)
Drake's Island open early May to Aug. Guided tours depart from Mayflower Steps in the Barbican. Refreshments available.
Mount Edgcumbe House House and Higher Gardens open May to Sep Mon and Tue pm. Park and Lower Gardens open all year daily.

Poldark Mining and Wendron Forge

Cornwall *p211 B1*

This area was mined for tin even before the Romans came and gave many Cornishmen their livelihood over several centuries. Vast amounts of tin were extracted before the industry finally went into a decline, but here at Poldark Mining visitors can see the old workings and a remarkable collection of historic engines and machinery. The site covers some three acres and the underground tour shows where the miners worked, the tools they used and the shafts which were their access to the world above.

A somewhat unexpected feature is the underground postbox, and souvenir postcards sent from here carry a special postmark. The tour progresses through a series of museum chambers where there are a large number of steam engines, many of which can be seen working. These include beam engines, pumps, a Horizontal Tandem steam engine and an Overhead Grasshopper engine. Not all of the exhibits are associated with mining, however. There are also printing presses, some tools of the cobbler's trade, cream, butter and cheese making equipment, and such household items as clothes mangles and ranges.

Wendron Forge was once very much in demand, serving a wide area, and later progressed into ornamental ironwork. After a period of disuse the forge is once more being worked and the blacksmith's craft is again being put to use, producing some lovely pieces of decorative ironwork. The licensed restaurant at the site contains a five-ton working waterwheel and there is also a craft shop and children's amusements.

Open Easter to Oct daily. Parking and refreshments available.

An industrial steam locomotive at Poldark Mining and Wendron Forge

Polesden Lacey

Surrey *p213 B2*

Polesden Lacey is situated on high ground with fine views from its south terrace across to Ranmore Woods. Thomas Cubitt built his Regency 'villa' here between 1821–23, on the site of the original house, and over the years a succession of owners have altered and enlarged the property. In 1906 Polesden Lacey was purchased by Captain Grevelle and his wife became a celebrated hostess. She entertained many famous people over a period of forty years, and even lent the house to King George VI and Queen Elizabeth for part of their honeymoon.

The house contains a fine collection of furnishings, painting, porcelain, tapestries and other works of art. The estate of over 1,000 acres is a delightful mixture of woodland and formal gardens and there is an open-air theatre here.

House open Mar and Nov, Sat and Sun pm only, Apr to Oct daily (except Mon and Fri) pm only. Open Bank Holiday Mon but closed on following Tue.
Gardens open all year daily. Refreshments available. NT.

Polperro

Cornwall *p212 C1*

Picturesque little colour-washed cottages huddle together in a deep cleft cut from the cliffs by the river Pol, making Polperro one of the most popular and frequently photographed of the Cornish fishing villages. Its streets are narrow and winding, often with no pavements, and in the height of the season it is necessary for visitors' cars to be left outside the village.

The most attractive part of the village is the little harbour, still used by local fishermen, but now also offering pleasure trips out to sea. Before the rest of the world discovered Cornwall, these were secluded beaches for the local smugglers to land their contraband, a local industry which is now remembered in the Museum of Smuggling in Talland Street. Here the displays relate the activities of both past and present-day smugglers.
Museum of Smuggling open Easter to Oct daily.

Polesden Lacey, where George VI and Queen Elizabeth honeymooned

Poole

Dorset *p212 F2*

Poole is a modern resort with a large natural harbour which has four tides a day as the sea ebbs and flows around the Isle of Wight. The tides keep the golden sands clean and are a great boon to the many pleasure craft entering and leaving the port. The beaches and amusements of the Sandbanks peninsula are attractive, especially for families. Between there and the Town Quay, are the headquarters of several yacht clubs and colourful craft swarm in the harbour. Boats can be hired from Sandbanks and ferries run from there across to Shell Bay.

The town has had a colourful history. In the Middle Ages it was the county's main port, it became popular with smugglers in the eighteenth century and during the Civil War became a Roundhead stronghold. Some of the first settlers in Newfoundland came from Poole in the nineteenth century and a lucrative trade developed, mostly in timber. This reached a peak at the time of the

Napoleonic Wars, and, as an expression of its wealth and civic pride, the town was almost completely rebuilt. To preserve the Georgian buildings and the few older houses which survive, fifteen acres near the Quay have been designated a Historic Precinct. Amongst the interesting buildings are the Customs House of 1813, the Harbour Office and St James Church, both built in 1820, and the former Guildhall of 1761, now a museum illustrating Poole's social history during the eighteenth and nineteenth centuries.

Also on the quay is the Maritime Museum, housed in the Town Cellar which dates from the late fifteenth century. The exhibits depict Poole's strong links with the sea since prehistoric times up until this century.

Here too is the world-famous Poole Pottery which was founded in 1873, although the characteristic pottery known today began in 1921. The various stages involved are demonstrated by craftsmen.

For leisure facilities Poole Park, with its large boating lake, miniature railway, and small zoo is deservedly popular. The more unusual animals in the zoo include wild cats, otters and porcupines.

Guildhall Museum open all year daily (except 1 Jan, Good Fri, 25 and 26 Dec), Sun pm only.
Maritime Museum open as above.
Poole Park Zoo open Mar to Oct daily, Nov to Feb, weekends and public holidays only. Daily during school holidays. Parking available.
Poole Pottery open all year (except Christmas week and Bank Holidays).

The harbour scene at Polperro, typically and unmistakably Cornish

Porchester Castle

Hampshire *p213 A2*

On a long spit of land projecting into Portsmouth Harbour stands Porchester Castle. It was built as a fort by the Romans in the third century as one of the many defences strung around the south and east coasts of England. The original twenty-foot high wall still stands, as do fourteen of the twenty round bastions, covering some nine acres.

A priory and its church was built in 1133 outside the inner walls of the castle, although only the church has survived, of which its west front and carved font are particularly fine features.

The great tower was added in the fourteenth century by Sir Robert Assheton, Constable of the Castle, and it became known as Assheton's Tower.

Buildings within the inner courtyard were converted into a palace by Richard II at the end of the fourteenth century and the ruined remains of the kitchen, hall and great chamber can still be seen.

The castle had been popular as a residence with royalty visiting Portsmouth including King John, Henry V who embarked from here for Agincourt and Henry VIII who came to the castle with Anne Boleyn.

During the seventeenth century the castle gradually fell into disrepair, although prisoners from the Napoleonic Wars were kept here.

See AM info. Also open Sun am, Apr to Sep. Parking available.

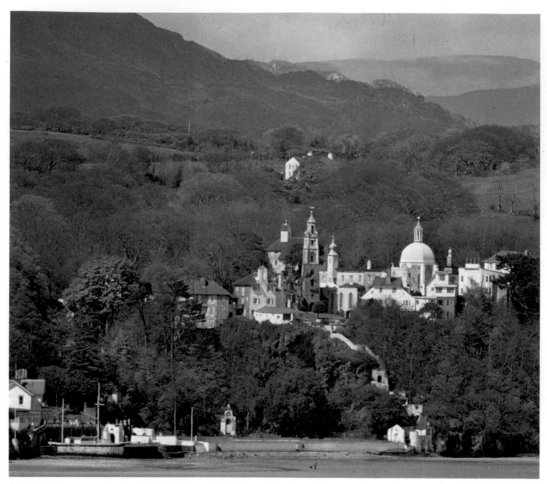

Sited between the estuaries of the Glaslyn and the Dwyryd, Portmeirion resembles a Mediterranean village

Portmeirion

Gwynedd *p216 C2*

This unique, fairy-tale village is situated on a rocky tree-clad peninsula on the shores of Cardigan Bay. Here, Welsh architect Sir Clough Williams-Ellis built his own dream village amidst exceptionally beautiful scenery.

At the nucleus of the estate is a sumptuous waterfront hotel – rebuilt from the original house and still containing a fine eighteenth-century fireplace, and a library which was moved here from the Great Exhibition of 1851. All around are many architectural fancies, among them an Italianate campanile (detached bell-tower), castle and lighthouse. Colonnades, a watch tower, grottoes and cobbled squares all combine harmoniously with pastel-shaded picturesque cottages. The buildings have been sited to the best advantage of the natural heights and slopes, with much of their materials being rescued from demolished buildings throughout Britain.

One - hundred-and-seventy-five acres of sub-tropical coastal, cliff and wooded gardens surround this harbour village occupying a mile or so of the Portmeirion peninsula. The estate encompasses the sixty-acre Gwyllt Gardens, considered to be one of the finest wild gardens in Wales. They include miles of dense woodland paths, and are famous for their fine display of rhododendrons, hydrangeas, azaleas and sub-tropical flora. Among the many varieties of trees here are palms, eucalyptus, cypresses and magnolias, together with various ferns and lilies.

The village has been used as a film set on numerous occasions and was the setting for the successful television series *The Prisoner*. Here, in one week, Noel Coward wrote his comedy *Blithe Spirit*. The village is run as a holiday complex but is open to toll-paying visitors. Apart from the hotel itself, accommodation is mainly self-catering in the cottages.

Village and Gwyllt Gardens open Apr to Oct daily. Parking and refreshments available.

Portsmouth

Hampshire *p213 A1*

There has been a harbour at Portsmouth since Roman times, and the city has been important in the history of the Navy since the fourteenth century.

Although 'Pompey' was heavily bombed during World War II, much of the original town survives. Old Portsmouth, the area around the Isle of Wight car-ferry embarkation point, is particularly interesting with its cobbled streets, narrow lanes and tall slim houses. One in the High Street is named after the Duke of Buckingham who was murdered here in 1628. From the gun ports and ramparts of the seventeenth-century gun-battery and sally-port, there are good views of the harbour mouth and Spithead, where Fleet Reviews are traditionally carried out.

The city has several literary ties: Sir Arthur Conan Doyle practised as a doctor at Bush Villas, Elm Grove, Southsea and wrote his first story, *A Study in Scarlet*, there; H. G. Wells worked as a drapery assistant in a local shop, and Charles Dickens was born in the town in 1812. His Georgian house, furnished in the style of the 1800s, contains the author's personal relics and an extensive library of his works, including many rare first editions.

Refurbished in 1972, the City Museum and Art Gallery houses the Fine and Decorative art collections, together with social history material and a display on the history of Portsmouth.

HMS *Victory*, Lord Nelson's famous flagship at the Battle of Trafalgar, which is moored in the harbour, has been described as 'the proudest sight in Britain', and because of her age and historic significance the ship is unique as the world's most outstanding example of ship restoration. Nearby is the Portsmouth Royal Naval Museum. It complements the ship by housing those relics of Nelson and Trafalgar which cannot be conveniently displayed on board as well as exhibiting a large collection of ships and figureheads. The interesting Nelson-McCarthy Collection consists of prints, paintings, ceramics, medallions, letters and miniatures.

The Royal Marines have a long association with Portsmouth. Their imposing Victorian Officers' Mess has been converted for use as the Royal Marines' Museum which was opened by the Duke of Edinburgh in 1975 and tells the story of the Marines throughout their 300 years of history.

Dickens Birthplace Museum open Mar to Oct daily.
City Museum and Art Gallery open all year daily (except Christmas). Parking and refreshments available.
HMS Victory open all year daily, Sun pm only.
Royal Naval Museum open all year daily, Sun pm only. Refreshments available.
Royal Marines' Museum open all year daily, am only on Sat and Sun.

HMS *Victory* in Portsmouth Harbour

Powderham Castle

Devon *p212 D2*

The ancestral home of the Earls of Devon, Powerham Castle is delightfully set in beautiful parkland beside the Exe Estuary.

The original fourteenth to fifteenth-century building was more a defensive manor than a castle, and was converted into today's stately mansion during the late eighteenth century, after suffering damage during the Civil War. Today's structure is therefore a blend of styles, the term castle being well suited though to Powderham's solid masonry and embattled towers.

Of particular interest inside are the medieval chapel, the elaborately decorated staircase and the music room. The very pretty chapel is the only medieval room to be seen and has an arched and braced timber roof, along with excellent old carved bench ends. The magnificent staircase rises the entire height of the building. The plasterwork by John Jenkins has drops of fruit and flowers modelled and arranged between panels. The music room was designed by James Wyatt in the 1790s and has a central dome and musical instruments modelled in its fine plasterwork, all lit by the room's bow window.

Outside there is a fine terraced garden and the mansion's extensive wooded parkland, with its deer, almost reaches the river. The parkland was once part of the marshland and bogs of the river Exe before it was reclaimed during the eighteenth century and planted with cedar, lime and oak trees.

Open Easter, Sun to mid May, then daily (except Fri and Sat) until Sep, pm only. Refreshments available.

Prinknash Abbey and Bird Park

Gloucestershire *p212 F4*

There are two abbeys at Prinknash, both set among the trees on opposite sides of the lovely parkland. The old abbey, which dates in parts from the fourteenth century, spent some 400 years in private ownership, following the Dissolution, until it was given back to the Benedictine monks in 1928. It is a pleasant building of mellow stone, and much of its history can be traced through the heraldic features in its carved woodwork and stained glass. An attractive feature of the old abbey is the charming medieval chapel. When the monks returned to Prinknash in 1928 they found the original building hopelessly inadequate for their expanding community, and in 1939 the foundation stone was laid for the new abbey. Completed in 1972, it is a bright, clean and modern building of total simplicity.

During the excavation of the foundations for the new building a bed of clay was discovered which prompted the monks to establish a pottery and today Prinknash Pottery is world-famous. Visitors can see the monks and their employees at work in the pottery and guides are available. The pottery is just one of the industries followed by the monks which include farming, ironwork stained glass and incense making.

Nine acres of the park have been set out as a Bird Park with many varieties of birds and waterfowl. Several types of swans and geese, notably a flock of Snow geese, are free flying and can be fed by visitors. There are also Pygmy goats and Jacob sheep, and the monk's fish ponds which were built before the Reformation, are still alive with trout.

Abbey open all year daily.
Pottery Mon to Fri also Sat am and Sun pm (shop open all day).
Bird Park open Mar to Oct daily, Nov to Feb weekends only. Parking and refreshments available.

A thatched replica of an Iron Age Dorset dwelling

Queen Elizabeth Country Park

Hampshire *p213 A2*

The park covers 1,400 acres of forest and downland including level plains, deep valleys and woodland which shelter numerous varieties of wildlife. Several marked routes throughout the park guide the visitor amongst forests and hills, over plains and down valleys; the length and stamina required for each differs according to the trail chosen.

A nineteenth-century shepherd's hut can be seen in the sheep management area, and many items used in the farming of these hills throughout the centuries are kept in the forest craft demonstration area.

The Butser Ancient Farm is a working reconstruction of an Iron Age settlement, operated according to the methods used around 2,300 years ago. The largest building on the farm is a thatched round house, made of oak stakes, woven with hazel rods, and daubed with clay. This house was based upon an Iron Age dwelling found in Dorset. The animals being raised on the farm are Exmoor ponies, Dexter cattle and Soay sheep, the nearest equivalent to historic breeds. Two fields are planted with crops commonly grown during Iron Age times, these were spelt and emmer, primitive varieties of wheat. A hand mill, weaving loom and kiln are amongst working replicas to be seen at the farm.

Open all year daily. Parking and refreshments available.

The last Abbot of Gloucester rebuilt an old hunting lodge into this lovely manor house – Prinknash Abbey

Raby Castle

Co Durham *p217 B4*

Dating from the latter part of the fourteenth century when Sir John Neville, High Admiral of England fortified it, Raby Castle is reputed to incorporate a tower built by King Canute in the eleventh century. The most notable features of the castle are the nine towers, including the Neville Tower, which was built in such a way that carriages were able to drive up to an inner staircase.

An outstanding collection of paintings from English, Dutch and Spanish schools are contained within the castle, as well as numerous pieces of French furniture and porcelain. There is also a collection of horse-drawn vehicles from the eighteenth and nineteenth centuries, and a superb medieval kitchen.

Open Easter to Sep daily, pm only, Easter weekend including Tue; Wed, Sun and Bank Holiday weekends until June then daily except Sat until Sep. Parking and refreshments available.

Raglan Castle

Gwent *p212 E4*

This fine example of a medieval castle was probably the last of its kind to be built in Wales, and although damaged during the Civil War, remains impressive.

The walls of the castle enclose the Pitched Stone Court, named after its cobbled surface, and the Fountain Court, where only the foundations remain of the large marble fountain which once sent water as high as the walls themselves. Dividing the two courtyards is the great hall and the adjacent buttery – both parts of the later additions which made the castle more comfortable.

When the castle was first built in the fourteenth century, there was still a certain amount of unrest in Wales, and the main keep, known as the Yellow Tower of Gwent, was built outside the castle walls with its own moat and drawbridge. In this way the five-storey hexagonal keep watched over the two gateways to the castle and could, at the same time, be isolated from the main part of the building. The Cromwellians set charges under the tower, but even they could not completely destroy it. From the top of its staircase there are superb views of the surrounding countryside.

See AM info. Also open Sun am Apr to Sep. Parking available.

Ragley Hall

Warwickshire *p216 F1*

Ragley Hall stands at the highest point of a 400-acre park. It is a magnificent seventeenth-century porticoed Palladian mansion with an imposing exterior which is more than matched by the craftsmanship displayed within.

It was the 1st Marquess of Hertford who commissioned James Gibbs to design the great hall, some seventy feet long and forty feet high. With its exquisite rococo plasterwork on the walls and ceiling, it is considered to be one of the finest baroque rooms in England. Many great artists have contributed to the decoration of the house over the centuries and the whole atmosphere is one of wealth and luxury.

Ragley Hall is filled with treasures, including collections of Sèvres porcelain, period furniture and fine paintings, such as the *Raising of Lazarus* by Cornelis van Haarlem. There are also portraits of the Hertfords' ancestors, among them Horace Walpole, a cousin of the 1st Marquess.

The Prince Regent visited the Hall during the late eighteenth century and the bedroom he occupied has been preserved.

The park was laid out by Capability Brown in 1750 and, despite nineteenth-century alterations, has retained most of its original pattern. More recent attractions include a children's adventure wood, a country trail and pleasant lakeside picnic areas.

Open Easter to Sep, Tue, Wed, Thu, Sat, Sun and Bank Holidays, pm only. Parking and refreshments available.

Ravenglass and Eskdale Railway

Cumbria *p216 D5*

Ravenglass lies on the Cumbrian coast, at the mouth of the river Esk. Once a Roman port, this delightfully unspoilt little fishing community is the starting point of the Ravenglass and Eskdale Railway. Originally constructed in 1875 to carry iron ore, this miniature fifteen inch narrow-gauge railway, known affectionately as L'aal Ratty has carried passengers since 1876. Its steam and diesel locomotives, open and saloon coaches, operate over seven miles of beautiful scenery. Running from Ravenglass to Dalegarth, near the attractive village of Boot in Eskdale, the train stops at both Irton Road and The Green en route. There is a small railway museum at Ravenglass.

Open Apr to Oct daily. (reduced services at other times. One train a day during winter, except Christmas). Parking and refreshments available.

Rhuddlan Castle

Clwyd *p216 D3*

This great castle ruin stands on a mound overlooking the banks of the river Clwyd, which was diverted into a channel so that the garrison could be supplied from the sea, two miles away. The present structure was built on the orders of Edward I as part of his plan to subdue the Welsh Princes, and he used it as his headquarters during campaigns. It continued in use until the Civil War, when it was wrecked by order of Parliament and subsequently used by the local people as a quarry.

It is still possible to appreciate the power of this once substantial fortress. One of four strictly concentric castles in Wales, it was built to a diamond-shaped plan with round towers, gatehouses, and nine-foot-thick curtain walls. In the east gatehouse near the centre of the passage, are the holes which accommodated the portcullis and gate.

See AM info. Also open Sun am, Apr to Sep. Parking available.

The baron hall at Raby Castle is 136 feet long and used to hold as many as 700 knights

Riber Castle Fauna Reserve

Derbyshire *p217 B1*

Standing at a height of 800 feet, overlooking the delightful town of Matlock, is Riber Castle – a prominent landmark for many miles around. Although its turrets and battlements give the impression of an ancient fortress, the castle was built in 1862 by Mr John Smedley, a local textile manufacturer who developed Matlock as a spa. For a good many years the castle was utilised as a school, but following this, between 1930 and 1950, it lay empty and fell to ruins. However, in 1962, a group of zoologists acquired the grounds, which cover over twenty acres, and established a nature reserve in them.

A comprehensive collection of British and European birds and animals live here now in natural surroundings. Of special interest are the breeding colonies of European lynx, whose kittens can be seen from June to September. The large collection of domestic animals include rare breeds of sheep, pigs, cattle, goats and poultry. Other features of the reserve are a butterfly exhibition, a model railway, models of prehistoric creatures, and some vintage cars.

Open all year daily (except 25 Dec). Parking and refreshments available.

Richmond

North Yorkshire *p217 B4*

Richmond is a pleasant mixture of narrow, twisting lanes and large open spaces. It contains examples of many architectural styles, incorporating buildings of the medieval, Georgian and Victorian periods. Two of the town's oldest features are the castle, which towers above the river Swale, and Grey Friars Tower. The latter dates from the fourteenth century and stands in Friary Gardens; it was once part of a Franciscan Friary and a curfew bell is still sounded.

The castle is an impressive example of early military architecture with a hundred-foot-high keep, built, curiously enough, on top of the gatehouse, and surrounded by some of the oldest defensive walls in the country. From the roof of the keep there are fine views of the river Swale. Scollards Hall, beside the east wall, dates from around 1080 and is probably the most ancient

It is easy to see why Richmond's castle, 100 feet above the river Swale, was an ideal military stronghold

domestic building in England.

Holy Trinity Church, which stands in the cobbled market place, is the oldest church in Richmond and, in 1971, was converted into the Green Howards Museum. The museum covers the history of the regiment and contains a collection of uniforms, weapons and medals, some of which date back as far as 1688. A separate chapel has been retained so that services may still be held in Holy Trinity.

Apart from its historical associations, Richmond is a popular touring centre, lying in a superb position at the entrance to Swaledale, and within easy reach of the rest of the Yorkshire Dales National Park. It is a favourite starting point for walkers and cyclists and there is a very pleasant local walk beside the Swale, which ends near the remains of twelfth-century Easby Abbey to the south-east of the town.

Castle See AM info. Also open Sun am, Apr to Sep.
The Green Howards Museum Open all year (except Dec and Jan); Apr to Oct daily, Sun pm only; Nov, Feb and Mar Mon to Sat only.

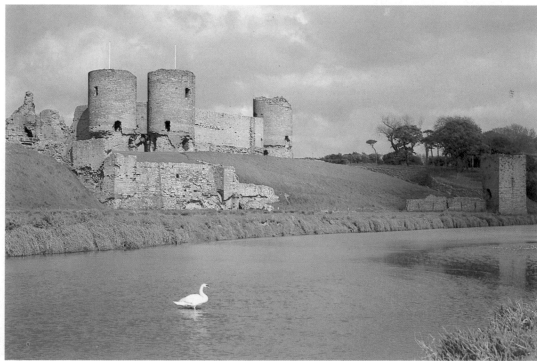

Although moated on three sides and bounded by the Clwyd on the fourth, Rhuddlan Castle fell in the Civil War

Rievaulx Abbey

North Yorkshire *p217 B4*

The grandeur of the setting and the considerable remains of this beautiful abbey, make Rievaulx one of the most magnificent monastic ruins in the country. The lofty walls of the abbey church and monastic quarters occupy a secluded and sheltered site in the valley of the river Rye, from which it took its name in 1131 on becoming the first Cistercian foundation in northern England.

On the hill above the abbey is Rievaulx Terrace, now the property of the National Trust. This is a winding, landscaped terrace of some half-a-mile in length, which was laid out in the mid-eighteenth century for Thomas Duncombe of nearby Duncombe Park. There are Classical temples at either end and the landscaping has been cleverly designed to reveal superb views all along the terrace.

Abbey see AM info. Also open Sun am Apr to Sep. Parking available.
Terrace open Apr to Oct (except Good Fri) daily. Parking available. NT.

Ripon

North Yorkshire *p217 B3*

Standing at the confluence of the rivers Ure, Skell and Laver, Ripon is often referred to as the Gateway to the Dales.

The large Market Square is dominated by a ninety-foot-high obelisk, where a forest horn is still sounded at each corner every night at 9.00 pm. At the south-west corner of the square is the Wakeman's House, a fourteenth-century half-timbered building. Formerly the official residence of the Wakeman and later the Mayor, it now houses a small museum of local history.

Built on an east-facing ridge in the middle of this busy market town is the small, but very impressive, cathedral. There has been a church on this site for over 1,300 years, but it was not until 1836 that Ripon was granted cathedral status.

The thirteenth-century west front is quite plain in contrast to the east, with its magnificent fifty-foot-high window in Decorated style, supported by gabled buttresses.

Inside, the notable fifteenth-century choir stalls are the work of local carvers. Above the south transept is the library, which contains books dating from before 1500 – including a twelfth-century manuscript copy of the Bible. Beneath the grand sixteenth-century Gothic nave is the oldest part of the cathedral, a seventh-century Saxon crypt, now a strongroom in which ancient silver and other church treasures are displayed.

Wakeman's House Museum open Spring Bank Holiday to Sep daily, Sun, pm only. Sat only during winter.

Roche Abbey

South Yorkshire *p217 B2*

This Cistercian house was named after a rock formation which resembled a cross and was a place of pilgrimage. Founded in the twelfth century by two local landowners, the abbey was colonised by monks from Newminster Abbey near Morpeth. During the sixteenth century the Dissolution of the monasteries led to the surrender, and subsequent plundering, of Roche Abbey. Centuries later the ruins were placed in the care of what was then the Ministry of Public Building and Works, by the 10th Earl of Scarborough.

In the valley of the river Ryton, close to Sandbeck Park, the ruins lie amidst lawns and woods landscaped by Capability Brown. The vaulted gatehouse, partly rebuilt in the fourteenth century, is particularly well preserved, and parts of the transept walls still stand to their full height.

See AM info. Parking available.

Rochester

Kent *p213 C3*

The strategic importance of Rochester was recognised by the Romans – who first fortified it, the Saxons – who incorporated the remains of Roman walls into their own fortifications, and the Normans – who built a castle of which the walls and an enormous keep survive. At the top of the spiral stairway there are superb views of the area. Just across the road from the castle is the great cathedral. Bishop Gundulf of

In its heyday, Rievaulx, one of the great abbeys of the north, housed a community of over 600; for more than 400 years it has stood in ruins

Bec, chief castle builder to William the Conqueror, was responsible for replacing the Saxon church, but only the lower part of the tower remains from the eleventh century. The rest of the cathedral is largely twelfth-century, with additions from the thirteenth and fifteenth centuries – all much restored and rebuilt after the depredations of the Civil War. Of particular interest is the elaborate Romanesque carving of the west door, the choir stalls, the chapter house doorway of 1340, and a series of bishops' tombs spanning seven centuries.

The city has many associations with Charles Dickens, who spent his boyhood here. In his story *The Seven Poor Travellers*, he describes the Watts Charity building. The charity, founded in 1579 by Sir Richard Watts, provided for any poor travellers, who were given dinner, accommodation for one night, and fourpence to help them on their way. Other buildings described in his books include the Royal Victoria and Bull; Restoration House – so called because Charles II stayed a night there on his return to London; the Tudor Eastgate House – now a museum with a display of Dickensia; and Chertsey's Gate – one of three surviving monastic gates.

Another person closely associated with Rochester was Admiral Sir Cloudsley Shovell. He built the Corn Exchange and paid for renovations to the Guildhall which dates from 1687 and has a 1780 copper weathervane in the form of a ship.

Castle see AM info, but closed all day Tue and pm Fri. Parking available.
Eastgate House open all year daily (except Sun).

Rockingham Castle

Northamptonshire *p213 B5*

Many old thatched cottages line the steep hill of the pleasant village of Rockingham. High above it on a hill stands Rockingham Castle, commanding scenic views ranging over five counties. First built by William the Conqueror, the castle occupies the site of an earlier fortification. Almost every style of architecture from the eleventh century blend harmoniously together, although the present house within the Norman walls is predominantly Tudor. The sixteenth and seventeenth centuries saw considerable modernisation of the castle, trans-

Rockingham Castle, once a royal hunting lodge, looks down on the pleasant old houses of Rockingham village

forming the once dilapidated fortification into a comfortable country house.

Many treasures are to be found within, including two chests, one belonging to King John, the other to Henry V. Indeed, it was believed that King John had hidden his jewels on the castle premises, but excavations carried out in 1935 to find the hoard proved fruitless.

The servants' hall and great kitchen give the visitor a glimpse of what life must have been like 'below stairs'; other domestic buildings include a brewhouse, woodshed, dairy, and servants quarters.

Within the grounds is a famous 400-year-old yew hedge shaped in the form of elephants. Charles Dickens is reputed to have seen Lady Dedlock's ghost behind it on one occasion. An iron gate leads to the delightful Wild Garden, a ravine containing some 200 varieties of trees and shrubs. A

vast expanse of lawn, called the Tilting Ground, is headed by a beautiful avenue of sycamore trees, providing a majestic setting for this once royal castle.

Open Easter to Sep, Thu, Sun, Bank Holiday Mon and following Tue pm only. Parking and refreshments available.

Romsey

Hampshire *p213 A2*

Lying on the banks of the river Test – one of England's finest trout and salmon streams, is this ancient market town which grew up around its now famous abbey.

Founded in the tenth century, the abbey church is a splendid Norman construction built in the shape of a cross. A carved (possibly Saxon) seven-foot-high crucifix can be seen outside against the south transept wall, and an early sixteenth-century painted wooden reredos standing

Rochester, onetime guardian of the river Medway, is still a major port

in the north transept. Within the vestry is the Romsey Psalter (a fifteenth-century illuminated manuscript). Today the abbey is a popular place of pilgrimage, for it is here that the much loved Lord Louis, Earl Mountbatten of Burma, who was horrifically assassinated in August of 1979, is laid to rest.

Not far from the abbey is King John's House, a thirteenth-century flint building which was used as his hunting lodge, and is now a museum.

Broadlands, home of the late Lord Mountbatten, lies just south of the town, and is one of the finest examples of mid-Georgian architecture in England. The elegant eighteenth-century house is set in lovely landscaped grounds beside the river Test which remain a tribute to the genius of Capability Brown. Robert Adam, William Kent and Henry Holland the Younger, all contributed to the creation of this masterpiece, with its richly decorated interior and fine works of art. Broadlands has many historic associations and has long been famous as a centre of hospitality for royalty and distinguished visitors. It was once the country house of the great Victorian Prime Minister, Lord Palmerston, and Queen Elizabeth II and Prince Philip began their honeymoon here.

Broadlands open Apr to Sep daily. Closed Mon except Aug, Sep and Bank Holidays. Parking and refreshments available.
King John's House open Spring Bank Holiday to end Sep, Tue pm only; Thur, Fri and Sat all day.

Rufford Old Hall

Lancashire *p216 E4*

One of the finest examples of its type, this medieval black and white timbered building stands on the banks of the Leeds and Liverpool canal. The only additions to the building were the brick wings, one was added in 1662 (now demolished), and the other in 1821. The original great hall is of particular interest, as it has an ornate hammerbeam roof and an intricately carved sixteenth-century wooden screen.

Inside the manor is some excellent period furniture, tapestries, armour and arms which, together with the house, were presented by Lord Hesketh to the National Trust in 1936. Also housed here is the Philip Ashcroft museum of country life.

Open Mar to Dec, Tue to Sun and Bank Holiday, pm only (closed Wed in Mar, Oct, Nov and Dec). NT.

The great hall at Rufford – the blocked doors once led to the other brick service wing

Rydal Mount

Cumbria *p220 E1*

This sixteenth-century yeoman's house was the home of William Wordsworth from 1813 until his death in 1850. The house stands on a hill above the small village of Rydal, overlooking the lower extremities of Rydal Water, and is surrounded by four-and-a-half acres of gardens laid out under the personal supervision of the poet. Wordsworth became Poet Laureate whilst living here, and, with his fame and popularity reaching its height, received a constant stream of admiring visitors – the forerunners of the tourists who throng the area today.

The house is now owned by a descendant of Wordsworth, and contains a collection of family portraits and many relics of the poet's life, including furniture and first editions of his works. A neighbouring meadow, Dora Field, (National Trust property) is named after Wordsworth's daughter who was particularly fond of the area.

What was once Wordsworth's favourite walk, is now a well-trodden footpath leading from Rydal Mount around Rydal Water – a small lake dotted with islands lying below the 2,000 foot Rydal Fell – to Grasmere, where the poet previously lived.

One of Wordsworth's lakeland homes – Rydal Mount

Rydal village has other literary connections. De Quincey and Hartley Coleridge were both former occupiers of Nab Cottage, situated near Rydal Water, and St Mary's Church has a memorial window dedicated to the poet Dr Arnold and his family.

Open daily all year (except mid Jan to Feb). Parking and refreshments available.

Ryedale Folk Museum

North Yorkshire *p217 C4*

This fascinating museum superbly illustrates the life and work of an agricultural community from the sixteenth to twentieth centuries. Tools, implements, domestic appliances and furniture are on show in authentic settings, which include a mock smithy and cobbler's shop. Sometimes there are demonstrations of various old country crafts. Outside are many reconstructed cruck buildings, including a medieval longhouse, a manor house, crofters' cottages, a barn and a wheelshed. There is also a particularly interesting medieval glass kiln, believed to be unique.

The museum is within one of the most enchanting villages in the country – Hutton-le-Hole. Its houses face each other across the wide grassy banks of the picturesque Little Beck.

Open Easter to Sep daily, pm only (all day mid July to Aug).

St Albans Hertfordshire *p213 B3*

St Albans, named after Britain's first Christian martyr, Alban, has developed over a period of 2,000 years. Present day St Albans combines narrow, medieval streets where some half-timbered houses with overhanging upper storeys survive, with wide roads of elegant Georgian residences and modern buildings.

The massive tower of the Norman cathedral can be seen from most parts of the town, and there are pleasant gardens and open spaces such as Verulamium Park, with its large ornamental lake. French Row is where French mercenaries were quartered in 1216, whilst employed by the Barons in their squabbles with King John. Here stands the fifteenth-century Fleur de Lys Inn, partly built of timbers from an earlier inn where King John of France was imprisoned in 1356. Situated in Abbey Mill Lane is Ye Old Fighting Cocks, an unusual octagonal timber-framed building, claimed to be the oldest inhabited licensed house in England, although originally a monastic fishing lodge.

The Cathedral

The Paul de Caen, a Norman abbot, reconstructed the original Saxon abbey, built in the eighth century of flint and brick from the ruins of the Roman town. Parts of the Norman structure which have survived include the transept (the pillars of which may be Saxon), the choir, the tower, and the bays to the east of the tower. The 300-foot nave and aisles, built in the thirteenth century, make the abbey one of the longest in the country. Particularly noteworthy are the thirteenth and fourteenth-century paintings on the piers of the nave; the Purbeck marble Shrine of St Alban (a Roman soldier beheaded for concealing a Christian priest) which was reconstructed from shattered pieces discovered in the nineteenth century, and above this the chamber of the monk who kept watch over it. Interesting brasses include one of a fourteenth-century abbot, and monuments dating back to the fifteenth century.

City Museum

The Natural History section of this museum also includes some live specimens, whilst in the Social History and Folk Life section there is a remarkable collection of craft tools, set in reconstructions of craftsmen's shops.

Verulamium Theatre, Museum and Hypocaust

The Roman town was built on the banks of the river Ver to the west of the town centre – a site now occupied by Verulamium Park. Although much of the remains were plundered for building materials in Saxon times, excavations have revealed parts of the third-century walls, foundations of a street of shops and a section of a hypocaust – the Roman system of underfloor heating. Nearby is the Roman theatre, the only known example in Britain to have a stage, rather than an amphitheatre. It has been excavated and restored and measures some 180 feet across. The Verulamium Museum contains the best collection of Roman decorated wall plaster in Britain, and there are also sections of mosaics, a painted ceiling and Roman artifacts. A model shows how the town would have looked during the third century.

Kingsbury Water Mill

This sixteenth-century water mill in St Michael's Street has been restored to working order and is now open as a museum. There is also an art gallery, and a craft shop displaying woodwork, pottery, pewter, jewellery and lace.

St Albans Organ Museum

A colourful collection of fairground and other mechanical organs and musical instruments is housed in this museum. There is also a saleable selection of records and books about various mechanical instruments.

Gorhambury House

This late Georgian mansion – home of the Earl of Verulam – contains Chippendale furniture, Grimston portraits and sixteenth-century enamelled glass. Francis Bacon, Viscount St Albans, philosopher and statesman, lived in the previous house on this site, and there are several mementoes of his family on show.

St Albans' clock tower from the church gateway

Royal National Rose Society's Garden

Lovely rose gardens here incorporate a trial ground for new species. The fragrant and colourful displays to be seen include 30,000 plants of some 1,650 varieties.

City Museum open all year daily (except Sun).
Verulamium Theatre open all year daily (am only Nov to Feb) **Museum** open all year daily, Sun pm only.
Kingsbury Water Mill open all year daily (except Christmas Day).
St Albans Organ Museum open for recitals Sun pm.
Gorhambury House open May to Sep, Thu pm only. Parking available.
Royal National Rose Society's Gardens open mid June to Sep daily (except Bank Holiday Mon), Sun pm only. Parking and refreshments available.

St Michael's Mount – an early centre of Christianity in these isles

St Mawes Castle

Cornwall *p211 B1*

One of Henry VIII's coastal defence fortifications, St Mawes Castle was completed in 1543 and together with Pendennis Castle on the opposite bank, guarded the entrance to Falmouth harbour. It follows the trefoil, or cloverleaf, pattern much favoured by Henry VIII, with circular bastions protecting the round central tower. It has been well restored, and is more or less complete with some carvings, Tudor fireplaces, and Latin engravings on the walls. The slots in the walls where the drawbridge mechanism was operated, and where soldiers could defend the walls are still visible. Below the castle are some nineteenth-century gun emplacements. The whole site is now surrounded by extensive gardens, and there are superb views across Carrick Roads, Falmouth harbour, and out to sea.

See AM info. Also open Sun am, Apr to Sep. Parking available.

St Michael's Mount

Cornwall *p211 A1*

Rising 230 feet out of the sea in Marazion Bay, is a rocky island crowned by a building of fairytale battlements and pinnacles. It was called St Michael's Mount because legend has it that St Michael appeared in a vision on the outcrop in 710, and Benedictine monks from Brittany subsequently built a monastery there. This accounts for its resemblance to Mont St Michel in France.

After the Dissolution of the monasteries it was a royal fortress until, in 1659, it became the home of the ancient Cornish St Aubyn family, and has remained so ever since. The Mount can be reached either by a causeway at low tide or, during the summer at high tide, by boat from Marazion or Penzance. The interior has some beautiful Georgian Gothic decoration, some intricately carved wooden and period furniture, and a collection of armour and pictures.

Open all year Mon, Wed and Fri. NT.

St Osyth

Essex *p213 D4*

The little village of St Osyth is a charming old-world community, centred around the Norman church and the ancient ruins of St Osyth Priory. Founded in the twelfth century by Augustinian Canons, the priory was named after the martyred daughter of Frithenwald, first Christian king of the East Angles. Only a few fragments of the original building remain, but they include an impressive late fifteenth-century flint gatehouse, complete with battlements and patterned with stone. St Osyth Priory is set in extensive and beautiful grounds of parkland and gardens. Red and Fallow deer roam free in the deer park, and peacocks grace the shady lawns. The gatehouse building contains apartments which house a collection of ceramics and jade.

Gardens and original priory remains open May to Sep daily. Private apartments, ceramics and jade, Aug daily, pm only.

Salisbury Wiltshire *p212 F3*

This great city, county town of Wiltshire, situated at the confluence of the rivers Avon, Bourne, Nadder and Wylye, spans the centuries with architecture from all periods.

The roots of Salisbury lie in Old Sarum, now on the outskirts of the city. Originally a cathedral and a castle stood at Old Sarum, with attendant town, but the close proximity of Church and State gave rise to friction. This, combined with the high winds which were damaging the cathedral, and a shortage of water near the site, compelled the clergy to leave Old Sarum, and rebuild their cathedral two miles away, down in the meads. Gradually the townspeople followed, and Old Sarum fell into decay although until 1832 it retained two members of parliament, despite the electorate numering only ten.

Today Salisbury is a thriving market town, and people from all over the south-west come to meet and trade. Apart from the normal market, there is a large cattle market and a Corn Exchange.

Salisbury and South Wiltshire Museum

A visit to this museum is a valuable precursor to exploring the city. There is a large collection of local exhibits, among the most exceptional are a group of mounted Great Bustards, all shot on Salisbury Plain and now a bird extinct in this country and models of Stonehenge and Old Sarum with a fascinating collection of objects found on these sites. There are also exhibits of finds from the city's past, such as Guild relics, including a processional giant, used in Guild pageants.

The Cathedral

On Easter Monday, 1220, the first foundation stones were laid, and thirty-eight years later the main building of the cathedral was finished. Before the end of the century the towering spire was added, which with the tower, soars 404 feet above the surrounding plain.

Unlike many medieval cathedrals Salisbury, because of the short time it took to build, has a uniformity of style unmatched anywhere else. It has an entrance for every month of the year, a window for every day, and a column for every hour – 8,760 altogether. The imposing west front has tier upon tier of niches in which statues once stood, but most have disappeared and those left are mainly nineteenth century.

There are many impressive tombs within the cathedral, the earliest, with a magnificently

An open-air market is held in Salisbury every Tuesday and Saturday

Salisbury

mailed and armoured figure reclining upon it, is that of William Longespere, who witnessed the signing of the Magna Carta and was laid here in 1226. In the north transept is the oldest clock in working order in Britain. Made in 1386, it has no dial, but strikes the hour.

The thirteenth-century roof painting in the choir has been restored, and beautiful sculptures decorate the walls of the octagonal chapter house. The cloisters, the largest of any English cathedral, contain some medieval glass, and in the library over the east walk one of the four remaining copies of the Magna Carta is kept.

Mompesson House

On the north side of Chorister's Green stands one of the finest houses in the cathedral Close. Mompesson House was built in 1701 for Thomas Mompesson, a rich merchant. A restrained, dignified building, the plain well-proportioned exterior contrasts with the lush interior decoration. It contains a finely carved staircase, elaborate plaster ceilings and overmantels, and some original panelling.

The House of John A'Port

Six times Mayor of Salisbury, John A'Port built this half-timbered, three-storeyed house in 1425. In 1930 restoration began and the plaster and paint removed to reveal the original beams. Alterations to the building were slight, and none of the old timbers had to be replaced.

Today it is a shop, but visitors are welcome to look at the stone fireplaces, the old staircase, Jacobean oak panelling of the upstairs room, and the carved oak mantel piece made in 1620.

Poultry Cross

Built to provide shelter for vendors at market, this octagonal building was probably erected as an act of penance by a wealthy citizen which was the custom at the time. It is the only one of four market crosses left, and is still used by market folk as it has been since the fifteenth century.

St Thomas of Canterbury

The original church was built in 1238, but the building as it stands is fifteenth century, with some of the earlier features retained. Notable here is the Tudor roof of the nave, and the remarkable, if crude, painting above the chancel arch. Restored in the nineteenth century, this sixteenth-century work shows Christ atop a rainbow, the Virgin Mother and St John with saints beneath sending the damned to hell below.

Salisbury and South Wilts Museum open all year Mon to Sat, also Sun pm July and Aug. Closed Christmas and Good Fri.
Old Sarum see AM info. Also open Sun am Apr to Sep. Parking available.
Mompesson House open Apr to Oct daily (except Thu and Fri) pm only. NT.

Sandringham House has been a favourite royal residence since 1862 and it is the present Royal Family's traditional New Year venue

Samlesbury Hall

Lancashire *p216 E4*

This fine old half-timbered building was first built in 1325, but restored in the sixteenth and nineteenth centuries. Particularly interesting is the banqueting hall, complete with a minstrel's gallery and several valuable antiques and paintings.

Throughout the year a wide variety of exhibitions are held at the Hall, sometimes with craftsmen demonstrating their work.

Open late Jan to mid Dec daily (except Mon). Refreshments available.

Sandringham

Norfolk *p218 E1*

Sandringham was purchased in 1862 by Queen Victoria, following the wishes of her husband, Prince Albert, who felt that their eldest son Edward, Prince of Wales, should have his own home. The house had many additions and alterations made to it in order to accommodate the Prince's family and household. Amongst the many treasures contained within the mansion are several paintings of the Royal Family, and members of European royal families.

Well laid out routes through the grounds surrounding the house, provide a good way to appreciate their colourful beauty. North of the mansion is a lovely flower garden created by King George VI, and nearby stands an eighteenth-century statue of Father Time – purchased by Queen Mary in 1950. Also within the grounds is the Church of St Mary Magdalene, which contains many memorials and gifts connected with the Royal Family.

A former Royal Retiring Room used specifically by kings and queens en route to Sandringham can be seen at Wolferton Station, about two miles west. Built in 1898, the rooms contain fine oak panelling, the original fittings (some gold plated), period posters, important small railway relics and Edwardian curios – including some from royal train journeys.

Sandringham House, Grounds and Museum open Apr to late Sep (except mid July to early Aug), Apr: Tue, Wed and Thu; May to Sep daily (except Fri and Sat), also open Easter Mon. Parking and refreshments available.

Wolferton Station (down side) open Apr to Sep (plus Bank Holidays) daily (except Sat), Suns pm only. Parking available.

Samlesbury Hall originally surrounded three sides of a courtyard but now stands as an L-shaped building

Scarborough North Yorkshire *p217 C4*

Scarborough – historic town, working fishing port and host to various national festivals, is nevertheless best known as a large, popular east-coast holiday resort.

The old harbour at Scarborough and the lighthouse which guides vessels

Scarborough first began to develop as a spa in about 1649, when water from a stream flowing across the South Sands was discovered to have curative properties. The next century saw the first bathing machine here (local people claim it was invented here), and since then crowds have flocked to Scarborough in order to enjoy the invigorating North Sea air.

The twin bays either side of Scarborough's promontary provide great stretches of sandy beaches. North Bay, backed by beautiful gardens, is studded with rocks which dry out at low tide and provide numerous pools to explore, although north-easterly gales result in exceptionally heavy surf which makes swimming dangerous. However, the main part of the resort is centred along South Bay, and here there are sheltered sands and safe bathing. Around the old harbour, still used by commercial vessels carrying timber, stand picturesque eighteenth-century buildings, including Customs House,

King Richard III's house (now a café) and some interesting old pubs, including the Three Mariners Inn in Quay Street. This dates from the fourteenth century and, once the haunt of smugglers, is now a Fisherman's Craft Centre.

The several Victorian villas which remain in the town include the Medicinal Baths, the Lonsborough Natural History Museum, and the Art Gallery which contains a permanent collection by local artists – all three are in The Crescent. The Rotunda Museum, situated in Vernon Road, has an interesting collection of regional archaeology and Scarborough bygones.

Wood End

This is the home of the Sitwell family, who all became famous writers. The house is set in charming gardens and contains a collection of first editions and portraits belonging to the family.

St Mary's Church

The novelist Anne Brontë, a frequent visitor to the town with her

sister, Charlotte, is buried in the churchyard. The church, built in the early twelfth century, was rebuilt in the fifteenth, but severely damaged during the Civil War. However, it still retains its medieval arcades, piers and south-aisle chapels.

The Castle

Scarborough Castle has dominated the town for 800 years, and stands on the magnificent headland between the two bays. The Normans built the large keep, the barbican and the curtain wall which can still be seen today. Although besieged six times, the castle was never taken by force.

Northstead Manor Gardens

These gardens contain Scarborough Zoo and Marineland, Yorkshire's largest amusement park, a miniature railway and an open-air theatre.

Fisherman's Craft Centre open daily during summer season.
Art Gallery open all year Tue to Sat and Sun pm, Spring Bank Holiday to Sep only.
Londesborough Lodge open as above.
Wood End open as above.
Castle see AM info. Also open Sun am Apr to Sep.
Scarborough Zoo and Marineland open Easter to Oct daily. Refreshments available.

Scone Palace

Tayside *p220 D5*

Scone was the capital of the ancient Pictish kingdom until 843, after which Kenneth MacAlpine, King of the Scots, overthrew the Picts and united the two nations. MacAlpine brought the Stone of Destiny to Scone, and Scottish kings were crowned on it for 400 years before it was removed to Westminster Abbey.

The present palace is an enlargement of the house built in 1580 by the Earls of Gowrie. By 1805 the architect had completed the Gothic restyling of the palace, with its turrets and castellations which were reminiscent of the medieval royal abbey that once stood here.

Among the many treasures within the Palace is fine French furniture from the eighteenth and nineteenth centuries, including a piece made for Marie Antoinette shortly after her wedding, and a superb collection of china (housed in the library) including an armorial tea service from the 1700s. Beautiful family portraits adorn the walls of the long gallery, a room measuring some 168 feet – an unusual feature in Scottish homes. Other items of interest include a collection of French and English clocks, and a rare set of Vernis Martin vases.

The spacious grounds of the Palace are famed for the beautiful walks they afford through giant oaks, limes, copper beeches and sycamore trees. Magnificent displays of colour are provided throughout the seasons by daffodils, azaleas, and rhododendrons.

A huge collection of conifers grows in the Pinetum, some reaching a height of 140 feet. Giant sequoias and Sitka spruces are just two of the varieties to be seen here. Also in the grounds is an agricultural machinery exhibition, and a children's adventure playground set in a small wood.

Open end Apr to early Oct daily, Sun pm only. Parking and refreshments available.

Severn Valley Railway

Shropshire *p216 E2*

The famous Severn Valley Railway is the foremost standard-gauge railway in the country, and has one of the largest collections of former British Rail locomotives. Over thirty are on show at the terminuses at Bewdley and Bridgnorth, and as many as five can be seen in steam when the service is in operation. There is also a vast amount of rolling stock, much of which is ex-Great Western, restored to its original livery.

The line runs for twelve-and-a-half miles, following the winding river Severn through some beautiful scenery. North from Bewdley it crosses the edge of the Wyre Forest where wooded slopes reach right down to the river, then across the massive Victoria Bridge, a 200-foot span, high above the river. With superb river views, the line passes through several village stations before entering Bridgnorth, a pleasant town built on two levels, with a strangely leaning castle keep.

Passenger services operate at frequent intervals every weekend Mar to Oct and most weekdays from May to Sep, plus all Bank Holidays. Refreshments on most trains. Parking at Bewdley and Bridgnorth.

Sewerby Hall, Park and Zoo

Humberside *p217 D3*

This fine Georgian mansion was built between 1714 and 1720, and now serves as an art gallery and museum. Its collections include historical and archaeological items, and paintings by local artists. However, the principal feature here is the Amy Johnson Room. Exhibits include the pilot's awards and trophies, and her pilot's log book which spans 1928 to 1938.

The Severn Valley Railway travels through gloriously open country

The grounds extend to some fifty acres and are attractively laid out with gardens, notably an Old English walled garden. Deer and wallabies can be seen in the park and there is also a mini-zoo and aviary. Recreational facilities here include a miniature golf course, archery, croquet, bowls, putting, and a children's corner.

Grounds open all year daily.
Museum open Easter to Sep daily, Sat pm only.

Shaftesbury

Dorset *p212 F3*

Perched high on the edge of the Mendip Hills, this ancient town looks down over the wide expanse of Blackmoor Vale. Shaftesbury's famous Gold Hill, a steep cobbled street lined with old cottages, is one of the most photographed street scenes in the country, and at the top of this hill the Local History Museum is to be found. Exhibits include agricultural and domestic items, toys, needlework,

Picturesque Gold Hill in Shaftesbury – originally a West Saxon town where Edward the Martyr was buried in 981

fans, pottery and finds from local excavations. Some of the relics relate to the old Benedictine Abbey for nuns, which was founded here in the ninth century by King Alfred. Although the abbey was demolished after the Dissolution, its foundations can still be seen near the Town Hall.

Museum open Easter to Sep daily, Sun, pm only.

Sheffield Park

East Sussex *p213 C2*

Many centuries ago the house at Sheffield Park belonged to King Harold's father. However, expensive remodelling in the eighteenth century created the beautiful Tudor-style mansion of today, with its towers, parapets, pinnacles and, at the east end, enormous church-style window.

One of the outstanding interior features of the house is the reproduction Gothic staircase, adorned by a glass dome and fluted fan-shaped moulded ceiling. The music room has fine side-panelling complemented by a very ornate plasterwork ceiling and frieze. Among the furnishings here are a nineteenth-century piano, harp and church organ.

The house stands in fifty acres of wooded parkland, in an advantageous position between the downs. It has sweeping lawns, flowering shrubs and some unusual trees. The house, although adjoining the National Trust Garden, is quite separate.

Open Easter to Oct Wed, Thu, Sun and Bank Holiday Mons, pm only. Parking available.

Sheffield Park Gardens

East Sussex *p213 C2*

These very large gardens, landscaped by Capability Brown, were part of the grounds of Sheffield Park before being acquired by the National Trust in 1954. The gardens have been enhanced by the addition of rare and unusual trees and shrubs, which have been planted by A. G. Soames, who owned the Park earlier this century. There are a hundred acres of wooded parkland with grassy swards, waterfalls and large lakes whose still waters, partly covered by waterlillies, reflect the colourful foliage of the trees and shrubs surrounding them. Spanning the lakes are ornate bridges with stone balustrades.

Open Apr to mid Nov Tue to Sat, Sun pm only, but open Bank Holiday Mons. Refreshments available. NT.

One of the four landscaped lakes in Sheffield Park Gardens

The 15th-century St John's almshouses at Sherborne from the abbey gate

Sherborne

Dorset *p212 E3*

The quiet country town of Sherborne stands on the edge of the lovely Blackmore Vale, on the north bank of the river Yeo. Sherborne school is famous, founded in the sixteenth century and now occupying some of the former abbey buildings. Adjacent to the school is the beautiful abbey church, burial place of the ninth-century kings Ethelbald and Ethelbert, which possesses some fine fan vaulting and old monuments. The abbey gate house contains the Sherborne Museum, with local history and Roman material, local photographs and natural history. Particularly interesting are a model of a Norman castle and a Victorian dolls house.

Sherborne has two castles. The Old Castle, built by Roger, Bishop of Salisbury, in the early twelfth century, is now a ruin. In 1592 Sir Walter Raleigh acquired the castle, but his attempts to modernise it for his own use proved futile, and soon afterwards he began the New Castle. This is more of a stately home than a castle, and is surrounded by lovely woods and parkland. In the seventeenth century the Earl of Bristol, whose descendants still live at Sherborne today, added two wings to the castle, creating an ornate and impressive exterior. Capability Brown planned the twenty acres of pleasure grounds which include a lovely lake, a cascade and an orangery. Special events take place here on Sundays during the summer.

Museum open all year, Apr to Oct daily (except Mon), Sun pm only, Nov to Mar Tue, Sat and Sun pm only.
Old Castle see AM info. Also open Sun am Apr to Sep.
New Castle open Apr to May Thur to Sat and Bank Holiday Mons; June to Sep daily, pm only. Parking and refreshments available.

Shrewsbury Shropshire *p216 E2*

This charming old county town is famous for its superb setting, its half-timbered buildings and its picturesque streets. Magnificently set on a virtual island in a huge loop of the river Severn, no less than nine bridges connect the town to the opposite bank of the Severn.

Shrewsbury was traditionally founded by the Britons who abandoned Wroxeter, the Roman City of *Viroconium* lying just five miles to the south-east, and subsequently adopted this strategic site.

Much of the character of this historic town has been retained in its narrow old streets. Gullet Passage and Grope Lane exemplify the bizarre alley and street names here which have changed little from the days of Elizabeth I; with their quaint, narrow passageways and leaning upper storeys almost meeting over them. Everywhere there are superb black and white buildings of plaster and weathered timber. Among some of the numerous notable examples of these are: Rowley's House in Baker Street; Bear Steps in St Alkmund's Square; Abbot's House in Butcher's Row; the tall gabled Ireland's Mansion and Owen's Mansion in the High Street; Rooke's House in Dogpole; King's Head in Mardol and the Old Council House Gateway.

The Castle

Commanding the once vulnerable north-eastern approach to the town, the castle was built soon after the Norman Conquest, but the present structure dates chiefly from about 1300. In 1790 the building was refurbished as a house by the engineer and architect, Thomas Telford. The keep is square, with circular corner turrets and a good proportion of its walls and inner bailey still survive, together with a Norman gateway.

Bear Steps

This group of picturesque buildings is of considerable antiquarian interest, and consists of a recently restored timber-framed fourteenth-century cottage with shops and a lovely old meeting hall. The hall itself has a mid-fourteenth-century crown post roof.

Clive House Museum

An interesting eighteenth-century Georgian town house, this was once occupied by Clive of India, during his period as Mayor of Shrewsbury in 1762. It now houses a collection of Caughley and Coalport china, maw tiles, costume, and church silver, together with a Georgian room and the Regimental Museum of the 1st Queen's Dragoon Guards.

Shrewsbury Castle defends the river approaches to the ancient capital

Rowley's House

Rowley's House is a restored sixteenth-century timbered house which contains impressive Roman remains from Wroxeter, and a collection of Shropshire bygones.

Longden Coleham Pumping Station

Situated on the south side of the river, facing the town, is this fine old pumping station. Now a museum, it preserves its two compound beam engines which were originally installed in 1900 and are now restored to working order.

St Mary's Church

The fine stone spire of the largest church on the Shrewsbury skyline, is one of the three tallest in England. St Mary's is Norman, with Early English and later work. Its stained glass is particularly beautiful and the fourteenth-century jesse window in the chancel is especially rich in colour.

St Alkmund's Church

The other major spire of the skyline belongs to St Alkmund's, which was built in the late eighteenth century on the site of a medieval church. This, too, has good stained glass, with an east window portraying an adaptation of Reni's *Assumption of the Virgin*.

St Chad's Church

The most unusual-looking of the town's churches and one of the very few round churches in the country is St Chad's. It has an oddly-shaped tower – the top half being shaped like a minaret crowned with a dome.

Abbey Church

Some Norman work is preserved in this impressive abbey church, founded in about 1080 by Roger de Montgomery. The west tower has a fine Perpendicular window and the font is reputedly made from a Roman capital. There are also some interesting tombs and monuments dating from about 1300 onwards.

The Quarry

On the town side of the river lies this huge park, which bears witness to the talents of famous gardener Percy Thrower. The splendid formal gardens of The Dingle, near its centre, are his great work.

Statues commemorate two great men associated with the town; Charles Darwin (1809–82), born and educated in Shrewsbury, together with Robert Clive (1725–74). Whilst among the famous nineteenth-century visitors at The Lion – a Georgian coaching inn partly built on a fifteenth-century timber-framed house – were Charles Dickens, the singer Jenny Lind and the violinist Paganini.

Castle open Easter Sat to Oct daily. Oct to Easter, Mon to Sat only.
Bear Steps open all year daily (except Sun).
Clive House Museum open all year (except Sun and Bank Holidays).
Rowley's House open all year daily (except Sun and Bank Holidays).
Longden Coleham Pumping Station open all year Wed to Fri, pm only.

Shugborough

Staffordshire *p216 F2*

The white colonnaded mansion, lying in a shallow valley on the northern edge of Cannock Chase, is the ancestral home of the Earls of Lichfield.

The house was built in 1693 and greatly enlarged in the eighteenth century. Along with the 900 acres of grounds it passed to the National Trust in 1966, and is now a museum – although the present Earl still lives in part of it.

The Museum of Staffordshire Life takes up the kitchen wing and stable block, and has displays illustrating agricultural development, rural crafts and social history. Among the exhibits is the Shrewsbury collection of horse-drawn vehicles, and an eighteenth-century brew-house and laundry. The house itself contains a fine collection of French furniture and much porcelain and silver. Drawings and sketches by Landseer are on display, as well as a long series of portraits of the Earl's ancestors.

The gardens and park, landscaped by James Stuart, are decorated with temples and follies, and at the park farm rare breeds of livestock are reared.

Open Mar to Oct Tue to Fri; pm only, Sat, Sun and Bank Holiday. Parking and refreshments available. NT.

Sissinghurst Castle Gardens

Kent *p213 D2*

Situated in the Weald between the North and South Downs, this magnificent garden has been created around the remaining buildings of the original medieval castle. They are the result of work in the 1930s by the writers Vita Sackville-West and her husband Sir Harold Nicolson. Extensive and colourful, the enchanting gardens are a collection of varying shapes and sizes, interspersed with beautiful lawns and separated by a yew, lime and a moat walk. The white garden in front of the old Priest's house features, as its name implies, plants which have a profusion of white blooms. Borders of flowering shrubs, trees, bulbs and the orchard, with its dogleg moat, all add to the beauty of Sissinghurst, and the rose garden is at its best in June and July.

The long library and the Elizabethan tower, from which

166

The Priest's House at Sissinghurst seen from the unique garden which contains white flowers only

there is an excellent panoramic view of Kent, are also open to the public. A delightful room in the tower was Vita Sackville-West's study.

Open Apr to Oct daily (except Mons) pm only. Sat, Sun and Good Fri all day. Parking and refreshments available. NT.

Sizergh Castle

Cumbria *p220 E1*

Home of the Strickland family for more than 700 years, Sizergh Castle was begun in the mid fourteenth century as a simple pele tower (defensive border fort). Later additions have created a sizeable property, one of the largest, in fact, of the border fortresses which were built in the turbulent days before the Union of Crowns. The exterior, surmounted by battlements, is still impressive, although eighteenth-

century modifications considerably softened its appearance.

Inside the castle there is particularly fine wood panelling and carving, decorated plaster ceilings and seventeenth-century Flemish tapestry. The furniture is both English and Continental, and items collected by the family over the centuries include Stuart and Jacobite relics, a fourteenth-century two-handed sword, a collection of family portraits and a medieval document describing Sir Walter Strickland's allegiance to the Earl of Salisbury in 1448. The grounds extend to more than 1,500 acres and contain gardens, terraces, a lake and rock garden with pools and waterfalls.

Open Apr to Sep. House open Wed and Sun, also Thu in July and Aug; pm only. Closed Bank Holiday Mon. Gardens open Wed, Thu and Sun, plus Wed and Thu during Oct, pm only. NT.

Skegness

Lincolnshire *p217 D2*

'Skegness is so Bracing' was the slogan advertising the Great Northern Railway's trips to this seaside resort in 1908, and it was the coming of the railway that led to the development of the resort. Today, its wide sandy beach, attractions and entertainments, are as popular as ever.

Although it is a vastly different place from the tiny fishing village so loved by the poet Tennyson in the early nineteenth century, its history is not forgotten. The Church Farm Museum is housed in a farmhouse and outbuildings which have been restored to show the life and work of a Lincolnshire farmer at the end of the nineteenth century. Displays include the Bernard Best collection of farm implements and machinery, and an interesting exhibition of veterinary equipment. During the summer craftsmen demonstrate their skills at weekends.

The promenade at Skegness is very attractive with its large areas of colourful gardens and seafront attractions. At North Parade is the popular Natureland Marine Zoo. Seals, sea lions and penguins are kept here in modern enclosures; a tropical house features creatures such as snakes, scorpions, and crocodiles, and the aquarium has both tropical marine tanks and a large fresh water fish collection. The Floral Palace is a riot of colour with its exotic plants and free-flying tropical birds, while more familiar animals can be found in the pets corner. The zoo also cares for baby seals which have been orphaned and washed up locally.

Opposite the Lifeboat Station there is a pottery where craftsmen can be seen at work and a model village.

Church Farm Museum open Apr to Oct daily. Parking available, refreshments at weekends.
Natureland Marine Zoo open all year daily (except Christmas Day). Refreshments available.
Pottery open all year daily.

Skipton

North Yorkshire *p217 A3*

To the north of Skipton lie the Yorkshire Dales, to the south rugged moorland extends along the Pennine chain into Derbyshire. Skipton stands near the northernmost point of the Leeds and Liverpool canal on the banks of the Eller Beck, a tributary of the river Aire.

A variety of interesting buildings in the town include the Old Town Hall, or Toll-Booth, with its remains of the town stocks. Popularly regarded as The Gateway to the Dales, Skipton is essentially a market town although even the introduction of textile manufacturing in the eighteenth century, which is now giving way to light industry, did nothing to lessen its rural atmosphere.

Standing on high ground, with an impregnable ravine to the north, are the few remains of the original castle. Built by the Normans in the twelfth century, it suffered extensive damage in the thirteenth century and was largely rebuilt by the Clifford family. Today it provides a fine example of a medieval fortress. Fully roofed, it has a picturesque interior courtyard and a massive

gatehouse flanked by six fourteenth-century round towers.

The Town Hall contains the Craven Museum which includes exhibits of folk life, lead mining and prehistoric and Roman remains, with special reference to the Craven District.

Situated in the High Corn Mill, parts of which date from the thirteenth century, the George Leatt Industrial and Folk Museum is built on a site where milling has been carried out since before the Normans came to England. Both restored and operational machinery includes two waterwheels, and flour milled on the premises may be purchased. Other points of interest here are a working blacksmith's forge and a collection of horse-traps and carts.

Some two miles to the northeast of Skipton, the Yorkshire Dales Railway Society have created the Embsay Steam Centre. Attractions here include steam locomotives, vintage carriages, and a shop selling models.

Castle open all year (except Sun am, Good Fri and Christmas Day) daily.
Craven Museum open Apr to Sep daily (except Tue), Sun pm only, Oct to Mar open daily (except Tue and Sun) pm only, Sat all day. Parking available.
George Leatt Industrial and Folk Museum open most Suns and Bank Holidays, pm only.
Embsay Steam Centre open Sun during Summer.

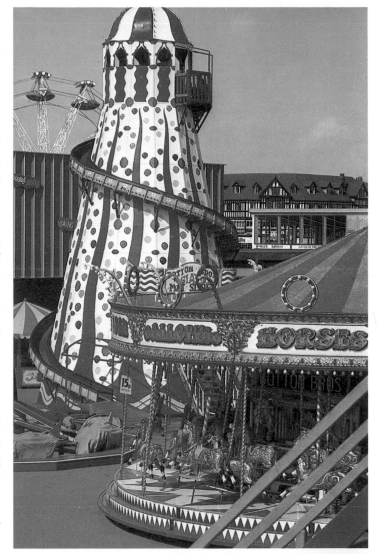

Right: Seaside entertainment is the trademark of Skegness

Skipton Castle was the last Royalist stronghold to surrender in the north

Skye

Highlands *p221 A2*

Skye, an historic isle of romance, is a wild area of mountains and lochs, inhabited by gaelic-speaking crofters and fisherfolk. This loveliest of Scottish islands is quickly reached from the mainland; but, beyond Skye, scattered islets streach away to the ocean. Its mountains are slashed by sea lochs up the western coast and in the north-west and south-west lie fertile areas with farms and woods. The land is often shrouded in mist, and when the sun shines on the red granite and black gabbro of its peaks, blue waters, and whitewashed crofts, it presents a timeless picture.

There are two ways of enjoying Skye: to feast the eyes and breathe in the atmosphere; or, for the strong and active, to walk, climb and explore. The island's natural phenomena include the Lealt Falls, where salmon may sometimes be seen leaping; the Old Man of Storr, a remarkable basalt column on the Trotternish ridge; and the Kilt Rock and waterfall where the rock has been eroded into pleats, all of which lie north of the island's capital of Portree.

In the southern part of the island, the magnificent Loch Coruisk is encircled by the famous Cuillin hills, best reached by boat from the hamlet of Elgol. Dunvegan Castle is the home of the Chief of Clan Macleod, where Rory Mor's two-handed sword and the MacLeod's Fairy Flag are preserved.

Two folk museums of note are the Skye Cottage Museum at Kilmuir and the Skye Black House Folk Museum at Colbost. The former consists of three one-hundred-year-old thatched croft cottages. The museum also houses a fine selection of implements and tools used by the people of the Highlands, together with interesting collections of old letters, papers and pictures.

The Skye Black House Folk Museum is housed in a well-restored typical nineteenth-century Black House, and contains implements and furniture of bygone days. Behind the museum is a replica of a whisky still.

Also of interest is the Skye Watermill, situated at Glendale on the shores of Loch Pooltiel. This grain mill and kiln (200 years old) has recently been restored to working order and is open to the public. At Armadale, the visitor can find the Clan Donald Centre which is located in the recently restored north wing of Armadale Castle, the seat of the Macdonalds. Although the main part of the building is now derelict, it was originally built in 1815 in the Gothic style and is set in romantic grounds. These sheltered woodland gardens overlook the waters of the Sound of Sleat.

Skye Cottage Museum open mid May to Sep daily (except Sun). Parking available.
The Skye Black House Folk Museum open Easter to Oct daily. Parking available.
Skye Watermill open Easter to Oct daily (except Sun.). Parking and refreshments available.
Dunvegan Castle open Easter to mid Oct Mon to Sat pm only, late May to Sep all day. Refreshments available.
Clan Donald Centre open Apr to Oct Mon to Sat, also, Sun pm from July to mid Sep. Gardens always open. Refreshments available.

The ruin of Caisteal Maol stands guard over the waters between Skye and the mainland

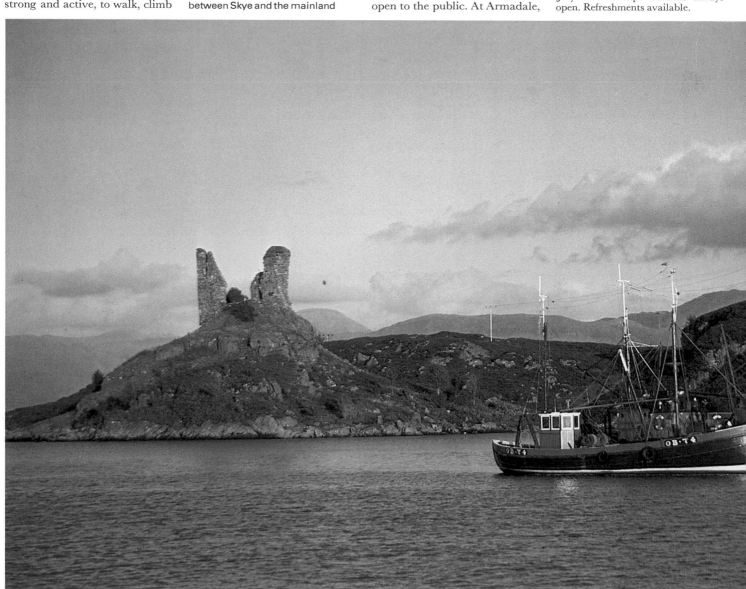

Sledmere House

Humberside *p217 C3*

This handsome, solid looking Georgian building has been the home of the Sykes family since it was originally built in the late eighteenth century. In 1911 a fire gutted the entire building, although much of the furnishings were rescued. It was restored to its original state by the architect W H Brierly. The park that surrounds the house was laid out in a semi-formal design by Capability Brown, and includes formal gardens, vast lawns, a lake and an Italian fountain.

The rooms are large and airy, the largest being the enormous library which has a semi-circular vault and is divided into three compartments. The contents include furniture by Chippendale and Sheraton, a set of Louis XVI

A vast sweep of park in front of Sledmere House makes the house look shorter than it actually is – 120 feet

seat furniture, and an early eighteenth-century tea table in Canton enamel. Paintings and portraits, including one by Benjamin West, adorn the walls. Of particular interest is the Turkish Room (built after the fire) which is decorated with tiles obtained in Damascus.

Special events take place here some weekends during the summer, and a children's playground is in the grounds. One unusual feature is the organ recital held on the second and last Sundays of each month and on Bank Holiday Sundays.

Open Easter Sun and Mon then Sun only till mid May; mid May to Sep daily (except Mon and Fri, but open Bank Holiday Mon) pm only. Parking and refreshments available.

Slimbridge Wildfowl Trust

Gloucestershire *p212 E4*

Sir Peter Scott founded the Trust in 1946, in order to aid the conservation of birds, and the centre at Slimbridge was the first of seven to be opened. Over 3,000 birds are kept here, making this the largest collection of wildfowl in the world.

Some seventy-three acres of landscaped pens, lakes and paddocks are open to visitors, where numerous species of ducks, geese and swans can be watched at close quarters. Observation towers and hides afford a closer look at the more wary birds. Appropriate food for wildfowl can be

purchased from the gatehouse, and binoculars may be hired.

The collection includes many rare and exotic varieties, and has the largest flock of flamingos in captivity. In the tropical house several fascinating species of birds sensitive to the British climate live amidst jungle foliage and exotic flora.

The visitor reception area houses a permanent exhibition centre, a cinema and a gift shop.

Open all year daily (except Christmas). Parking, refreshments and picnic facilities available.

Flamingos in characteristic pose at Slimbridge Wildfowl Trust

Snowdonia National Park Gwynedd

'There is no corner of Europe that I know which so moves me with awe and majesty of great things as does this mass of the northern Welsh mountains'. These sentiments of the novelist Hilaire Belloc echo a response which has stirred visitors for centuries.

Snowdonia National Park comprises 840 square miles of beautiful and varied countryside – mountains, lakes, forests, estuaries and twenty-five miles of coastline. Within its boundaries are sixteen nature reserves, which testify to the unusual store of wildlife, stark villages whose people still make their living off the hillsides, and numerous relics of ancient tribes and cultures.

Nearly all the early remains of man's settlement in Snowdonia are found along the northern coastline – from near Bangor to Conwy – and from the estuary of the Traeth Mawr to that of the Dyfi. People settled upon these slopes facing the sea because of the milder climate and the wind, which kept tree growth down. The valleys were uninhabitable, due to marshes and impenetrable forest.

Between 4,000 and 2,000 BC, settlers arrived either by way of St George's Channel, or by the land which once linked southern Britain with Ireland. These people left behind them great Megalithic tombs, built of huge slabs of stone. Examples can be seen a little inland between Harlech and Barmouth, and at Maen Y Bordel and Capel Garmon in the Conwy Valley.

Inland from Aber to Penmaenmawr, and from Talsarnau to Tywyn are many round cairns, or barrows, dating from 2,000 BC, in which the ashes of the cremated dead were placed in pottery vessels. This form of burial persisted for well over 1,000 years. Druids Circle above Penmaenmawr is the best example of a stone circle. Simple standing stones are frequent, and probably marked ancient pathways over the mountains from the ports on the coasts.

With the arrival of iron and the weaponry that accompanied it, came the necessity to build hillforts, fortified by walls of earth and stone. There are examples on Conwy Mountain, at Pen y Gaer, half a mile south-west of Pont Aberglaslyn, and in western Merioneth. These date from about 500 BC, and probably played a major part in the struggle against the Romans, who held Wales as a frontier for over three centuries from AD 73. They built a series of forts linked by roads. From the fort at Caerhun, four miles south of Conwy, the Roman road known as Helen's Causeway

The Snowdon Mountain Railway was first opened on Easter Monday, 1896

runs through the centre of the National Park, linking Caerhun to forts at Bryn y Gefeiliau near Capel Curig, Tomen y Mur, a well-preserved example, Brithdir and Pennal. Another fort is Caer Gai, on the shores of Bala Lake.

The principal remains of early Christian settlements are the gravestones of the founding missionaries of the sixth and seventh centuries, who arrived shortly after the Romans left. A collection of these can be found in the church at Penmachno. At Beddgelert and Tywyn, parts of the existing churches date back to the twelfth and thirteenth centuries, and many parish churches in Snowdonia show work from the thirteenth to sixteenth centuries.

Snowdonia's highest point is a mere 3,650 feet above sea level, yet it appears a mountainous area, perhaps because of the abrupt nature of the landscape – its sudden rise from the coast, deep valleys and great bare slopes, a ruggedness left by the ice-age glaciers. Consequently there is an enormous variety of habitat, from the milder coastal regions to the spectacular eroded peaks upon which grow alpine plants, such as Purple and Mossy saxifrage, found on the north facing rock ledges of Cwms.

An easily identifiable upland bird is the raven, which makes its home among the crags, and is quite numerous throughout upland and lowland Snowdonia. The buzzard also nests in the high crags and shares the raven's diet of beetles, worms, carrion sheep and voles. The peregrine, though rarely seen, still lives here and it is hoped will recover its numbers – so drastically cut as a result of them eating prey poisoned by insecticide. The ring ouzel and wheatear are the two most interesting small upland birds, and of course the wren, which is a true mountain bird and can live at a height of 2,000 feet. On heather moors, such as Berwyn, are grouse, and where young conifer plantations meet the heatherland the blackcock is found

The competition of cattle and sheep has banished deer from the hillsides, although Fallow deer which have escaped from parks are spreading in the larger Forestry Commission plantations. Farmers blame the forests for harbouring foxes, of which there are many. Due to limited game keeping, other predators have survived here which have been persecuted to the point of extinction in most other areas of Britain. The polecat, hardly known outside Wales, is quite common, and the rare Pine marten, whose dark red-brown fur is known as sable in the fur trade, still exists in the remoter woods. The otter is also rare, although weasels, stoats and badgers are fairly common. These predators feed on an abundant supply of Field voles, Bank

voles, Water voles, Wood mice, shrews and hedgehogs.

Walking, climbing, skiing, canoeing, sailing, fishing and pony trekking are popular activities in the National Park of Snowdonia and there are several facilities for these throughout.

The Carneddau and Rhinog ranges provide challenging walks in mountainous scenery, whereas walks through the easier terrain of the Gwydyr, Beddgelert, Coed y Brenin and Dyfi forests, the Cregennen lakes and the north side of the Mawddach estuary, avoid high mountains but reveal fine views, moorlands, valleys, trees and open water.

Snowdon itself is the most popular summit, and was the attraction of North Wales which drew the first tourists in the eighteenth century. There are six major routes to the top, and for the less energetic, the Snowdon Mountain Railway climbs to the 3,650-foot peak at a steady 5mph. Beginning at Llanberis, the track runs nearly five miles to a bar, restaurant and shop at the summit, each train consisting of a single coach propelled by a Swiss-designed rack and pinion engine – the only one in Britain.

Snowshill Manor

Gloucestershire *p212 F5*

This small manor house built of warm Cotswold stone is Tudor in origin, and once belonged to Catherine Parr – wife of Henry VIII. The interior reflects the character of its last owner, Charles Wade, who was a compulsive collector of a wide variety of items, and it is these collections which make Snowshill Manor particularly remarkable. Some take over whole rooms, such as the nautical collection of old compasses, the model ship and the telescopes. Another is devoted to early forms of transport – old bicycles, sedan chairs, models of farm carts and hobby-horses. There are also old musical instruments, weaving and lacemaking

Snowshill Manor is a treasure house of curios and a tiny model village is laid out in the terraced gardens

A wealthy Victorian railway magnate rebuilt Somerleyton Hall in the 19th century

exhibits, and many other fascinating, unusual, rare and valuable objects.

Open Apr to Oct, Wed to Sat and Bank Holiday Mon, (Apr and Oct, only open Sat, Sun and Bank Holiday Mon). NT.

Somerleyton Hall

Suffolk *p214 E5*

The magnificent red brick and mellow stone mansion, rebuilt in Anglo-Italian style in 1846, stands surrounded by twelve acres of beautiful gardens.

On the east side of the house there is a French Renaissance arcade, and the north end supports a charming campanile, or bell-tower. The west, or garden, side has an ornate three-storey, square porch, inset with a fine oriel window and topped by pinnacles at each corner. These, combined with the stone parapets and stone-faced dormer windows, present a delightful façade.

The interior has some rich carved panelling, particularly in the oak parlour and on the staircase, and there are some superb pieces of antique furniture, tapestries and big game trophies.

The gardens, including a statuary, are well laid out with lawns, flowering shrubs, rare trees, shaped hedges, and the remains of a winter garden surrounds a sunken garden. A fine pagoda stands in the centre of the maze, and there is a nature trail and miniature railway.

Open Easter to Sep Thu, Sun and Bank Holidays pm only; also Tue and Wed also in July and Aug. Refreshments and parking available.

Southampton

Hampshire *p213 A2*

Southampton is a modern commercial port with a fine shopping centre, new civic buildings, a good deal of industry, a splendid university, fine sports and leisure facilities. However, the secret of its character is that it has been a modern port for upwards of a thousand years – always adapting to change, rebuilding, strengthening, growing. The docks, situated where the rivers Itchen and Test join Southampton Water, have expanded over the centuries into the giant passenger and container services for which the city is now famous. The liner *Queen Elizabeth II* moors here.

Southampton has had the status of city since 1964, although it has no cathedral. The mother church is St Mary's, a handsome late-nineteenth-century building, and the oldest church is St Michael's which dates back to Norman times. The base of the tower is the earliest part and inside is a twelfth-century French font. The tower of Holy Rood, a fourteenth-century church which was badly damaged by bombing in 1940, has been preserved as a memorial to men of the Merchant Navy. Other memorials are the Mayflower column commemorating the Pilgrim Fathers who sailed from Southampton in 1620, and a sculpture in East Park dedicated to the crew of the *Titanic*.

Tudor House, now used as a museum of antiquarian and historical interest, is a fine example

of a timber-frame town house with overhanging upper storeys. The Bargate, a striking medieval gateway and now the focal point of the city centre, was originally the northern entrance to the medieval town. Its upper floor, once the Guildhall, contains a museum of local history. An interesting maritime museum is housed in a fourteenth-century wool warehouse which has buttressed stone walls and old roof timbering.

The Spitfire Museum, dedicated to R J Mitchell, houses historic aircraft, including the Spitfire Mk 24 and the Seaplane S6A which made world speed records in 1929.

The Art Gallery housed in the Civic Centre includes a collection of eighteenth to twentieth-century English paintings, Continental Old Masters of the fourteenth to eighteenth centuries, and modern French paintings, including works by the Impressionists. There is also a small collection of sculpture and ceramics here.

The small zoo on the Common is attractively laid-out and contains a comprehensive collection of animals and birds.

Tudor House Museum open all year Tue to Sat, Sun pm only. Parking available.
Bargate Guildhall Museum open all year (except Good Fri, and Christmas) Tue to Sat, Sun pm only.
Wool House Maritime Museum open all year Tue to Sat, Sun pm only. Parking available.
Spitfire Museum open all year Tue to Sat, Sun pm only.
Art Gallery open all year (except Good Fri and Christmas Day) Tue to Sat, Sun pm only.
Southampton Zoo open daily. Refreshments available.

Southend-on-Sea

Essex *p213 D3*

Within easy reach of London's east end, Southend has extended its reputation as a day-tripper's paradise to become a commuter colony, at the same time retaining its position as a favourite holiday resort. In the process it has swallowed a number of villages, encouraged industry, and undertaken a good deal of rebuilding and development, including a shopping centre which attracts a new variety of day-tripper – Continental shoppers who fly in to Southend Airport or come by ship. The town is situated on the Thames estuary and the tide goes out a long, long way, uncovering

Vessels ranging in size from ocean-going liners to hydrofoils ply up and down Southampton Water

mud which is said to have curative properties. To provide enough depth of water for ships, the pier has to stretch out beyond the sand and silt and is, at one-and-three-quarter miles, the longest in the world.

The pierhead is the focal point of an area devoted to gaiety – fairground, amusement park and entertainment centre rolled into one, with facilities for a variety of sports into the bargain.

To the east, Thorpe Bay has a quieter atmosphere, with a beach of sand and shingle. There are ornamental gardens and an Edwardian bandstand at Westcliff, and further up the estuary is the fishing village of Old Leigh, where cockle boats can be watched unloading.

Other villages which have become part of Southend include

Prittlewell with its twelfth-century priory housing the southeast Essex museum; and Southchurch, with a fourteenth-century moated manor house called Southchurch Hall. This has been restored and is furnished as a medieval manor house, although one wing is Tudor in style.

Near Southend's airport is the Historic Aircraft Museum which has collections of aircraft, aircraft engines and all sorts of aviation equipment.

Prittlewell Priory Museum open all year (except Good Fri and Christmas). Apr to Sep daily, Sun pm only. Oct to Mar Mon to Sat.
Southchurch Hall open all year (except Good Fri and Christmas) Mon to Fri pm only, Sat all day, Sun pm Apr to Sep only.
Historic Aircraft Museum open June to Sep daily, Oct to May Sat and Sun.

Southend's pleasure pier is packed with amusements from beginning to end

Southport

Merseyside *p216 D4*

Donkeys still take children jig-jogging along the sands of Southport, and in the mornings race-horses are exercised on the beach. This combination of traditional entertainment and refinement is typical of the town. Amusement areas such as Happiland (for children) and Pleasureland contrast with beautiful parks and gardens; kiosks and shops along the front are complemented by boulevards of select emporiums; sporting facilities include a skate-board rink and a golf club; and entertainment varies from ballet to brass bands, and from zoos to steam engines.

Southport Zoo in Princes Park, covering two-and-a-half acres, contains aviaries and an aquarium as well as an assortment of mammals and reptiles. In Churchtown, the older part of Southport, are thatched cottages, old pubs, and the splendid Botanic Gardens, where there is a section specialising in ferns, a pets' corner and a small museum. The town's most distinctive feature is Lord Street, which runs parallel to the sea front and for more than a mile forms a wide boulevard with attractive shops on one side, and gardens, fountains and public buildings on the other. These include the Atkinson Art Gallery, which has both permanent and temporary exhibitions of painting and sculpture, and an Arts Centre which caters for theatre and music lovers.

The Steamport Transport Museum houses ex-BR locomotives and also buses, tram-cars and traction engines, while the Model Village and Model Railway on the promenade is marvellously detailed.

Southport Zoo open all year daily (except 25 Dec). Refreshments available.

Atkinson Art Gallery open all year daily (except Sun), Thu and Sat am only. Refreshments available.

Botanic Gardens Museum open all year, Tue to Sat and Bank Holiday Mon, Sun pm only. Closed Good Fri, Christmas and New Year's Day and Fri following Bank Holiday Mon. Parking and refreshments available.

Model Village and Railway open Mar to Oct daily. Refreshments available.

Steamport Transport Museum open June to mid Sep, Mon to Fri pm only. Also open from mid morning on Sat and Sun, May to Sep, and during July and Aug daily. Oct to Apr Sat and Sun pm only. Parking and refreshments available.

Above: Wayfarers' Arcade – a shoppers' paradise – typifies Southport's Victorian elegance

Spalding

Lincolnshire *p217 D1*

Spalding stands in a flat landscape interwoven with dykes and streams, which make it very similar to parts of Holland. Both ancient and modern buildings blend harmoniously together in this delightful town – world famous for its bulb and horticultural industry.

One of the outstanding features of the town is the impressive Ayscoughfee Hall. Dating back to the fifteenth century, the house was later restored in the Gothic style. Many rare and beautiful stained glass windows can be seen here, encompassing all periods from fourteenth to the eighteenth centuries. The Hall is also the home of a bird museum, and contains several hundred British specimens.

The most famous of Spalding's attractions however must be Springfields, a unique twenty-five-acre spring flower park on the eastern out-skirts of the town. Over a million bulbs flower here in springtime amidst lawns and lakes, and under glasshouses. The summer rose gardens, a recent addition, are a collection of over 12,500 rose bushes, in a hundred varieties. The flower parade takes place here each spring, a spectacular procession of floats decorated with numerous colourful tulip heads, watched by crowds of some 200,000 people. After the procession, the floats are displayed at a four-day exhibition, together with many other exhibits of both an educational and commercial nature.

Ayscoughfee Hall and Gardens open all year daily. Parking available. **Springfield Gardens** Flower parade and exhibition usually mid May. Spring gardens open Apr to mid May, summer gardens open mid June to Sep daily. Parking and refreshments available.

Speke Hall

Merseyside *p216 E3*

Speke Hall, a particularly fine half-timbered, black and white house, stands in a wooded park on the north bank of the river Mersey. It was started in 1490 by Sir William Norreys, but it was not until the sixteenth century that it assumed its present form. A red sandstone Elizabethan bridge, which once spanned the moat, leads to the gloomy inner, cobbled, courtyard where two yew trees, over 400 years old, grow.

The interior of the house presents a fascinating blend of styles ranging from the seventeenth century to the mid nineteenth century. Among the furniture there are some fine antiques, and of particular interest are the Mortlake tapestries. The great chamber, or hall, has a sixteenth-century plasterwork ceiling of inimitable quality, fine wainscoting of Flemish origin and an Elizabethan chimney-piece. The kitchen has stone mullioned windows and contains a display of polished brass and copper cooking implements, a collection of smoothing irons, and some interesting early vacuum cleaners.

Open all year daily (except New Year, Good Fri and Christmas), Sun pm only. NT.

Spetchley Park

Hereford and Worcester *p212 F5*

The lovely early nineteenth-century neo-Classical home of the Berkeleys, although not open to the public, adds a great deal of charm to the gardens which surround it. These extend to more than thirty acres with many rare trees, shrubs and plants, and a lake inhabited by ornamental wildfowl. Springtime at Spetchley is particularly delightful, although the gardens are colourful throughout the summer. In the park wander herds of Red and Fallow deer and there is a garden centre selling plants and shrubs.

Open Apr to Oct daily (except Sat), Sun pm only. Garden centre also open on weekdays during the winter.

Stamford

Lincolnshire *p213 B5*

Stamford's Town Bridge, just by the ford used since prehistoric times, is the heart of a town whose position has brought it importance and prosperity. It is quieter since a bypass took through-traffic away from its streets and retains so much charm that it is now a conservation area.

During the Middle Ages it had six religious houses; little remains of these but five out of fourteen medieval churches are still used. In Red Lion Square are All Saints, an Early English building which has a separate fifteenth-century tower with a tall spire, and St John's, which also dates from the fifteenth century. St Mary's has a thirteenth-century tower with a fine fourteenth-century spire, and a chapel which has a roof decorated with stars. St Martin's, south of the river, is late fifteenth century and contains a monument to the first Lord Burleigh.

Nearby are almshouses founded by Burleigh in 1597, the year before his death. Brasenose Gate, a pointed arch in the old grammar school wall, is a reminder of those Oxford students who set up a short-lived rival university in the fourteenth century.

Browne's Hospital, founded in the fifteenth century, by a rich wool merchant, enlarged in 1870 and now modernised, is one of the finest examples of medieval almshouses in the country. Riverside meadows, an open-air swimming pool, and the Friday Market are other attractions of the town.

About one mile south, is Burghley House, the largest and grandest Elizabethan house in existence. Arranged around a courtyard, it has towers, turrets, and the tall decorated chimneys which typify Tudor architecture. The interior is equally magnificent, containing over 700 works of art. In the grounds are a lake, a rose garden and an orangery.

Browne's Hospital open all year daily.
Burghley House open Apr to early Oct daily (except Fri and Mon, but open Bank Holidays) Sun pm only. Refreshments and parking available.

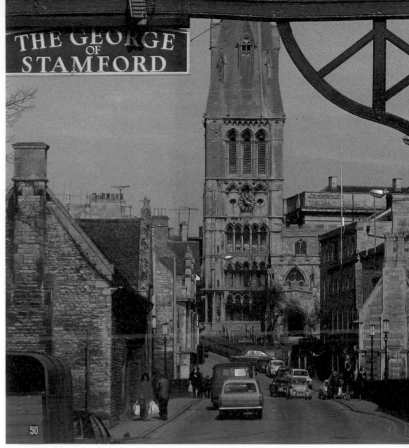

The sign of Stamford's ancient coaching inn stretches across the street

The Dutch introduced the tulip industry to Spalding over 60 years ago and now the area grows more than half Britain's bulbs

The river Avon provides a lovely setting for distinguished Stanford Hall

Stanford Hall

Leicestershire *p213 A5*

This fine William and Mary mansion was built in about 1690 on a lovely site overlooking the river Avon. The Hall remains largely unaltered and contains some fine antique furniture, family portraits and a collection of Italian works of art. Seventeenth-century Flemish tapestries adorn the walls and the ballroom has particularly good decorative plasterwork with hunting scenes painted on the walls.

The stable block which stands next to the house, now houses a collection of old cars and motorcycles. There is also an aviation museum set up to commemorate Lt. Percy Pilcher RN, who was the first man in the country to get a flying machine off the ground. The centre-piece of the museum is a replica of his plane, *The Hawk*, which took to the air in 1898. Unfortunately Pilcher died the following year when his plane crashed in the park and a memorial erected by the Royal Aeronautical Society now marks the spot.

Other interesting features at Stanford Hall include an old forge, and a working craft centre which operates at weekends. There is a colourful walled rose garden, and the park has a nature trail and facilities for fishing.

Open Easter to Sep Thu, Sat and Sun pm only; Easter, Spring and Late Summer Bank Holiday Mon and Tue pm only. Parking and refreshments available.

Steamtown Railway Museum

Lancashire *p216 E5*

Once the meeting point of three of the old railway company lines, Carnforth is now the home of the Steamtown Railway Museum. The engine shed, covering thirty-seven acres with almost four miles of track, is the home of thirty steam locomotives of various sizes. They have been collected here, not only from Great Britain, but also from France and Germany and range from the little *Gasbag*, formerly in use at Cambridge Gas Works, to the magnificent *Flying Scotsman*. The museum also has a restored automatic electric coal plant, a 75,000-gallon water tank, a carriage and wagon repair shop and a seventy-foot turntable. A fifteen-inch gauge miniature passenger railway also operates on this site. Locomotives can be seen 'in steam' on Sundays from Easter to October and daily during July and August.

Open all year daily (except Christmas Day). Parking and refreshments available.

Stirling Central *p220 C4*

Stirling is a very pleasant town of lovely gardens and great historical interest. It is a busy shopping centre and a junction of several of Scotland's main highways lying at the heart of an area of great beauty.

Known as the Gateway to the Highlands, the town is surrounded by fertile agricultural land which is watered by the meandering river Forth. It is overlooked by the lovely wooded Ochil Hills and even loftier peaks appear away on the horizon. In the past Stirling has paid the price for its strategic position and battlefields such as Sauchiburn (1488), Stirling Bridge (1297) and Bannockburn (1314) can be seen nearby. An equestrian statue of Robert the Bruce looks over Bannockburn and a presentation by the National Trust for Scotland illustrates this decisive battle in Scotland's struggle for independance. Today Stirling is a centre of learning, with its new university built on the banks of the loch within the Airthrey estate to the north of the town. The public are free to wander in its parkland setting and its MacRobert Centre provides opera,

concerts and exhibitions for all.

Although the town is dominated by its castle, there are many other historic buildings. Argyll's Ludging (Lodging), now used as a Youth Hostel, is a remarkable example of seventeenth century domestic architecture. Cowane's Hospital, or Guildhall, was built for 'the support of twelve decayed gild breithers' by John Cowane, Dean of Guild. The Tollbooth was the work of the famous Scottish architect, Sir William Bruce, and features a fine pavilion roof and clock tower. Nearby is the Mercat Cross, a tall column surmounted by a unicorn and flanked by cannons. Standing in the middle of the road, this was for many centuries the focal point of the town for events, announcements and public punishments. More ancient than all of these is Stirling's Auld Brig (Old Bridge) over the Forth which was built in 1415 and is now pedestrianised.

Mar's Wark
These ruins were once the magnificent palace built by the Earl of Mar in the fifteenth century but never completed. It was a building which went from riches to rags for it housed the newly-wed James VI and his bride soon after it was built, but later became a workhouse.

Church of the Holy Rude
This impressive fifteenth-century church has an unusual open timber roof and a five-sided apse in the choir. Its 90-feet-high tower bears the scars of hostilities which may have occurred during the Civil War or the Jacobite rebellion. Mary Queen of Scots was crowned here as a child and, following her abdication, it was the scene of the coronation of her son James VI, also an infant monarch.

Wallace Monument
To the north of Stirling, overlooking Causewayhead, is this famous pinnacled monument to Sir William Wallace, who defeated the English at the Battle of Stirling Bridge in 1297. It is a tall tower on top of the 362-feet-high Abbey Craig and incorporates a bronze statue of the patriot. The Tower Hall contains a display of armour which includes Wallace's 5ft 4in two-handed sword, together with a collection of portrait busts of famous Scots such as Robert the Bruce, Robert Burns, Sir Walter Scott and many more. Over 200 steps lead up to the top of the monument from where there are magnificent views.

The Castle
Perched on a 250-foot sheer crag dominating the town, this imposing castle seems to have grown from the stone on which it is built. It figured prominently in the wars of Scottish succession during the thirteenth and fourteenth centuries, passing back and forth between Scots and English until it was finally won by the Scots in 1342. From 1370 to 1603 the castle was the home of the Stuart Kings and it was they who shaped the castle as it is seen today, replacing an earlier wooden structure. It was an era during which the castle was witness to coronations, festivities and all the intrigue which surrounded the Royal Court. It was the birthplace of James II and James V and both Mary Queen of Scots and James VI (James I of England) spent several years in the castle. It was James V who created the magnificent Renaissance palace within the castle walls, one of the best examples of its type in the country. From the castle's lofty position there are some splendid views extending well into the highlands, particularly from the 420-foot high Queen Victoria's lookout and from Ladies Rock. The upper rooms of the palace contain the Museum of the Argyll and Sutherland Highlanders, the castle's 'home regiment', and items on display include the regiment's silver and plate, uniforms and a collection of medals from the time of Waterloo to the present day.

King's Knot
This ancient mound is thought to be an Iron Age burial mound but was long ago incorporated into the castle garden. Bordering the old jousting grounds, it was used as a sort of medieval grandstand for royal spectators of the tournaments. It is now a popular picnic area amid wooded lawns.

Landmark Visitor Centre
A multi-screen presentation, complete with sound effects, traces the history of Stirling and brings to life such events as the Battle of Bannockburn, a tournament at the castle and the commercial life in the town. There is also an exhibition of life in Stirling one hundred years ago and a shop with Scottish crafts, books and records.

Cambuskenneth Abbey
The remains of this Augustinian abbey, founded by David I in the eleventh century, lie beside the river Forth to the east of the town. It was the scene of Bruce's first Scottish parliament in 1326 and is the burial place of James III and his wife. The abbey was dissolved during the Reformation and some of its masonry was used for new buildings in the town.

Castle open all year daily (Sun pm only from Oct to Mar). Parking available. AM.
Museum of the Argyll and Sutherland Highlanders open Apr to Oct daily, pm only on Sun. Parking available.
Landmark Visitor Centre open all year daily. Refreshments available.
Mar's Wark open at all times. AM.
Wallace Monument open all year.
Cambuskenneth Abbey open Apr to Sep daily, Sun pm only. A.M.

For over 800 years Stirling has looked up to a protective castle

It is remarkable to think that the massive stones at Stonehenge were moved with levers and ropes

Stokesay Castle

Shropshire *p216 E1*

Stokesay Castle, reputed to be the oldest fortified manor house in England, dates back to the eleventh century. Many additions were carried out during the thirteenth century and during the Civil War the house was surrendered to Parliament, but survived relatively unscathed.

The courtyard is oblong in shape and surrounded by a wide moat. The oldest part of the house is thought to be a wing projecting into the moat in the north-west corner. The beautiful sixteenth-century gatehouse has an ornately timbered upper section, and replaces an earlier drawbridge house. Good examples of Early English windows can be seen in the fine thirteenth-century hall, heated by means of a central brazier.

Open Mar to Oct daily (except Tue). Parking available.

Stonehenge

Wiltshire *p212 F3*

To the west of Amesbury on the broad expanse of Salisbury Plain lies Stonehenge, one of the most impressive Megalithic monuments in Europe. Uncertainty shrouds its purpose, but it is believed that this was the site of ancient sun-worshipping ceremonies. The pattern consists of an outer ring and an inner horseshoe of sarsen, or 'foreign', stones which came from the Marlborough Downs. Some of the larger sarsens are over twenty-one feet in height and embedded to a depth of more than eight feet. Set up inside and outside the horseshoe are eighty bluestones with the largest, the so-called Altar Stone, at the centre of the horseshoe. The bluestones are thought to have been brought from the Preseli Hills in Dyfed. An outer ditch, banking, and fifty-six late-Neolithic holes mark the outer perimeter of the stones.

Open all year daily. Parking and refreshments available. AM.

Stourhead House and Gardens

Wiltshire *p212 F3*

This fine Palladian mansion was built for the wealthy banker, Henry Hoare, in the early eighteenth century. Although the interior is superb, the whole house is somewhat overshadowed by the magnificent gardens – acknowledged as having one of the finest layouts in Europe.

It was the second Henry Hoare who was responsible for the original landscaping, and he devoted many years to its development. The area covered is vast and the combination of water, lawns, trees, shrubs and Classical temples is delightful. Carefully designed vistas have been made to appear completely natural, whilst others which are more obviously

Wellington chose Stratfield Saye House, an unpretentious country retreat, as his home

contrived are no less enchanting. Each generation made useful additions to the flora at Stourhead, notably the many varieties of rhododendrons and azaleas, but the basic landscape remains the same.

House open daily (except Fri) between May and Aug, pm only. Mon, Wed, Sat and Sun, pm only, Apr, Sep and Oct.
Gardens open all year daily. NT.

Stratfield Saye House

Hampshire *p213 A3*

Originally built in 1630 by Sir William Pitt, Stratfield Saye was later purchased by the Nation in 1817 for the first Duke of Wellington after his victory at Waterloo.

The Duke's life and work is reflected throughout the rooms of this Jacobean-styled house: Napoleon's Tricolours hang from marble columns; the library con-

Stone Bridge and the Pantheon at Stourhead

tains leather volumes from his early days in India, and paintings and bronzes portray his beloved Copenhagen – the charger who carried the Duke at Waterloo, and whose grave is marked in the grounds. The house is full of beautiful pieces of French furniture, Sèvres china, silver, and a fine art collection. Of particular historic interest is the Roman mosaic pavements excavated from nearby Silchester.

Open daily (except Fri) end Mar to end Sep. Parking available.

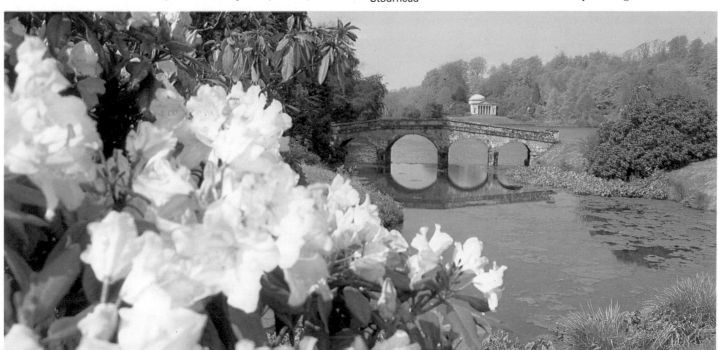

Stratford-upon-Avon

Warwickshire *p216 F1*

Famous as Shakespeare's birthplace, Stratford is a charming old market town in its own right. Mellowed buildings, many half-timbered, line broad streets. Lush meadows lead to the gently flowing river Avon, and brightly-coloured boats on the canal lend a holiday atmosphere to this pleasant town in the heart of England.

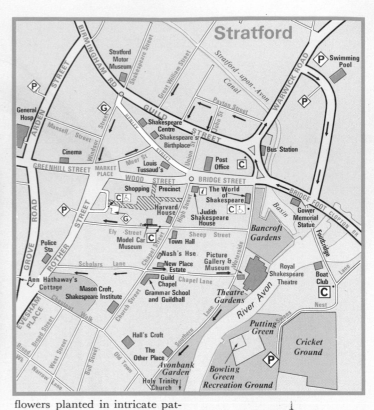

The town first grew from a Bronze Age settlement, was succeeded by a Romano-British village, and then in Anglo-Saxon times a monastery was founded. Recognition as a town came when it was granted the right to hold a weekly market in about 1196. In the thirteenth century, the powerful Guild of the Holy Cross built its chapel and hall, and virtually ran the town. When Henry VIII suppressed such religious organisations, the municipal power went to a bailiff, fourteen aldermen and fourteen burgesses. John Shakespeare, William's father, held the office of bailiff in 1568.

Stratford is surprisingly unspoilt, for there is no doubt that since the first Shakespeare Festival, 200 years after his death, a large part of the town's prosperity is due to its Shakesperian connections. This medieval and Georgian town is now second only to London as a tourist attraction.

A portrait assumed to be of Shakespeare, our greatest dramatist

Holy Trinity

Approached down a long avenue of limes, this partly thirteenth-century building stands in quiet, pleasant grounds beside the river Avon. The great panelled door has a sanctuary knocker; any criminal who reached it could gain thirty-seven days' grace. In the chancel set, in the wall above his gravestone, is a bust of Shakespeare. It was made within a few years of his death and is supposedly a fairly accurate likeness. His wife lies on one side and his daughter Susanna on the other.

A particularly beautiful feature of this church are the choir stalls, richly carved with figures. Among them is a scolding wife pulling a man's beard, a monkey drinking from a jug and a mermaid with a mirror, combing her hair.

Nash's House

The name of this splendid half-timbered building comes from Thomas Nash, who was the husband of Elizabeth Hall, Shakespeare's grand-daughter. It is now a museum depicting Stratford's history since prehistoric times, and provides an accurate record of England in Skakespeare's day.

Behind Nash's House is the Knott garden, with herbs and flowers planted in intricate patterns, and the Great garden. A mulberry tree, said to have been grown from a cutting of a tree Shakespeare planted, shades the lawn.

Royal Shakespeare Theatre, Picture Gallery and Museum

The red-brick block of the theatre's buildings was the country's first National Theatre. Built from a public fund and completed in 1932, it is best seen at night when its riverside position is enhanced by floodlighting. The Royal Shakespeare Company which performs here is world famous, and the auditorium and huge stage, with its mechanical contrivances, were designed specifically for Shakespeare's plays.

The gallery contains portraits of Shakespeare, famous Shakespearian actors and actresses, scenes from plays performed at the theatre, and theatrical relics.

Harvard House

From this house John Harvard left his parents and set out for America. Educated at Cambridge, he died at the age of thirty but left a legacy of £779 17s 2d for the founding of Harvard University. His grandparents, Thomas and Alice Rogers, whose initials are carved on the front of the house, built it in 1596. The rambling interior is full of passages and winding stairs with rough beams in the rooms.

The rambling cottage at Shottery where Anne Hathaway's family lived

Now the property of Harvard University, it contains some interesting exhibits, including the walking stick of Jefferson Davis, the Southern leader in the Civil War.

Shakespeare's Birthplace

The house in Henley Street where Shakespeare was born is visited by more than 500,000 people every year. It has been restored to its old condition as far as possible and is a typical middle-class home of the period. The stone-paved living rooms open straight on to the street, and in the kitchen the great fireplace with its roasting spit and cast-iron pots includes an unusual feature, a seventeenth-century 'baby-minder', which prevented children from getting too close to the fire.

Upstairs is the room Shakespeare was born in. The walls and ceiling, even the glass in the windows, are scratched with the names of visitors. These include those of Walter Scott, Robert Browning, Isaac Walton and other literary figures. Among the treasures in the house are a sword and a ring said to be Shakespeare's, his school desk, documents, portraits and a letter sent to him by his friend Richard Quiney asking for a loan of thirty pounds.

Hall's Croft

Perhaps the most impressive medieval house in Stratford, Hall's Croft was the home of John Hall, an eminent local doctor and husband of Susanna, Shakespeare's elder daughter. The house contains an exhibition illustrating sixteenth and seventeenth-century medical practice. The walled garden is a delight, and the house is seen at its best from here. When Susanna's daughter, Elizabeth, died in 1670, Shakespeare's direct line of descendants came to an end.

Stratford-upon-Avon Motor Museum

This pleasant Victorian building, once a church and school, is the home of an excellent motor museum, recommended to every vintage motoring enthusiast.

The vintage cars and motorcycles are displayed in a setting with a theme of the Roaring Twenties – the Golden Age of Motoring. Specialities include exotic sports cars and grand tourers from that age – often recovered from places like India, and professionally restored to showroom condition. Also here is the music, fashion and decor of the twenties; a replica of one of the early roadside garages; and many collections of motoring memorabilia. A shop, picture gallery and picnic garden complete the attractions.

There is another museum of cars, the Model Car Museum in Ely Street. Here a collection of about 19,000 miniature vehicles from forty countries can be viewed.

Ann Hathaway's Cottage

Two miles from the centre of Stratford is the village of Shottery. The Hathaway family lived here, and did so until 1892. Shakespeare married Ann in 1582, and the house is kept much the same as they must have known it. The fifteenth-century building with its country garden looks like a typical English cottage, although in fact it has twelve rooms. One of these has a settle beside a large fireplace where Shakespeare is said to have courted his bride-to-be. The kitchen is a fascinating place where old cooking utensils, tableware and other tools of a working Elizabethan kitchen are kept.

In one of the bedrooms is an oak bed over 400 years old. It has five carved figures at its head, the original rush mat beside it and a needlework cover made by Ann Hathaway's sister.

Nash's House open all year Mon to Sat, also Sun pm Apr to Oct. Closed Christmas and Good Fri.

Royal Shakespeare Theatre, Picture Gallery and Museum open Apr to Nov daily, Sun pm only. Dec to Mar Sat and Sun.

Harvard House open all year Mon to Sat, also Sun pm Apr to Sep.

Hall's Croft open all year (except Good Fri am and Christmas) Mon to Sat, also Sun pm Apr to Oct.

Shakespeare's Birthplace open all year daily. Closed Sun am Nov to Mar, Good Fri am and Christmas.

Motor Museum open all year daily (except 25 Dec).

Model Car Museum open all year daily. Parking available.

Anne Hathaway's Cottage open all year daily (except Good Fri am, Christmas and Sun am Nov to Mar). Parking available.

Sudbury Hall

Derbyshire *p216 F2*

Sudbury Hall, a seventeenth-century Jacobean mansion set in attractive parkland, was the home of the Vernons until 1967.

Its fine 138-foot long gallery is decorated with murals by Laguerre, Grinling Gibbons carvings and an elaborately carved staircase by Edward Pearce. The east wing of the house contains the Museum of Childhood which has a permanent exhibition entitled Exploring Childhood; each room has activities for children and there are galleries for temporary exhibitions of arts and studies.

In the grounds is the twelfth-century All Saints Church which has a stained glass window presented by Queen Victoria.

Open Apr to Oct Wed, Thu, Fri, Sat, Sun and Bank Holiday Mon pm only NT.

Sudeley Castle and Gardens

Gloucestershire *p212 F5*

This very large and very grand castle has a history stretching back for over 1,000 years, but owes its present grandeur to the extensive restoration undertaken during the nineteenth century. The exterior was treated most sympathetically and adheres to the style of the remaining parts of the fifteenth-century edifice, with towers and battlements.

The interior, however, is almost completely nineteenth-century, with occasional reminders of the illustrious past of Royal Sudeley. The chapel contains the tomb of Catherine Parr, sixth wife of Henry VIII, who out-lived her husband and came to Sudeley as wife of its owner, her second husband Sir Thomas Seymour. She died soon afterwards, followed shortly after by her husband who was executed for treason. The tomb of the dowager queen is not the original, which was destroyed by Parliamentarians, but is a nineteenth-century replacement. The castle contains a magnificent art collection including works by Constable, Poussin, Van Dyck and Turner. There is also some fine period furniture, tapestries, one of which is reputed to have belonged to Marie Antoinette, and an exhibition of costumes. The grounds are extensive and include formal gardens and a lake with a large collection of waterfowl. A more recent addition is the large adventure playground for young visitors, complete with its own replica castle.

Open Mar to Oct daily, grounds from late morning, castle and exhibitions pm only but from late morning on Bank Holiday Sun and Mon. Parking and refreshments available.

Suffolk Wildlife and Country Park

Suffolk *p214 E5*

In a gently sloping, part-wooded country park just outside Kessingland, is this interesting collection of birds and animals. Some will be familiar to all, such as the goats, sheep and waterfowl; others include the more elusive native species such as Red and Fallow deer. Animals from far off continents are the monkeys, llamas, wallabies and, most impressive of all, the big cats. There are many varieties of birds in the park including colourful parrots, macaws, owls, toucans, stately peacocks, cranes, rheas and the sacred ibis. Many of the birds and animals are free-roaming and special food can be purchased to feed the ducks and geese on the lake.

Open Mar to Oct daily. Parking and refreshments available.

Sulgrave Manor

Northamptonshire *p213 A4*

The oldest part of Sulgrave Manor was built in the sixteenth century by Lawrence Washington. At that time it was a modest building and additions were made during restoration in the early part of this century. It was the ancestral home of George Washington; his great-grandfather, John Washington departed from Sulgrave Manor for America in 1656. After having several owners the house was eventually bought by a body of British subscribers in 1914, then restored and refurnished by American subscription for the peoples of Great Britain and America to celebrate the hundred years of peace.

The house is now a museum containing portraits, contemporary furniture and many relics associated with George Washington and his family. The most treasured possession in the manor is an original oil painting of George Washington which hangs in the great hall. Above the main door is the Washington coat of arms.

Sulgrave's fourteenth-century church contains many memorials related to the manor, including the tomb of Lawrence Washington and the Washington family pew.

Open all year daily (except Wed and Jan). Parking available.

Sutton Park

North Yorkshire *p217 B3*

This is an elegant seventeenth-century building, much influenced by the Palladian style of architecture. The interior is for the most part light and extremely attractive with rooms of modest proportions and some superb plaster ceilings. Much of the contents originated from the ancestral home of the Dukes of Buckingham at Normanby Park in Lincolnshire, including some fine pieces of furniture and a large array of family portraits. In the entrance hall is a drawing of the first Duke's London home which is now Buckingham Palace. Throughout the house there are a large number of attractive and valuable clocks, and collections of enamelwork and porcelain. The latter collection is housed in the porcelain room, which has a particularly lovely porcelain chandelier. An interesting feature is the Chinese room with its rare Chinese wallpaper.

The house is surrounded by parkland, landscaped by Capability Brown, and delightful gardens.

Open Easter Fri, Sun and Mon, then Suns in Apr. From end Apr to end Sep Sun, Tue to Thu and Bank Holiday Mon, pm only. Refreshments available, pm.

Sweetheart Abbey

Dumfries and Galloway *p220 D2*

The tiny, picturesque village of New Abbey is situated in a wooded setting on the Pow Burn. Overlooking the village is Sweetheart Abbey, one of the most beautiful monastic ruins in Scotland. Dating from the thirteenth century, it was constructed of red sandstone brought from the quarries at Caerlaverock, and colon-

---

The Jacobean front of Sudbury Hall, with diapered brickwork and Baroque porch designed by Sir William Wilson ised by monks from nearby Dundrennan Abbey.

This, the last pre-Reformation Cisterican abbey to be built in Scotland, was founded by Devorgilla, Lady of Galloway. She also founded Oxford's Balliol College in memory of her husband, John Balliol the elder. Upon her husband's death, Devorgilla kept his embalmed heart in a casket and it was from this that the abbey got its name.

Lying in a secluded hollow, the roofless remains of the abbey include the ninety-foot-high central tower and much of the nave and transepts. The short choir is dominated by a great rose window and the precinct wall is amazingly well preserved. This encloses about thirty acres and was built from particularly large stone boulders.

Devorgilla was buried in front of the abbey altar, together with her husband's heart, in 1289. The original monument fell into decay but a replacement was set up in the south transept chapel in 1933.

The isolated Abbot's Tower stands to the north-east with the estuary of the river Nith and Solway Firth beyond.

See AM info. Parking available.

Above: Sulgrave Manor kitchen, with its great fireplace, contains old cooking implements and antique guns
Below: Sudeley Castle dates from the 14th century and once belonged to Yorkist kings Edward IV and Richard III

T

Talyllyn Railway

Gwynedd *p216 C2*

The small seaside town of Tywyn is the terminus for the narrow-gauge Talyllyn Railway which was once used to carry slate and passengers from the Bryn Eglwys Quarry, south of Abergynolwyn, to the coast at Tywyn. It now carries visitors for some seven miles up a beautiful valley, close by the Dolgoch Falls to Nant Gwernol, near to the foot of the Cader Idris range.

Maintained by the Talyllyn Railway Preservation Society since the early 1950s, it was the first railway in Britain to be saved by volunteers – and the first to provide a continuous public service since 1866. Adjacent to Talyllyn Wharf Station is a museum which contains one of the finest collections of relics representing narrow-gauge railways, including a number of locomotives and wagons.

Railway open Easter to Oct, regular daily services (except Oct). Timetables available. Refreshments available.

Railway Museum open Easter to Oct daily, Nov to Mar by arrangement.

Tamworth Castle Museum

Staffordshire *p216 F2*

In 1897, the Corporation of Tamworth acquired the castle to commemorate the Diamond Jubilee of Queen Victoria, and to establish a museum. So it remains today – a remarkably well-preserved building in a variety of styles which show something of its long history. The oldest part is a section of early Norman herringbone masonry which leads to the keep, a remnant of the days when the Marmions, Royal Champions of the Kings of England, lived here.

One of the finest rooms in the castle is the fifteenth-century banqueting hall with its lofty open-timbered roof and mullioned windows. The majority of the castle buildings are of seven-

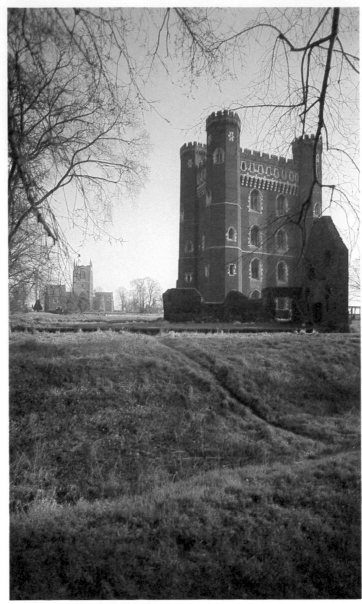

The great tower of Tattershall Castle once housed about 100 servants

teenth and eighteenth-century construction and contain richly carved woodwork, period furniture and there is a painted heraldic frieze in the state apartments.

Many of the rooms contain art exhibitions and items of local history, but during the course of the present programme of restoration work, some sections may be closed.

Adjacent to the castle is a sixty-five-acre park on the banks of the rivers Tame and Anker. Three-and-a-half acres have been laid out with lawns and flower beds – the rest is laid out with a playground and sports and swimming facilities.

Open all year daily (except 25 Dec and Fri Oct to Mar), Sun pm only. Parking available.

Tattershall Castle

Lincolnshire *p217 D1*

Both the village of Tattershall and the surrounding flat fenland are dominated by the massive square keep of Tattershall Castle, which rises to a height of over a hundred feet. It was built in the fifteenth century of locally made bricks as an extension, to provide more comfortable accommodation than the existing castle offered. At the end of the seventeenth century the castle was left empty and subsequently fell to ruin. At the beginning of this century is was rescued by Lord Curzon from transportation and re-erection in America, and he restored the keep before donating it to the National Trust in 1926.

Today, the keep stands alone, the earlier buildings having all gone, surrounded by smooth lawns and two moats. It is a solid and impressive structure with four corner turrets, the walls surmounted by battlements which enclose five storeys and forty-eight rooms. Particularly interesting are the stone fireplaces, carved with heraldic detail, which were recovered and reinstated by Lord Curzon.

Open all year (except Good Fri, 25 and 26 Dec) daily, Sun pm only. NT.

Tatton Park

Cheshire *p216 E3*

In a magnificent deer park of some 2,000 acres, stands Tatton Hall. The grounds were landscaped by Humphry Repton in the middle of the eighteenth century and today leisure pursuits, such as horse riding, exploring nature trails and picnicking, can be enjoyed in them. On a large lake called Tatton Mere there are facilities for sailing, fishing, swimming and model yachting; whereas Melchett Mere is the home of many species of wildfowl.

Home of the Egerton family since the late sixteenth century, the present house was designed by the architect Samuel Wyatt at the end of the eighteenth century; after his death in 1807, his nephew Lewis Wyatt completed the work. There are spectacular views of the gardens and park from the state rooms and bedrooms. The interior is entirely furnished with the Egerton family collection, which includes furniture by Gillow, china, glass and silver. There are also many excellent paintings, including works by Van Dyck and Canaletto. A family museum has been established in the tenants hall, and the last Lord Egerton's remarkable collection of curiosities and hunting trophies, veteran cars, estate fire engines and a state coach can be seen here as well.

The fifty acres of grounds with an orangery, Japanese and Italian gardens and a hundred-yard-long broad walk of tall trees leading to a replica of a Greek monument, complete the attractions of Tatton Park.

Park and Gardens open all year daily, Gardens pm only mid Oct to Apr.

House open Apr to mid Oct daily, pm only. Mar and mid Oct to mid Nov Sun and Bank Holidays, pm, only. All closed Mon, except during Aug and Bank Holidays. N.T.

Tenby

Dyfed *p211 B4*

The centre of Tenby, with its charming Georgian houses and winding narrow streets enclosed by well-preserved medieval walls, has as much appeal as the beautiful stretch of Welsh coastline on which it is built.

Prominent from all angles is the ruined Norman castle on its hill; a statue of Prince Albert surveys the fragmented castle walls and there is a museum in the renovated keep. To the north of Castle Hill lies the little harbour – now a popular yachting centre – the lifeboat station and North Sands.

Beyond these high limestone cliffs are broken by a series of coves. To the south are Castle Sands and South Sands backed by low cliffs and dunes. All the beaches provide safe bathing.

A small zoo is housed in a Napoleonic fort on St Catherine's Rock which can be reached on foot at low tide, and ferries run to Caldy Island where there is a Cistercian monastery

The municipal buildings, station and new housing estates lie outside the old walls, and camp-

High cliffs and sandy beaches spread out on either side of Tenby's old fishing harbour

Tatton Hall is one of England's best pieces of Regency architecture still in existence

ing and caravanning areas on the outskirts are evidence of Tenby's popularity as a holiday centre, but the town's expansion has not interfered with the attraction of the older part. In the town centre the Tudor Merchant's House, with its gabled front, and Plantagenet House, are both National Trust properties. The former houses a small museum. Laston House in Castle Square was designed as a public baths when Tenby was a fashionable watering place in Victorian times, and

North Bay House, built to a design which won an award at the 1851 Exhibition, is known as Prize House.

St Mary's Church is the largest parish church in Wales. It is Perpendicular in style and contains some interesting monuments. Tenby Museum has, amongst other exhibits, items from caves which indicate that they were inhabited by prehistoric man.

Castle open at all times.
St Catherine's Rock open Whit to Sep daily.
Tudor Merchant's House open mid Apr to Sep Mon to Fri, Sun pm only.
Tenby Museum open daily all year.

A Bristol Fighter, built in 1917, during one of Shuttleworth's summer flying displays. All the exhibits in the collection are kept in working order

Tewkesbury

Gloucestershire *p212 F5*

The ancient town of Tewkesbury occupies a delightful site at the confluence of the rivers Avon and Severn, where several smaller tributaries join them. It is a small town of half-timbered buildings and historic inns, including The Black Bear, which is one of the oldest in the country, and The Royal Hop Pole, associated with Dickens' *Pickwick Papers*. Tewkesbury's literary connections are many, for it was featured as Nortonbury in Mrs Craik's *John Halifax, Gentleman* and was the home of the author, John Moore. Mementoes of both are collected in the John Moore Museum in Church Street. Adjacent to this museum is the Little Museum, and both are housed in particularly interesting old buildings. The latter has been restored as a medieval shop, showing how goods were offered for sale centuries ago. Tewkesbury's third museum, the Town Museum, is in Barton Street and contains items of local history and archaeology. There is also a reconstructed carpenter's workshop here and a model of the Battle of Tewkesbury – one of the bloodiest

events of the Wars of the Roses. These are housed in an equally interesting building which, formerly a merchant's house, contains fine wood panelling and decorated ceilings.

The town is dominated by its magnificent abbey church which has the largest Norman tower in existence. The climb to the top is well rewarded with panoramic views over such local landmarks as Bloody Meadow, named after the terrible battle which took place there, and Gupshill Manor, which was used as a headquarters during the battle. The tower was, in fact, a lookout point throughout the hostilities. The abbey, which was once part of an extensive Benedictine monastery, is most noted for its superb vaulted ceilings, its vast Purbeck marble altar and the organ, which is the oldest in the country. There are a large number of monuments and memorials within the abbey, including a plaque which marks the burial place of Prince Edward, son of Henry VI, who was brutally murdered by the Yorkists within the abbey when he took refuge from the battle.

Museums open daily throughout the summer. John Moors Museum closed Sun and Mon; Little Museum Sun.

The Shuttleworth Collection

Bedfordshire *p213 B4*

The aerodrome at Old Warden holds this fascinating collection of historical aircraft, cars, bicycles and other items of transport.

Founded more than half a century ago by the late Richard Shuttleworth, it was his aim that each exhibit must work, and this still applies today. The aviation exhibition includes a Blériot similar to the model used for the world's first crossing of the English Channel in 1909, a reproduction of a British Boxkite of 1910 – especially designed for the film *Those Magnificent Men in Their Flying Machines* – and the famous de Havilland Moth. Genuine veterans of World War I are represented, as are fighters of World War II, such as Spitfires and Hurricanes.

There is an extensive programme of road vehicle restoration and those already restored include a 1903 de Dietrich racer and a 1902 Baby Peugeot. An old fire engine dating from 1780 is among the many other interesting exhibits.

Visitors now have the chance to see servicing and restoration

being carried out on exhibits as an area of the workshops has been opened to the public. During the summer there are several flying displays and pageants featuring aeroplanes from the collection.

Open all year daily (except Christmas). Special flying days on last Sun in month, May to Sep. Two special pageant days July and Sep. Parking and refreshments available.

Thetford

Norfolk *p213 D5*

Thetford was the capital of the Saxon Kings of East Anglia and for a short period after the Norman conquest was the seat of the Bishopric of East Anglia. Its ecclesiastical importance continued until the Reformation, and there were four religious houses and twenty churches during the reign of Edward II.

After the Dissolution of the monasteries its importance waned, but as a market town in an agricultural area it remained reasonably prosperous. In the early nineteenth century an attempt was made to turn it into a spa – the pump house in Spring Walk was built in 1818 – but this was unsuccessful. With the closure in the 1930s of the long-established engineering firm which had been Thetford's main industry, the town's population dwindled. It was in these circumstances that Thetford became an overspill area for London.

Only three of the medieval churches survive, the most interesting being the part-Saxon, part-Norman Church of St Mary the Less; all three have been much rebuilt and renovated. The mound of a motte and bailey castle is preserved in Castle Park, and the remains of the twelfth-century Cluniac Priory stand amidst mature trees, contrasting strangely with new houses which overlook the area. The Ancient House, now a museum, has carved beams in the main room and is believed to have been a Tudor merchant's house. The Georgian King's House (now the Council offices) stands on the site of a house used by James I, and other buildings of interest include an old lock-up behind the Guildhall, the gaol of 1816 in Old Market Street, and almshouses. There is a riverside promenade in the town centre where the rivers Thet and Little Ouse meet.

Ancient House Museum open all year (except Good Fri, Christmas and New Year's Day) daily, Sun pm only.
Castle accessible at any time.
Priory see AM info. Also open Sun am Apr to Sep. Parking available.

The Thursford Collection

Norfolk *p218 E1*

This is a memorable museum containing perhaps the best collection of engines and organs to be found anywhere in the world. Each exhibit has been lovingly restored, and today's visitors can experience the sight, sound, fun and excitement of the heyday of the fairground.

Exhibited here are many mechanical and keyboard organs ranging from huge, carved and richly decorated fairground, cinema and dance organs, to small barrel organs, all to be heard demonstrating the variety and richness of their nostalgic music. Among these exhibits is the mighty Wurlitzer cinema organ, the fourth largest in Europe, which was built by the Rudolf Wurlitzer Company in New York for the Paramount Cinema in Leeds. It boasts 1,339 pipes, arranged in nineteen ranks half an inch to sixteen feet in length.

After the Dissolution of the monasteries part of Tewkesbury Abbey was used as the parish church

Forming the centrepiece of the main museum building is the Savage's Venetian Gondola switchback ride, a unique example from the traditional travelling fair. Some fifty-six feet in diameter and thirty feet high, this amazing Gondola ride is covered in beautiful ornate decoration carved in solid wood. Its musical accompaniment is provided by a Gavioli organ.

The museum also has a considerable collection of magnificent engines, ranging from showman's engines, traction and ploughing engines, and steam road locomotives. An outstanding example of this age of steam is portrayed here by the King Edward VII Showman's Engine, weighing some twenty tons with drive wheels of eight feet diameter.

During the summer season there are rides on a narrow-gauge steam railway which runs around the beautiful grounds of Thursford. The engine is a traditional saddle tank steam engine (built during the late nineteenth century) which spent much of its working life in the Dinorwic Slate Quarry in Wales. There is also a picnic area, a children's adventure playground and a souvenir shop in the grounds.

Open all year, Easter to Oct daily pm only, rest of year Sun and Bank Holidays pm only.
Midsummer musical evenings Tue mid June to Sep.
Parking and refreshments available.

A musical organ from The Thursford Collection's bizarre assortment of fairground exhibits

The Vyne's Classical portico is the earliest example of this style to be found on an English country house

The Vyne

Hampshire *p213 A2*

This beautiful Tudor manor house was built early in the sixteenth century by William Sandys, who later became Lord Chamberlain. Woodland surrounds three sides of the H-shaped house and the north side, to which John Webb added a Classical portico a century later, overlooks lawns and a lake stocked with waterlilies. The small private chapel in the grounds has some excellent stained glass which depicts Henry VIII and Catherine of Aragon amongst its nobilities; the screen and canopies are also noteworthy. After the Civil War, the Chute family bought the mansion and were responsible for the interior alterations during the eighteenth and early nineteenth centuries. The most outstanding is the Palladian-style staircase hall, with its fluted columns, panelling and decorative plasterwork ceiling. The long gallery was altered by the addition of beautiful oak linenfold panelling. The furnishings have been collected over the centuries, and include elegant porcelain figures and Venetian painted glass plates.

Open Apr to Oct pm only. Closed Fri and Mon but open Bank Holiday Mon. Refreshments available. NT.

Thoresby Hall

Nottinghamshire *p217 C2*

Around the pretty little village of Edwinstowe, in Sherwood Forest, is an area known as The Dukeries because of its stately homes. Some three miles to the north of the village, deep in the heart of

the forest, is Thoresby Hall, until recently the only Dukeries mansion still occupied by descendants of the original owners. Now the property of the National Coal Board, it is the third house to have been built on the site. Lady Mary Wortley Montagu, one of the greatest English women letter writers, occupied the first one which was destroyed by fire in the eighteenth century; the second, demolished in the nineteenth century, was the residence of the Duchess of Kingston. The present Thoresby Hall, built between 1864 and 1875, was designed by Anthony Salvin for the Pierrepont family.

Standing in 12,000 acres of parkland, this impressive Victorian mansion with some 200 rooms has retained much of its original character. The state apartments are open to the public, and include the great hall with its portrait of Lady Montagu; the

historic library with its carved fireplace and statues of Robin Hood and Little John; the Rococo blue salon and the state dining room. The grounds consist of gardens, river walks, fine avenues of chestnut trees and an ornamental lake. To the west of the lake there is a folly called Budby Castle, and a miniature steam railway. Other attractions include the Thoresby Hall Pottery, a resident wood craftsman, a deer park and an adventure playground.

Open every Sun in June, July and Aug (also Easter Sun and Mon, Sun and May Day, Sun and Spring Bank Holiday, Late Summer Bank Holiday) pm only. Parking and refreshments available.

Thorpe Park

Surrey *p213 B3*

Converted gravel pits have been attractively landscaped to provide a lake and parkland setting

A castle has faced the wild Atlantic at Tintagel for over 800 years

for this unusual new leisure park.

Elaborate displays record the lives of peoples that have inhabited Britain through the ages. For example, there is a reconstruction of a Celtic farm and a Saxon hall; a Norman motte and bailey castle; a Roman galley; and a Viking long ship.

There are also replicas of historical sea and air craft that have featured in Britain's heritage. These include a *Supermarine SJ* and planes from the Schneider Trophy Seaplane races.

A space-like domed pavilion houses exhibition and entertainment areas and numerous other facilities.

Open all year daily (except 25 Dec).

Tintagel

Cornwall *p211 B2*

Legend has it that Tintagel Castle was the stronghold of King Arthur, but in fact the castle was built 600 years after the romantic King's supposed lifetime. The rock on which it stands, known as The Island, was connected to the mainland by a natural bridge of rock, but this collapsed long ago and was replaced by a footbridge.

There are traces of a settlement in AD 500, but this is believed to have been monastic. Built in the twelfth century by the Earl of Cornwall, a bastard son of Henry I, the castle later belonged to the Black Prince. It then became a prison for a while but eventually fell into decay. However, the Arthurian legend, first mentioned in 1145, persists; but Tintagel is exciting whether or not Arthur lived here. Waves crash in Merlin's Cove and a waterfall drops forty feet into Tintagel Cove, from which great cliffs rise with dark slate caverns at their base.

The village itself has expanded in recent years, with new bungalows outnumbering the thick-walled stone houses. However, the old Post Office, a small fourteenth-century manor house, remains a rare survival of domestic building from the Middle Ages with many interesting features. It was used as a receiving office for post during the nineteenth century and is now owned by the National Trust.

Castle see AM info. Also open Sun am Apr to Sep.
Old Post Office open Apr to Oct daily, but pm only on Suns. Dec, Jan and Feb key available from caretaker. Closed Nov. NT.

Tintern

Gwent *p212 E4*

One of the finest relics of Britain's monastic age, the abbey owes almost as much of its beauty to its idyllic setting as to the serene beauty of its roofless walls. It is set in the Wye Valley, amid peaceful meadows by the river and is flanked by steep-sided wooded slopes.

The noble ruins of the abbey church date back to the thirteenth century and still preserve an aura of sanctity. Its walls, almost intact, display Gothic architecture at its best. Particularly noteworthy are the majestic arches, fine doorways and elegant windows, including a fine traceried rose window over sixty feet high, set in the east end. Remains of many of the domestic buildings also survive and include the sacristy, chapter house, parlour, refectory and kitchen.

The abbey was founded in 1131 by the Cistercians, the monks

Tintern Abbey became a favourite haunt of William Wordsworth in the 18th century and its beauty inspired him to write a poem about it

from Citeau in France, and was suppressed by Henry VIII's Dissolution of monasteries during the sixteenth century. The monks of this order were noted for their austere lives and farmed on a large scale, maintaining lay brothers to do all their manual labour. The Anchor Inn, near the river, is connected to a slipway by a thirteenth-century arch, and was probably once the abbey's water gate.

Tintern's former railway station now houses a small exhibition telling the story of the old Wye Valley railway line. Here there are also refreshment facilities together with a picnic site. At Wyndcliff, some two miles south, a walk leads to a 770-foot-high hill which offers exceptional views. Walkers can also enjoy fine views of the Wye Valley from the Tintern Forest, Chapel Hill and Barbadoes Forest trails – controlled and waymarked by the Forestry Commission.

Abbey see AM info. Also open Sun am Apr to Sep. Parking available.
Tintern Station Railway Exhibition open Easter to Christmas daily (except Tue and Wed). Parking and refreshments available.

Torquay Devon *p212 D2*

Torquay's setting of natural beauty and mild climate have helped to make it the Queen of Watering Places, famous holiday resort and favoured residential area. Terraces of elegant houses encircle lushly-vegetated hillsides, palm trees stand amid gardens of blossom and pleasure craft ride at anchor in the harbour.

Wooded slopes and terraces encircle Torquay's colourful harbour

Until the Napoleonic Wars Torquay was a fishing village, but while Europe was in upheaval wealthy Britons had to find a substitute for holidays abroad and Torquay offered a gentle climate and beautiful surroundings. The Palk family, who owned much land in the area, were quick to see the possibilities of this sudden popularity and employed architects to lay out the town, consciously choosing an Italianate style to enhance its Mediterranean appearance. Their plan, with its fine houses and gardens, is the core of the present-day Torquay.

Boat trips and fishing expeditions start from the harbour, and regattas and powerboat races are held at intervals throughout the year. Tennis and bowls championships are held in Torquay and other sports are well-catered for.

Kent's Cavern

The natural cave contains weird formations of stalactites and stalagmites, now effectively illuminated. It is one of the oldest known caves to be inhabited by man and bones were found here, along with those of bears and a sabre-toothed tiger believed to date from the Ice Age.

Natural History Society Museum

Founded in 1844, the museum contains archaeological finds from Kent's Cavern and other caves in South Devon, as well as natural history exhibits.

Babbacombe

Over 400 models and 1,200 feet of model railway are laid out here in four acres of ingenious miniature landscaped gardens. Modelled to represent the English countryside, the gardens show a comprehensive range of conifers, flowering shrubs and trees, with an emphasis on dwarf conifers, and the buildings have the smallest details.

Torre Abbey Mansion

This eighteenth-century house is used as an art gallery and museum and has some interesting pictures and furniture. Nearby are the ruins of Torre Abbey, founded by monks from northern France who were responsible for building the first quay. The twelfth-century tithe barn is known as Spanish Barn because sailors from the Spanish Armada were imprisoned there in 1588.

Aqualand

This is the largest aquarium in the West Country and its speciality is tropical marine fish. Aqualand also has a fine exhibition of various types of local marine life, tropical freshwater fish and even a pair of otters from Asia.

Kent's Cavern open all year daily.
Natural History Society Museum open all year (except Good Fri and Christmas) Mon to Sat. Parking available.
Babbacombe Model Village open all year daily (except 25 Dec). Parking available.
Torre Abbey Mansion open daily Apr to Oct.
Aqualand open Apr to Oct daily.

Totnes

Devon *p212 D2*

Folklore has it that Brutus, grandson of Aeneas, came from Troy to found Totnes and the British race. Verifiable fact shows that Totnes was mentioned in Domesday Book and by the thirteenth century was a Borough with a Merchant Guild and a town wall. The East Gate and North Gate remain from those times, and the former has a flight of steps leading to the Rampart Walk, which follows the line of the medieval wall. The curfew and angelus bells are still rung, and every Tuesday in summer Elizabethan history comes to life when the people of Totnes create a colourful spectacle by wearing Elizabethan dress.

There are many old buildings in the town centre, among them the Guildhall, an ancient stone building of great charm where the Council has met since 1624. Here are kept samples of Saxon coins minted in Totnes, a list of Mayors back to 1359, and other historical items. Elizabethan House, a half-timbered, gabled building with overhanging upper storeys, is now used as a museum and has an exhibition tracing the development of computers. The red sandstone parish church of St Mary, mainly reconstructed in the fifteenth century although founded much earlier by the Normans, contains a superb stone rood screen and a winding stairway which led to the rood-loft. The Butterwalk and Poultrywalk have projecting upper storeys supported on pillars, providing a covered area where produce was displayed for sale. Nowadays a pannier market is held here on Fridays and there is a cattle market on Tuesdays.

The Normans built a castle to defend the crossing place of the river Dart at the northern end of the town, but only parts of the keep and walls remain.

Totnes also has a Motor Museum which covers fifty years of motoring with a collection of vintage, sports and racing cars.

There is splendid walking country both in the immediate environs of Totnes and on Dartmoor. Sports facilities include bowls and tennis in the Borough Park and a covered, heated, swimming pool.

Guildhall open Easter to Sep Mon to Fri, Oct to Mar by appointment.
Elizabethan House open Mar to Oct Mon to Sat (also occasionally during winter). Parking available.
Castle see AM info. Also open Sun am Apr to Sep. Parking available.
Motor Museum open Easter to Oct daily. Parking available.

Tramway Museum

Derbyshire *p217 B1*

This most unusual and fascinating open-air museum is situated in the hill village of Crich. Once an important mining centre, the village is now famed for its unique museum, set in a disused limestone quarry. The quarry itself was the site of a former narrow gauge mineral railway, built by the great railway pioneer, George Stephenson, to link the quarry with the main line railway at nearby Ambergate.

Here vintage tramcars from all over Britain and abroad have been painstakingly and beautifully restored, many of them to working order, by volunteer members of the Tramway Museum Society. The museum is a live one, with a number of lines laid out so that the trams can still run, and visitors may ride them along three-quarters-of-a-mile of electric tramway, following part of the trackbed of the original railway. An air of authenticity has been created by the museum's period setting. This is achieved by the use of the reconstructed façade of Derby's Georgian Assembly Rooms, an Edwardian bandstand, gates from London's Marylebone Station, Victorian gas lamps, street furniture, a pillar box, stone paving and granite setts laid between its tram rails, together with many other tram relics from this bygone era. All this has enabled the trams to be shown today in the surroundings in which they once operated. At the passenger-loading island there is an elegant cast-iron tram shelter and at the Wakebridge terminus one can see a replica of an old Derbyshire lead mine.

High above the Tramway Museum is the 940-foot summit of Crich Stand, a lofty vantage point crowned by a monument to the Sherwood Foresters – the Nottingham and Derby Regiment.

Open Easter week to end Oct Sat, Sun and Bank Holidays, mid May, June, July and Aug also Tue, Wed and Thu. Tram services operate at frequent intervals when the museum is open. Parking and refreshments available.

Traquair House

Borders *p220 E3*

Traquair House, the oldest consistently inhabited house in Scotland, originally dates from the tenth century, although much of it was rebuilt in the seventeenth century.

The main staircase leads to an eighteenth-century library which remains as it was some 250 years ago, and contains an original collection including a fourteenth-century bible and Nuremberg Chronicle, hand-printed in 1493. Other treasures to be seen in the house are tapestries, silver, glass, embroideries from the thirteenth century, and relics of Mary Queen of Scots – one of twenty-seven monarchs to have stayed at the house. Among exhibits connected with her are a rosary and a cradle – reputed to have been used for her son, James VI of Scotland, James I of England.

Outside an eighteenth-century brewhouse is still used to produce ale which is bottled and sold to visitors. In an old farm workman's hut there is a wood workshop; the adjacent old stables house the pottery; a screen printing workshop is in the old grain loft and nearby Bachelors Hall has a weaving workship. Here also are cottage tea rooms, small antique shop, nature trails and woodland walks by the river Tweed and Quair Burn.

Open Easter week then remaining Sun in Apr; May to early Oct daily, pm only; July and Aug all day. Parking and refreshments available.

Inhabited since 950, Traquair House is occupied now by a descendant of the 1st Laird of Traquair – James Stuart

Tramway Museum has collected over 40 trams from all over the world

Trelissick Gardens

Cornwall *p211 B1*

This beautiful wooded park affords splendid views of the river Fal and Falmouth Harbour. A fine collection of trees such as magnolias, cedars, maples and great beeches surround the spacious, well tended lawns which are so much a feature of Trelissick. Throughout the seasons, the garden is alight with colourful flora, and a comprehensive range of rhododendrons, azaleas, fuchsias and hydrangea provide a glorious display. Many winding walks lead through tunnels of foliage, under massive trees, and eventually to a summer house and a Saxon cross.

A house has stood in the gardens since 1280, but the present building (not open) dates from 1750. It was subsequently altered and extended during the course of its varied ownership.

Gardens open Mar to Oct daily, Sun pm only. Refreshments available. NT.

Trentham Gardens

Staffordshire *p216 F2*

These gardens surround an elongated lake and cover over 700 acres. They are particularly renowned for their formal sections, originally created by Capability Brown, and believed to be the largest in Europe.

The various gardens make a blaze of colour throughout the year; in the spring over a quarter of a million bulbs burst into bloom and the famous Italian gardens are best seen in summer, whilst the autumnal colours of the trees reflected in the waters of the lake create a marvellous spectacle. There are also rock, peat and woodland gardens, together with a perfumed garden for the blind, and demonstration gardens.

Trentham has an outdoor heated swimming pool in an attractive woodland setting, a children's adventure playground complete with tree houses, pony rides and crazy golf. For those who prefer more leisurely entertainment, rides are available on a miniature railway through trees along one side of the lake, or a trip on a motor launch around the lake.

Open all year daily (except 25 Dec). Parking and refreshments available.

Trerice

Cornwall *p211 B2*

Situated in some fourteen acres of grounds, Trerice, partly screened by elm trees, is approached along narrow Cornish lanes. A picturesque Elizabethan mansion, it is the second house to occupy the site (although no records remain of its predecessor) and dates from 1573, when it was rebuilt by a member of a famous Cornish family, Sir John Arundell.

The house has unusually distinctive curved gables which crown its silvery grey limestone façade. A popular theory is that Sir John may have got the idea for them when soldiering in the Netherlands and Belgium. Now a National Trust property, it was purchased in 1954 with money bequeathed by Mrs Annie Woodhouse. Restored by the Trust, with help from various quarters, the house remains much as it did in the sixteenth century.

Its turfed forecourt enclosed by high walls leads into an E-shaped entrance front beside which is the vast latticed window of the main hall. The house follows a familiar medieval pattern of a passage from the porch leading to the great hall beyond, and contains tapestries and oak and walnut furniture.

A notable feature of Trerice is the fine quality of its plasterwork which was probably modelled by the same master craftsman who plastered Buckland Abbey. The main hall contains a contemporary fireplace, dating from 1572, and beyond the row of recessed arches above the screens passage

The châteaux of the Loire inspired the architect of Waddesdon Manor, and the splendid gardens were laid out by a French landscape artist, Lainé lies a little musicians' gallery. The principal sitting room on the first floor has a barrel ceiling and the Arundell arms are incorporated into both the frieze and the overmantel. There is a shop in the main house and a restaurant in the barn.

Open Apr to Oct daily. Refreshments available pm only. NT.

Tucktonia

Dorset *p212 F2*

Tucktonia is a model landscape featuring the famous, and not so famous, buildings and landmarks of Britain. A network of old and modern railways, roads, canals and rivers connect over 200 faithfully reproduced buildings which are accurate to the smallest detail.

The city of London, with its fascinating sights, is recreated here at Tucktonia. St Paul's Cathedral, the Tower of London, Buckingham Palace and Tower Bridge are amongst many that have been scaled down to form this impressive miniature of England's capital.

Here also a typical Cornish fishing village, complete with fishing boats, forms a picturesque part of the model coastline, along which is moored a perfect scale replica of the famous liner *Queen Elizabeth 2*. Other models depict places of Scottish historical interest, including the romantic Eilean Donan Castle, the cottage where Robert Burns was born, and Hadrian's Wall.

Britain's heritage, from prehistoric Stonehenge to an ultra modern nuclear power station, is delightfully illustrated and after dusk the models are illuminated to provide the visitor with a spectacular last glimpse of this world in miniature. There is also a leisure complex here with amusements for all ages.

Open Mar to Oct daily. Parking and refreshments available.

Twycross Zoo

Leicestershire *p213 A5*

This modern zoo, set in fifty acres of parkland, specialises in breeding animals in danger of extinction. The only group of proboscis monkeys in the country are included in one of the finest collections of primates. Other larger animals at the zoo are elephants, camels, giraffes, lions, tigers,

Ruined Tynemouth Priory stands with the castle built to protect it

cheetahs and leopards. Attractive waterfowl and flamingos can be seen in large pools, and a bird house contains a colourful display of tropical birds. Also of interest is the Rural House with its blacksmith shop and the farmhouse kitchen depicting life of fifty years ago.

Open all year (except 25 Dec) daily. Parking and refreshments available.

Tynemouth Priory and Castle

Tyne and Wear *p217 B5*

These majestic ruins stand on a headland, with excellent views of the coastline, the harbour entrance and Tyne estuary. The eleventh-century priory occupies the site of a previous monastery, destroyed by the Danes in 865. The fourteenth-century castle and curtain wall was originally built to protect the Benedictine priory, but served later as a coastal defence.

The mellow old ruins, which include the grave of Malcolm III of Scotland and fine lawns, are reached through the ruined gatehouse with its towers and keep. Hiding behind the ruins is the coastguard station. An excellent view of the ruins can be had from the end of the north pier.

See AM info. Also open Sun am Apr to Sep. Parking available.

Waddesdon Manor

Buckinghamshire *p213 A4*

This mock French Renaissance chateau was built between 1874 and 1889 by Destailleur, for Baron Ferdinand de Rothschild.

Inside there is a fine collection of furnishings, paintings and personal mementoes of the family. Items of particular interest in the collection are two writing tables, one made for Marie Antoinette and another for Louis XVI. Paintings include works by Gainsborough, Reynolds, Romney and Rubens. A museum of small arms can be seen in the bachelors wing.

The grounds, decorated with fountains and sculptures which have been collected from France, Italy and the Netherlands, include two deer enclosures and a well-stocked aviary.

Open late Mar to late Oct, Wed to Sun, pm only. Open from late morning on Good Fri and Bank Holiday Mon (closed Wed following Bank Holiday). Parking and refreshments available. N.T.

London Bridge, as it appeared in medieval times, perfectly reconstructed in the model world of Tucktonia

The picture gallery at Wallington, with pre-Raphaelite wall-paintings

Wakehurst Place Garden

West Sussex *p213 C2*

The estate of Wakehurst Place was bought in 1903 by Gerald Loder, and later by the first Lord Wakehurst, who was a president of the Royal Horticultural Society, and he began to create the gardens as we see them today. They were bequeathed to the National Trust and later leased to the Royal Botanical Gardens at Kew as an extension of their scientific and experimental work. Much of the estate is given over to woodlands, but about a hundred acres is cultivated and contains many exotic plants and rare species. The flowering shrubs give a superb show and a pic-turesque water course links a series of ponds and lakes.

Open daily (except Christmas Day, New Year's Day and May Day Holiday). Parking available. NT.

Wallington

Northumberland *p220 F2*

Although it was built in 1688, this fine mansion has a predominantly eighteenth-century flavour, owing to the considerable alterations which were made at that time. Originally owned by the Blackett family, it passed by inheritance to the Trevelyans and both families are much in evidence in the many portraits which adorn the walls here. Much of the furniture is Dutch and there are also some fine pieces by Chippendale, Hepple-white and Sheraton. The extensive collection of porcelain, including Oriental, Bow, Meissen, Wedgwood and Sèvres, are on show in specially constructed cabinets. There is also some fine silverware and an enchanting collection of old dolls houses now kept in the common room. Nearly twenty of these are on show, with pride of place given to a particularly large model of a mansion. This has thirty-six rooms, all with electricity and some with running water, and is populated with more than seventy dolls. The adjacent store is now a children's room with old toys, games and books and a fascinating Noah's Ark. Elsewhere in the house a large number of model soldiers can be seen.

Having seen the main part of the house with its lavish furnishings and beautiful plasterwork, a visit to the kitchen provides an interesting contrast. It is furnished as it would have been around the turn of the century, with a scrubbed pine table and huge dresser. All the old cooking utensils and clothes-washing equipment can be seen too. The house is set amid wooded park and moorland with three lakes and some lovely gardens, much still adhering to the formal layout of the eighteenth century. An interesting feature is a set of four stone dragons' heads, which were once a part of the old Bishopsgate – one of the entrances to the City of London.

Open Apr to Sep daily (except Tue) pm only. Oct, Wed, Sat and Sun, pm only. Grounds open all year daily. Refreshments available. NT.

Walsingham

Norfolk *p218 E1*

Walsingham, or Little Walsingham, a market town beside the river Stiffkey, has always been famous for its Shrine of Our Lady of Walsingham. The town arose around the shrine and later its Augustinian priory, sometimes referred to as an abbey. The shrine was built in about 1061 to commemorate a vision of the lady of the manor and became a famous medieval place of pilgrimages. Richeldis de Favraches founded the priory in the twelfth century, incorporating the shrine into its church. In the fourteenth century a Franciscan friary was established, but a century later all the monastic buildings were de-stroyed and the statues from the shrine burnt at Smithfield. Walsingham again became a place of pilgrimages in 1922 and there are now two modern shrines: an Anglican and, a mile to the south-west, the Roman Catholic. The most striking aspect of the priory ruins is the east wall of the fourteenth-century church which is now a handsome archway with elaborate buttresses and turrets. The noble fifteenth-century gatehouse led from the church into the town. It is thought that the original chapel lay inside the precinct wall near the north aisle, but nothing remains today. The surviving walls of the refectory, rebuilt in the thirteenth-century, lie to the south. Adjacent to the former precinct walls of the priory is the Anglican church built in 1931.

Shirehall Museum – a Georgian building, formerly a courthouse where Sessions Courts were held, has now been converted into a museum. Its former courtroom has retained its original fittings including the prisoners' lock-up.

Abbey grounds open Apr to Sep, only Wed only in Apr. May to July and Sep, Wed, Sat and Sun. August, Mon, Wed, Fri, Sat and Sun. Also Bank Holidays from Easter to Sep. **Museum** open May to Sep daily; Oct: Sat and Sun only.

Warkworth Castle

Northumberland *p220 F3*

The builders of Warkworth Castle in the eleventh century, found here a site with remarkable natural defences. The river Coquet loops protectively around the castle and the village, and its steep banks provide additional defences. The castle occupies the highest point on this little peninsula and towers over the quaint village below. The remains are extensive with an impressive gatehouse and an unusual keep which still retains a vivid picture of its former strength.

Not far away, and accessible by boat from the castle, is Warkworth Hermitage – a tiny chapel with living quarters which were hewn out of the sandstone by an unknown hermit. Another interesting feature of Warkworth is the ancient fortified bridge which spans the Coquet across to the northern end of the village.

Castle and Hermitage see AM info, but Apr to Sep only. Parking available at castle.

Warwick Warwickshire *p216 F1*

Warwick, the historic county town of Warwickshire, grew around its impressive castle. This turreted fortress rises above the lovely river Avon which flows past the castle and lends Warwick much of its charm.

Although the town was devastated by fire in 1694, when over two hundred buildings were destroyed, there are some notable survivors from the Tudor period. The High Street, Mill Street, Bridge End and Castle Street have some fine examples of the characteristic half-timbered and gabled buildings. Two of the old town gates also survive, both surmounted by chapels. The West Gate bears the chapel of the nearby Lord Leycester Hospital and at the other end of the High Street the East Gate carries the fifteenth-century St Peter's Chapel.

The Castle

The present castle, one of Britain's most splendid castle-mansions, dates from the fourteenth-century and was built on the site of a Norman castle, which itself replaced a Saxon motte and bailey. The gatehouse bears the crest of the Earls of Warwick, a bear and a ragged staff. Within are the Bear Tower and Clarence Tower, built by that Duke of Clarence who was reputedly drowned in a butt of malmsey. Below is a dungeon with a horrific display of torture instruments, the walls bearing graffiti attributed to Royalist soldiers during the Civil War.

The armoury contains the sword of Guy of Warwick, a Saxon knight who slew the Danish champion, the giant Colbrand. A suit of armour of particular interest is that made for a son of the Earl of Leicester, who was only three years old when he died in 1584; it is displayed in the great hall of the state apartments overlooking the river. The armour collected here includes Oliver Cromwell's helmet, and his death mask may also be seen. The furnishings and paintings in the hall are of great interest.

Lord Leycester Hospital

This group of buildings dates from the twelfth-century and had been used as Guildhall, council chamber and grammar school before 1571, when Robert Dudley, Earl of Leicester, had them renovated and extended. He endowed the hospital for occupation by men wounded in the service of the Queen and her successors. The hospital is still the home of ex-servicemen.

Collegiate Church of St Mary

The nave and tower of this cathedral-like church were built after the disastrous fire of 1694, to a design by Sir William Wilson. The Beauchamp Chapel houses the tomb of Richard Beaumont who died in 1439, one of the most perfect medieval tombs extant. On a Purbeck marble base lies an effigy of Beaumont, his hands raised to a figure of the Virgin in the roof. The Chapel also houses the tombs of Ambrose Dudley, created Earl of Warwick by Elizabeth I when the Beauchamp line died out, and his brother, Robert Dudley, Earl of Leicester.

Market Hall and St John's House

Originally built on arches to provide space for stalls underneath, the Market hall, which dates from 1670, is used as the Warwickshire County Museum, the arches now being filled by doors and windows. A branch of the County Museum, specialising in crafts, costume and musical instruments, together with the museum of the Royal Warwickshire Regiment, is housed in St John's House, a lovely seventeenth-

The tower of Warwick Church

century building with gardens and beautiful wrought-iron gates.

Warwick Doll Museum

This fascinating collection of antique period dolls and toys was put together by Mrs Joy Robinson and is now housed in one of Warwick's best surviving medieval buildings. The black and white Tudor Oken's House was the home of Thomas Oken, one of the foremost sixteenth century-citizens of Warwick.

Castle open all year daily (except 25 Dec). Parking and refreshments available.
Lord Leycester's Hospital open all year daily (except Sun, Good Fri and 25 Dec). Parking and refreshments (Mar to Sep) available.
Warwickshire County Museum open all year Mon to Sat. Also Sun, May to Sep, pm only.
St John's House open Mon and Wed to Sat. Sun pm May to Sep only.
Warwick Doll Museum open all year daily.

Winkhurst House at the Museum

Weald and Downland Open Air Museum

West Sussex *p213 B2*

Historic buildings re-erected on a magnificent forty-acre site of wood and parkland make up this museum. Among these buildings, which were threatened by demolition, are farmhouses from the fifteenth and sixteenth centuries, a large aisled barn (particularly well preserved) and a working tread-wheel dating back to Elizabethan times. A charcoal burner's camp has been recreated here, together with a blacksmith's forge and wheelwright's shop. Most of the buildings are accessible and are authentically furnished and equipped.

The Hambrook Farm houses an introductory exhibition with information on the type of people who would once have inhabited these buildings, plus a brief outline of the building techniques and materials used in their original structure. A nature trail runs through the woodland area which has many interesting features.

Open Apr to Sep daily (except Mon but including Bank Holidays and Mon in July and Aug,). Oct Wed, Sat and Sun. Nov to Mar Sun only. Parking available.

Wedgwood Museum and Visitor Centre

Staffordshire *p216 F2*

This centre has been especially designed to give visitors every opportunity to see the skills of the craft of pottery being performed, using the traditional and modern techniques that have made Wedgwood so famous. The museum contains a comprehensive collection including works by Josiah Wedgwood, made when he founded his first factory in 1769. Exhibits dating from the eighteenth century to present day include the famous Queens Ware, Jasper and Black Basalt, as well as the development of bone china in the nineteenth century and interesting examples of Josiah Wedgwood's experimental designs.

Open all year Mon to Fri. Appointments preferred.

Wells Somerset *p212 E3*

Wells is England's smallest city and it nestles below the sometimes gentle, sometimes dramatic scenery of the Mendip Hills. It takes its name from the underground streams which rise to the surface here, watering the moat of the Bishop's Palace before joining the river Sheppey. Were it not for its magnificent cathedral and the adjoining ecclesiastical buildings, Wells would be no more than a country market town.

In spite of its traffic and the thousands of visitors who flock to the city, Wells retains an unusual air of tranquillity, a characteristic which has held true throughout the centuries for it has seen none of the hostilities which have beset other cities. The worst disturbance would seem to have been when William Penn, founder of Pennsylvania, USA, attracted a crowd of around 2,000 to his preaching in the courtyard of the Crown Hotel, for which he was forcibly removed.

The area around the cathedral is the most peaceful of all and the Vicar's Close is particularly picturesque. This is a row of fourteenth-century buildings (the only complete medieval street remaining in Britain) whose exteriors have changed little from the original. The street is occupied now by the singers of the cathedral and is linked by a bridge to it. Access from the street is via the Chain Gate, above which is the communal dining room, still with much of its original furniture.

Other historic buildings include the Guildhall and some fifteenth-century almshouses; the City Arms – a gaol until the nineteenth century; and St Cuthbert's Church which dates from the fifteenth century and has an imposing tower, a tie-beam roof and a carved font cover.

The Cathedral

Thought by some to be the world's finest example of a secular church with its subordinate buildings, the present cathedral was begun by Bishop de Bohun in 1174 and was one of the first attempts in English Gothic architecture. It was extended during the following centuries and the cloisters and some of the subsidiary buildings are fifteenth and sixteenth century.

The west front is superb with its canopied statues of saints, angels and prophets, and although depleted in number during the Civil War, many survive looking down over the vast lawn which spreads before the entrance. The central tower was built in the fourteenth century and led to the addition of the inverted support arches at the east end of the nave which, though practical in origin, are one of the visual delights of the cathedral. The two squat, yet elegant, towers at the west end were later additions. On a smaller scale, the amusing and beautifully executed carvings in the transepts reward study. The sweeping double staircase, its worn stone treads eloquent of succeeding communities of monks and clergy in procession from the cathedral, leads to the bridge which crosses the public road to the houses of the vicars choral and, by its second branch, to the thirteenth-century polygonal chapter house. This is elevated on an undercroft once used as a

The 14th-century gateway to the moated Bishop's Palace at Wells

treasury, and has a fan-vaulted roof supported by a ribbed central column.

A great attraction within the cathedral is the fourteenth-century astronomical clock, one of the oldest working clocks in the world, which features jousting knights among its moving parts. Other points of interest include medieval window glass and the

Wells Museum

Alongside the cathedral is a row of old buildings which includes the former Deanery and it is here that the Wells Museum has its home. Several rooms contain its collections which include finds from the nearby Wookey Hole and items of local history. There is also a collection of samplers.

Bishop's Palace

To the south of the cathedral lies the beautiful moated Bishop's Palace, one of the oldest inhabited houses England and home of the Bishop of Bath and Wells. Access from the town market place is through a medieval gateway known as the Bishop's Eye. The Palace is surrounded by a high wall, which dates back to the beginning of the thirteenth century, and the lovely wide moat upon which swans glide. They are famous for their habit of ringing a bell for food, a trick which they seem to have inherited from their Victorian ancestors who were taught to do this by the daughter of the Bishop. The earliest parts of the Palace are the undercroft, the Bishop's chapel and the banqueting hall ruin. Portraits of past Bishops hang on the walls of the long gallery.

Wells Museum open all year (except Christmas) Mon to Sat (pm only from Oct to Mar). Also open Sun pm June to Sep.

Bishop's Palace open Easter, then May to Oct Sun pm only; daily during August, pm only. Grounds only on Thu pm. Refreshments available Aug only.

carvings under the misericord choir seats.

Welney Wildfowl Refuge

Norfolk *p213 C5*

Over 800 acres of the Ouse Washes have been designated as a refuge for migratory birds and native species under the protection of the Wildfowl Trust. Thousands of Bewick's swans have their winter home here, together with tens of thousands of ducks which include wigeon, teal, shoveler and mallard. In springtime the refuge is alive with nesting birds including redshank, snipe, ruff, Black-tailed godwit and mallard. Wild flowers also benefit from the seclusion here and provide a lovely show in summer. The birds can be watched undisturbed from the hides and from the spacious observatory. During the winter a lagoon containing hundreds of swans is floodlit for the benefit of visitors.

Open all year daily (except Christmas). Visits escorted by a Warden weekends, only at 10 am and 2 pm. Parking available.

Welsh Folk Museum

South Glamorgan *p212 D4*

This open-air museum has old buildings from all over Wales which have been reconstructed to illustrate the Welsh way of life over several centuries. It occupies the grounds of St Fagans Castle which is itself interesting – a fine Elizabethan mansion with beautiful furnishings and a fascinating kitchen. The gardens are formal with fishponds, statues, topiary work and a lovely avenue of lime trees.

The castle out-buildings now

house the workshops of a wood-turner and a cooper – barrel maker – who can both be seen at work.

The modern main block of the museum contains four separate galleries. The gallery of material culture has an enormous range of exhibits from Welsh dressers to medical equipment; from Eisteddfod chairs and crowns, to carved love-spoons. The costume gallery not only displays a variety of modes of dress but sets them out in authentic surroundings. The other two galleries are devoted to agriculture, the first illustrating the development of farming methods with implements, machinery and photographs and the second housing a collection of old carts and wagons from the horse-drawn era.

The remainder of the site, which extends to about a hundred acres, is dotted with the reconstructed buildings in lovely settings. They include a number of farmhouses, the earliest of which dates from the fifteenth century, a North Wales quarryman's cottage and a toll-house displaying its eighteenth-century tariffs.

More unusual items are a circular pigsty and a cockpit, which once provided gory entertainment in the yard of a Denbigh inn. The fishermen of Wales are not forgotten and the boat house contains a unique collection of coracles, a wide variety of freshwater and sea fishing equipment in the net house and, at the end of the pool, several salmon traps.

Open all year daily (except Christmas, New Year's Day and May Day Holiday). pm only on Sun. Parking and Refreshments available.

The old smithy is one of many traditional buildings that have been re-erected in the grounds of St Fagan's Castle. The interior is authentic

Powis Castle was built in 1250 by Owain ap Gruffydd. Capability Brown landscaped the grounds which contain oak trees many centuries old

Welshpool

Powys *p216 D2*

The little town of Welshpool is situated to the south-east of Lake Vyrnwy on the Shropshire Union Canal. Lying in the Severn river valley close to the border with England, it is an important agricultural and market centre with a long and stormy history. The site of an early Celtic settlement, the town was called Y Trallwng in Welsh, which means pool, because of the surrounding waterlogged countryside. It received its first charter in the thirteenth century, and became known as Welshpool in the nineteenth century to distinguish it from Poole in Dorset. A compact town – its north-western edges skirt steep hillside, whilst the heights of Long Mountain rise to the east beyond the river. In recent years Welshpool has been extensively modernised, but a few of its original narrow streets still survive along with some interesting half-timbered buildings. High on a bank at the north end of Church Street stands the parish church of St Mary of the Salutation, notable for its roof and tower architecture. In the churchyard lies a great stone known as the Maen

Llog. Once used as a throne by the Abbot of Strata Marcella, a Cistercian monastery to the north-east of Welshpool, it was brought to the town upon the Dissolution of the monastery. Other interesting buildings include the railway station and the nineteenth-century Town Hall.

Set amidst terraced gardens and lawns, reputed to have been landscaped by Capability Brown, Powis Castle stands on the south-west outskirts of Welshpool. This well-preserved red sandstone medieval castle with twin towers has been continuously occupied for more than 500 years. The interior contains some fine sixteenth-century plasterwork and panelling, along with tapestries, paintings and late Georgian furniture. Many relics and possessions of Clive of India are also on display and the castle was given to the National Trust in 1952 by a great-great-great grandson of Lord Clive.

Powysland Museum, started in 1874 by Morris Jones, displays a striking collection of relics illustrating the social history of Powysland. Its archaeological, domestic, agricultural and craft exhibits include an Iron Age shield and Roman antiquities.

The Welshpool and Llanfair Light Railway was originally built to carry general goods, and it ran from the 1930s to 1956 when it was closed by British Railways. However, after being rescued by railway enthusiasts, the five-and-a-half-mile stretch between Llanfair Caereinion station and Sylfaen station was opened in 1963. It is hoped that the line will continue to Welshpool in the near future.

Powis Castle open Easter, then May to Sep Wed to Sun pm only. Also open Bank Holidays. Parking and refreshments available. NT.
Powysland Museum open all year daily (except Sun), pm only on Sat. Closed Wed Oct to May.
Welshpool & Llanfair Light (Steam) Railway open at weekends from Easter to Oct. Daily from early June to early Sep. Parking at Llanfair and Castle Caereinion Stations.

West Midland Safari and Leisure Park

Hereford and Worcester *p216 E1*

The West Midlands park was established in the early 1970s and is now one of the most popular Safari Parks in Britain. It covers some 200 acres and includes drive-through reserves of lions,

monkeys, bison, tigers, giraffes, zebra, elephants and rhinos. Outside the reserves there is an extensive leisure park with a pets' corner, sea lions, boating ponds and children's amusements. These include a playground, roundabouts, trains, rocket rides and a skatepark. The park is attractively laid out with landscaped picnic areas.

Open mid Mar to Oct daily. Parking and refreshments available.

Westonbirt Arboretum

Gloucestershire *p212 F4*

One of Europe's most comprehensive collections of trees can be seen here at the Westonbirt Arboretum. Some of the trees date back as far as 1829, when Robert Holford began planting in what was then open pasture. Set in 247 acres of gently rolling parkland, the arboretum is incorporated into a 600-acre Forestry Commission estate. Each season brings a different beauty; budding trees in spring, summer flowering shrubs, the russet tones of autumn leaves, and the severity of winter. Many kinds of rare specimens can be seen here, and particularly impressive are the large varieties of conifers, maples, birches and oaks.

Open all year daily. Refreshments available Apr to Oct. Parking available.

Weston Park

Staffordshire *p216 E2*

This lovely Classical mansion is the home of the Earl and Countess of Bradford and has been in their family for some 300 years. The interior has been considerably altered since it was built, emphasising the fact that Weston Park is a home as well as a great historic house. It contains a fine collection of furniture and paintings, which include works by Holbein and Van Dyck, and there is a large collection of letters on show which were written by Disraeli to the 3rd Countess. The tapestry room contains a late eighteenth-century Gobelins tapestry.

The house is the centre of an estate which covers about 14,000 acres. Much of this is given over to forestry and farming, but the area around the house was laid out by Capability Brown in one of his famous landscape gardens. Mature sweeping lawns, watered by three lakes were embellished in 1760 with the addition of the Roman Bridge and the Temple of Diana, which looks back towards the house. The park is also the home of a herd of Fallow deer and some rare breeds of sheep, and visitors can enjoy rides in horse-drawn vehicles. For the younger visitor there is a woodland adventure playground, a pets' corner and an aquarium, while their parents will probably enjoy seeing a potter at work in the Taurus Pottery, or a visit to the garden centre. Each year at Weston Park there is a programme of special events and exhibitions.

Open Easter to Sep daily (except Mon and Fri but open on Bank Holidays), House, pm only. Parking and refreshments available.

Weston-super-Mare

Avon *p212 E3*

Weston has expanded rapidly since the Victorians started to develop this small fishing village into a seaside resort, and it is now the largest town on this stretch of coast.

The town is well laid out with wide roads and lawns along the seafront and plenty of open spaces. The tide goes out a long

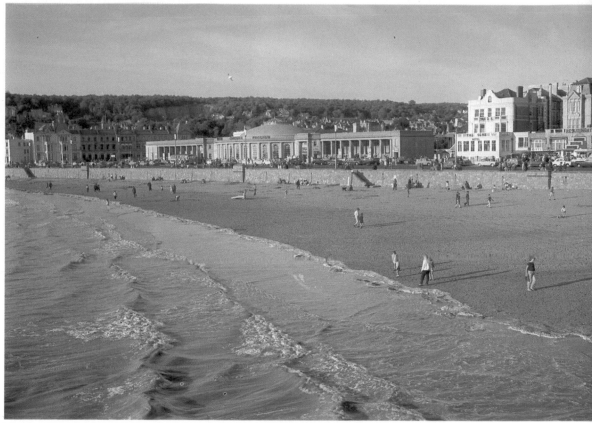

The view from the Grand Pier across the bay to the famous Winter Gardens at Weston-super-Mare

way over the beach, leaving mud exposed as well as the golden sands. This type of beach is ideal for ball games and sun-bathing, but at high tide swimmers have a long walk to deep water. However, the sea-water pool on the beach caters for bathers of all ages and abilities and has a multi-stage diving board; there is an indoor pool too, if the weather is inclement. In the attractive Winter Gardens are tennis courts,

bowling and putting greens; there is a seafront golf course and good facilities for other sports. Two piers provide traditional seaside amusements and there are two theatres offering year-round entertainment, regular concerts in the Rozel Music Garden, a three-screen cinema, several discothèques and ten-pin bowling. Children are well catered for too; amongst the many pleasures are donkey rides and pony carts on

the beach, a model boat pond, paddling pools and mini-zoo.

The Woodspring Museum, housed in workshops of the old Gaslight Company, has a wide variety of exhibits including an old chemist's shop, a dairy, and a display illustrating Victorian holidays.

Woodspring Museum open all year Mon to Sat (except Good Fri, Christmas Day and New Year's Day). Parking and refreshments available.

The east front of Weston Park; the present house was designed by Lady Wilbraham in the 17th century

Whipsnade Park Zoo

Bedfordshire *p213 B4*

Originally planned as a sort of convalescent home for sick animals from London Zoo, Whipsnade has developed into a major zoo in its own right. It now covers some 500 acres of lovely Chilterns countryside and is home to over 2,000 animals. When the zoo opened in 1931, it was quite revolutionary in that it provided large open enclosures for animals that would previously only have been kept in heated cages. The experiment was a resounding success and the creatures from warmer climes adapted well to their new surroundings; so well in fact that the zoo has achieved a remarkable breeding record, and about eighty per cent of its inhabitants have been born at the zoo.

One of the zoo's major successes is in the conservation of endangered species, including North American bison, Père David's deer, Przewalski's horses, Great Indian rhinos, African Black rhinos and, of course, the White rhino which now form a sizeable herd at Whipsnade. As well as these rare breeds the zoo contains all the usual mammals and birds, far too numerous to list, a delightful children's zoo and the ever popular animal rides. It is possible to take vehicles into the zoo and a novel way of seeing part of it is via the Whipsnade and Umfolozi Railway, a two-foot-six-inch gauge steam operated line which follows a circular route through the African region.

Open all year daily (except 25 Dec). Steam Railway Apr to Oct. Parking and refreshments available.

Although the great Thomas Telford designed Wick harbour, large steamers can only dock here at high tide

Whitby

North Yorkshire *p217 C4*

For hundreds of years gulls have screamed over the incoming fishing boats of Whitby, and fishermen and their families have lived under the East Cliff on the banks of the river Esk. Terraces of cottages still rise tier on tier from the water's edge, a fishing fleet plies from Whitby harbour, and nets are mended outside cottage doors. The Victorians started to develop the town as a resort, building hotels and houses to the west of the river mouth, and now the town relies on holidaymakers for its prosperity.

Much of the provision for outdoor activity is on the West Cliff and the Spa complex, which includes a theatre and Floral Pavilion (often used for dances) can be found here. A lift links the cliff top with Whitby Sands, where there are a number of chalets for hire, donkey rides and safe bathing.

Shakespeare's mother, Mary Arden, spent her childhood here at Wilmcote

On West Cliff is a statue of Captain James Cook, who learnt his seamanship sailing colliers from the port, making his home at a house in Grape Street which bears a memorial plaque. Another sailor remembered in the town is Captain William Scoresby, who invented the 'crow's nest' and is reputed to have captured 533 whales in his lifetime. Relics of Cook and Scoresby are displayed in the Whitby Museum, which also has a fine collection of fossils.

Adding to the sense of timelessness which gives Whitby its especial character, are the abbey ruins on East Cliff. The first abbey, founded by St Hilda in 657, was destroyed by Danes in 867, and the buildings of the later Benedictine monastery, dissolved in 1539, have disappeared. Stripped of its roof, battered by the elements, and shelled by the Germans in 1914, the ruins are nevertheless austerely impressive. Close by is the medieval parish church of St Mary with a squat Norman tower, and it is approached by a flight of 199 steps.

Museum open all year (except Christmas and New Year's Day). May to Sep daily, pm only on Sun. Oct to Apr daily am only Wed and Sat open all day, pm only on Sun.
Abbey see AM info. Also open Sun am Apr to Sep. Parking available.

Wick

Highland *p222 E4*

The townspeople of Wick said harsh things about Thomas Stevenson's ability as a civil engineer when a breakwater he constructed was smashed by a violent storm, so perhaps his son, Robert Louis (who wrote *Treasure Island*), was feeling disgruntled when he described Wick as 'the bleakest of God's towns on the baldest of God's bays'. It is true that the cliffs are forbidding, the hilltops windswept and devoid of tree or shrub, yet the coast and surrounding countryside have a fascination of their own.

The town does not deserve to be called bleak these days, and it welcomes holidaymakers.

Swimming from the beach is safe only in the calmest weather, but there are two open-air swimming pools, and facilities for bowls, tennis and putting, with a golf course at the nearby village of Reiss. There are boats for hire on the river, and sea angling is popular – though it needs an expert to navigate around this coast.

The obelisk on the South Head honours James Bremner, a great engineer, and there is a plaque commemorating Robert Louis Stevenson on the Customs House. This is a land of castles, most of them now gaunt ruins. A landmark, nicknamed by seamen Auld Man O' Wick, is the ruined fourteenth-century Castle of Old Wick, also known as Castle Oliphant; to the north are the ruins of seventeenth-century Sinclair Castle and Girnigoe Castle, dating from 1500. The latter has a dungeon where the 4th Earl of Caithness held his son until he died of 'famine and vermin'.

Until 1800 the herring fleet was based at Staxigoe a few miles to the north, where the old red-tiled houses can still be seen. Then the building of Pulteneytown harbour to the south of the river signalled the expansion of Wick and a boom period for fishermen. The people of Wick have sought new industry and the town is now famous for Caithness glass. Both industries have great appeal, the fishing fleet bringing life and colour to the harbour, and a visit to the glassworks, where the manufacture of subtly-coloured hand-blown vessels can be seen, being both informative and interesting.

Castle of Old Wick accessible except when adjoining rifle range is in use. AM.
Castles Girnigoe and Sinclair accessible at all times.

Wilmcote

Warwickshire *p216 F1*

This village of local stone cottages and timber-framed houses, set on the Stratford-Upon-Avon Canal, is famous as the birthplace of Shakespeare's mother, Mary Arden. Her birthplace is the picturesque Tudor farmhouse of the Arden family, now owned and preserved here by the Shakespeare Birthplace Trust. The interior of the house, laid out as it might have been during her day, has a huge fireplace with one of the largest ovens to be seen in England, and a table believed to have been used by monks in the fifteenth century. Outside there is a cider-mill and dovecote, along with other attractive stone outbuildings housing a museum of farming and rural life.

Mary Arden's House open all year (except 24 to 26 Dec. and Good Fri am, Apr to Oct daily, but pm only on Sun; Nov to Mar, Mon to Sat only. Parking available.

Wilton House

Wiltshire *p212 F3*

Standing on the banks of the river Wylye, Wilton House has been described as one of the most beautiful houses in England. The mansion was started by Inigo Jones with the aid of his nephew John Webb, in the sixteenth century, and later additions were made by Holbein and James Wyatt in the eighteenth century. It has been the seat of the Earls of Pembroke for 400 years. Inside the house is a world famous collection of paintings and furniture, including pieces by Kent and Chippendale. There are magnificent double and single 'cube' rooms, elaborately decorated with bundles of fruit, flowers and foliage gilded in gold. Paintings include works by Rembrandt, Rubens and Van Dyck. An interesting exhibit of 7,000 nineteenth-century miniature model soldiers can be seen here.

The grounds are beautiful, with their superb setting of twenty acres of cedar-shaded lawns, with Cedars of Lebanon and an eighteenth-century Palladian bridge which spans the river Nadder.

Open early Apr to early Oct daily (except Mon, but open Bank Holidays) Sun pm only. Parking and refreshments available.

Wimborne Minster

Dorset *p212 F2*

This ancient town once owed its prosperity to the wool trade, but now its wealth comes from market gardening. One of the great churches of Dorset is situated here; the twin-towered Church of St Cuthberga, built of brown and grey stone, and encompassing almost every architectural style from Norman to Gothic. The quarter-jack clock on the minster's west tower features a grenadier wielding a hammer in each hand with which to strike the bells on each quarter-hour.

There is a model town, just off the cornmarket, built to a scale of one-tenth, using authentic materials to recreate Wimborne Min-

---

The 18th-century whalers saw Whitby's greatest days as a seaport

ster in miniature. The site occupies a third of an acre and incorporates beautiful gardens with miniature trees, flowers, and fish. Narrow streets lined with houses, shops, and churches are faithfully reproduced to the smallest detail. The most impressive of these buildings must be the minster itself – an exact replica reaching over twelve feet high. Its clock strikes two minutes after that of the real minster to enable visitors to watch both performances.

Many items of local interest are contained in the Priest's House Museum in the High Street. Items from Roman times are exhibited here, together with a section devoted to rural implements. The museum houses some of the best horse brasses in the country.

About one-and-a-half miles south of Wimborne are the Merley Tropical Bird Gardens. Three acres of lawns and gardens, enclosed by an eighteenth-century wall, contain large cages of a wide variety of birds, including many tropical species.

Model Town open Mar to Nov daily.
Priest's House Museum open early Apr to Sep daily (except Sun).
Merley Bird Gardens open all year daily. Parking and refrehments available.

Winchester *Hampshire*   *p213 A2*

When the Romans left Winchester – having made it one of their largest towns – King Alfred designated it capital of England. Since then the city has continued to be an important administrative centre and, having the oldest public school in England, a venerable seat of learning.

Like so many English cities, the heart of Winchester is its cathedral and its precincts. However, the whole of this compact city is a delight to explore, with its architecture spanning over eight centuries and the river Itchen flowing through its charming back streets. There are many reminders of Winchester's history scattered around its streets; a bronze statue of King Alfred faces up the High Street, and near to it is the City Mill. This sixteenth-century building stands across the river Itchen and, now a youth hostel, is a good starting point for riverside walks to both the north and south. A stretch known as The Weirs is particularly pleasant and this runs alongside the old city walls. The High Street (now mostly pedestrianised), apart from having a number of good shops has many interesting features. These include the Victorian Old Guildhall and, although now occupied by a bank, echoes the past daily at 8.00 p.m. by sounding the bell which rang out the curfew in Norman times. Close to it is the old Butter Cross – a Gothic monument with a fifteenth-century statue of John the Baptist set in to it.

The Cathedral
The history of the cathedral dates as far back as the seventh century to St Peter's Church which oc-

Winchester Cathedral, interior

cupied the site. When the Normans arrived in Britain they brought with them their own distinctive architectural style and the tower, transepts and the crypt of the present cathedral built by William the Conqueror reflect this. As one of the longest cathedrals in Europe, it measures 556 feet and stands majestically in the spacious Close. Here can be seen Pilgrims' Hall, where pilgrims used to rest on their journey to Canterbury in the Middle Ages; the Deanery and the attractive half-timbered Tudor Cheyne Court. One of the cathedral's bishops in the ninth century was St Swithun, and the legend goes that he wished to be buried in the churchyard where the rain would fall on him. However he was not, and to express his anger he caused rain to fall for forty days – hence the expression that if it rains on St Swithun's Day (July 15th) it will rain for the next forty days. In any event there is a shrine to St Swithun in the cathedral. Treasures to be seen inside include a square font made of black marble, which is carved with scenes depicting the life of St Nicholas; medieval wall paintings and elaborate tombs dedicated to such notable people as King Canute, Jane Austen and Izaak Walton.

Wolvesey Castle
Near to Cathedral Close lie all that remain of the former residence of the Bishops of Winchester – Wolvesey Castle. Built in the twelfth century, it was reduced to ruins during the Civil War.

The present Bishop's Palace, standing next to the castle, was built to the designs of Christopher Wren in 1674. Only one wing of the original building still stands, and incorporated in to this is a Tudor chapel that was once part of Winchester Castle.

Winchester College
When founded by the Bishop of Winchester, William of Wykeham, in 1382, the school was for poor scholars only. However fee paying pupils gradually began to attend and by the end of the nineteenth century had increased to such an extent that many new boarding hostels had to be established and it became England's first public school. The college is made up of a number of buildings grouped around a quadrangle and they vary in age from a hundred to 600 years. Inside the chapel are a sixteenth-century Flemish tapestry, seventeenth-century altar rails and fourteenth-century carved stall ends. Other buildings include the cloister, where summer lessons used to be held, and the hall where boys used to eat from wooden platters. Pupils today are still called Wykehamists, after the college founder.

Castle Hall
The Hall stands on the site of William the Conqueror's defence point and is all that remains of the castle which Henry III built, but was later demolished during the Civil War by Cromwell's armies. Inside hangs the famous Round Table which was made to commemorate King Arthur and his knights. The Tudor rose was painted on it in 1522 to honour the visit of Emperor Charles V when Henry VIII entertained him here. The Hall has seen many royal personages and a number of trials have taken place here, including the one at which Sir Walter Raleigh was condemned to death.

Westgate Museum
Westgate, at the western end of the High Street, is one of the five gates of the city walls that enclosed the city in the thirteenth century. At one time Westgate was used as a prison, but it is now a museum with exhibits that include weaponry, armour, and weights and measures that were used in Tudor and Elizabethan times.

St Cross Hospital
Founded by Bishop Henry de Blois during the twelfth century, this establishment is still used as

We know that this table has existed since at least the 15th century

almshouses today and is therefore the oldest in Britain. The inhabitants are dressed in two different distinctive robes. Those belonging to the original order founded by de Blois wear black and are decorated with a silver cross; those belonging to the other Order, founded by Cardinal Henry Beaufort around 1445, wear purple cloaks. These elderly gentlemen can often be seen walking around the city. Hospitality is still extended to visitors at St Cross by the offering of the Wayfarer's Dole, which consists of a piece of bread and a mug of ale.

The Royal Green Jackets' Museum
This specialist museum is divided into three sections. One is devoted to the Rifle Brigade, one to the King's Royal Rifle Corps and one to the Oxfordshire and Buckinghamshire Light Infantry. Incorporated in to all the displays are collections of uniforms, weapons, regimental silver and medals.

Pilgrim's Hall open all year daily (except when closed for private functions).
Winchester College accessible all year daily Sun pm only. Guided tour available (except Sun am).
Castle Hall open all year daily (except Good Fri and Christmas Day) Sun pm only (Sat pm only from Oct to Mar).
Westgate Museum open all year daily (except Good Fri, Christmas and New Year); Sun pm only.
St Cross Hospital open all year daily. Parking available.
The Royal Green Jackets' Museum open Apr to Sep, Mon to Fri. Sat pm only. Oct to Mar, Mon to Fri only.

Windermere
Cumbria *p220 E1*

Nineteenth-century conservationists protested that a railway would ruin the peace of Lake Windermere and its environs, as a result of which the line was terminated at the hamlet of Birthwaite, and the station was called Windermere. The present town of Windermere grew up around the station, expanding until it joined with Bowness to make a lakeside town devoted to tourism. The invention of the internal combustion engine further popularised the area, and roads, towns, places of interests, and even the lake itself, suffer from congestion during the holiday season.

However, no influx of people can spoil the beauty of Windermere. To the north, where the lake is fed by the rivers Brathay and Rothay, the country is mountainous, affording protection from the colder winds, and ten miles to the south the lake waters join the river Leven on its way to the sea. The banks of the lake are well-wooded, so that from the road the water is rarely glimpsed, and conversely, from a boat one is almost unaware of road traffic. In fact the best way to enjoy the scenery is by boat, whether from a ferry plying between the major towns, a hired motor cruiser, a rowing boat, or one of the yachts which add colourful movement to the scene. There are often as many as 1,500 craft on the lake and wardens enforce a strict code of conduct.

One of the best overall views of Lake Windermere can be obtained from Orrest Head (reached by a footpath from the station).

The biggest island in the lake is Belle Isle, where an eighteenth-century circular mansion, built on the site of a Roman villa and surrounded by landscaped grounds, is open to the public. This unique house was the first completely round house built in England and contains portraits of the Curwen family, views of Lake Windermere by Philip de Loutherburg and specially designed furniture by Gillow of Lancaster.

The Steamboat Museum has a covered dock where Victorian and Edwardian craft are preserved. The oldest exhibit is *Dolly* of 1850, salvaged from Ullswater in 1962 and restored. Situated in the village of Near Sawrey, is Hill Top, where Beatrix Potter worked on many of her *Peter Rabbit* stories. However visitors often have a long wait to enter this charming little seventeenth-century house which contains some of her original drawings, furniture, china and pictures.

The parish church of Windermere is St Martin's at Bowness and was founded in the tenth century. The present church dates from 1484 and was restored in 1870. It contains chained books and some interesting stained glass windows. One depicts a packhorse, and in the east window is the coat of arms of John Washington, an ancestor of the American President.

Steamboat Museum open Easter to Oct, daily but pm only on Sun. Parking and refreshments available.
Belle Isle (Motor Launch runs continuously from far end of Bowness Promenade) open May to Sep, Sun, Mon, Tue and Thu. Refreshments available.
Hill Top open Apr to Oct daily (except Fri) pm only on Sun.

Passenger boats ply from end to end of Lake Windermere, a 10-mile trip

Windsor Berkshire *p213 B3*

Royal Windsor, a town which has given its name to the Royal Family, owes its existence to the great fortress, the largest inhabited castle in the world, upon the chalk bluff high above the bend of the river Thames.

Saxon kings had hunted the forests in this area for centuries, based in a settlement known as Windelsora. When the Norman kings built the first fortress on Windsor's present site, four miles upstream from the old settlement, and Henry I held his court there in safety from the hostile Saxons, the town began to grow.

The architecture of Windsor today is largely Georgian and Victorian, but there are buildings far older. One mile from the castle is Clewer parish church, which was virtually completed by the eleventh century. The font is Saxon, and there is also a tomb with Saxon lettering.

Windsor parish church, rebuilt in 1820 although dating from 1168, records in its register the burial of Charles I. The Three Tuns Hotel was built in 1518 and in St Alban's Street is the seventeenth-century home of Nell Gwynne, mistress of Charles II.

There are many narrow cobbled streets in Windsor, especially between Church Lane and Castle Hill, lined with seventeenth- and eighteenth-century buildings. The river too lends its own special atmosphere to Thames-side towns and Windsor is no exception. Boating is to be had and there are pleasant riverside walks, gardens and pubs.

The Castle

For nearly nine centuries Windsor Castle has been the home of kings and queens, and it is the oldest royal residence still in use.

The thirteen-acre site was chosen by William the Conqueror who built a concentric castle of earthworks and wooden defences here. Because it lay near a large tract of forest which provided good hunting, the castle soon became a residence of Norman kings, who loved the hunt as much as their Saxon predecessors. However, it was not until the reign of Henry II that stone buildings were erected as the royal apartments.

Open to the public are the precincts, the state apartments and Queen Mary's Doll's House.

The state apartments are in the upper ward, and the sixteen magnificent rooms hold a remarkable collection of furniture, porcelain and armour. The carvings of Grinling Gibbons are everywhere, and on the walls hang many masterpieces, especially those by Van Dyck and Rembrandt.

Everything in the remarkable Doll's House works, even the minute light bulbs the size of dewdrops. The scale of this house, built by Sir Edwin Lutyens, is one inch to one foot. Famous artists, craftsmen and writers (the library has real leather-bound books of original works) contributed to this gift to Queen Mary in 1924. The detail is amazing, even the linen in the pantry is initialled – a task which took 1,500 hours of work, and the cars in the garages are constructed to run 20,000 miles to a gallon of petrol!

The Chapel of the Order of the Garter, St George's Chapel, was begun in the reign of Edward IV and completed by Henry VIII. It forms the setting of the ceremonious annual service of the Sovereign and Knights Companion of the Order. Here, among the magnificent architecture, heraldry and decoration, Charles I, Henry VIII and Jane Seymour are buried.

Within the walls of Windsor Castle lies St George's Chapel

Eton College

Eton, north of the river, is linked to Windsor by Windsor Bridge. Henry VI founded Eton in 1440 as a collegiate church with a grammar school and almhouse attached. The epitome of the public school, it has produced a string of famous names, and still clings to the traditions which have made it famous.

College Hall and the kitchen survive from the original design, and most of the rest is fifteenth century. College Chapel is the choir of the original Founder's Church, whereas the west range of the cloisters, the great gatehouse, and Lupton's Tower were added in the early sixteenth century; Upper School was built in about 1690.

Guildhall

Built in 1689 by Sir Thomas Fitz, but finished by Wren, the Guildhall houses an exhibition of local history from the Palaeolithic period to the present day. Notable is the collection of royal portraits from the time of Elizabeth I, and a series of dioramas showing historical events at Windsor from early times to the celebration of George III's Jubilee in 1809. There is also a natural history display.

The pillars and arches of Portland stone which support the roof were declared by the townsmen to be unable to take the weight. Wren insisted they were ample but was forced to add columns in the middle. However, close inspection shows these to fall short by an inch or so of the beams they are supposed to support. Wren proved his point.

Household Cavalry Museum

This is one of the finest military museums in Britain. Situated in Combermore Barracks, it traces the history of the Household Cavalry from the Monmouth Rebellion in 1685 to the present day. Exhibits include uniforms, weapons, horse furniture and armour. Terrain models illustrate the Life Guards and Royal Horse campaigns.

Windsor Great Park

This royal park covers approximately 4,800 acres south of the castle, and includes parkland, woods and magnificent gardens.

The Long Walk stretches from the towers of Windsor to Snow Hill, a distance of three miles. On Snow Hill stands a huge bronze of George III on horseback, erected in 1831. Queen Anne added the three mile ride to Ascot in the eighteenth century. In George III's reign Thomas Sandby and his brother laid out the two-mile-long lake of Virginia Water. It has a fine cascade and on the banks stand a group of Roman columns brought from Tripoli.

Lodges in the park include Cumberland Lodge, named after 'Butcher' Cumberland of Culloden. From here the famous Rhododendron Walk stretches for a mile to Bishop's Gate, where the poet Shelley once stayed.

The Savill Gardens started by Eric Savill in 1931, show to their

The Long Walk, lined with chestnut and plane trees, was created in 1685

best advantage rhododendrons, magnolias, cherries and camellias, and beside the ponds and streams grow primulas, irises and lilies. There are beds of roses, rock plants and alpines – almost every manner of plant found in English gardens. The Valley Garden, near Virginia Water, is similar, and the Kurume Punch Bowl is an amphitheatre of thousands of Japanese Kurume azaleas.

Castle Precincts open all year daily. State apartments open all year Mon to Sat and Sun pm May to late Oct. Queen Mary's Doll's House as state apartments (except Good Fri, 25–27 Dec and 1 Jan). Castle is always subject to closure at short notice.
Eton College open daily pm only, but also am during school holidays. Chapel closed Sun during school holidays.
Guildhall open Good Fri to Sep daily, pm only.
Household Cavalry Museum open all year Mon to Fri, except Bank Holidays, also Sun from Apr to Aug.
Savill Gardens (Windsor Great Park) open Mar to Oct daily. Parking and refreshments available.
Valley Gardens (Windsor Great Park) open all year daily.

Wisley Gardens

Surrey p213 B3

These are the famous and extensive gardens of the Royal Horticultural Society. At all seasons there is something to enjoy at Wisley: crocuses in early spring; a sudden flourish of rock plants; glorious rhododendrons in bloom; tranquil green lawns set with formal rose beds; cheerful borders; the mellow colours of the heather garden – particularly lovely in autumn.

The gardens cover 300 acres and include testing grounds for fruit and vegetables, as well as flowers, shrubs and trees, and there are also a number of glasshouses. At the information centre gardeners can obtain advice about horticultural problems, and there is a shop selling books on gardening and related subjects, gifts, preserves, and, in season, fruit from the gardens.

Open all year daily (except 25 Dec). Sun, pm only. Parking and refreshments (Mar to Oct) available.

Woburn Abbey and Wild Animal Kingdom

Bedfordshire p213 B4

Probably Britain's most famous stately home, Woburn Abbey is the ancestral home of the Dukes of Bedford and has been open to the public since 1955. One of the world's greatest private collections of works of art, including paintings by Rembrandt, Gainsborough, Reynolds, Van Dyck, Franz Hals, and many other famous and important works are housed in the palatial mansion of Woburn. The magnificent state apartments are decorated in the superb elegance so typical of the seventeenth and eighteenth centuries, and contain an abundance of treasures. The state bedroom is particularly impressive, with its fabulous ceiling and furnishings, and it was here, in the splendid four-poster state bed, the newly married Queen Victoria and Prince Albert once slept. The exquisite Chinese room is hung with hand-painted oriental wallpaper, and contains a host of beautiful Chinese porcelain and furniture.

Some 300 acres of the surrounding woodland has been given over to a superb Wild Animal Kingdom. The drive-through safari park includes a lion reserve, tiger range, and monkey jungle, where animals can be seen roaming in almost natural habitats. Amongst other species to be seen in the Kingdom are Brown bears, giraffes, rhinos, elephants, and bison.

A cruise on the Boat Safari over the Drabeloe Lake encircles the island home of the chimpanzees, from which one can see flamingos and swans, and watch the amusing antics of the sealions. Amongst other animal life to be seen here at Woburn are the many species of deer in the park, and the delightful entertaining dolphins in the Dolphinarium.

Within the grounds of Woburn there are many recreational facilities. A Chinese dairy overlooks a pond where Chinese ducks can often be seen swimming; a pottery, art gallery and craftshop display work by international artists, with many pieces available for purchase; and the fairground, pets' corner, and children's playground provide amusement for the younger visitor.

Open all year daily. Parking and refreshments available.

Woburn Abbey was built on the site of a medieval monastry in the 17th century

Robert Smythson, who also worked at Longleat, designed Wollaton Hall

Wollaton Park and Hall

Nottinghamshire *p217 B1*

Lying on the outskirts of Nottingham is the 774-acre Wollaton Park, with its formal gardens, deer park and nature trail set around a lovely lake.

Standing within the park is the striking sixteenth-century Wollaton Hall. This is now a natural history museum, exhibiting mammals, birds and fishes arranged in natural habitat groups. Also displayed here is a large series of insects, and various archaeological finds.

The eighteenth-century stables house an industrial museum connected with printing, engineering, pharmacy and mining. Machinery connected with lace, hosiery and tobacco making can also be seen. In the courtyard is a colliery horse-gin, once used to wind both men and coal up and down a mine.

Industrial Museum open all year daily from Apr to Sep, Sun pm only; Oct to Mar Thu and Sat, also Sun pm. Refreshments available Apr to Sep in Park.
Natural History Museum open all year daily (except 25 Dec) but pm only on Sun. Parking and refreshments available.

Woodstock

Oxfordshire *p213 A4*

Woodstock is a charming busy place on the river Glyme – full of hotels, pubs, teashops and lovely old stone houses. The town has many royal links, but is most famous for its magnificent Blenheim Palace.

This palatial Italian-style mansion by Sir John Vanbrugh was started in 1705 for John Churchill, the 1st Duke of Marlborough. The enormous palace took seventeen years to build at a cost of £300,000, of which £240,000 was defrayed by Parliament as a reward for the Duke's victory over the French and the Bavarians at Blenheim. Unfortunately it was not completed until after the Duke's death in 1722.

The palace is rich in exotic furnishings and art treasures and it was here that Sir Winston Churchill was born in 1874. He was buried in the nearby Bladon churchyard on the southern fringe of the park and within sight of Blenheim.

The immense grounds, covering some 25,000 acres, were originally conceived by Henry Wise but later exquisitely remodelled and landscaped by Capability Brown. He created an artificial lake from the river Glyme, with its unfinished bridge, and a column 134 feet high in honour of Marlborough, the victor of Blenheim. Trees surrounding the column were planted in groups to represent the battle.

The grounds also play host to a garden centre, a narrow-gauge passenger-carrying steam railway and there are launch trips on the lake. The deer park is always open to walkers.

Also of interest in Woodstock is the Oxfordshire County Museum which is located in the sixteenth to eighteenth-century Fletcher's House and houses an exhibition of Oxfordshire from earliest times to the present day.

Blenheim Palace open daily mid Mar to Oct. Garden Centre open daily. Refreshments available.
Oxfordshire County Museum open all year daily (except Good Fri and 25, 26 Dec and Mon Oct to Apr); pm only on Sun. Refreshments available.

Wookey Hole Caves and Mill

Somerset *p212 E3*

Over many thousands of years the river Axe has worn away the rocks here to form the vast underground caverns in the heart of the Mendips at Wookey Hole. The guided tour leads through several of the caverns and they are truly spectacular. Unlike the caves at nearby Cheddar, there are no pretty rock formations here, but the immense size of the caverns more than compensates for this. The only exception is a strangely shaped rock known as the Witch of Wookey which casts an eerie shadow and is associated with morbid legends of child-eating and suchlike. The tour proceeds deeper into the more recently opened seventh, eighth and ninth caverns, crossed by high metal bridges, with the river Axe rushing far below. On emerging from the caves which gave shelter to man more than 2,000 years ago, the path passes the Hyena Den once occupied by those predatory creatures between 35000 and 25000 BC.

The circular tour continues by entering the old paper mill where high quality paper has been hand made since the seventeenth century. The recently restored works now make paper again and the long process of pulping, pressing, drying and finishing can be seen in operation.

Further rooms in the mill have been given over to some colourful and unusual collections, for example, Lady Bangor's Fairground collection of bygone fairground items from the age of steam. The superbly carved and painted figures from the old-time rides are an art form of their own and can be viewed to the accompanying music of a Marenghi fairground organ.

In 1973 Madame Tussaud's bought the caves and mill and the most unusual attraction of the tour is the fascinating storeroom of moulds and figures from the famous waxworks. The moulds are a strange collection of heads, limbs and torsos, all named but totally unrecognisable. Other shelves contain row upon row of familiar faces such as Henry VIII, Diana Dors and Harold Wilson. There are also costumes and accessories, many of which actually belonged to the person portrayed. The final display before re-emerging from the mill is an exhibition of archaeological finds from the caves.

Open all year daily (except 25 Dec). Parking and refreshments available.

The damp, chilly caverns of Wookey Hole are still being explored

Worcester

Hereford and Worcester *p216 F1*

The ancient cathedral city of Worcester lies within an area of rich farmland and meadows, of apple and cherry orchards and hopfields. It is famous for sauce and china; for having the country's oldest surviving newspaper; and for its fine cricket ground.

In medieval times, the eastern boundary of Worcester was marked by defences which ran parallel to City Walls Road. These have been excavated and Worcester's oldest buildings lie between them and the riverfront. Friar Street and its continuation, New Street, contain several historic houses including the sixteenth-century Nash House and the fifteenth-century Greyfriars, one of the few monastic buildings to survive the Dissolution of the monasteries.

The Cathedral

The cathedral was founded as a Saxon monastery by St Oswald in 983. The crypt, one of the most inspiring parts, was constructed by St Wulston, the only Saxon bishop to keep his office after the Norman invasion in 1066. In the centre of the exquisite chancel, in front of the high altar, is the tomb of King John. Above, in the choir, is the oldest royal effigy in England. This is made of Purbeck marble and was originally painted and bejewelled. The arches of the Lady Chapel behind the high altar are perhaps among the most beautifully proportioned thirteenth-century work to be found in the country.

Prince Arthur's Chantry, an elaborately carved chancel, was built in 1504 by Henry VIII in memory of his son Arthur, who had died at Ludlow. It is remarkable for its fine tracery, heraldry and sculptures.

The cathedral library, over the south aisle of the nave, contains a large collection of early manuscripts, including fragments of an eighth-century Gospel and deeds of land from the same period. A thirteenth-century gateway opens out on to College Green. It leads on to the cloisters, the King's School and the chapter house as well as the ruins of the old Guester Hall – the guesthouse the monks built in 1320.

Just to the west of the gateway (also called the Edgar Tower) is the deanery, an early eighteenth-century house with a particularly beautiful pedimented doorway.

The Commandery

Founded in 1085 as a hospital by St Wulston, this timber-framed building with its most impressive great hall, was used by Charles II as his HQ during the Battle of Worcester in 1651. The magnificent Elizabethan staircase leads to upper rooms, one of which has fine sixteenth-century wall paintings.

Royal Worcester Porcelain Works and The Dyson Perrins Museum

The porcelain industry was started in 1751 by Dr Wall and a group of local businessmen. Their factory soon produced its own successful lines of Chinese blue-printed ware, and later richly ornamented ware, that ranks with some of the world's greatest. Dr Wall died in 1766, but the royal seal of approval was given by King George III some twelve years later.

Adjacent to the factory is the Dyson Perrins Museum, which contains the finest collection of Worcester china in the world. Exhibits cover the period from 1751 (when the factory was founded) to the present day.

Tudor House

This 500-year-old timber-framed building, once an inn, has been turned into a folk museum which depicts daily life in the city from Elizabethan times. Amongst its exhibits is an old-fashioned kitchen with a cast-iron cooking range.

King Charles's House

King Charles II hid in the house after his defeat in the Battle of Worcester in 1651 outside the city walls, and fled through the back door as Parliamentary troops entered at the front. The house is now a shop.

Guildhall

One of the most gracious Queen Anne buildings in the town is the Guildhall. It was designed in 1721 by Thomas White, a pupil of Sir Christopher Wren. Inside the building is a beautifully decorated assembly room and a collection of armour, including some which was left on the field after the Battle of Worcester.

City Museum and Art Gallery

This museum has a collection of Civil War relics together with archaeology and natural history. One section of the museum is devoted to the Worcestershire Regiment raised in 1694, and the county's Yeoman Cavalry formed exactly a hundred years later.

The Commandery open all year Tue to Sat. Also Sun pm from Apr to Sep. Open Bank Holiday Mon.
Dyson Perrins Museum open all year Mon to Fri (except Bank Holidays), also Sat Apr to Sep. Parking and refreshments available.
Tudor House open all year Mon to Sat (except Thu).
Guildhall open all year Mon to Fri.
City Museum and Art Gallery open all year Mon to Sat.

Worcester Cathedral occupies a commanding site above the river Severn

Ancient remains of a Roman wall

Wroxeter
Shropshire p216 E2

A Roman legionary fortress was established at Wroxeter in about the middle of the first century, but later the garrison moved further north to Chester and a new town – the fourth largest in Britain during the Roman occupation and tribal capital of the Cornovil – grew up on the site. Aerial surveys show that this town – *Viroconium Cornoviorum* – covered about 180 acres, most of which is now farmland. The town was inhabited long after the Roman legions were withdrawn, probably into the eighth century.

Although the forum was excavated in the 1920s, it has since been covered in except for a line of column stumps. On the site which is now open to the public were a market hall, a public latrine, a baths complex, and a *palaestra*, or exercise hall. The largest remaining section of masonry is an old arch, part of the wall which divided the hall from the baths. These consisted of a series of rooms providing hot baths, moist heat, dry heat, and cold plunges. A swimming pool was also built, but never seems to have been used – possibly because an extension to the baths, providing a second set of rooms which may have been for women, blocked access to the pool. Visitors can see the *pilae* (some of them modern reconstructions) which supported the floors, stoke holes, and furnace chambers.

A museum contains, besides an assortment of interesting artifacts, a cast of the inscription stone from the forum which shows that the building was dedicated to Emperor Hadrian in AD 130. Another inscription stone mentions Cunorix, believed to be an Irish settler, probably one of the *foederati*, or allies, brought to Britain by the Romans in their endeavour to protect the country from invaders when the military occupation came to an end. The original forum inscription stone and many other finds from the Wroxeter site, are in Rowley's House Museum in Shrewsbury.

See AM info. Also Sun am Apr to Sep. Parking available.

208

York *North Yorkshire p217 B3*

Two thousand years of history are crammed within the walls of York – one of Europe's most interesting and historic cities. It is a city to be walked in, so the alley ways and corners of medieval domesticity can be discovered, and the glory of the Minster can be wondered at.

York Minster from the south-east, a superb example of English Gothic

The Romans called York *Eboracum*, and, as capital of Lower Britain, became one of the leading cities of the Roman empire. Emperor Hadrian used it as a base, and when Emperor Constantine died here, in AD 306, his son became the only Emperor proclaimed in Britain – Constantine the Great, one of the most famous men in history.

During Saxon times York declined, because the Saxons did not like living in the old Roman cities, and it was not until AD 867, when the Danes took York, that it once more became an important trading centre and port.

The three-mile circuit of the medieval walls, which enclose the old city, stands on earth ramparts erected by the Anglo-Danish kings. It takes two hours to walk the walls, and they provide a fascinating sight of the tight-knit, jumbled centre of a medieval town. Close to the Minster is a maze of narrow streets of ancient shops and inns. The Shambles is perhaps the most famous street – here are still the shelves and hooks in front of shops used to display meat beside the cobbled thoroughfare. Many of the old houses have boot-scrapers outside their doors, harking back to the days when the unsurfaced streets were often a sea of mud, and others display firemarks – badges which proved a property was insured with a company possessing fire-engines, before the days of a municipal fire brigade.

The Minster
The Gothic cathedral of York was begun in 1220, but was not completed until 250 years later. The earliest part is the south transept, and then came the beautiful octagonal chapter house, the nave, the choir, the finely carved twin west towers and finally the massive central lantern tower, completed by about 1480 in replacement of an earlier one which had collapsed. One of the Minster's greatest treasures is the wealth of stained glass, spanning the ages between the twelfth and twentieth centuries. About eighty of the 130 windows were taken down for safety reasons during World War II, and this gave re-

York

Some of the houses in the Shambles almost touch across the street

storers a chance to put right the mistakes of past glaziers, where the wrong glass had been put in to replace broken pieces, or had been put in the incorrect place. The great east window is approximately the size of a tennis court and was created between 1405 and 1408. At the apex God is depicted with the words 'Ego sum Alpha et Omega' – I am the beginning and the end – which is the theme of the whole window.

King's Manor
Originally the home of the abbot of St Mary's Abbey, it became the residence of the King's Council of the North in Henry VIII's time. New apartments were added and Henry VIII and Catherine Howard may have stayed here in 1541. From this period there remains a cellar and a room with a Tudor doorway, open fireplace and ornamental plaster frieze.

From 1628 the house was greatly enlarged, and after the Civil War the house was used for various purposes until 1964 when it was restored to become part of the University of York.

Merchant Adventurers' Hall
This fourteenth and fifteenth-century hall was the meeting place of the powerful Company of the Merchant Adventurers. It is a superb example of a medieval guildhall, with the banners of the various guilds still displayed. The building is made almost entirely of wood as the Black Death killed the majority of masons in the city. The Pancake Bell in the under-

croft, where guild pensioners lived, was rung every Shrove Tuesday to tell the apprentices it was pancake time.

Yorkshire Museum and Gardens
The museum, founded in 1827, is housed in a fine neo-Classical building in grounds containing the Botanical Gardens and the majestic ruins of St Mary's Abbey. It houses large collections of archaeology, geology, pottery and natural history. Among the unique finds from Roman York is the head of a statue of Constantine the Great. The sixteenth-century guesthouse of the abbey is a separate museum exhibiting relics of prehistoric, Viking and medieval times. Also here is an extensive and important geological collection, including dramatic twenty-five-foot-long fossils of ichthyosaurs and pleisiosaurs – animals which lived 160 million years ago.

The Botanical Gardens, laid out in the early nineteenth century,

form York's most beautiful park – full of fascinating trees and plants, pleasant lawns and walks.

Castle Museum
Dr J. L. Kirk presented his outstanding collection of bygones to the City of York in 1935. It is displayed in the Female Prison, designed in 1780. There are among the reconstructions a Victorian parlour, moorland kitchen, Georgian dining room and Jacobean hall. The outstanding attraction is Kirkgate and Alderman's Walk in the prison exercise yard. This is a Victorian cobbled street complete with shop fronts and waiting hansom cab.

Across the circular lawn from the Female Prison is the Debtors Prison. Upstairs is kept a collection of firearms, armour, uniforms, medals and decorations, and general militaria. Downstairs there are costumes, period rooms and toy collections.

National Railway Museum
This museum is the largest rail-

way collection in Britain. Housed in a former British Railways steam locomotive shed, the central hall covers two acres and contains twenty-five locomotives and twenty items of rolling stock. The museum also illustrates railway history through uniforms, posters, models – every conceivable thing connected with railway development.

King's Manor open all year daily (except 25 Dec).
Merchant Adventurers' Hall open all year Mon to Sat and Bank Holidays (except New Years' Day, Good Fri and Christmas). Closed when Hall is being used for functions.
Yorkshire Museum open all year daily (except Christmas) but pm only on Sun. Hospitium open Mon to Sat in summer only. Gardens open all year daily (except Christmas).
Castle Museum open all year daily (except Christmas and New Year's Day).
National Railway Museum open all year daily (except New Years' Day, Good Fri, May Day Holiday, Christmas and some other public holidays); pm only on Suns. Parking and refreshments available.

Key to Location Atlas

Motorway

Motorway under Construction

Motorway junction

Primary Route

A Roads

B Roads

B9999   **Road Numbers**

Country Boundary

River and Lake

Killerton
House   **Place of Interest**

212   **Overlaps and numbers
of continuing pages**

The cities and towns in the gazetteer which
have a street plan are underlined in red.

221

222

219

220

Stornoway

Thurso

Wick

Portree

Banff

Inverness

Peterhead

Aberdeen

Fort William

Montrose

Pitlochry

Dundee

Oban

Perth

Inverary

Stirling

Glasgow

Edinburgh

Berwick

Peebles

Ayr

Dumfries

Stranraer

Newcastle

Carlise

Durham

Hadrian's Wall
See Pages 88, 89

Workington

Isle of Man

Kendal

Lake District
See Pages 108, 109

Lancaster

Scarborough

217

218

Blackpool

Bradford

York

Leeds

Hull

Liverpool

Manchester

Grimsby

215

Anglesey

Chester

Stoke

216

Lincoln

Caernarvon

Derby

Nottingham

Snowdonia National Park
See Pages 170, 171

Shrewsbury

Leicester

King's Lynn

Norwich

Norfolk Broads
See Pages 134, 135

Aberystwyth

Birmingham

Warwick

Peterborough

Bury
St Edmunds

Worcester

Stratford
upon Avon

Cambridge

Ipswich

**Pembrokeshire Coast
National Park**
See Page 143

Fishguard

Carmarthen

Hereford

Cheltenham

Oxford

St Albans

Colchester

Pembroke

Swansea

Gloucester

213

214

Newport

Bristol

Bath

Reading

Windsor

London

Canterbury

Cardiff

Maidstone

211

212

Taunton

Salisbury

Winchester

Dover

Dartmoor
See Pages 64, 65

Bournemouth

Southampton

Chichester

Brighton

Exeter

Isle of Wight

New Forest
See Pages 132, 133

Plymouth

Penzance

Scale 16 miles to 1 inch (approx)   1 : 1,000,000

5   0   10   20   30   40   Miles

5   0   10   20   30   40   50   60   Kilometres

Page No.		Grid Ref.
10	Abbotsbury	E2
14	Arlington Court	C3
15	Avebury	F4
18	Bath	E4
21	Berkeley	E4
22	Bickleigh	D2
22	Bicton Gardens	D2
26	Boscastle	B2
27	Bournemouth	F2
28	Bourton-on-the-Water	F5
29	Breamore House	F3
32	Bristol	E4
34	Broadway	F5
35	Brownsea Island	F2
35	Buckfast	D2
35	Buckfastleigh	D2
38	Caerleon	E4
39	Caerphilly	D4
44	Cardiff	D4
45	Carnglaze Slate Caverns	C2
45	Castle Combe	F4
48	Cheddar	E3
48	Chedworth Roman Villa	F4
49	Cheltenham	F5
50	Chepstow	E4
53	Chipping Camden	F5
54	Chysauster	A1
54	Cilgerran Castle	C5
54	Cirencester	F4
55	Cleeve Abbey	D3
56	Clovelly	C3
58	Compton Acres Gardens	F2
58	Compton Castle	D2
58	Compton House	E3
60	Corfe Castle	F2
60	Cotehele House	C2
61	Cricket St Thomas Wild Life Park	E3
62	Cwmcarn Forest Drive	D4
66	Dartmouth	D2
67	Dodington House	E4
67	Dorchester	E2
70	Dunster	D3
72	Dyrham Park	E4
77	Evesham	F5
78	Exeter	D2
80	Farway Countryside Park	D2
81	Fleet Air Arm Museum	E3
81	Forde Abbey	E3
83	Glastonbury	E3
85	Gloucester	F5
90	Hailes Abbey and Museum	F5
92	Hereford	E5
104	Kidwelly Castle	C4
105	Killerton House and Gardens	D2
107	Lacock	F4
110	Lanhydrock House	B2
110	Launceston Castle	C2
112	Lelant Model Village	A1
116	Llandaf Cathedral	D4
124	Longleat	F3
125	Lydford	C2
126	Margam Country Park	D4
128	Mevagissey	B1
128	Milton Abbas	F2
129	Monmouth	E4
130	Montacute House	E3
130	Morwellham	C2
134	Newquay	B2
139	Oakhill Manor	E3
142	Paignton	D2
142	Pembroke Castle	B4
144	Pendennis Castle	B1
147	Plymouth	C2
148	Poldark Mining and Wendron Forge	B1
148	Polperro	C1
148	Poole	F2
151	Powderham Castle	D2
151	Prinknash Abbey and Bird Park	F4
152	Raglan Castle	E4
158	St Mawes Castle	B1
158	St Michael's Mount	A1
158	Salisbury	F3
163	Shaftesbury	F3
164	Sherborne	E3
169	Slimbridge Wildfowl Trust	E4
172	Snowshill Manor	F5
175	Spetchley Park	F5
178	Stonehenge	F3
178	Stourhead House and Gardens	F3
182	Sudeley Castle and Gardens	F5
185	Tenby	B4
186	Tewkesbury	F5
188	Tintagel	B2
189	Tintern	E4
190	Torquay	D2
191	Totnes	D2
192	Trelissick Gardens	B1
192	Trerice	B2
193	Tucktonia	F2
196	Wells	E3
197	Welsh Folk Museum	D4
198	Westonbirt Arboretum	F4
199	Weston-super-Mare	E3
201	Wilton House	F3
201	Wimborne Minster	F2
206	Wookey Hole Caves and Mill	E3

Newlyn, near Penzance, in the days when fish, not tourists, were Cornwall's livelihood and visitors to these picturesque coasts were a rarity

A

B

Page No.		Grid Ref.
12	Abingdon	A3
12	Alfriston	C2
12	Allington Castle	C3
13	Alresford	A2
14	Arundel	B2
14	Audley End	C4
17	Banham	D5
17	Battle	C2
20	Beaulieu	A1
20	Bekonscot Model Village	B3
22	Bignor Roman Villa	B2
24	Bluebell Railway	C2
24	Bodiam Castle	C2
26	Boughton House	B5
28	Bradgate Park	A5
29	Bressingham Gardens and Live Steam Museum	D5
30	Brighton	C2
34	Broadstairs	E3
35	Bucklers Hard	A1
36	Bungay	D5
36	Burford	A3
37	Bury St Edmunds	D4
40	Cambridge	C4
42	Canterbury	D3
47	Chartwell	C2
52	Chichester	B2
53	Chilham	D2
55	Clandon Park	B2
55	Claydon House	A4
56	Cliveden	B3
57	Colchester	D4
60	Courage Shire Horse Centre	B3
66	Deal	E3
68	Dover	D2
72	East Bergholt	D4
72	Eastbourne	C2
73	Easton Farm Park	D4
76	Ely	C5
80	Fishbourne Roman Palace	B2
81	Folkestone	D2
82	Framlingham Castle	D4
82	Furzey Gardens	A2
86	Great Dixter	D2
86	Great Yarmouth	E5
87	Greys Court	A3
87	Grimes Graves	C5
87	Guildford	B2
91	Hastings	D2
92	Hatfield House	B3
94	Herstmonceux	C2
94	Heveningham Hall	E5
94	Hever Castle	C2
96	Hughenden Manor	B3
97	Ickworth House	C4
97	Ingatestone	C3
100	Isle of Wight	A1
105	Kilverstone New World Wildlife Park	D5
106	Knebworth House and Country Park	B4
106	Knole	C2
111	Lavenham	D4
111	Leeds Castle	D2
112	Leicester	A5
113	Lilford Park	B5
116	Littlecote House	A3
124	Long Melford	D4
124	Loseley House	B2
125	Lullingstone Castle	C3
125	Luton Hoo	B4
126	Lympne	D2
126	Mapledurham	A3
126	Marwell Zoo	A2
138	Norwich	D5
140	Oxburgh Hall	C5
140	Oxford	A3
144	Penshurst Place	C2
145	Peterborough	B5
146	Petworth	B2
148	Polesden Lacey	B2
149	Porchester Castle	A2
150	Portsmouth	A1
151	Queen Elizabeth Country Park	A2
154	Rochester	C3
155	Rockingham Castle	B5
155	Romsey	A2
157	St Albans	B3
158	St Osyth	D4
163	Sheffield Park	C2
163	Sheffield Park and Gardens	C2
166	Sissingshurst Castle Gardens	D2
172	Somerleyton Hall	E5
172	Southampton	A2
173	Southend-on-Sea	D3
175	Stamford	B5
176	Stanford Hall	A5
179	Stratfield Saye House	A3
182	Suffolk Wildlife Country Park	E5
182	Sulgrave Manor	A4
186	The Shuttleworth Collection	B4
186	Thetford	D5
188	The Vyne	A2
188	Thorpe Park	B3
193	Twycross Zoo	A5
193	Waddesdon Manor	A4
194	Wakehurst Place Gardens	C2
196	Weald and Downland Open Air Museum	B2
197	Welney Wildfowl Refuge	C5
200	Whipsnade Park Zoo	B4
202	Winchester	A2
204	Windsor	B3
205	Wisley Gardens	B3
205	Woburn Abbey and Wild Animal Kingdom	B4
206	Woodstock	A4

Once a thriving Kentish port, Deal is now a modern town and a favourite week-end haunt for Londoners

E

Page No.		Grid Ref.
12	Aberystwyth	C1
13	Alton Towers	F2
14	Arley Hall Gardens	E3
20	Beaumaris	C3
21	Betws y Coed	C3
23	Blackpool	D4
24	Bodnant Gardens	C3
26	Boscobel House	E2
29	Bramall Hall	F3
38	Caernarfon	C3
47	Charlecote Park	F1
48	Chatsworth	F3
50	Chester	E3
53	Chirk Castle	D2
59	Conwy	C3
60	Coughton Court	F1
61	Criccieth Castle	C2
68	Drayton Manor Park and Zoo	F2
69	Dudley Castle and Zoo	F1
76	Elan Valley Reservoirs	D1
76	Erdigg	E2
80	Eye Manor	E1
80	Festiniog Railway	C2
81	Fort Belan	C3
82	Furness Abbey	D5
83	Gawsworth Hall	F3
90	Harlech Castle	C2
91	Harvington Hall	F1
92	Heaton Hall	E3
95	Hodnet Hall Gardens	E2
95	Holker Hall	D5
99	Ironbridge Gorge Museum	E2
102	Jodrell Bank	E3
103	Kenilworth Castle	F1
110	Lakeside and Haverthwaite Railway	D5
110	Lancaster	E5
112	Leighton Hall	E5
112	Levens Hall	E5
113	Lichfield	F2
116	Little Moreton Hall	E3
116	Llanberis	C3
117	Llandudno	C3
117	Llywernog Silver-Lead Mine	C1
125	Ludlow	E1
126	Lyme Park	F3
130	Morecambe	E5
137	Norton Priory	E3
142	Packwood House	F1
144	Penrhyn Castle	C3
146	Pilkington Glass Museum	E3
150	Portmeirion	C2
152	Ragley Hall	F1
152	Ravenglass and Eskdale Railway	D5
152	Rhuddlan Castle	D3
156	Rufford Old Hall	E4
160	Samlesbury Hall	E4
162	Severn Valley Railway	E2
164	Shrewsbury	E2
166	Shugborough	F2
174	Southport	D4
175	Speke Hall	E3
176	Steamtown Railway Museum	E5
178	Stokesay Castle	E1
180	Stratford-upon-Avon	F1
182	Sudbury Hall	F2
184	Talyllyn Railway	C2
184	Tamworth Castle Museum	F2
184	Tatton Park	E3
192	Trentham Gardens	F2
195	Warwick	F1
196	Wedgwood Museum and Visitor Centre	F2
198	Welshpool	D2
198	West Midlands Safari and Leisure Park	E1
199	Weston Park	E2
201	Wilmcote	F1
207	Worcester	F1
208	Wroxeter	E2

The setting has not changed since Victorian times but Beddgelert's traditional costumes and occupations are a thing of the past

CAERNA[RFON] BAY

Kirk Mich[ael]
Peel
Foxdale
Port Erin
Calf of Man
Castleto[n]

Holyh[ead] Bay
Holyhead
Val[ley]

Bardsey Sound

A

B

Cardigan
Cilgerran Castle
Fishguard

211

Page No.		Grid Ref.
20	Belton House Park and Gardens	C1
21	Belvoir Castle	C1
22	Beverley	C3
24	Blickling Hall	F1
25	Bolsover Castle	B2
25	Bolton Abbey	A3
36	Burton Constable Hall	D3
44	Carlton Towers	C3
46	Castle Howard	C3
46	Castle Rising	E1
46	Castleton	B2
56	Clumber Park	C2
63	Darlington	B4
70	Durham	B5
76	Elvaston Castle and Country Park	B1
80	Flamingoland	C4
82	Fountains Abbey	B3
87	Haddon Hall	B2
90	Hardwick Hall	B1
90	Harewood House and Bird Garden	B3
90	Harrogate	B3
92	Haworth	A3
94	High Force Waterfall	A4
95	Holkham Hall	E1
96	Hornsea Pottery	D3
96	Houghton Hall	E1
102	Jervaulx Abbey	B4
103	Kelling Park Aviaries	E1
106	King's Lynn	D1
110	Lambton Pleasure Park	B5
114	Lincoln	C2
124	Lotherton Hall	B3
127	Melbourne	B1
131	Newby Hall	B3
134	Newstead Abbey	B1
136	Norfolk Wildlife Park	E1
136	North Norfolk Railway	E1
137	North of England Open Air Museum	B5
146	Pickering	C4
152	Raby Castle	B4
153	Riber Castle Fauna Reserve	B1
153	Richmond	B4
154	Rievaulx Abbey	B4
154	Ripon	B3
154	Roche Abbey	B2
156	Ryedale Folk Museum	C4
160	Sandringham	E1
161	Scarborough	C4
162	Sewerby Hall, Park and Zoo	D3
166	Skegness	D2
167	Skipton	A3
169	Sledmere House	C3
174	Spalding	D1
182	Sutton Park	B3
184	Tattershall Castle	D1
187	The Thursford Collection	E1
188	Thoresby Hall	C2
191	Tramway Museum	B1
193	Tynemouth Priory and Castle	B5
194	Walsingham	E1
200	Whitby	C4
206	Wollaton Park and Hall	B1
208	York	B3

An idyllic view of rural life in the last century in a remote valley not far from Barnard Castle, County Durham

Page No.		Grid Ref.
12	Alnwick	F3
14	Argyll Forest Park	B4
16	Ayr	C3
16	Bamburgh	F3
17	Barnard Castle	F1
25	Border Forest Park	E3
34	Brougham Castle	E1
42	Cameron House	C4
44	Carlisle	E2
45	Castle Bolton	F1
56	Cockermouth	D1
62	Culzean Castle and Country Park	B3
62	Dalemain	E1
68	Doune	C4
69	Drumlanrig Castle	D3
69	Dryburgh Abbey	E3
69	Dumfries	D2
74	Edinburgh	D4
82	Galloway Forest Park	C2
86	Grasmere	E1
95	Holy Island	F3–4
96	Hopetoun House	D4
96	House of the Binns	D4
98	Inveraray Castle	B5
102	Jedburgh	E3
103	Kendal	E1
104	Keswick	D1
105	Kilmarnock	C3
117	Loch Lomond	C4
127	Mellerstain	E3
128	Melrose	E3
131	Muncaster Castle and Bird Garden	D1
136	Norham Castle	F4
139	Oban	B5
145	Perth	D5
156	Rydal Mount	E1
162	Scone Palace	D5
166	Sizergh Castle	E1
176	Stirling	C4
182	Sweetheart Abbey	D2
191	Traquair House	E3
194	Wallington	F2
194	Warkworth Castle	F3
203	Windermere	E1

A 19th-century view of Derwentwater, looking towards the high peaks of Skiddaw

Tiree
Gott Bay
Coll
Canna
Rhum
Figg
Muck
Tobermory
Calgary Bay
Claggan
Lochaline
Salen
Fishnish

THE MINCH

5
4
3
2
1

A
B
C
D

Sandwood
Loch
Loch Inchard
Loch Laxford
Rhiconich
Laxford Bridge
Scourie
Eddrechillis Bay
Clashnessie Bay
Kylestrome
Unapool
Kylesku
Loch Glendhu
Loch Glencoul
Loch Veyatie
Inchnadamph
Enard Bay
Loch Assynt
Ledmore
Knockan
Ullapool
Strath Kinnaird
Gruinard Bay
Laide
Aultbea
Ardessie
Dundonnell
Inverewe Gardens
Poolewe
Gairloch
Talladale
Kinlochewe
Shieldaig
Achnashellach Lodge
Kishorn
Lochcarron
Strathcarron
Stromeferry
Balmacara
Kyle of Lochalsh
Kyleakin
Breakish
Broadford
Dornie
Inverinate
Ardelve
Auchtertyre
Invershiel

A838
Tongue
Loch Hope
Loch an Dherue
Bettyhill
Strathy
Portskerra
Melvich
Reay
A836
Thurso
Loch Loyal
A836
Altnaharra
Loch Meadie
Loch Naver
Forsinard
A897
Kinbrace
Loch Badanloch
Kildonan
Helmsdale
Overscaig
A838
Loch Shin
Lairg
A839
Rogart
Dunrobin Castle
Brora
Rosehall
Oykell Bridge
A837
Invershin
Mound Station
Golspie
Bonar Bridge
Clashmore
Ardgay
Kincardine
Edderton
A9
Tain
Braemore Junction
A835
Aultguish
Garve
Dingwall
Strathpeffer
Contin
A832
A834
Conon Bridge
Evanton
Alness
Cromarty
Rosemarkie
Fortrose
Avoch
Munlochy
North Kessock
Inverness
Culloden Battlefield
Nairn
Forres
Auldearn
A96
Cawdor
Croy
Cawdor Castle
Ferness
A939
Drumnadrochit
Daviot
Tomatin
Grantown-on-Spey
Carrbridge
Boat of Garten
Aviemore
Coylumbridge
Glen More Forest Park
Invermoriston
Torgyle
Cluanie
Fort Augustus
Invergarry
Highland Wildlife Park
Kincraig
Kingussie
Newtonmore
Laggan Bridge
Dalwhinnie
Dalnaspidal
Blair Atholl
Killiecrankie
Moulin
Pitlochry
Logierait
Ballinluig
Grandtully
Aberfeldy
Kenmore
Fearnan
Lawers
Dunkeld
Amulree
Bridge of Orchy
Spittal of Glen

Mallaig
Morar
Arisaig
Lochailort
Glenfinnan
Kinlocheil
Corpach
Banavie
Spean Bridge
Roy Bridge
Tulloch Station
Kinlochmoidart
Acharacle
Salen
Strontian
Ardgour
Onich
North Ballachulish
Inversanda
Ballachulish
Glencoe
Kinlochleven
Fort William
Portnacroish

Duntulm
Kilmaluaig
Staffin
Uig
Edinbane
Berrisdale
Dunvegan
Skeabost Bridge
Portree
Bracadale
Drynoch
Sligachan
Sconser
Scalpay
Kyleakin
Raasay
Rona
Isle Ornsay
Armadale
Ardvasar

SKYE

219

Page No.		Grid Ref.
10	Aberdeen	F2
16	Balmoral Castle	E2
28	Braemar	E2
47	Cawdor Castle	D3
60	Crathes Castle	F2
61	Culloden Battlefield	D2
69	Dufftown	E2
70	Dunrobin Castle	D3
76	Elgin	E3
81	Fort William	C1
83	Glamis	E1
84	Glencoe	C1
84	Glen More Forest Park	D2
95	Highland Wildlife Park	D2
98	Inverewe Gardens	B3
98	Inverness	D2
146	Pitlochry	D1
168	Skye	A2
200	Wick	E4

Ben Nevis, Britain's highest (4406ft) mountain, has been a favourite subject for illustrators for over 100 years

Acknowledgements

The publishers gratefully acknowledge The Mansell
Collection Limited for the use of engravings
and the following for the use of photographs:

Barnabys Picture Library

Martin Body

British Tourist Authority

J Allan Cash Ltd

C M Dixon

England Scene Colour Picture Library

Philip Llewellin

Oliver Matthews

Colin Molyneux

Picturepoint Ltd

Peter Reynolds

Chris Ridley

Peter Russell

Geoff Silcock

Spectrum Colour Library

Trevor Wood

Woodmansterne Ltd

John